IMPERIAL HEARST
A SOCIAL BIOGRAPHY

Imperial Hearst

A SOCIAL BIOGRAPHY

BY FERDINAND LUNDBERG

WITH A PREFACE BY DR. CHARLES A. BEARD

GREENWOOD PRESS, PUBLISHERS
WESTPORT, CONNECTICUT

Originally published in 1936
by Equinox Cooperative Press

First Greenwood Reprinting 1970

Library of Congress Catalogue Card Number 74-98850

SBN 8371-2963-X

PRINTED IN UNITED STATES OF AMERICA

TO
HEYWOOD BROUN
AND THE
AMERICAN NEWSPAPER GUILD

A PREFACE
and a Farewell to William Randolph Hearst

>>>>>>>>>>>>><<<<<<<<<<<<<

WILLIAM RANDOLPH HEARST has passed the mark of three score years and ten. Even now he stands within the shadow that in due course enshrouds all mortals. Yet a few years and he too will come to that judgment meted out to things earthly and human. Then his stocks, bonds, and titles to castles, estates, and mines, his hirelings, servitors, beneficiaries, and banker-sponsors will avail as naught.

But before he goes to face that verdict, it is fitting and proper that he should receive the judgment of contemporaries on this side—the judgment of experience and documentation. It is fitting also that this judgment should be rendered to his heirs and legatees into whose hands the Hearst heritage will soon pass, under whose jurisdiction the Hearst empire will doubtless dissolve and crumble into ruins. For the judgment on the creator of this aggregation of wealth, terror, and ambition will be the verdict of the American nation upon its tormentor, or at least of that part of the nation interested in the preservation of those simple decencies without which no people can endure.

Summarily, what is this judgment of contemporaries in no way fearing or beholden to William Randolph Hearst? It is that Hearst, despite all the uproar he has made and all the power he wields, is a colossal failure and now holds in his hands the dust and ashes of defeat. He will depart loved by few and respected by none whose respect is worthy of respect. When the cold sneer of command at last fades from his face, none will be proud to do honor to his memory.

What is the supporting evidence for this judgment?

The first is the popular verdict at the polls. In early manhood

Hearst had political ambitions. He wanted to be the governor of a great state, and there can scarcely be any doubt that he regarded this as a stepping stone to the Presidency of the United States. In this quest for political power Hearst offered himself to the citizens of New York as the candidate for governor in 1906, and he received their sentence of banishment in the autumn of that year. It was a smashing repudiation. Never afterward was he able to set foot in the path that leads to the White House.

The second piece of evidence supporting the judgment of ostracism and oblivion for Hearst was provided by the actions of the superintendents of American schools assembled in convention at St. Louis in February, 1936. For years the Hearst papers, with characteristic disregard for truth, had been attacking leaders in American education—such men as Professor Charles H. Judd and President Hutchins, of Chicago University, President Chase, of New York University, and President Graham, of North Carolina University. Hearst had been calling them communists and enemies of the American Republic. He had fostered "red scares" and made drives on the public schools, alleging that they were centers of disloyalty and sedition. Men favoring Hearst's methods went to the convention of superintendents at Atlantic City in 1935, with a view to winning educational endorsement of the Hearst "campaign." It was thought that teachers were "timid" and could be easily herded into the Hearst camp—thus adding moral strength to Hearst sensationalism, and increasing the circulation of the yellow press.

With the deadly swiftness of the lightning's flash, teachers denounced Hearst at Atlantic City, and sent his henchmen scurrying for cover. Accustomed to raking the underworld and intimidating political gangsters, Hearst there had his first encounter with an organization of men and women trained in the nobler traditions of American life, and found out what they thought of him. At St. Louis the next year the superintendents, with scarcely a dissenting voice, condemned two of Hearst's "pet" projects in unmeasured terms. They denounced the "red-rider" attached to school appropriations in the District of Columbia. They denounced the methods employed to oust from the office of Commissioner of Education in Massachusetts, Dr. Payson Smith, outspoken opponent of legislation branding teachers as unfaithful and compelling them to take oaths of loyalty. The superintendents did not dignify Hearst by mentioning his name, but they put the finishing touches to his hope of dominating education in the United States by threats, sensationalism, and terrorism. Their verdict is that rendered against him years ago by Charles W. Eliot—the verdict of ostracism and oblivion.

The third piece of supporting evidence for the judgment on Hearst is his own record, revealed in its broad outlines by the documentation of Mr. Lundberg's pages. We have only to compare it with the record of men who command the esteem of the American nation—such as Washington, Jefferson, Lincoln, and Emerson—to discover the long-term and final verdict of this nation on William Randolph Hearst.

This is not to say that Mr. Lundberg has told "the whole story." To tell the whole story of any man like Hearst is an achievement beyond human powers. Owing to the shadowy and complicated nature of Hearst's operations, the exact truth in many particular instances is difficult to unearth. This is not to say that Hearst possesses no virtues. Nero and Caligula had virtues.

It is to say that enough authentic and indubitable facts are presented in the following pages to show what manner of man Hearst has been and still is—to disclose his ambitions, his conceptions of decency, his methods, his standards of public morals, his lack of reverence for truth and character, his tastes, the means he employs to attain his ends, his treatment of his own servitors, the ramifications of his economic greed, the sum and substance of his career. Mr. Lundberg destroys William Randolph Hearst by producing the cold, brute facts of the record.

It is impossible to believe that any person literate enough to read Mr. Lundberg's pages can come to any other verdict than that of ostracism and oblivion for Hearst. Perhaps a few who stand in dread of him or desire to use him for their purposes may express no judgment publicly—now. But unless we are to believe in the progressive degradation of the American nation, we are bound to believe that Hearst's fate is ostracism by decency in life, and oblivion in death.

Odors of his personality may linger for a time—until his estate is divided and his journalistic empire is dissolved; but they will soon evaporate in the sunlight of a purer national life. Even school boys and girls by the thousands now scorn his aged image and cankered heart.

No doubt, Hearst, while he lives, and his legatees, until his empire is dissolved, will continue to make sensations in American life. They will be as merciless as tigers in attaining their ends. As unwonted strength sometimes comes to dying men just before the *rigor mortis* sets in, they may rouse themselves to even more passionate and vindictive outbursts. But their doom has already been pronounced by the American people, by public spirited men and women whose loyalty to the fine things of the American tradition gives the promise of endurance to their judgment. Hearst may buy writers of distinction to adorn his pages; he may bring pressure to bear on men whose interests he can advance or injure; he may wring commendations from those who fear his power in material affairs; but the verdict of the American spirit has been rendered in tones which even he cannot mistake. It goes with him to the vale of shadows.

Any doubts which the young generation may have, through lack of authentic information, will be resolved by Mr. Lundberg's documented account of the Hearst career.

CHARLES A. BEARD

Washington, D. C.,
March 9, 1936

Author's Foreword

Although the present work is the only complete exposition of the financial, political and social results of the career of William Randolph Hearst, there are some omissions. Descriptions of his personal life have been omitted. Some events and exploits which are similar to those described in the text have also been omitted.

The appearance of this material, while it may still be valuable in a defense of democratic forms against the onslaught of black reaction behind the banners of yellow journalism, has been made possible only by helpful textual changes, corrections and suggestions made by Mr. Charles Angoff, editor of *The American Spectator*, Dr. Charles A. Beard, Mr. Henry Hart, and various others in the newspaper, teaching and legal professions; and by the encouragement offered in the defense of democratic liberties by Professor George S. Counts of Columbia University, Professor E. A. Ross of the University of Wisconsin, Dr. Harry F. Ward of Union Theological Seminary, Professor Robert Morss Lovett of the University of Chicago, and many others.

Without the assistance of my wife, Isabel Lundberg, in the reading of documents, manuscript and proofs, and in the preparation of indices, the work would have been seriously delayed and lacking in many of those virtues which it may have.

F. L.

Contents

Chapter
I
Page 19

Parentage and birth in San Francisco. The source of the Hearst fortune. The Comstock lode. William Randolph Hearst's expulsion from St. Paul's and Harvard. He works for the New York *World*. His father gives him the San Francisco *Examiner*. Death of Senator George Hearst.

Chapter
II
Page 23

The *Examiner* is patterned after Pulitzer's *World*. Hearst's parties for his staff. The arrival of Sam S. Chamberlain. The *Examiner* and political graft. Its journalistic fakes. The *Examiner* attacks the political allies of the late Senator Hearst. The *Examiner* prints the advertisements of disorderly houses. The *Examiner* blackmails the Southern Pacific Railroad.

Chapter
III
Page 49

Hearst purchases the New York *Journal* and arrives in the metropolis in 1895. Hearst's raid upon Pulitzer's staff. The *Journal's* methods for getting circulation. Hearst as the friend of union labor. The Venezuela Boundary Treaty. The Guldensuppe case. The *Journal's* role in fomenting the Spanish-American war and Hearst's economic motives therefor. Falsification of news from Cuba. The explosion of the *Maine*. Intimidation of the McKinley Administration. The war in Cuba. The *Journal* obtains the Spanish-American peace treaty through bribery.

Chapter
IV
Page 83

Hearst espouses Bryan in 1896. The reasons. The campaign. The *Journal* gains circulation. The second Bryan campaign and the reasons for Hearst's continued support. Bryan's second defeat leaves the *Journal* stronger than before. The Hay-Pauncefote Treaty. Mrs. Hearst finances an archaeological expedition to Peru. It surveys the Cerro de Pasco mines, which the Hearst Estate then acquires. Hearst's attacks upon McKinley. Brisbane's editorials discussing personal violence against the State heads. McKinley is assassinated. National boycott against Hearst.

He weathers the storm and seeks political office. Tammany sends him to Congress in 1902. Seventeen people killed in an explosion of fireworks to celebrate Hearst's election. Hearst in Congress. He marries at the age of forty. Candidacy for Mayor of New York in 1905. Tammany balks and Hearst attacks Charles F. Murphy. Cartoons of Murphy. Tammany steals the election from Hearst. Tammany endorses Hearst for Governor the following year. Charles Evans Hughes exposes Hearst. Hearst the only Democrat on the State ticket to be defeated. The theft of the Standard Oil letters. A few of these are published in 1908. Hearst's attacks upon Mayor Gaynor. The attempt to assassinate him. Collier's exposes the nature of Hearst's exposure of the Standard Oil letters. The Senate orders an investigation. The inconclusive ending of the committee's investigation, and the reasons.

Chapter V

Page 139

Hearst enters Chicago. The views on Hearst of Charles Edward Russell. Hearst's use of Socialists. Andrew M. Lawrence of the Chicago *American*. The beginning of the Chicago gangs. Max Annenberg and the circulation war. Murder and a reign of terror. The entire American press is silent. Chicago *Tribune* buys Annenberg from the *American*. Chicago police and judiciary controlled by the owners of Chicago newspapers. Hearst influence appears in the American Federation of Labor. Union workmen killed, slugged and arrested. Newspaper thugs attack citizens. Union labor traduced by Hearst.

Chapter VI

Page 174

Labor on the Hearst properties in Peru and South Dakota. American fascism in 1910. Hearst exploits Chinese labor. The devious policies of his papers toward labor. His efforts to crush unions of newsboys and editorial workers. His opposition to child labor legislation. His attack upon the American Newspaper Guild. Roosevelt's attitude to the Guild in Hearst's behalf. The Guild fights on and strikes a Hearst paper in Milwaukee.

Chapter
VII
Page 201

Hearst's drive for Champ Clark. The Democratic nominating convention of 1912. Hearst's antipathy to Wilson. His attacks upon him as President. Hearst's Peruvian reason for fighting Wilson on the Panama canal. The World War. Hearst's imperialism goes with the German rather than the Ally imperialism. Reasons for Hearst's pro-German and anti-British orientation. Hearst's attempts to foment wars between the United States and Mexico and Japan. His purposes. The Senate investigates his connection with Germans. Hearst men in pay of Germany. Brisbane gets $500,000. Boycott against Hearst. German-Americans and Irish-Americans support him. Paul Block.

Chapter
VIII
Page 211

The Associated Press sues Hearst for the theft of its news. Hearst loses in the Supreme Court. How the AP news was stolen. Federal courts enjoin Hearst. But the AP does not try to punish Hearst. Why? Oswald Garrison Villard's answer. Hearst's power in the AP.

Chapter
IX
Page 248

Fails to get Democratic nomination for Governor in 1918. Supports Hiram Johnson's Presidential ambition in 1920. Mayors Hylan and Thompson and their anti-British antics. Hearst and Al Smith. Why Royal S. Copeland is U. S. Senator. Coolidge. The Teapot Dome scandals. William B. Shearer and armaments propaganda. The forged Mexican documents. Andrew W. Mellon and tax rebates for Hearst. The Couzens report. Anti-Hoover intrigue. Role of the National City and Giannini banks. Franklin D. Roosevelt and 1932. Hearst's mining interests and the Roosevelt policies. The Committee for the Nation. Father Coughlin. On the eve of 1936.

Chapter
X
Page 308

Analysis of Hearst's economic domain. The misleading *Fortune* article. Unloading $50,000,000 worth of stock upon the public. The power of the banks over the Hearst properties. The "missing" $68,000,000. Is Hearst putting all his assets into mining? Real estate. Real estate and politics.

Chapter XI

Page 343

Hearst's imperialism. His reaction. His fascism. His about-face from Roosevelt and the New Deal. Hearst's visit to Hitler. Hearst and the San Francisco strike. Hitler's government is paying Hearst $400,000 a year. Hearst's fascist drive in this country as a "defense against Communism." Hearst attacks courageous teachers and professors. His anti-Soviet campaign and its falsifications. What does his life mean?

Index

Page 393

IMPERIAL HEARST
A SOCIAL BIOGRAPHY

I

WILLIAM RANDOLPH HEARST is a product of the turbulent Old West. His methods and morals are those of the San Francisco of the seventies and eighties.

His father, George Hearst, was the son of a wealthy Missouri farmer who had interests in lead mines. When George Hearst joined the gold rush of '49, the Missouri farmer's wealth supported the boy until, in 1859, George Hearst bought an interest in the Comstock silver lode for $450, which he sold two years later for a small fortune. Thereupon he formed a partnership—Hearst, Haggin, Tevis and Company—to operate in mining shares. He acquired the Homestake property in South Dakota for $70,000 in 1877 and the Anaconda property in Montana in 1884 for a pittance. After serving a few weeks of an appointive term in the United States Senate in 1886, he financed the Democratic campaign in California in that year and a year later was rewarded by being elected United States Senator. He was at once made a member of the Senate Indian Affairs Committee, by virtue of which he was able to learn well in advance of the public that the Apache chief, Geronimo, had been caught by the United States Cavalry. This information enabled Senator Hearst to buy 200,000 acres of land in northern Mexico, depreciated because of Geronimo's presence, for twenty cents an acre.[1] This land is now the Babicora ranch, worth about two million dollars, and owned by William Randolph Hearst. Senator Hearst married Phoebe Apperson, a Missouri school teacher whom wealth transformed into a philanthropist and shrewd business manager.

William Randolph Hearst was born April 29, 1863, in a San Francisco that was internationally notorious. A thousand murders a year occurred there; the Barbary Coast was wide open. He was an only child, his parents were over-indulgent, he was unruly. The environment did not provide an example of restraint.

[1] *National Cyclopedia of American Biography*, Vol. I.

He attended the Washington Grammar School in the city. Bad deportment was his chief distinction. He was sent to St. Paul's School, at Concord, N. H., but was quickly ejected "for the good of the school." He was then placed under a tutor who prepared him at home for Harvard. At Harvard, from the very first, he was continuously embroiled with the university authorities.

At this period he was unsure of himself, and tried to hide a feeling of inferiority by spending large sums of money on clothes and campus pranks. Some of these pranks were cruel, as when Hearst and his cronies humiliated performers at a Boston theater by throwing pies and ripe fruits. It was apparently necessary for Hearst to assert himself in a robust fashion; his voice had turned out to be high-pitched—in an era that preferred the basso profundo in a man. Indispensable to most of Hearst's Harvard parties were young ladies not from Boston's Back Bay, and plentiful supplies of liquor.

The only significant activities which interested him were journalistic. He became business manager of the *Lampoon*, the campus comic paper, and a frequent visitor at the plant of the Boston *Globe*, where he picked up information about newspaper mechanism. He studied the daily editions of Pulitzer's New York *World* very closely. Journalistic plans may have been budding in his mind. His father owned the San Francisco *Examiner*, acquired for a bad debt of $100,000 in 1880.

Harvard expelled Hearst for having a messenger deliver an elaborately tied package to every faculty member. Each package contained a chamber pot, the photograph of the recipient adorning the inside bottom.[2] Among the members of the faculty who received them were William James, Josiah Royce and others among the best minds of the day. Hearst's attitude toward things and persons of intellect was set. It is significant that very few of the Hearst executives have been university men, and that some of his own sons have flunked out of institutions of higher learning.

After Hearst entered politics many stories about him emanated from Harvard and were printed, to the dismay of his mother, who

---

[2] "W. R. Hearst—Epitome of Capitalist Civilization," by Lawrence Martin, *Social Frontier*, February, 1935.

withdrew her annual donation to the university in favor of the University of California, where many buildings today bear the Hearst name.

After his expulsion, and before he returned to California, young Hearst worked for a short time on the New York *World*. When Senator Hearst asked what his son proposed doing after the Harvard escapade, the young man said he wanted the *Examiner*. His father could not have been more surprised. Newspapers, in California, were not looked upon as legitimate enterprises by the public, although the journalists themselves may have entertained illusions. Newspapers were necessary adjuncts for men who sought political office, but the social standing of professional journalists was not much higher than that of runners for those hotels which rented rooms by the hour.

George Hearst, therefore, was surprised, and Mrs. Hearst was alarmed, for the family now belonged to the élite of the city. But the boy was adamant, and his father eventually capitulated, though not until his son's tears and appeals to his mother won her support.

On March 4, 1887, William Randolph Hearst, rejected by two distinguished American schools as incorrigible, became the editor and owner of the San Francisco *Examiner*, and embarked upon a career that impugned the combined work of Harvard's Eliot, Royce, James, Peirce, Munsterberg, Wendell Phillips, Santayana, Lowell and Emerson.

The *Examiner's* circulation was then negligible, and possibly Senator Hearst hoped his offspring would fail as a journalist. There is definite reason to believe that Senator Hearst later regretted this indulgence of his son's desire.

Senator Hearst died in Washington in 1891; he was eulogized in the Senate as a Western pioneer. The funeral service in the Hearst mansion on New Hampshire Avenue was attended by Senators, Congressmen, members of the diplomatic corps, and President and Mrs. Harrison.

The Senator's final commentary on his son was to leave his entire fortune of $17,000,000 to his wife. He did not disinherit William Randolph, who was then twenty-eight years old, nor did he make stipulations that would prevent him from inheriting eventually; but his action indicated he preferred that the day of his son's inheritance be postponed until the death of the mother, who was still quite young. In the code of the Old West, from which Senator Hearst came, the male always inherited—unless there were reasons compelling another course.

But Senator Hearst might as well have left his fortune to his son. Young Hearst experienced no difficulty in securing more than half of it from his mother.

>>>>>>>>>>>> II <<<<<<<<<<<<

WITH the title to the *Examiner* coaxed from his worried father, William Randolph Hearst, at the age of twenty-four, when most young men out of college are seeking some modest niche, proceeded to distract the citizens of San Francisco with journalistic jazz while he despoiled their municipality.

Young Hearst was not primarily after money: he was after power, and money was indispensable to the attainment of it. He squandered money. Had he done nothing but let his father's wealth accumulate, he would be incalculably richer today than he is.

But young Hearst, expelled from St. Paul's and Harvard, needed power; he wanted to make other people dance as he cracked the whip. Personal justification and psychological reassurance were essential to him at this period, no less than later.

It was undoubtedly his father's money, plus donations from his mother, who wanted her only child to prove himself as much a man as the rest, which kept him from going under, for at first the *Examiner* was not a financial success. It was not until the *Examiner*, following the advice of hardier souls whom Hearst gathered around himself, sank a siphon into the city treasury, that the *Examiner* ledger began to balance.

Although professors of journalism have discoursed learnedly about the "Hearst method," the essentials of a Hearst newspaper, of yesterday, today, and tomorrow, can be understood by anyone after a trip to Coney Island. There one finds Hearst journalism in terms of real life—false stimulation and the simultaneous perpetration of fraud. The spirit of Coney Island is the spirit of Hearst. Ambrose Bierce, who worked for Hearst, put it even more bluntly: "The Hearst method has all the reality of masturbation."

Hearst had trouble building the *Examiner* into a profitable business. But the community was growing, everything in it was growing, and this circumstance was on his side. Despite the lavish use of money to purchase the directing talent which he, unlike Pulitzer, lacked, young Hearst made little headway for more than a year. Advertising was not then what it is today. Although the *Examiner* snared in all the possible, and impossible, advertising, it was probably more than a decade before it was making a substantial profit from legitimate and quasi-legitimate sources. But there were many dark alleys.

The *Examiner* was then an imitation of the New York *World*, even typographically. Hearst has never been diffident about appropriating another man's ideas. One of his first innovations was to subscribe to the *World's* news service, which brought a cosmopolitan note into San Francisco journalism.

Under Senator Hearst the *Examiner* had been printed on a single web-press, one side of a sheet at a time; it looked sloppy and unprofessional. Young Hearst ordered all the equipment offered in the catalogue of a printing machinery house in the East. This action has often been cited by Hearst followers as an example of pure inspiration.

Two months after the new owner took charge the Hotel Del Monte at Monterey burned to the ground. Hearst sent a brigade of staff men to report it and issued a fourteen-page extra edition with zinc etchings. The public bit at this novelty and bought heavily.

At first Hearst had difficulty getting himself accepted as a serious newspaper proprietor by the staff. A rich man's son, expelled from Harvard, reputed to be a snob, and also a wastrel, given the paper by his father—such facts did not predispose the staff in his favor nor earn its respect. Hearst's first job was to get himself accepted as a "regular" fellow.

It was not an impossible task, however. The tall, bashful, pallid and blue-eyed young man with a straggly straw-colored mustache and the high-pitched voice, attired in flaming scarf and clothes direct from Piccadilly, set out to woo the *Examiner* men. He wined, dined and fêted his staff in a way never before seen in American journalism. All salaries were raised as a matter of course, so that everybody was quite willing to endure whatever might come. Hearst probably enjoyed the staff parties for their own sake, yet the gatherings served, as others had at Harvard, to rally about him persons who might not otherwise have accepted him at his own valuation. Some members of the *Examiner* staff remained with him for years as key lieutenants.

Hearst took over the old family summer home at Sausalito, overlooking the Bay, and acquired two yachts, the first of many in his career. With these as social bases, he invited the staff to divert itself singly and collectively. The men were given the best entertainment money could buy in the Frisco of the 'eighties. The vagrant journalists—poor, bitter, and cynical men—had a grand time, perhaps for the first time in their lives.

Most of the parties were at Sausalito; there were also wild yachting parties and affairs at a city resort called the Maison Riche. About the Sausalito house, until it was demolished in 1931, there clung a "bad odor," according to one memoir[1] of the period. San Franciscans, perhaps out of envy, were inclined to consider the Sausalito parties scandalous. Young Hearst, it is true, was girl-crazy. There is nothing unique about that. What was somewhat unusual was that he apparently felt some need to flaunt his amorous adventures in public. In San Francisco at this period—as well as during the early New York period—Hearst would go about, not with one girl, but with *two*, one on each arm. This gave him an air of apparently excessive masculinity.

Once Hearst had won the *Examiner* staff, the parties ended. He terminated them by absenting himself in Europe and closing the Sausalito place, forgetting to resume them upon his return.

"To talk with one of the survivors of that crew is to get the flavor of a happy and extravagant world, now gone forever," wrote George P. West, an old California newspaper man.[2] "The *Examiner* office was a madhouse inhabited by talented and erratic young men, drunk with life in a city that never existed before or since. They had a mad boss, one who flung away money, lived like a ruler of the late Empire at his house above the water at Sausalito, and cheered them on as they made newspaper history."

[1] "Hearst: A Psychological Note," by George P. West, *American Mercury*, November, 1930.
[2] *American Mercury*, November, 1930.

In every city with a Hearst newspaper the Hearst office has always been known to the profession as "the madhouse."

There were additions to the *Examiner* staff. Arthur McEwen, Hearst's friend at Harvard, an associate on the *Lampoon* and a companion in many of the campus pranks, was brought on as editorial writer. It was McEwen who epitomized the Hearst objective: "What we're after is the gee-whiz emotion."[3]

But it was not until the late Sam S. Chamberlain, whom Hearst first met in the barroom of the Hoffman House in New York, took charge as managing editor that the *Examiner* really hit its stride. Chamberlain—drunken, profane, corrupt—reeled into the scene in 1888 and was given an enormous salary. The black art of nineteenth-century journalism was at Chamberlain's white, cynical, pudgy fingertips.

His presence on the Pacific Coast resulted from close association with John W. Mackay, who had founded *Le Matin* in Paris, where he had learned the *sub rosa* refinements of journalism at a time when French public life, never much above the level of boudoir melodrama, was at its lowest. Mackay and his partner, James Fair, who became United States Senator from California, had conspired[4] with agents of the dissolute Louis Napoleon, in the wake of the Franco-Prussian War, to corner the world's wheat market. *Le Matin* was an offshoot of this grandiloquent scheme, which almost ruined Mackay and Fair. Chamberlain had also worked for Pulitzer and the elder James Gordon Bennett, the leading sensationalists in American journalism up to that time.

Chamberlain was rarely seen in San Francisco sober. There is a story that A. B. Henderson, Hearst's business manager, cabled Hearst, who was in Europe, for permission to discharge Chamberlain for habitual drunkenness. Hearst replied: "If he is sober one day in thirty that is all I require."[5]

Henderson, according to an uncensored version of this episode,

---

[3] "The American Newspaper," by Will Irwin, *Collier's*, January 21, 1911, et seq.
[4] *The Big Bonanza*, by C. B. Glasscock, Bobbs-Merrill Co., Indianapolis and New York, 1931.
[5] *W. R. Hearst: An American Phenomenon*, by John K. Winkler, Simon and Schuster, New York, 1928.

had more to complain of than drunkenness. Chamberlain had been so drunk in his office that he had had an unfortunate accident of which he was unaware. In this condition a lady from one of San Francisco's women's clubs found him when she breezed in on a publicity errand, and hastily withdrew with a painful impression of the Hearst management.

It was from the corrupt Continental journalism, rather than from the staid Anglo-Saxon, that Hearst, through Chamberlain, learned how to go beyond the tamer Pulitzer sensationalism.[6] The Anglo-Saxon tradition, far from perfect and twisted beyond recognition in the newspapers of the early West, required a certain sobriety of statement, an adherence to matters of general public interest and some relation to facts. Parisian journalism, always frankly bought and paid for, "inspired" behind the scenes, ruled by the personal element, featuring the *crime passionel* in all gory details, has never pretended to serve even a general ideal of truth. Frankly, cynically, the Parisian newspapers belonged to groups and factions with private points of view. Today in Paris *boulevardières* know, or suspect, at any given moment, which special interest is behind each newspaper. The Foreign Office, the munitions cartel, the colonial concession hunters, the wealthy wife of an ambitious Deputy, political parties, the Church, the Royalists—each has a newspaper.

Chamberlain had two problems to solve for the *Examiner*. One was to get circulation, the other to get money. Senator Hearst's indulgence was problematical from the first.

In the quest for circulation the *Examiner* began to feature the pious utterances of the city's clergy. It denounced crime and corruption, sedition, treason and all the traditional sins. It invariably threw in some piquant morsel of sex.

During this shaping of editorial policy, Hearst worked with the staff as he has never worked since. At night he wrote detailed instructions for each staff member. Chamberlain's office was the rallying center. Hearst was usually found there, accepting without question whatever Chamberlain advised.

[6] Few newspaper readers today remember that Pulitzer, in his early days, published highly sensational newspapers. His New York *World* was not always the respectable publication it subsequently became.

The *Examiner* also began to assail petty municipal abuses, to sneer at the big corporations, and to scuttle the Republican and Democratic machines of the city. Its readers assumed all this to be on behalf of civic righteousness. With Hearst and Chamberlain, however, it was a necessary step to getting money independently of Senator Hearst, and it was not an advertising age.

Opposing established political bosses was dangerous to Senator Hearst, but for this the Senator's offspring apparently did not care. The *Examiner* exposed Chris Buckley, the saloon-keeper who had placed Senator Hearst in the United States Senate, and Buckley's crony, Sam Rainey. It disclosed that Buckley's saloon on Bush Street was the rendezvous of Jimmy Hope, a notorious bank bandit, and that Hope, though wanted for crimes in many states, freely moved about San Francisco under political protection. Buckley and Rainey were indicted and had to flee. The *Examiner* also turned on Martin Kelly and Phil Crimmins, the Republican bosses, and virtually stripped them of power.

According to Hearst's biographer, John K. Winkler,[7] Senator Hearst approved of this, after mildly remonstrating with his son. Yet Senator Hearst, whatever his defects, was never disloyal. So far as the record shows, he had never double-crossed anyone.

Chamberlain and Hearst were after big game. They wanted to operate the political machinery themselves, and after Buckley was deposed the first Hearst political venture occurred—with a group of Democrats composed of Hearst himself, Franklin K. Lane, who became Wilson's Secretary of the Interior, Gavin McNab, Frederick Lawrence, the brother of Andrew Lawrence and himself a Hearst reporter, Judge D. G. Sullivan and Frank H. Dunne.[8]

The first booty that fell into the maw of the *Examiner* was a contract for all the city and county printing and for the publication of official notices. This is a plum often angled for by American newspapers. It was "legitimate" political spoil for loyal party papers. In the case of Hearst, the spoils were procured by scuttling one faction of his party in order to install his own jerry-built faction. No principle, or political need, underlay the maneuver.

[7] Former reporter on the New York *Journal*.
[8] *W. R. Hearst, an American Phenomenon*, by John K. Winkler.

The coup placed the *Examiner* on its financial feet. In addition to the printing contracts, it now had a ground-floor insight into plans for future civic improvements which made many private real estate deals very profitable. Hearst's rôle as one of the nation's big real estate operators dates from this early period. Political machines in Chicago, New York, Los Angeles, Boston and elsewhere were to yield similar opportunities.

Simultaneously with his development of a political machine Hearst was buying talent. Winifred Black ("Annie Laurie," the first sob-sister and precursor of the countless Beatrice Fairfaxes offering advice to the lovelorn) was among the first feature writers. Bud Fisher, creator of "Mutt and Jeff," T. A. Dorgan ("Tad"), Homer Davenport and Harrison Fisher were others. Edward W. Townsend, creator of "Chimmie Fadden" and his gas-house lingo, was in the business office. Phineas Taylor wrote "Casey at the Bat" for the *Examiner*. Then and later the *Examiner* used material from Gertrude Atherton, Mark Twain, Max O'Rell, Bret Harte, Edwin Markham, Jack London, Ambrose Bierce and many others. Edwin Markham's "The Man With the Hoe" was printed by the *Examiner* in 1899. This celebrated poem served as the model for the following parody on Hearst published by the San Francisco *News-Letter* of May 8, 1904:

THE MAN WITH THE DOUGH

Bowed by the weight of infamy he leans
Upon his tub, and gazes at his gold,
The emptiness of folly on his face,
And on his back the brand of good men's hate.
Who made him dead to decency and truth—

A thing that feels not, and can never think,
Stupid and dull, own brother to the ass.
Who gave his face its vacuous, leering grin?
Whose was the hand that shaped those trembling lips,
Slobbering with weakness, tremulous with vice?
Whose breath blew out his light, and made a beast?

*Is this the thing that dare aspire and hope
To place his name where honest men have writ?
To make decrees and work his bestial will—
To sell his land to anarchy and strife?
To play the fool with our great destiny?
And is this gold the instrument he wields?—
The filthy gold oozing in yellow drops.*

*The color of the sheet that shouts his name,
The color of the blood in his poisoned veins,
The gold his father gathered by his toil,
The gold his mother spends in deeds of love,
The gold that in his vicious hand becomes
A tool of treason and a villain's aid.*

*What gulfs between him and great Jefferson!
Slave of destroying vices, what to him
Are Honor and the calls of Chivalry?
What the integrity which strong men prize,
The blush of modesty, the strength of truth?
The barrel that he hugs is all his God,—
He knows no music but the jingling coins,
And with such music he has charmed the minds
Of fawning things, prostrating their cheap souls
In mute obedience to his filthiness.*

*O citizens and Masters of the State,
How will your reason reckon with this man?
How answer his brute question when he seeks
To brand his infamy upon this land?
How will it be with all his treasure then,
When honest men shall thrust him into Hell
And let him shrivel through the centuries?*

Hearst was an aspirant to the Presidency of the United States when it appeared.

IMPERIAL HEARST

To get Bierce on his staff Hearst called at the writer's lodgings. Bierce at first thought it was one of the office boys sent to invite him to the lair of the much-talked-about *enfant terrible*. But no!

"That unearthly child," Bierce later wrote in his memoirs,[9] "lifted its blue eyes and cooed, 'I am Mr. Hearst,' in a voice like the fragrance of violets made audible, and backed a little away."

Bierce worked for Hearst for twenty years—a long interval. At the end of that time he wrote, "I am not sorry that, discovering no preservative allowable under the Pure Food Law that would allow him to keep his word overnight, I withdrew."

Bierce's literary talent was useful to Hearst. It struck fear into influential San Franciscans; but Bierce, lacking realistic social insight, probably did not realize the full extent of his usefulness. Chamberlain, however, with his Paris training, knew that the acidulous utterances of the columnist are a magic key that opens strong boxes. Bierce rarely chewed the same cud twice, and, one may confidently suppose, on the basis of insight provided by documents in other connections, that when Bierce's rapier flashed a collector from the *Examiner* appeared somewhat later in the innocent guise of an advertising agent. Bierce may not have known about this, but it would have been odd, after two decades with Hearst, if he had not.[10]

Circulation was essential. An audience gave Hearst his power.

In 1888 the *Examiner* instituted a campaign to have the Democratic convention brought to the then uncouth San Francisco. Hearst went to Washington: President Cleveland had to intercede to keep the convention in the East. This campaign cost $80,000 but was worth infinitely more in the national advertising it gave Hearst. The young blade who, two years before, was distributing chamber pots

---

[9] "In Motley," p. 305 *et seq.*, in *The Collected Works of Ambrose Bierce*, Neale Publishing Co., New York and Washington, 1909-1912.

[10] A perfect illustration of this confirmed Hearst practice was reported by the New York *Call* on June 23, 1911, shortly after the fire in the Triangle shirt-waist factory in New York City, in which scores of girls were burned to death. The *Call* alleged that the New York *Journal* was sending reporters to promise proprietors of sweatshops that the *Journal* would reestablish public confidence in the shirt-waist industry by issuing a booklet containing editorials and articles if they would take advertisements costing from $100 to $150. The alternative to buying an ad and obtaining a whitewashing was—publicity.

to the Harvard faculty, was now causing the President of the United States to bestir himself.

There were many *Examiner* "stunts" to attract attention and circulation. Winifred Black simulated a fainting spell in Market Street and was taken to the City Receiving Hospital, and two days later the *Examiner* exposed "horrendous" conditions at the hospital. Miss Black did not neglect the sex factor: attendants at the hospital subjected women patients to various titillating indignities. Were the doctors conducting necessarily intimate examinations? The *Examiner* preferred the innuendo.

When a baby was born to a prostitute in the city prison, young Hearst (or Chamberlain) saw a way to turn this event to advantage. The *Examiner*, its heart bleeding with pity, started a fund for this infant, fortunate enough to be born when Hearst needed publicity. The fund was named after an anarchist in jail on a charge of dynamiting a street railway. (Hearst was soliciting the support of organized labor and indiscriminately applauded dynamiters, bombers, anarchists and nihilists, to the consternation of conservatives and responsible labor leaders.) The *Examiner* readers subscribed $20,000 toward a fund of $250,000 for a children's hospital, which Hearst, in a rash moment, had underwritten. The *Examiner* put more and more effort into a campaign to get the public to put up the money. Balloon ascensions, contests, and catch-penny prizes were resorted to, but Hearst in the end was personally involved for about $200,000. It was a long time, however, before he gave the money.

The *Examiner* dispatched a trainload of school children to the World's Fair at Chicago, interviewed a pair of bandits in the mountains when the police could not get at them, captured a live grizzly bear, but did not campaign against the Red Light district of the Barbary Coast, whence it derived solid revenue. But it did send a staff man to Canada who returned with a detailed story of the smuggling of Chinese labor and opium into the United States. The *Examiner*, true to the California spirit, was against the influx of the Chinese. The irony of this was that the Hearst family was then, and for many years, the biggest employer of cheap Chinese labor in California. When "Chinese on your ranch" was later shouted at Hearst with telling effect in political campaigns, it was one of the few charges which could make him writhe. Fifteen years later Hearst offered $10,000 to anyone who could prove that he had employed Chinese labor, but when mining engineers and neighboring ranchers stepped forward they could not collect the reward.

By 1889 the *Examiner* had a circulation of 55,000 daily, 62,000 on Sunday. A forty-page edition was issued on October 20, 1889, to commemorate two successful years, and in it the *Examiner* announced itself as "The Monarch of the Dailies." With this edition Hearst began the commemoratory racket later used by all the Hearst papers on all occasions—Easter, Christmas, Fourth of July, and Labor Day. For these special editions the Hearst advertising agents comb the cities. All true-blue businessmen want to mark the occasion by appropriately large notices at specially advanced rates. They don't? Well, that is too bad, for the city tax collector, the health department or the police may be obliged to find infractions of at least one ordinance.

At the end of 1889 the *Examiner* published a forty-page New Year's edition. The inspiration for much of its contents came from the books of Jules Verne, and this type of material established a pattern for thousands of journalistic fakes perpetrated by Hearst. The second section of the "mammoth" New Year's issue was called "The Edition of the Future." It was devoted to a melange of fantasy *presented as news*, with a line, in small type, that it was not fact. Few noticed the disclaimer, and nobody was supposed to; but it was a loophole if unpleasant repercussions occurred.

But that was not all. The *second* section was placed *first* and newsboys shouted such headlines as this:

BOSTON IS DESTROYED
ANOTHER EARTHQUAKE CALAMITY IN THE EAST

There followed a long, graphic and detailed story about the destruction of Boston by a mysterious temblor, in which thousands of lives were lost.

The next day the *Examiner* noted with bland satisfaction that an old lady and others with relatives in Boston had been given a pleasing thrill of terror.

Hearst has never had scruples against printing fiction and intentionally false statements as fact. Even in his early San Francisco days there was an accumulation of open-and-shut libel suits that had been brought against him. He has probably been sued for libel more often, and paid more libel damages, than any other American. He has also, for the purpose of *pretending* to contest accusations, probably brought more libel actions than any other living individual. He has won very few. In more recent years he has avoided bringing libel actions—for excellent reasons.

Some professors of journalism have been surprised by what they considered to be the journalistic innovations Hearst introduced. There is no evidence that between 1887 and 1895 Hearst showed any originality at all. All of the *Examiner's* ideas were borrowed. Hearst has been credited with inventing the "exposé," but it was old even in San Francisco when he began. The New York *Times* had already exposed the Tweed Ring in New York, perhaps the first spectacular "exposé" in the history of American journalism. Pulitzer was using the "exposé" while Hearst was at Harvard. The "human interest" story is also supposed to have been invented by Hearst, but Pulitzer was using it when Hearst was still placing pins on adults' chairs. And E. W. Scripps established the first newspaper chain in 1875.

Though it posed as the public protector against public wrongs in its news columns, the *Examiner* in its advertising columns gave itself dead away.

It was an unmoral decade in an unmoral city, and newspaper standards generally were not high. But the *Examiner,* in the words of one of its staff, was "The Whore's Daily Guide and Handy Compendium."

A stranger in San Francisco, perusing the *Examiner*, would have his steps guided by such advertisements as these, *which appeared every day:*

MASSAGE: Ethel Lacost, young French lady, gives massage. 20½ Fifth Street, Room 15.
MME. AIMEE, with newly arrived assistants; new system of magnetic and massage treatment. 517 Post St.
GENUINE massage treatment by an Eastern lady. 19 Sixth Street, Room 2.

Patrons of the *Examiner*, male or female, who encountered classic difficulties as a result of the massage treatments, needed only to consult the *Examiner* for further guidance, as follows:

MEDICAL. A written guarantee given; my process, without medicine, restores every case of monthly or other conditions, from whatever cause; womb complaint a specialty; home for confinements; pills or powders, $1; send stamps. Mrs. Dr. Dale, 404 Golden Gate Avenue.
ALL female monthly periods are restored at once, after all others failed, by my Safe Specific, no matter from what cause; pills, powders, $1; latest Regulator with or without medicine. Mrs. Dr. Strassman, 916 Post Street.
MRS. WILSON of 312 Sixth Street is now at 77 Ninth Street; confinement $15; women's diseases a specialty; sure cure for catarrh.

"Catarrh" is the trade name for gonorrhea.

A NEW PROCESS discovered by Dr. E. Vice, the celebrated female physician of Berlin, for irregularities.
WOMEN who have fallen and wish to reform. Will find Christian home and friends by addressing J. W. Ellsworth.

As for the gentlemen, they could find in the *Examiner* advertisements of "sure cures" for gonorrhea and syphilis, tuberculosis, cancer and other plagues as well.

Despite this unsavory record, of which the foregoing is only a sample, Hearst was not prevented some years afterward from having investigators track down evidence against the "Agony Column" in the New York *Herald*. As a result of Hearst-procured evidence the younger Bennett was indicted, *in absentia*, in Federal court, of using the mails to facilitate immoral traffic. He was fined $10,000, and he paid without demur.

With a political apparatus of its own, and circulation, the *Examiner* was ready to turn its attention to Big Business, in accordance with the best French tradition.

The Southern Pacific was the biggest thing in California. It controlled everything from the Governor and the Legislature down to the judges on the bench and below. The ranching and mining interests, which had experienced prosperity because of it, kowtowed even while grumbling about its rates. The railroad interlaced all of California. By fair means and foul the Southern Pacific had built itself into the strongest single force in the state. Behind it stood, or had stood, the state's biggest men: Leland Stanford, Collis P. Huntington, E. H. Harriman, Darius Ogden Mills.

The *Examiner* did not challenge the railroad to open combat until Senator Hearst was in his grave; to Senator Hearst, as to many old-timers, the Southern Pacific was sacred. It represented progress. Senator Stanford was Senator Hearst's colleague and friend, and delivered a funeral oration for him in 1891.

Neither Hearst nor Chamberlain had any reverence for the Southern Pacific or its managers. Young Hearst had met the whole Southern Pacific crowd at his parents' home on Nob Hill and regarded them as museum pieces, and fair game. Nor had Chamberlain, who had been on intimate terms with Mackay, any admiration for them.

The campaign against the Southern Pacific swept the circulation of the *Examiner* to heights which all the feature stories, contests and prizes of the earlier years had failed to reach. The *Examiner* had touched a live wire in the form of a basic social issue. Unwittingly, it had stumbled into the midst of the class struggle, though it had no intention of sincerely fighting on the people's side.

The *Examiner* charged the Southern Pacific and Collis P. Huntington with legislative bribing, franchise stealing, tax juggling, maltreatment of labor and the farmers, and general perfidy. Evidence, dubious and valid, was produced. Fiction was interwoven indiscriminately with fact. Huntington was represented as some sort of beast, in a way that capitalists are not represented even in radical publications today. The public response to this typically Parisian journalism, and not the campaign itself (it was not intended to bring about any reform), worried the directors of the Southern Pacific. For more than a year the assault continued furiously and then—it suddenly stopped.

People were as astonished by its abrupt cessation as they had been by its beginning. They purchased the *Examiner* to learn of some new nefarious phase of the "Octopus." There were rumors that the *Examiner* was merely waiting in order to produce a greater dramatic effect in the disclosure of some crushing piece of new evidence. But nothing appeared. San Franciscans began to call at the *Examiner* office and to write letters. Stories that the paper had sold out to the railroad, that the railroad now really owned the paper, very naturally went through the city. Threatening letters were sent to the newspaper by the inflamed individuals among a gulled public. Hearst and Chamberlain became alarmed. Hearst went to Egypt, leaving Chamberlain to weather the storm. And it was a real storm!

The circulation began to go down. So the *Examiner*, after several months of silence, commenced a feeble sniping campaign. It is because of this sniping that the full and amazing story of the blackmail of the Southern Pacific by Hearst's *Examiner* came out. This story does not appear in any of the standard histories of American journalism.

In 1897 Collis P. Huntington was in Washington testifying, as the head of the Southern Pacific, before the Committee on Pacific Railroads of the House of Representatives. The questions, for the most part, were based on material which had appeared in the Hearst papers. Huntington contended that Hearst was merely persecuting him and the railroad.

In conversation with reporters and Congressmen after the committee session, Huntington was asked what he thought animated Hearst.

"We won't keep him on the payroll," Huntington growled.

The audience gasped. Among those who heard this revelation was C. C. Carlton, Washington correspondent of the San Francisco *Call*. He sent the story to his paper, which published it.

The *Examiner* immediately wired Bierce, then in Washington, and asked whether Huntington had said it. Bierce made inquiries, and laconically wired back: "Carlton was right. Huntington said it."

The *Examiner* boldly gave the lie direct to the *Call*, which was owned by John Spreckels, sugar magnate and head of a group trying to reform San Francisco politics, beginning with Hearst, whom it considered a cancer on the body politic. This group had its own economic interests to serve, too.

For more than a year after the Huntington remark, agents for the *Call* put pressure on the Southern Pacific and the Wells Fargo Bank to do something about Hearst. These institutions were finally convinced that something had to be done to stop Hearst or he would be running the whole state for his own benefit and not theirs. Thereupon the *Call* was provided with all the documents, which were published in October, 1898.

They are among the most bizarre mementoes in the tortured history of American journalism.

In the end they forced Hearst to transfer his principal political activities from California to New York.

Exhibit A:

San Francisco
June 29, 1892

C. M. Palmer, Esq.,
Business Manager of the *Examiner*,
San Francisco, California.

Dear Sir—We hereby agree to engage space in the Grand Special World's Fair edition of the San Francisco *Examiner*, matter to be furnished by us, including cuts, for twenty pages, or one hundred and forty columns, for which the Southern Pacific Company agrees to pay Thirty Thousand Dollars ($30,000) gold coin of the United States, payable at the rate of One Thousand Dollars ($1,000) per month or in larger instalments at the option of the Southern Pacific Company, and all in accordance with an agreement entered into between the *Examiner* management and C. F. Crocker, A. N. Towne and William H. Mills on behalf of the Southern Pacific Company, it being understood that the said edition shall have a minimum issue of five hundred thousand copies, and shall be published simultaneously at San Francisco and Chicago on or about the date of the official opening of the Columbian Exposition.

And it is further agreed that the said matter shall be subject to enlargement, alteration and revision at the option of the Southern Pacific Company at any time prior to February 1, 1893.

> Yours truly,
> W. H. Mills, for the Southern Pacific Company
> Charles F. Crocker, Vice-President

IMPERIAL HEARST   39

On September 24, 1893, Colonel Crocker wrote to Mr. Palmer as follows:

Some time in August last W. T. Herrin met yourself and your manager, Mr. Henderson, relative to the instalments unpaid on the contract between your paper and the Southern Pacific Company, dated June 29, 1892. I understand from Mr. Herrin that in your interview with him you agreed at that time that the contract was made providing for the payment of $30,000 to the *Examiner*, it was stated by your agents as an inducement to the railroad for making this contract that the *Examiner* would accord to the railroad company fair treatment in its columns.

Mr. Herrin then informed you that it was my opinion, as well as that of other directors of the Southern Pacific Company, that the *Examiner* had not, especially during the strike, given the company fair treatment. To this you replied that you believed that the *Examiner* had fairly treated the railroad company and that if you thought it had not done so you would not expect the company to make any further payments on the above-mentioned contract.

It was certainly a part of the contract between the *Examiner* and the railroad company that the *Examiner* should accord fair treatment to the railroad. In view of this contract, I do not assume for a moment that you would insist upon the railroad's paying the *Examiner* the full sum of $30,000 if the *Examiner* had not fully performed the stipulation made in its behalf.

The *Call* also printed the following undated letter from H. E. Huntington, of the Southern Pacific, to T. T. Williams of the *Examiner* business office:

You admit that in consideration of the sum of $30,000 to be paid in monthly instalments to the *Examiner* by the Southern Pacific Company, the company was to receive certain advertising and fair treatment. There can be no question that the chief consideration to inure to the Southern Pacific Company in its transaction was the fair treatment to be accorded by your paper; that it would not have entered into an agreement to pay $30,000 for advertising merely, as the benefit to accrue from such advertising alone was grossly inadequate to the sum of money involved.

It is now assumed, on behalf of the *Examiner*, that the question of fair treatment is one which could be determined by the *Examiner* management only, and could not possibly be a question of debate or arbitration . . . During the negotiations which led to this contract it was not suggested nor intimated that Mr. Hearst would solely and arbitrarily determine all questions as to such negotiations which led up to this contract. Had we been apprised of such intention it is not likely that the contract proposed would have been entered into.

Hearst, reacting characteristically to the exposure by the *Call*, retorted with abuse against the paper, describing its proprietor as "John Degenerate Spreckels, Fool and Failure." (The *Examiner*, October 23, 1898.) Hearst tried to evade personal responsibility by saying his subordinates had exceeded their authority while he was in Egypt and that as soon as he found out about this contract he proceeded to rescind it. But the *Call* nailed Hearst's explanation by showing that he personally had assigned the contract for cash to the First National Bank of San Francisco. The assignment[11] was dated July 24, 1893, and read:

"For value received I hereby assign the within claim against the Southern Pacific Company, balance due therein at this date being $19,000, to the First National Bank of San Francisco." It was signed "The *Examiner*, W. R. Hearst," and this signature was witnessed by I. C. Stump.

Commenting on this, the *Call* said:

"Now, when Hearst assigned this contract to the bank, putting this assignment and signature on its back alongside of Crocker's certificate to it, what were the legal facts? Crocker certified that the contract was valid and would be paid when due 'according to the terms thereof.' If there was no agreement behind the contract Hearst had performed his part, for the *Examiner* had completed and delivered the advertising called for, and had thereby completed his undertaking openly written in the contract. But Crocker's indorsement implied legally that Hearst's undertaking was not completed; that 'according to the terms thereof' Hearst had something to do besides advertising, which had been completed and delivered. . . .

"When he personally hypothecated that contract, with the clause which made the secret agreement a part of it, and with Crocker's indorsement of its validity it performed 'according to the terms thereof,' Hearst could not be ignorant of the condition of the sale nor of the time lock it had upon his lying and blackguardism for the space of thirty months.

[11] Reproduced by the San Francisco *Call*, October 24, 1898.

"At the date of this hypothecation there was due on the contract $19,000, and the Southern Pacific continued payment until June, 1894. The next payment, due July 11, 1894, was defaulted on the ground that the 'terms thereof' had been violated by the *Examiner*."

The contract itself, one of the most astounding documents in the history of American journalism, was dated June 29, 1892, and reads:[12]

"The company is to enjoy immunity from hostility in the columns of the *Examiner*, and it is not to be the victim of malicious attack or criticism or misrepresentations; that the *Examiner* will not seek to create hostile sentiment in the minds of the community against the Southern Pacific Company, or any of the interests it represents, and that while not stipulating as against all criticism, it agrees that criticism shall not proceed from any motive of malice or malignity and that such criticism as may be found necessary to keep and maintain the confidence of the public to the extent that any public sentiment may have been created from other sources, is to be avoided as much as possible."

Underneath were the following notations:

"Col. Crocker: The above is my understanding. How does it conform with your understanding? W. H. Mills" [land agent of the railroad].

"This agrees with my understanding quite fully. Certainly nothing less would be satisfactory. Charles F. Crocker."

"As I understand the talk, the above covers the understanding fully. A. N. Towne."

The signer on behalf of the Examiner was Frank Gassaway of the business office. Gassaway placed parentheses around the clause "is to enjoy immunity from hostility in the columns of the *Examiner* and," but approved the balance:

By this contract, the *Call* said, Hearst promised, for $30,000, not to be "a liar and a blackguard."

"That the money was paid for another purpose was clearly understood by Hearst and the Southern Pacific people," the *Call* con-

---

[12] Published by the San Francisco *Call* in October, 1898, and by the New York *Herald*, October 30, 1906.

tinued. "The proprietor of 'The Monarch of the Dailies' demanded $30,000 as the price to cease malicious attacks upon the railroad and the varied interests it represents. The officials of the road recognized the wisdom of acceding to the demands, but in doing so they forced from Hearst a secret agreement that in consideration of the money received he would show no malice or malignity in his paper toward Southern Pacific interests.

"The railroad men did not ask for fairness. They framed a contract that Hearst accepted, and in accepting admitted that he had been paid $30,000 to be decent in his treatment of a great corporation. . . . If there was no secret blackmail agreement referred to in the advertising contract of June 29, 1892, the Southern Pacific Company owes Hearst a balance of $8,000 on that contract. Let him bring suit for that amount. If the statute of limitations has run, the *Call* will agree to pay any judgment that Hearst gets against the Southern Pacific Company if the company will waive the statute."

Hearst did not bring suit.

After the turn of the century, despite the Southern Pacific scandal, Hearst's influence in California became more decisive than ever. In the San Francisco elections of 1901, Hearst, from headquarters in New York, backed the ticket of the new Union-Labor Party which elected Mayor Eugene E. Schmitz, a former union theater musician. In 1903 and 1905 Schmitz, backed by labor, was reëlected. Schmitz's campaign manager was Abraham Ruef, a former honor student at the University of California.

The Ruef-Schmitz machine, backed by Hearst, gave San Francisco the most corrupt administration in its history. It took money wherever it could be found, specializing in the sale of franchises to such corporations as the United Railroads, the Spring Valley Water Company (which supplied San Francisco with its water), the Home States Telephone Company, the Pacific Telephone and Telegraph Company, the Southern Pacific Company and others. And of course it exacted tribute from prostitutes and gamblers.

San Francisco was governed by a board of eighteen supervisors who belonged to the Ruef-Schmitz machine, and who grafted independently. There was no coördination in the graft. The direct

Hearst representative on this board was Jennings J. Phillips, the *Examiner's* circulation manager and boss of its strong-arm men. These thugs functioned in boosting circulation, in political campaigns, and on private errands for Hearst himself.

The first adverse development for the Ruef-Schmitz-Hearst combination was the election by the machine itself of William H. Langdon as District Attorney in 1906. Langdon immediately appointed Francis J. Heney, who had won fame as the government prosecutor in the Oregon land scandals, as his assistant. Preparations were at once made for proceeding against the Ruef-Schmitz-Hearst machine. His backers in this fight were Senator James D. Phelan (large-scale San Francisco realty operator tired of paying tribute, and who had previously been double-crossed in a political alliance with Hearst), Spreckels and Fremont Older, editor of the *Bulletin*.

It was not a principled opposition that was waged by Spreckels, Phelan and Older, as it turned out later, although during the period of conflict there were many appeals to idealism against the depravity of Hearst. Scrutinized closely, the anti-Hearst forces were more dangerous socially, for they convincingly drew about themselves the mantle of righteousness. Spreckels and Phelan were after the very political power that Hearst had, and Older, as editor of the *Bulletin*, was one of their instruments. Older participated in many of the campaigns against Hearst until he joined Hearst in 1918, becoming editor of the *Call-Bulletin*, the result of Hearst's merging his two old enemies, the *Call* and the *Bulletin*. In 1936 Mrs. Older published an "authorized" biography of William Randolph Hearst[13] which either ignores or distorts the significant facts in Hearst's career. Older's autobiography[14] does relate, however, that the old *Bulletin*, as well as Hearst's *Examiner*, was on the payroll of the Southern Pacific.

In 1906 the Ruef-Schmitz-Hearst machine placed James L. Gallagher in the Mayor's chair and on October 25th of that year Gallagher ordered Langdon, whose investigators were sifting through old records, removed from office. The order was carried out by the

[13] *William Randolph Hearst: American*, by Mrs. Fremont Older, D. Appleton-Century Co., 1936.
[14] *My Own Story*, by Fremont Older, The Call Publishing Co., San Francisco, 1919. Hearst owned the *Call* when his company published this book.

servile Board of Supervisors. But Heney proceeded with the investigation while Langdon fought the removal order in the courts. Ruef and Schmitz were eventually indicted and were found guilty of extortion on June 13, 1907. Led by the *Examiner*, all the San Francisco papers at this time, except the *Bulletin* and the *Call*, were assailing the prosecution.

The District Court of Appeals upset the convictions in January, 1908, and Heney prepared a new case amid an atmosphere of intensified bitterness. After this court decision the *Examiner*, which had been circumspect in criticizing the prosecution, carried on a venomous campaign against the forces of law and order in San Francisco. Just before the Court of Appeals' reversal the *Examiner* had confined itself to protesting against conditions in the prison in which the sensitive Ruef and delicate Schmitz were confined, thereby showing the two convicts that it was still on their side, inducing them not to talk about Hearst.

Mayor Gallagher, seeing the handwriting on the wall, went over to the side of the prosecution before the second trial began. His former political associates bombed his home. Buildings which Gallagher owned in Oakland were also demolished. This wave of anarchism, creating public hysteria, was endorsed by the *Examiner*, which printed cartoons depicting the explosion of a bird cage. *Examiner* editorials described the escape of a parrot from the cage.

The excitement was only beginning. Prosecutor Heney was shot in the head in the court room during the second trial and for several weeks his life was in danger. His assailant was Morris Haas, a former convict, "planted" by the Ruef-Schmitz forces in the jury panel at the first trial. Heney had dramatically exposed Haas, and for this Haas was seeking personal vengeance. The shooting occurred on November 13, 1908. While Heney lay at the point of death, the *Examiner* published cartoons ridiculing him and the prosecution.

Public indignation was now thoroughly aroused. Mobs milled around the *Examiner* office and threatened the destruction of the property. Hearst hirelings were posted inside with shotguns, rifles and revolvers. The police dispersed the crowds with difficulty.

It was now obvious that the *Examiner* was closely in league with the criminal political element and could not speak out against it. Subscriptions to the paper were cancelled by the thousands. The *Chronicle*, which had been aligned with the defendants, now mildly supported the prosecution.

At length the prosecution, which had been taken up by young Hiram Johnson, was successful in placing Ruef and Schmitz permanently behind bars. Thereupon the *Examiner* resumed publication of stories about frightful prison conditions which were *injuring the health* of the two former political bosses, thus paving the way for their eventual parole.

An extraordinary picture of political corruption by the Ruef-Schmitz-Hearst machine was revealed during the course of the trials. Graft was regularly received from gambling dens, Barbary Coast dives, "French restaurants," and public service corporations. Schmitz was convicted in a "French restaurant" case.

The "French restaurants" were institutions peculiar to San Francisco. There was nothing really French about them. They were public restaurants where liquor and food were dispensed on the ground floor, but with private rooms upstairs to which gentlemen could retire with ladies.

The "French restaurants" were notorious. After the trials, many cried the loudest against them who had found them in the past to be veritable public utilities. But the public had not known about the political graft these places paid, nor realized that many were owned by so-called respectable citizens. For example, during the trial it developed that a conservative regent of the University of California who was also a bank officer had money invested in several "French restaurants."

The evidence against Ruef and Schmitz had been gathered by William J. Burns, who was later to be closely associated with Hearst. Hiram Johnson, the prosecutor (elected Governor of California in 1910 and again in 1914 on the Republican ticket), also soon became attached to the Hearst political retinue, for Hearst keeps company only with winners. In 1909 Republican Charles M. Fickert, who achieved international notoriety as the man who fabricated the evidence against Tom Mooney, was elected District Attorney and, in time, also became part of the Hearst political entourage in California.

As far as any overt action was concerned, the *Examiner* was immune from prosecution, although it had been deeply involved in the conspiracies of the Schmitz-Ruef machine and had been favored in tax matters. Also, Hearst had personally made tremendous real estate profits during the régime simply by being advised of new moves the administration planned and of franchises to be given to public service companies.

In 1912 William J. Burns was in the Hearst camp, and was called into the case of the bombing of the Los Angeles *Times*, owned by Harrison Grey Otis, a rabid labor-baiter. In its issues of January 6 and 7, 1912, the San Francisco *Bulletin* charged that Hearst, formerly an ostensible friend of union labor,[15] had turned against union labor because the American Federation of Labor would not support his absurd political ambitions. The *Bulletin* reported that District Attorney John D. Fredericks, of Los Angeles, prosecutor of the McNamara brothers for the bombing, was working with Hearst, who was grooming him for Governor of California.

Hearst was the "press-agent for the prosecution," the *Bulletin* charged, and went on to reveal "his quiet, under-the-surface campaign to punish organized labor for its failure to support him for the Presidency of the United States."

W. J. Burns, later head of the Bureau of Investigation of the Department of Justice, in return for the publicity given to him by the Hearst papers, which represented him as a superman, provided them with all the details of the man-hunt for the McNamaras. The Hearst papers were calling for J. J. McNamara's skin even before his arrest; they obtained the news of every new twist before any other paper. *The Hearst papers demanded the indictment of every labor union leader in the United States on the ground that the McNamaras had acted as part of a general labor conspiracy.*

When the McNamaras confessed, union labor received the worst setback in its history. Public opinion had been inclined to believe

---

[15] Hearst's Los Angeles *Examiner* had been founded in 1903 at the solicitation of local labor leaders.

that the McNamaras were being unjustly accused. Newspapers all over the country joined the assault on organized labor, and a movement developed in many places, with Hearst participating, to push the unions, conservative as well as radical, to the wall. In Chicago and San Francisco Hearst used the occasion to lock out his union pressmen. Until the confession, unions all over the country had contributed funds to the McNamara defense, of which Clarence Darrow was the chief. After the confession the leaders of the A. F. of L. were frightened by the cries of Hearst and others for their blood. "Hanging is too good for these fellows," said the Hearst papers, whose proprietor had been refused an endorsement by Samuel Gompers, president of the A. F. of L.

Very largely because of this case and its subsequent handling by Hearst and Otis, Los Angeles is one of the worst open-shop cities in the United States. The personal crime of two minor labor officials put into the hands of Hearst and Otis a weapon that is being wielded against labor in Southern California to this day.

In 1916 Hearst dealt another blow against labor, this time in San Francisco. The bombing of the Preparedness Day Parade by persons unknown was used by District Attorney Fickert to entangle Tom Mooney, organizer of the street railway workers of San Francisco. Mooney was convicted and sentenced to die, but was saved by the intercession of President Wilson after a storm of international protest, especially in Russia, threatened to injure the war efforts of the Allies.[16]

After Mooney's incarceration in San Quentin, all the influence of the anti-labor Hearst press was used to keep him there. Hearst was influential with the Harding, Coolidge and Hoover administrations, and used all his power, together with reactionary anti-labor elements in California, to prevent the freeing of Mooney, even though several state witnesses, the trial judge, and most of the jury had independently declared they were convinced that Mooney had been framed. In the Hearst papers, and by connivance with Hearst puppets in

---

[16] Wilson, as a private citizen, asked Governor Hiram Johnson to commute Mooney's death sentence.

California politics and on the California bench, the Hearst influence has been among the main obstacles to Mooney's release.

Mrs. Fremont Older in her authorized biography makes it appear that Hearst tried to help Mooney. She says her husband, when he joined Hearst, asked permission to bring the Mooney case with him. Older had campaigned for Mooney's acquittal on the old *Bulletin* and had done much to expose the frame-up. Hearst acquiesced. Mrs. Older neglected to point out that Hearst allowed Older to help Mooney only as long as Hearst was endeavoring to embarrass the war-time Allies. The Mooney case increased disaffection in foreign labor circles, especially in Russia. In 1917-18 Hearst, as we shall see, endorsed Vladimir Ilyitch Lenin, because it suited his economic purposes of the moment. After the war ended and Mooney could no longer be used to promote discord abroad that would have a cash value for Hearst, the Hearst organization turned against him. Mooney remains in jail. A man who surely could have secured his release, the outstanding man whose political creations sit on the judicial bench and occupy many political offices in California, is Hearst.

III

AGED thirty-three, emboldened by his San Francisco success, and with his mother's money in hand,[1] Hearst sent Charles M. Palmer, his manager, to purchase the New York *Morning Journal* from John R. McLean. A price of $180,000 was ultimately agreed upon.

The *Morning Journal* had a faintly unsavory reputation. It had been designed, in the elder Bennett's phrase, for the "delectation of love-sick chambermaids." McLean, publisher of the Cincinnati *Enquirer*, had acquired it only a little over a year before for $1,000,000 from Albert Pulitzer, brother of Joseph Pulitzer.

Before Hearst sent his agent to buy it, there had been a long family debate. Young Hearst, anxious to challenge Pulitzer's supremacy, had been imploring his mother since the death of his father to give him funds for a New York paper. Torn between her wish to please her unruly son and her prudence, Mrs. Hearst could not easily make up her mind. It was four years before the son carried his point. Even then she insisted that Edward Hardy Clark, her personal business manager, should be the controlling officer in all the new corporations Hearst created around the *Journal*. These corporations were useful for evasion of taxes and damage suits, and miscellaneous profitable intrigues.

Clark and Mrs. Hearst were cousins. Since 1895 he has been the financial brains behind the Hearst enterprises. A Missourian, like Hearst's parents, he had been summoned by Mrs. Hearst upon the death of the Senator. Mrs. Hearst familiarized him with the various Hearst mining and ranching enterprises, especially with the lucrative Homestake Mining Company. Clark was a quiet, efficient, sober young man. He absorbed all she and Senator Hearst's partners, with whom he worked hand-in-glove for many years, could teach him.

[1] Revealed in the probate of the will of Phoebe Apperson Hearst after her death in 1919.

The money for the purchase of the *Journal* came from the sale of the seven-sixteenths Hearst interest in the Anaconda Copper Mining Company to the Rothschilds of London for $7,500,000.[2] The transaction was handled through the National City Bank of New York. This was the first Hearst connection with this leading financial institution, in which he is now influential. As a result of this deal, National City became the banker for Anaconda, and has been involved in numerous sleight-of-hand stock deals with it, as was revealed in the Senate investigation of Wall Street in 1933.

From a business viewpoint the sale of the Anaconda stock was a first-class mistake. Had the stock been retained, Hearst would be one of the richest men in the world, probably topping Henry Ford and equalling Rockefeller, for in 1929 the Anaconda produced more than 40 per cent of the world's copper, and in the World War it reaped enormous profits.

But the property had become something of a white elephant to the Hearsts. As Mayor John MacGinnis, of Butte, told Clarence Barron of the *Wall Street Journal* in 1904, "Not one thousand, but many thousands of grafters are on the Amalgamated payroll. [George Hearst had been president of the Amalgamated, later merged with Anaconda Standard.] The Amalgamated loses $500,000 a year in Montana newspapers. The leases given to politicians have cost $500,000 a year alone. It is costing the Amalgamated also $1,000,000 a year for lawyers. Boston and Montana [an affiliate] pays all the political expenses. $5,000,000 a year has been lost or wasted in five years, or in all $25,000,000."[3]

Moreover, the Anaconda silver vein had been exhausted, and Marcus Daly, the dominant figure in the enterprise, lied to Mrs. Hearst about the amount of copper underground, and lied to Haggin and Tevis and the Rothschilds themselves a few years later.[4] Daly was a geological expert, with a degree from Columbia University

[2] *They Told Barron*, notes of Clarence Walker Barron, edited and arranged by Arthur Pound and Samuel Taylor Moore, Harper & Bros., New York, 1930.
[3] *More They Told Barron*, edited by Arthur Pound and Samuel Taylor Moore, Harper & Bros., N. Y., 1931.
[4] *The War of the Copper Kings*, by C. B. Glasscock, Bobbs-Merrill Co., Indianapolis and New York, 1935.

School of Mines. He eventually acquired the bulk of Anaconda's stock.

Logically, therefore, or so they thought, Mrs. Hearst and Clark chose this property, on which the political grafters were fattening, for sacrifice. Clark moved the offices of the Hearst Estate from San Francisco to the Mills Building in Wall Street. Possibly he foresaw some of the financial coups made possible by a connection with a big newspaper in the financial center of the nation. The coups materialized, at any rate.

Chamberlain took charge of the *Journal*. With him came Homer Davenport, the cartoonist, who later became angry with Hearst and toured the country telling to businessmen's clubs stories in which Hearst figured as Casanova; Arthur McEwen, who also withdrew and started a paper in San Francisco that aired many of Hearst's private affairs; Winifred Black, Charles Tebbs and F. L. H. ("Cosey") Noble. Noble was the first city editor in the new "madhouse" on Park Row, and the author of one of its best quips. Asked in a downtown beanery by a fellow journalist what he was doing now, Noble replied ruefully: "I was city editor when I left the office."

Title to the *Journal* passed to Hearst on September 25, 1895, but the paper was not published under his name until November 7. On the first day under Hearst's ownership the *Journal* devoted two-thirds of its front page to a drawing of the wedding procession of the Duke of Marlborough and Consuelo Vanderbilt. Julian Ralph wrote the story, which, with all the details, down to the sighs of the bride, took three inside pages.

Bennett had been outdone in kowtowing to nobility for the delectation of gaping chambermaids.

Hearst and Chamberlain were not aiming at Bennett. They had Pulitzer, their master, in mind. Pulitzer was the biggest thing in American journalism. Always the imitator, Hearst made his paper an exact copy of the *World* in size and typographical lay-out. He lowered his price from 2 cents to 1 cent, and Pulitzer soon followed.

The *Journal* sent band-wagons, covered with posters, through the streets. Billboards were used. Pennies were sent through the mail to registered voters, to enable them to purchase the *Journal*.

An early *Journal* feature about a faithless husband was advertised by sending a "confidential" postcard to New York housewives, suggesting that they read the *Journal* and learn more about their husbands. As these cards were written by clerks, they seemed to be anonymous warnings. They were signed: "A Friend." Thus Hearst, in his search for circulation, introduced into many households a helpful note of discord.

Hearst almost never developed his own talent. He took it at secondhand from more skillful executives. There has not been one outstanding journalist or writer, except the late Ring Lardner, who obtained his training in the Hearst organization. All the Hearst stars were stars before they came to him, attracted by the initial bait of high salaries.

A few months after he settled in New York, Hearst was hiring men away from the *World*. He would hire the head of a department and stipulate that he bring his whole staff. Salaries were doubled and even trebled, causing romantics among the newspaper gentry to believe that Hearst was generous and that permanent prosperity had arrived. Richard Harding Davis was paid $500 in the fall of 1895 for covering a Yale-Harvard football game and lending his publicized name to the *Journal*.

Hearst's raids upon his staff caused Pulitzer, then going blind, much mental anguish. In the end Hearst, despite efforts by Pulitzer to recapture his men, had his way. Some of this hiring was merely to embarrass; Hearst soon fired many of the men he had seduced from Pulitzer, leaving them stranded without jobs and *persona non grata* at the *World*.

Hearst's habit of firing men at a moment's notice after they had been lured away from good jobs gave rise to the demand for ironclad contracts on the part of prospective Hearst employees. The contract system subsequently caused Hearst heavy losses, for many men, hired on long-term contracts, did not fit into the dizzy Hearst scheme. To get rid of these hapless ones they would be reduced to chief of copy boys or custodian of out-of-town papers. Men who were more difficult to pry from the payroll would be made lavatory attendants, and there have been some who remained at "work" of this kind, drawing $500 a week, more or less, for a long period. One such person caused the lavatory drains to become clogged every few days by stuffing them with newspapers. The business office finally gave up and paid the contract in full. Another, simulating a person whose brain was cracking, told a reporter in a corner saloon that he often had an uncontrollable desire to set fire to the benzine in the composing room. His contract was also paid.

Throughout the long contest with the *World*, the *Journal* lost the original $7,500,000[5] from the Anaconda, plus money taken from the now profitable San Francisco *Examiner* and the Frisco political pool. Throughout this period the *World* made money. From a business viewpoint the contest was a complete failure for Hearst, although it has often been said that he "conquered" Pulitzer. Even after ten years Pulitzer was so far the master that he could condescend to support Hearst in some of his political campaigns, whipping others over Hearst's shoulders.

But Hearst made a lot of noise. In three months he pushed the *Journal's* circulation from 20,000 to 150,000. The average daily circulation of the *World* was 185,000 copies. Hearst's gain was bought at tremendous cost, approximately $7 per reader. In order to get more circulation and an Associated Press franchise, Hearst had to buy the *Morning Advertiser*, for Pulitzer, a member of the Associated Press, refused to sell Hearst a franchis . In three months Hearst had taken Pulitzer's whole Sunday staff of editors, artists and writers, headed by Morrill Goddard, a young genius in his line. The men in the *World* office would simply receive a note saying: "Mr. Hearst would be pleased to have you call."

Hearst's first New York offices were in the Pulitzer building, where he took an ornately furnished suite and lined it with costly California redwood. Pulitzer soon ousted him from this vantage point and Hearst moved to the *Tribune* building next door on Nassau Street, where the *Journal* was printed.

[5] The probate of his mother's estate showed that Hearst, anticipating his inheritance, never repaid this money.

54		IMPERIAL HEARST

The *Journal* staff, then as now, did not bother to gather news. The *Journal's* idea was to get "splash sensations" that would "paralyze" the public. Hearst's real news, like everything else, came from the pages of the *World*. Down to 1918, when it was stopped by court order,[6] the Hearst organization relied chiefly on opposition papers in various cities for real news.

When some sensation was not being concocted, the old *Journal* office was quiet. As soon as the first edition of the morning *World* appeared, it was galvanized into activity, the copy readers setting up a four-part chant:

"Sound the cymbal, beat the drum,
The *World* is here, the news has come."

During a lull one day in the *Journal* office Chamberlain suddenly emerged from his office, drunk. He lost control of himself when he saw the staff lolling about.

"Get excited, everybody," he bawled at the top of his voice. "Everybody get excited! Everybody get excited!"

The men responded nervously: one of the reporters seized a telephone and begged the telephone operator to ring all the phones. She did so and the office was soon in an uproar that satisfied Chamberlain.

Morrill Goddard was the first of the Pulitzer keymen to be lured away. After him went Arthur Brisbane, his successor as the *World's* Sunday editor; Solomon Solis Carvalho, the *World's* business manager, intimately familiar with all the devious ways in which a newspaper can raise money; Richard F. Outcault, who originated for Pulitzer the colored comics that brought the name "yellow journalism" into existence. From various New York papers, including the ever-reliable *World*, Hearst took Edgar Saltus, Stephen Crane, James Creelman, Robert H. ("Bob") Davis, Julian Hawthorne (son of Nathaniel Hawthorne), Alan Dale, W. J. Henderson, Richard Harding Davis, Alfred Henry Lewis and others.

Brisbane and Goddard survive to this day as Hearst executives, and Carvalho lasted until 1917. The latter is now in retirement on

[6] *Property in the News,* a transcript of litigation in the Federal District of New York through the United States Supreme Court of the Associated Press vs. International News Service, et al; New York, 1919.

an annual pension of $18,000. Brisbane has become "The Arch-Stooge" of American journalism, and Goddard remains, like Edward Hardy Clark, behind the scenes.

It was either Goddard or Brisbane, while on the *World*, who first conceived the "banner" headline. Brisbane has been said to claim this distinction but the evidence favors Goddard. One day Goddard noticed a crowd about a druggist's window. On display was the cross-section of a ship, with the inner sections shown in bright color and a shark swimming below. An explanation was printed in large type. It gave Goddard an idea. Banner headlines had not yet been used on news pages. Advertisers, however, were using large type in the papers, and bill-posters, faced with the necessity of projecting a message over a distance, had been indulging in it for years. The circuses and freak shows were also using large type and colored ink for their advertisements. The large-type headline was a natural and inevitable development of vaudeville journalism.

On the Sunday following his study of the drug-store display, Goddard filled a page with the cross-section of a human body, topped by a "banner" or "streamer" headline. In subsequent weeks he published illustrations (including cross-sections) of pre-historic monsters, ape-men, murderesses, unclad chorus girls, diseased and misshapen human bodies lying on the surgeon's operating table. The circulation of the Sunday *World* began to rise rapidly. Goddard drew his inspiration from Jules Verne, Edgar Allen Poe, Conan Doyle and Gaboriau. The grotesque Goddard features required a minimum of reading matter, which made them popular with the thousands of immigrants who could not decipher English.

Goddard took his whole staff to the *Journal*. Pulitzer immediately hired them back, but they remained only twenty-four hours, or until Hearst could reëstablish communications. On the *Journal* the Goddard imagination, steeped in the libraries which he has ever since frequented in his search for the unique, ran riot, and it is still at work.

Hearst's seduction of *World* men produced a celebrated quip. T. E. Powers, the cartoonist, was hired by Hearst on a contract. Pulitzer took him back on another contract. The Hearst office then gave Powers an iron-clad contract, which he signed. Pulitzer brought suit for the services of Powers, who was enjoined from working for either, although both the *World* and the *Journal* paid him his salary during the litigation. In the course of the arguments lawyers delved back for precedents to indentured servant and slave laws. After much impressive argument for both sides a decision in favor of Hearst was handed down. Powers felt his importance inflated and celebrated the decision appropriately. With a friend, who carried his roll of drawing paper, he ordered drinks for the house in a Park Row saloon. After several rounds Powers and his friend staged a skit. While his friend belabored him over the head with the roll of drawing paper, Powers, on his knees, his hands raised in supplication, piteously paraphrased the line from *Uncle Tom's Cabin*: "You can beat this poor old body but my soul belongs to William Randolph Hearst."

This was received so satisfactorily that it was repeated in front of City Hall. Spectators applauded. Powers and his friend repeated it all the way up Broadway.

Powers still contributes his grotesque drawings to the Hearst papers.

Probably the most embarrassing situation Hearst created for Pulitzer came when he hired Edward Farrelly, a *World* executive. Pulitzer had arranged a formal dinner as a surprise expression of appreciation. A few hours before the dinner Pulitzer was informed:

"Farrelly has gone over to the enemy."

"To Gush?" Pulitzer said incredulously. "Gush" was the telegraphic code-name on the *World* for Hearst.

The Farrelly dinner was cancelled.

Stephen Crane wrote a series on life in the "tenderloin," where *amour* was a profession. Alan Dale, the dramatic critic, interviewed Anna Held on her first visit to the States. The headline ran: "Mlle. Anna Held Receives Alan Dale Attired in a 'Nightie.'" A sob-sister wrote on "Why Young Girls Kill Themselves." The *Journal* serialized Henry James' *The Other House* under the headline: "Henry James' New Novel of Immorality and Crime; The Surprising Plunge of the Great Novelist Into the Field of Sensational Fiction." A novel by F. Marion Crawford was headlined as "A Story of Woman's Passions; Marion Crawford's New Italian Society Novel of Love, Revenge, Suicide and Poison."

In 1896 Hearst started an evening edition to compete with the *Evening World*. A few men rewrote the *Evening World's* news. The rewriting of news still takes place in the newspaper business, but no one except Hearst has appropriated the whole news report of competitors. Very often only the first paragraph was rewritten by the *Journal*, the rest being reprinted—without credit.

Pulitzer ignored the stigma of "yellow journalism," but Hearst hastily seized upon it as a way of getting more publicity. Everybody was discussing the new "yellow journalism." Hearst *announced* himself as a "yellow journalist," believing that would incite curiosity and cause people to read the Hearst papers, which adopted the familiar saffron covering sheet. The *Journal* today, the Chicago *American* and other Hearst afternoon papers have a front and back page of this yellow-brown paper.

Hearst's personal life was unchanged in the early New York years. He occupied a suite at the old Hoffman House. There, late at night, all the newspapers of the city would be spread out on the floor, and Hearst and his executives, on their knees, would rummage through the day's news and compare the "play" given the major stories. The "reader-interest" of each story would be analyzed, and what seemed unlikely to divert the lowest common denominator was pronounced unworthy of being included in the *Journal*.

It was at the Hoffman House that Hearst agreed to give Brisbane one dollar for every one thousand additional copies of the *Journal* sold while Brisbane's signed column of comment appeared on the first page. Pulitzer had wounded Brisbane's vanity, and so lost him. While Pulitzer was on one of his frequent European trips and Brisbane was in charge of the *World*, Brisbane experimented with placing one of his signed editorials on the front page several days in succession. As soon as Pulitzer saw the *World* with Brisbane's signed opinions on the front page, he telegraphed a peremptory order to cease. Hearst, however, was willing to try Brisbane. An initial salary of $200 a week was agreed upon. In recent years Brisbane's annual salary in the Hearst service has exceeded $250,000.

At this period Hearst was seen at all the theatrical first nights, he frequented Delmonico's and the other fashionable restaurants, rode in one of the newfangled expensive French automobiles. He was usually accompanied by two of the prettiest girls that could currently be found along Broadway. Hearst's hobbies, since the Harvard days, have been the theater and the girls.

The *Journal* staff, unlike that of the San Francisco *Examiner*, was not taken on the Hearst parties. Hearst was no longer obliged to get himself accepted. Many of the Hearst parties, then as later, reached the proportions of an Elks' convention; but it was the executives, politicians, prospective advertisers and the like who were fêted— along with the ladies of the theater.

In New York Hearst worked with his staff until he entered politics in 1902. After 1902 he appeared only spasmodically in his offices, and then chiefly to make sudden and arbitrary demands for money from his business managers.[7] After the master has passed through the city many a Hearst paper has been stripped of ready cash. Faced with the inability to meet payrolls and other items of expense, the business managers have had to scurry about for loans or draw against their personal bank accounts. Hearst held them strictly accountable for any difficulties even though he had been responsible.

The *Journal* in the early Hearst days covered a story in a unique way. A news development would cause a complete exodus from the office. Chamberlain, after a consultation with the city editor and news editor, would shout commands. Members of the staff, primed by "Cosey" Noble and other staff tacticians, would be struggling into coats and heading for the street. There would be a rush to capture hansom cabs, carriages and bicycles. (Hearst rewarded meritorious reporters with bicycles, insuring their early appearance on any scene of action.) The Hearst cavalry, known as "the wrecking crew," would then point for the scene of crime, revelry, political shivaree

---

[7] *Prophets True and False*, by Oswald Garrison Villard, Alfred A. Knopf, New York, 1928.

IMPERIAL HEARST

or disaster. Stephen Crane said that a man had to be either drunk, a lunatic or Sam Chamberlain, to run the *Journal*.[8]

Out of Park Row, sometimes late of an evening, would swing a cavalcade that set citizens gaping. Outriders on cycles rang warnings, the horses' hoofs struck sparks from the cobblestones. After Hearst came to Park Row the locality attracted the most reckless of the city's cabmen, and these were inspired, under the influence of heavy tips, to procure former fire and cavalry horses. Some bystanders always fell in with the dramatic spirit of these representatives of the "New Journalism," as Hearst called his farrago—messenger boys, delivery wagon drivers and stray dogs would follow pell-mell after the Hearst legion. Hearst himself would often come leaping, long-legged, wild-eyed, intent, out of the Tribune Building, and hop either into his French road-burner or a handy gig, to be whisked like a field marshal to the scene of battle.

Until Hearst arrived Park Row had been somewhat leisurely. This attitude had to be discarded by the other papers if they wanted to be able to inform *their* readers at breakfast, in competition with the *Journal*, that some harridan had been shot in the left breast, *not* the right. But the other papers could not compete. Pulitzer tried to form a "wrecking crew" of his own, but it lacked the demoniacal drive, and the numbers, of the Hearst phalanx. If Pulitzer sent ten men on a story, Hearst would send twenty. If it was a crime, Hearst would add to his forces some publicized detective or "reformed" murderer who would write an "expert" account. If Pulitzer sent fifteen men, the *Journal* would send thirty.

If another story broke while the whole staff was bogged down in the wilds of Brooklyn on the trail of a wild iceman, the *Journal* would hire another staff, new recruits being signed up for the duration of the war. Sub-editors would appear in the Park Row saloons looking for unemployed newspaper men, who would be hired on the spot. If the rumored story failed to materialize such wights would not be recognized in the *Journal* office. If they got a big front-page splash they would be welcomed with open arms.

Picked Hearst men at times posed as city detectives or even as

[8] "Hearst and Hearstism," by Frederick Palmer, *Collier's*, September 29, 1906.

Federal agents, as they do to this day. But in the early *Journal* days it was a novelty for a reporter to tap some public malefactor on the shoulder, jerk his head significantly, and say "Come along." The destination was always the *Journal* office, where the startled victim of the hoax would be photographed, interviewed and asked to confess whatever the *Journal* wanted confessed. Sometimes, of course, a *Journal* reporter making an "arrest" received a crack on the jaw.

The police technique was very successful with women, and the *Journal* men introduced the ruse of telling the ladies "their man" was in "trouble" and wanted to see them. They would be escorted to the *Journal* office, raw material for Hearst's presses and colored inks.

Hearst men always had plenty of money with which to purchase entry, to hire locomotives, to make love in the quest for stories. Hearst often went out on these stories with his storm-troopers, and as he moved about, he would say repeatedly, "We must beat every paper in town, we must beat every paper in town."

The Guldensuppe case[9] showed Hearst off to excellent advantage.

Mrs. Herman Nack, an East Side German midwife, and Martin Thorn, her lover, had murdered Guldensuppe, her former lover. Guldensuppe's body had been hacked to pieces in a bath tub and distributed around the city. A leading clue was the type of oilcloth in which various parts of the body were wrapped. The design of the cloth was reproduced by *Journal* artists and a piece given to a dozen staff men. They were assigned to discover its purchaser. An East Side dealer was found who remembered Mrs. Nack as the buyer of identical cloth. On hearing this, Hearst, followed by the entire *Journal* staff in hacks and on bicycles, proceeded to the house in which Mrs. Nack lived, and rented the entire building. The Hearst men moved into the tenement hallways and occupied some of the vacant flats. Guards were posted fore and aft to keep competing newsmen out. Scouting parties were dispatched through the neighborhood to take charge of every public telephone within an area of several blocks, snipping those wires which could not be held.[10] The "features" in the case were being developed hourly by the *Journal* in successive

---

[9] Reported by Frederick Palmer in *Collier's*, September 29, 1906, *et seq.*
[10] Detail supplied by a former Hearst reporter.

IMPERIAL HEARST

editions. Readers were advised not to miss an edition, to watch the business of crime detection from the inside, with the police hopelessly out of the race. The *Journal* got the whole story, down to confessions. Armed sluggers escorted the *Journal's* delivery wagons throughout the city to keep opposition papers from filching a copy. So great had mob hysteria become that riots occurred at busy corners as people strove to tear the papers out of the drivers' hands. The sluggers were slugged by the public. People were knocked down and trodden upon in the rush.

Hearst invented the slogan: "While Others Talk the *Journal* Acts." He started legal proceedings against various corporations which were allegedly mulcting the public. These suits served two purposes. They made news and they put the fear of Hearst into the corporations, which were not long in offering advertising contracts *à la* Southern Pacific. Most big corporations, once denounced in the language of fishwives and haled into court by the *Journal's* lawyers, are now heavy Hearst advertisers. The Hearst invective has been stilled by the lullaby of the cash register. The corporations are no better today than when he attacked them.

Hearst took the idea of crusading against "predatory wealth" (Pulitzer's phrase) from the *World*, but the *Journal* never matched its competitor in the opponents it tackled. The *World* exposed bigger fish than Hearst was after, and occasionally even went after some of its advertisers. The *Journal* never did.

In 1897 the *Journal*, with a tremendous outcry, obtained an injunction that prevented the Board of Aldermen from granting the gas company a franchise, which the *Journal* claimed was worth $10,000,000, in Brooklyn. The court ultimately found the franchise illegal. The *Journal* then sent questionnaires to mayors and prominent public men in all parts of the country asking their opinion of the "splendid fight." Replies favorable to the *Journal* were plastered over two pages in the *Sunday Journal*. On December 3, 1897, the *Journal* announced it had stopped "the gas franchise grab in Brooklyn, the trolley franchise grab in Brooklyn, the death terminal of the

[Brooklyn] Bridge, the dilatory work on Fifth Avenue, the $10,000,000 light monopoly in New York."

On March 29, 1897, Hearst fired point-blank upon Pulitzer and in print called the wizard of the *World* "a journalist who made his money by pandering to the worst tastes of the prurient and horror-loving, by dealing in bogus news, such as forged cablegrams from eminent personages, and by affecting a devotion to the interests of the people while never really hurting the interests of their enemies, and sedulously looking out for his own." This was written by Hearst, who, for nine years, had outdone any offenses of Pulitzer, and whom Edwin L. Godkin in *The Nation* called "the blackguard boy." Not only had the public crimes of Pulitzer been surpassed but, in his private life, Hearst was leaving a trail any description of which would not pass through the United States mails.†

There is much detailed, and highly technical, evidence of the various Hearst sell-outs to the public utility companies, the railroads and the political boodlers against which the *Journal* campaigned.

It is significant that the constituent companies of the Consolidated Gas Company of New York, controlling all the gas and electricity of the city, had no difficulty whatever after the *Journal's* first blast. New York today has the highest basic electric rate for domestic users in the nation. Hearst has carried Consolidated Gas advertising for years.

The New York Telephone Company, subsidiary of the American Telephone and Telegraph Company, despite the *Journal's* crusades against public utilities, has had no difficulty in maintaining the highest metropolitan domestic telephone rate in the United States: $4.25 a month for a private instrument. The telephone companies' ads have been a steady source of Hearst revenue for many years.

And despite Hearst indignation over the traction trust, the Hearst Estate participated in the wrecking of the Metropolitan Street Railway line, and consistently sold short the stocks of companies which the *Journal* attacked.[11]

Hearst's campaigns for public ownership have deceived many astute people. The effect of these campaigns was to take the leadership of the reform movement out of the hands of real reformers and

---

[11] New York *Herald*, throughout October, 1906.
† Congressional Record, January 8, 1897. Speech by Grove L. Johnson.

IMPERIAL HEARST

place it in the hands of Hearst, where it could be surreptitiously sold to interested parties. Wherever Hearst has had a dominating influence in "reforming" public utility companies—New York, Chicago, San Francisco—"predatory wealth" has had a clear track ahead.

Hearst soon perceived that the public was interested in prominent names and he loaded the *Journal* with prominent names affixed to the most puerile remarks. He sent former Senator John H. Ingalls to Nevada to cover the Corbett-Fitzsimmons fight, not because the Senator was a pugilistic expert, but because he had been a Senator. For several years Hearst worked the signed-statement racket for all it was worth. The method was simply to send an inquiry to any prominent personage. When a courteous reply was received it was immediately slapped into print.

At Hearst headquarters today in New York, and in every city where there is a Hearst paper, an index is kept of people who are willing to be quoted along certain lines. All have been publicized. When Hearst favors a big navy of heavy battleships, a list of retired admirals is taken from the files and the old gentlemen are approached for their ready opinions. If, however, the Hearst organization believes that lighter-than-air ships are to be preferred to heavy battleships (somebody may be wishing to sell the government airships and has spoken to Hearst about it), there is ready an equally imposing list of authorities who will give opinions on this question. For a small, mobile, mechanized army, there is another set of publicized nonentities waiting to be quoted, as there is for a large conscript army. On all questions of foreign relations there are groups of "experts" with all the necessary degrees, titles and badges of office who will be quoted in the manner desired. No direct falsification is needed. The falsification lies in the entire method.

Hearstian vaudeville was soon extended to the foreign field in the ceaseless search for sensation. Correspondents sent abroad were not known by this humble name. They were "Special Commissioners" of the New York *Journal*. Nor were reporters at home so designated. They were "representatives." A Hearst man sent to interview a banker or a favorite of the stage would go in a morning coat, carrying a gold-headed cane and engraved visiting cards containing these words: "A representative of the *Journal*." It might be anyone from the managing editor to the business manager, and the doors opened.

The same ruse worked very well abroad, where Hearst men moved in the highest circles. In London the Hearst man established himself so well that he was able soon after his arrival to bribe an under-official to give him a copy of the Anglo-American treaty which settled the Venezuelan boundary dispute, over which the United States had threatened war when Cleveland was President. The treaty, published in full by the *Journal* before it was released to the other papers, was a first-class "beat." It was of special interest to Wall Street, which had been very perturbed by Cleveland's bellicosity toward London, on whose favors Wall Street was then financially dependent.

Richard Harding Davis, the handsome and dashing war correspondent, was sent to Moscow in 1896 to report the coronation of Czar Nicholas II. In the capital of the Czars a newspaper man had the same status as a scavenger, and only a few European newsmen with "social" background were to be admitted to the coronation ceremony. But Davis was a "High Commissioner," not a plebeian newspaper man. He arrived several weeks before the ceremony, and when the Czar's agents refused his request for a ticket of admission, sighs went up from the ladies in the Moscow drawing-rooms. A cabal was immediately begun, with half of Petersburg society and the diplomatic corps involved, to get Davis into the coronation ceremony. Having him at its mercy thousands of miles away, the *Journal* meanwhile was continuously wrangling with him about money.

Writing to his brother about the affair, Davis said:

> I have just sent off my coronation story, and the strain of this thing ... is off. ... Edwin Arnold, who did it for The London *Telegraph* had $25,000, and if I told you of the way Hearst acted and Ralph interfered with impertinent cables, you would wonder I am sane. They never sent me a cent for the cables until I was so late that I could not get it out of the bank, and we have spent and borrowed every penny we have. Imagine having to write a story and to fight to be allowed a chance to write it, and at the same time to be pressed for money for expenses and tools so that you were worn out by that alone. The brightest side of the whole thing was the way everybody in this whole town was fighting for

me. The entire town took sides, and even men who disliked me, and who I certainly dislike, like C. W. and R—— of the Paris Embassy, turned in and fought for my getting in like relations. And the women— I had grand dukes and ambassadors and princes, whom I do not know by sight, moving every lever, and as Stanhope of the *Herald* testified, "every man, woman and child in the visiting and resident legation is crazy on the subject of getting Davis into the coronation."

An *imperial invitation* was sent to Davis at the last minute. It was a triumph of triumphs, marred only by the fact that the long-distance parsimony of Hearst had made it necessary for Davis to have the driver of his droshky extend him credit.

Ten years later Davis called at the *Journal* office to consult newspaper clippings for a book he was writing. "At the *Journal*," he noted in his diary, "Sam Chamberlain who used to pay me $500 a story, touched me on the shoulder as I was scribbling down notes and said, 'Hearst says to take you back at $17 a week.'

"I said, 'I'm worth $18 and I can't come for less.'

"So he brought up the business manager [S. S. Carvalho] and had a long wrangle with him as to whether I should get $18. The business manager, a Jew gentleman, didn't know me from Adam, and seriously tried to save the paper a dollar a week. When the reporters and typewriter girls began to laugh, he got very mad."

Carvalho was the watch-dog of the *Journal's* exchequer. While Hearst was out scattering money, Carvalho went about the office turning off lights and picking up stray bits of paper; once he even invaded the ladies' lavatory to snap off the lights. A young lady screamed, and Carvalho darted out just in time to be observed.

But Carvalho, while a watch-dog, took personal advantage of the loose organization of the Hearst enterprises. He formed his own ink company which sold ink at a profit to the Hearst organization.

For Queen Victoria's Jubilee celebration the *Journal* hired Mark Twain. Because he was the outstanding American writer, Twain was fêted in London, and was much in demand as an after-dinner speaker. This was another triumph for the *Journal*, which it reported as news. The *Journal* sent Stephen Crane, Julian Ralph, two women, two British newspapermen and one lowly "legman" to cover the

Greco-Turkish war in 1897. Hearst sold their correspondence to the Chicago *Tribune* and the Buffalo *Evening News*, and when the editors of those papers sent commendatory messages on their work, the *Journal* printed *them* as news of first-class importance. The *Journal* only printed what was said in praise of it. Two "expeditions" were sent to cover the Klondike gold-rush.

All this delighted Hearst and Chamberlain. They watched the *Journal's* circulation creep up on the *World's*. But the cup was not without its bitterness. The *World* had many more advertisements. Advertisers claimed the *Journal's* patrons could not read.

Both Pulitzer and Hearst saw an easy way to gain circulation by fomenting the Spanish-American War. Before war broke out, at a moment when it seemed as though the war-mongers grouped around Assistant Secretary of the Navy Theodore Roosevelt and William Randolph Hearst had been circumvented, Pulitzer said he "rather liked the idea of war—not a big one—but one that would arouse interest and give him a chance to gauge the reflex in his circulation figures."[12]

Pulitzer's mild desire for war was eclipsed by Hearst's mad passion for it. Both the *World* and the *Journal* stooped to every kind of falsification to gain their ends, but Hearst stooped lower.

It was just before the Spanish-American War that Hearst's mother ordered her servants not to let a copy of the New York *Journal* in the house. But she did nothing, with the monetary power in her hands, to stop her son's actions.

The possibility of a war with Spain for the Caribbean Islands had been agitated since 1825.[13] A number of insurrectionary expeditions had been outfitted on American soil and had landed crews of adventurers in Cuba. They were duly shot by the Spaniards. Long before Hearst came East, the preliminary conditions for war existed. All that was needed was the man who would set fire to the combustibles, and Hearst was the man.

[12] *Joseph Pulitzer*, by Don C. Seitz, Simon and Schuster, New York, 1924.
[13] *The Martial Spirit: A Study of the War with Spain*, by Walter Millis, Houghton Mifflin Co., Boston and New York, 1931.

IMPERIAL HEARST

The final plotting that led to the Cuban and Philippine shambles was directed by Hearst in the office of the New York *Journal*. The "Cuban Question" was handled exclusively by Hearst. Whenever a dispatch on Cuba reached the office, Hearst dropped whatever he was doing and gave it his personal attention. Most of the headlines on the Cuban-Spanish quarrel, until war was declared by the United States, were written by Hearst himself.

Hearst's first "editorial line" was to represent the Cubans in the clutches of cruel tyrants. The revolutionary party in Cuba was small, but the *Journal* soon made it seem as though all Cubans hated Spain. Actually the Cuban populace was apathetic toward the revolutionists. The Cuban conspirators thereupon redoubled their efforts. The Spaniards, in an effort to subdue the trouble-makers, decreed concentration areas within Cuban cities. Anyone outside the towns was considered an outlaw unless he carried a Spanish passport. The revolutionists responded by burning plantations and pillaging. The *Journal* described this destruction as the work of the Spaniards, without troubling to investigate, or to print, the Spanish version.

For some time the *Journal* had no correspondent in Cuba, but it nevertheless printed dispatches dated "Havana," giving detailed accounts of Spanish barbarities. The "information" on which these dispatches were based was supplied by the imaginations of Cuban emigrés in New York. Rewrite men in the *Journal* office pointed up their yarns. The method to create "atrocities" used so effectively during the World War was fully developed by Hearst in 1898.

Hearst found it necessary to send a man to Cuba when the Cuban Junta in New York began running short of ideas. This correspondent was Frederick Lawrence, whose outstanding contribution while on the island was to write a completely fictitious story about a gallant group of American volunteers who, manning a battery of Gatling guns, captured the city of Piñar del Rio from the Spaniards. The story electrified Americans, and even stirred Washington. American blood seemed, somehow, to be involved. This was what the story was intended to do. The Spaniards expelled Lawrence.

Hearst made arrangements in Washington—the McKinley Administration was in abject fear of the *Journal*—and Lawrence was summoned before the Senate Foreign Relations Committee. He was a conquering hero. He testified under oath that all the Spanish versions of Cuban affairs were "untrue." As to the fighting he witnessed in Cuba (there was no fighting according to the Spaniards and later American historians)[14] Lawrence was forced to admit:

"Personally I have no knowledge of it. I did not go outside the lines and did not count the dead and dying or anything of that kind; but the gentlemen who would bring me information—and I did not have to seek for it, they were only too willing to give it to me—were men of the very highest character. . . ."

"Q. Were these gentlemen on the side of the insurgents?"

"A. Yes, sir."

"Q. So for that reason you were inclined to give their accounts greater credit than that of the censor?"

"A. Yes, sir."[15]

The *Journal* had provided Lawrence with the names and locations of insurgents in Cuba. His dispatches did not indicate that he himself had been given information about the "battles" at second hand. Hearst was so pleased with Lawrence's work and his testimony that he rewarded him with a bonus.

James Creelman was sent to replace Lawrence and Frederick Remington was sent to draw pictures of the "gallant fight" for Cuban liberation. Remington found Cuba quiet. Although warned by the Spanish authorities not to leave Havana, he entered the interior. There was no fighting, no revolution. He returned to Havana, having seen only sugar plantations smoldering in the wake of the insurrectos, and sent this telegram:[16]

W. R. HEARST
JOURNAL NEW YORK
EVERYTHING IS QUIET. THERE IS NO TROUBLE HERE. THERE WILL BE NO WAR. I WISH TO RETURN.

REMINGTON

[14] *Ibid.*
[15] Compilation of Reports of (Senate) Committee on Foreign Relations, 1789-1901 (Vol. 7), pp. 655-672, May 20, 1896.
[16] *On the Great Highway,* by James Creelman, Lothrop Pub. Co., Boston, 1901.

Hearst immediately wired back:

REMINGTON
HAVANA
PLEASE REMAIN. YOU FURNISH THE PICTURES AND I'LL FURNISH THE WAR.

HEARST[17]

Meanwhile the *Journal* office itself was busy. On February 22, 1897, the *Journal* headlined a story as follows:

SHERMAN FOR WAR WITH SPAIN FOR MURDERING AMERICANS

John Sherman was the Secretary of State in the incoming McKinley Administration. The story was a lie.

Another deliberate fabrication of 1897 was this:

FLEETS OF THE GREAT POWERS BOMBARD THE CUBAN INSURGENTS

The next coup by the *Journal* (whose minor falsifications were too numerous to detail) was born in the brain of Hearst himself. A dispatch from Creelman described the heroic stand of beautiful Evangelina Cisneros, whose father, a revolutionary, had been captured and placed in jail by the Spaniards. The daughter, not wishing to desert, insisted upon accompanying her father to jail. The Spaniards gallantly permitted this, and were to be sorry ever afterward. Hearst exclaimed: "Enlist the women of America for Miss Cisneros." He himself wrote the headline: "Does Our Flag Protect Women?" The "Cuban girl martyr," said the *Journal*, was in the clutches of bestial Spaniards, destined for a fate, as the *Journal* hopefully said, "worse than death."

The *Journal* induced Mrs. Jefferson Davis, widow of the Confederate President, to appeal to the Queen Regent of Spain, to give Evangelina Cisneros "to the women of America to save her from a fate worse than death." Mrs. Julia Ward Howe was prevailed upon to appeal to Pope Leo XIII. A general petition was drawn up, with

[17] *Ibid.*

the signatures of Mrs. Mark Hanna, Frances Hodgson Burnett, Julia Dent Grant, Mrs. Nancy McKinley (mother of the President), and Mrs. John Sherman, wife of the Secretary of State. Their names served to give authenticity to the Cisneros story and to advertise the *Journal*, whose circulation was soaring and running even with the *World's*.

The Spanish Ambassador at Washington, perturbed by the political connections of the ladies whom Hearst had enticed into the petition, denied the truth of the stories about "the girl martyr." For giving the lie direct to Hearst, Sr. Dupuy de Lôme was to pay.

The Ambassador's denial only made the case more sensational. "Witnesses" were produced by the *Journal* who testified to Miss Cisneros' plight. They were recruited from New York's Cuban colony, but nobody had time to investigate them. The *Journal* took its case abroad and in London secured the signatures of 200,000 women to a petition imploring the release of the sainted Evangelina Cisneros.

Karl Decker, a Hearst "representative," was secretly sent from New York with orders to secure her escape.

On October 10th the *Journal* announced that Miss Cisneros, the "Cuban girl martyr," had been rescued by the *Journal*: "An American Newspaper Accomplishes at a Single Stroke What the Best Efforts of Diplomacy Failed Utterly to Bring About in Many Months."

Most of the front page was filled by two drawings, showing "Miss Cisneros Before and After Fifteen Months of Incarceration." On one side was a beautiful girl, on the other a debilitated woman.

The story began: "Evangelina Cosio y Cisneros is at last at liberty, and the *Journal* can place to its credit the greatest journalistic coup of this age."

How this heroic rescue actually took place is interesting. Miss Cisneros virtually had the run of an old decrepit jail, moving in and out of her cell at will. Decker had simply climbed to the roof of a building adjoining the calaboose, leaned over, and broken with his hand an ancient rusted window bar. Miss Cisneros leaned out and Decker pulled. She was with him in a trice. She was smuggled off the island and brought in triumph to New York.

IMPERIAL HEARST 71

With the "girl martyr" in New York, the fun began. Hearst ordered a gigantic celebration at Madison Square Garden, followed by a reception at Delmonico's, at which all the political hacks, retired military leaders, dusty wives of dead and forgotten heroes, were trotted out. Hearst himself merely looked in on the celebration at Delmonico's and was introduced behind a hedge of potted palms to Miss Cisneros, who looked the picture of health.

Creelman later wrote[18] that Hearst was acute enough to see the "sordidness" of the episode.

It was then arranged to have Mrs. John A. Logan, widow of General Logan, take Miss Cisneros to the White House, where she was introduced to President McKinley who, according to the *Journal*, "gave the exploit his unofficial blessing." He said, according to the *Journal* (and because the *Journal* said it the remark is of dubious authenticity), "It was a most heroic deed."

There can be no doubt that the Cisneros case did much to intensify anti-Spanish opinion.

The *Journal* raised the cry for an American war vessel to be dispatched to Cuba to protect American "interests," which were slight, and the government had obeyed by sending the *Maine*. A number of New York papers were trying to allay the growing war fever, among them the Republican *Tribune*, which supported McKinley in his weak efforts to avert war. The *Journal* savagely attacked the Administration for its "mildness"· toward Spain.

The time had arrived for Hearst to square accounts with Ambassador Dupuy de Lôme. Yet Hearst's correspondents in Cuba privately agreed with Spain's ambassador in Washington. Richard Harding Davis, on January 16, 1897, in a letter to his mother from Cardenas, Cuba, said: "Every one I met was an Alarmist and this is polite for liar."

Some months before, a Hearst agent had abstracted from the Havana postoffice a letter written by the Ambassador to a friend in Cuba.[19] It was a personal letter, which the Ambassador could have, but had not, entrusted to his diplomatic pouch. It contained some

[18] *Ibid.*
[19] *The Martial Spirit*, by Walter Millis.

personal reflections on life in Washington, among them an unfavorable opinion of McKinley. Lôme considered him a weakling and a "low politician, catering to the rabble."

The letter was sent secretly to New York and held until a psychological moment. In February, 1898, it was published by the *Journal* on the front page, in facsimile, under this headline:

THE WORST INSULT TO THE UNITED STATES
IN ITS HISTORY

Lôme immediately cabled his resignation to Spain.

The *Journal* called his letter "infamous," but its contents were less severe than the *Journal's* daily strictures on McKinley. Moreover, it was an ordinary letter, similar to countless thousands which appear in diplomatic memoirs. The only indiscretion was its theft and publication *at a crucial moment*. Lôme had been one of the obstacles to war. Now he was out of the way.

On February 10, 1898, the *Journal* announced: "Threatening Moves by Both Spain and the United States; We Send Another War Vessel to Join *Maine* in Havana."

This was untrue, but public hysteria had been lashed into fever. Only a spark was needed. The spark came.

The battleship *Maine*, partly because of the *Journal's* campaign, had moved into Havana harbor on January 25, 1898, had been saluted by Morro Castle and had replied to the salute. Her place of anchorage was designated by the harbor authorities according to custom.

On the night of February 15, 1898, one week after the Lôme incident, Secretary of the Navy Long, asleep in his Washington home, was awakened by a Navy Department messenger. The battleship *Maine* had been blown up in Havana harbor with 260 men killed! He could not believe the news. Had the Spaniards gone crazy?

At the *Journal* there was pandemonium. Artists were illustrating just how a torpedo was placed under the vessel and detonated by means of an electric wire from the shore. Hearst and Chamberlain were like madmen. The morning headlines were black and red, ominously demanding "Who Destroyed the *Maine*?" and offering $50,000 reward for "information" revealing the culprit.

An extra edition of the *Journal* on the morning of February 17th, flatly declared: "The War Ship *Maine* Was Split in Two by An Enemy's Secret Infernal Machine!"

The first eight pages were devoted to imaginary portrayals of how it had been done. Captain Sigsbee of the *Maine* later, with a flash of insight, considered these drawings and diagrams to be proof that there had been a plot and that the *Journal* knew of it. It was a shrewd guess, but the reasoning behind it was faulty. The *Journal* printed diagrams of everything.

The *World* sent a tug to Havana harbor to ascertain the "truth," and attempted to send divers down. The *Journal*, on Hearst's order, started a monster subscription campaign to build a memorial to the dead seamen. The circulation of both the *World* and the *Journal* crossed 1,000,000 copies daily.

The *Journal* approached former President Grover Cleveland for his endorsement of its campaign. Cleveland wired this reply: "I decline to allow my sorrow for those who died on the *Maine* to be perverted into an advertising scheme for the New York *Journal*."

What happened to the *Maine* is still a mystery, despite Naval investigations which terminated only in 1911 when the hulk was raised, towed to sea and committed to the deep with military honors.

There have been two principal theories. One is that, by accident, the vessel's magazine blew up. This may well have been so, although the Navy rejected the theory. The second is that Cuban insurrectos, seeking to involve the United States with Spain, did it. This is plausible, as all historians admit. However, the insurrectos were few in number, had no heavy explosives and the harbor of Havana was closely guarded against them by Spanish authorities. Moreover, the insurrectos had not previously demonstrated either cunning or bravery sufficient to effect the blowing up of a warship of a friendly power, which they were hoping would assist in ousting the Spaniards. They had not even succeeded in blowing up Spanish ammunition dumps or garrisons and, indeed, had not tried. It would have been politically suicidal for the insurrectos, had they been caught, to destroy the *Maine*. But, if the insurrectos did it, *they must have had money and supplies from the mainland*.

Historically, the Spanish government has been exonerated.

An unusual secondary circumstance is that nobody has come forward to acknowledge the deed, which suggests that it could not have been part of a general conspiracy. This makes the theory of accident stronger. Had insurrectos or Spaniards planned the explosion, some parties to the conspiracy, or members of their families, would surely have spoken out by now, if only on their death beds.

Studies of probable causes have erred, in my opinion, by not considering the Hearst organization, its character and its bias. The man in the United States most interested in plunging the country into war was William Randolph Hearst. The *Journal* had led the campaign to have a warship sent to Havana, although none was needed. An "incident" was, there is no doubt, hoped for by Hearst. The *Journal* made the first accusation against Spain, whom history has since exculpated, shielding the Cuban Junta *with which the* Journal *had very close connections*. All the Hearst men in Cuba carried letters from Cuban conspirators in New York. Richard Harding Davis, in one of his published letters, states: "We have the strongest possible letters from the Junta. . . ." This point is at least certain: *If the Junta directed the explosion, then it was caused by a group with which the* Journal *had intimate connections*.

In this connection Hearst's slogan flashes upon the mind: "While others talk the *Journal* acts."

Among the incidental incitements perpetrated by the *Journal* was an account of the detention and search at the customs of three Cuban girls on their way to the United States. Richard Harding Davis simply related the fact of the search. Hearst summoned Remington and instructed him to make a drawing for which Hearst supplied the details. This drawing, printed on the front page of the *Journal*, showed a young girl standing naked and helpless before Spanish officers who were rummaging through her clothing.

When the girls arrived in New York the *World* sought them out. They were furious at the *Journal's* false representation of their humiliation. They denied they had been stripped, or that men had searched them. A police matron had conducted the search, and they had not been undressed.

The *World's* story forced Davis, with an independent reputation to sustain, to send a letter to the *Journal*. This was printed inconspicuously. Davis pointed out that he had said nothing about the stripping of the girls or a search conducted by Spanish officers. Davis did not say these details had come from Hearst.

The *Journal* headlines of the time give some idea of the pressure brought to bear by Hearst, who wrote most of these headlines himself.

On Sunday, February 20th, the *Journal* was filled with photographs of the *Maine* wreck. On Sunday evening another of the many *Journal* "extras" declared: "How the *Maine* Actually Looks As It Lies, Wrecked by Spanish Treachery, in Havana Bay."

In the following week the *Journal* printed these headlines, all of them lies:

NO WAR—BUT NIGHT AND SUNDAY
WORK ON BIG GUNS GOES ON

SABBATH TOIL AND RUSH OF SOLDIERS
TO ALL SEASIDE FORTS

RECRUITING ALREADY BEGUN;
TROOPS IMPATIENT TO MARCH

DESPERATE WORK TO HOLD
THE UNITED STATES IN CHECK

THE UNION ABLAZE WITH PATRIOTISM
EVERY STATE READY TO SPRING TO ARMS
AT A MOMENT'S NOTICE

CITIZENS DEMAND THAT CONGRESS
SHALL TAKE ACTION

CITIZEN SOLDIERS EVERYWHERE
ARE ROUSED BY THE WAR SPIRIT

TWO MORE BIG CRUISERS ARE ORDERED
MADE READY FOR SERVICE

76   IMPERIAL HEARST

There was a good deal of distinguished anti-war sentiment, but none of this was published in the *Journal* or the *World*.

Congress finally appropriated a paltry $50,000,000 for "national defense." McKinley expected to obtain a full capitulation from Spain on every demand. Indeed, the Spanish agreement to all American demands had been dispatched, and official Washington knew it, when war was hastily declared.[20] But even about the defense appropriation the *Journal* lied, the headline saying: FOR WAR! $50,000,000.

Meanwhile, the *Journal* continuously maligned McKinley. Mark Hanna, the President's "adviser," was caricatured as the Goddess of Liberty in a robe plastered with dollar signs, holding a ribbon of ticker tape in his hands. The *Journal* charged that delay in declaring war was plotted by the "moneybund" to enable it to profit in the stock market.

On April 7, 1898, the *Journal* spread this across its front page:

MCKINLEY AND THE WALL STREET CABINET ARE READY TO SURRENDER EVERY PARTICLE OF NATIONAL HONOR AND DIGNITY

To support this the *Journal* carried an "interview" quoting Assistant Secretary of the Navy Theodore Roosevelt, as follows:

"The *Journal's* attitude as reflected in its Washington dispatches during the past few days, is most commendable and accurate. All who know the situation will concede that. It is cheering to find a newspaper of the great influence and circulation of the *Journal* tell the facts as they exist and ignore the suggestions of various kinds that emanate from sources that cannot be described as patriotic or loyal to the flag of this country."

Roosevelt, in a letter to the Associated Press, published in the New York *Evening Post*, said:

"The alleged interview with me in today's New York *Journal* is an invention from beginning to end. It is difficult to understand the kind of infamy that resorts to such methods. I never in public or private commended the New York *Journal*."

[20] *Ibid.*

IMPERIAL HEARST

The *World* published the letter on its front page, characterizing the *Journal's* news as "Written by Fools for Fools."

The declaration of war came in April, and both the *Journal* and the *World* were in ecstasies. On May 5, 1898, the distinguished Edwin Lawrence Godkin wrote in *The Nation*:

"The fomenting of war and the publication of mendacious accounts of war have, in fact, become almost a special function of that portion of the press which is known as 'yellow journals.' The war increases their circulation immensely. They profit enormously by what inflicts sorrow and loss on the rest of the community. They talk incessantly of war, not in the way of instruction, but simply to incite by false news, and stimulate savage passions by atrocious suggestions. . . . [The multitude] have already established a régime in which a blackguard boy with several millions of dollars at his disposal has more influence on the use a great nation may make of its credit, of its army and navy, of its name and traditions, than all the statesmen and philosophers and professors in the country. If this does not supply food for reflection about the future of the nation to thoughtful men, it must be because the practice of reflection has ceased."

Upon declaration of war, Hearst offered his yacht to the Navy, with himself as captain. He was politely refused, but the yacht was accepted. He later succeeded in obtaining an ensign's commission.

The Hearst "wrecking crew" was dispatched to Tampa, where a yacht had been chartered. All the big newspapers chartered private vessels, which often interfered with naval maneuvers.

Before troops were landed in Cuba, the U. S. Navy, after considerable confusion, at last located the Spanish fleet, which was known to have left Spain, in the harbor of Santiago. The American fleet, supplemented by an equal number of newspaper tugs and yachts, cruised outside. Not much was happening in the way of war. The troops which the *Journal* had "rushed" to seaports months earlier had not yet budged.

But the *Journal* was active. Among its many false headlines was this:

BIG BATTLE
Is Expected

The type in the second line was so minute that it could not be read at even a short distance from the newsstands.

In San Francisco the *Examiner* was whipping up sentiment for an invasion of the Philippines, to which the Navy department dutifully dispatched Dewey with his fleet, although the Philippines had not figured among the alleged reasons for going to war with Spain. Officially, the United States merely wanted to free bleeding Cuba. But Hearst, in close touch with business interests on the Pacific Coast, *was chiefly interested in seizing the Philippines.*

The *Examiner* had long been campaigning for the annexation of Hawaii, which American sugar planters seized in a fake revolution and wanted to retain. Congress had voted against annexation once. The *Examiner* also wanted the Philippines. Their possession by the United States would enhance the value of Hearst real estate in the Port of San Francisco, and would secure for him the gratitude, and the advertising, of maritime, banking, storage and transportation interests whose eyes were on Philippine trade.

When the American expeditionary force landed up the coast from Santiago, Cuba, a cutter filled with Hearst artists, writers, war authorities, biographers, photographers, medical men and astrologers hailed the leading boat by megaphone. The boat-load of soldiers, on the fringe of a jungle which might be infested with Spanish sharpshooters, paused, thinking a military order was being transmitted. The megaphonist merely wanted to learn the name of the private in the prow of the boat. The name was ascertained, and the first boat landed. Thus the *Journal* was able to give to the world the name of the first American soldier to set foot on Cuban soil. But it got the wrong name.

Mingled with the troops were newspapermen, with the Hearst "wrecking crew" the most numerous and the most prominent. Hearst himself was on the spot, which made the event historic.

At El Caney James Creelman of the *Journal* was shot, and fell in the tall grass as the troops pushed by. Creelman said later:[21]

"Some one knelt in the grass beside me and put his hand on my fevered brow. Opening my eyes, I saw Mr. Hearst, the proprietor of the New York *Journal*, a straw hat with a bright ribbon on his head, a revolver at his belt, and a pencil and a notebook in his hand. The man who provoked the war had come to see the result with his own eyes and, finding one of his correspondents prostrate, was doing the work himself.

"Slowly he took down my story of the fight. Again and again the tinging of Mauser bullets interrupted. But he seemed unmoved. That battle had to be reported somehow.

" 'I'm sorry you're hurt, but'—and his face was radiant with enthusiasm—'wasn't it a splendid fight? We must beat every paper in the world.'

"After doing what he could to make me comfortable, Mr. Hearst mounted his horse and dashed away for the seacoast, where a fast steamer was waiting to carry him across the sea to a cable station."[22]

Creelman had been an active apostle of the journalism that acts. It was he who suggested a bayonet charge to the American officers at El Caney. All the books Creelman had read told of a bayonet charge. The military, thus reminded, acted. The charge came off as desired by the *Journal's* tactician. El Caney was taken "gloriously," said the *Journal*.

The *Journal* reeked with the "heroic" deeds of the American army, before whom the "might" of Spain shrivelled. There was very little truth, but, for that matter, all the papers were lying.

Pascual Cervera, the Spanish admiral, when the Spanish forces had withdrawn to the fortified hills surrounding Santiago, made his forlorn dash out of the harbor. His ships were hopelessly outclassed and out-dated. He had come merely to be beaten; this was understood both by himself and by Spain. According to the *Journal*

---

[21] *On the Great Highway.*

[22] Edward Marshall, another Hearst reporter, was shot through the spine and lost a leg.

and other newspapers of the day, however, it was a first-class fleet, a menace to the American coast.

Admiral William T. Sampson had steamed down the coast in the cruiser *New York* for a conference with Shafter on the coordination of the military and naval forces. About the fleet hovered the newspaper tugs.

Suddenly the first Spanish ship emerged, followed by another. Out they came, and veered down the coast. The American vessels were in so close to shore that they had difficulty maneuvering, and, as the firing opened, endangered each other with their own shells. The Hearst press-boat moved forward under full steam and was soon under the guns of the American fleet. It passed in front of one man-of-war, causing fire to be withheld.

The fleeing Spanish ships raced down the coast, their wooden decks afire, their boilers bursting, their antiquated guns unable to shoot straight. The American fleet pursued, pouring shot after shot into flaming hulks. On the skirts of the fleet raced the newspaper tugs, Hearst well in the lead.

He was in at the kill.

As sailors from the burning Spanish battleships *Oquendo* and *Teresa* leaped overboard and swam for shore, the Hearst vessel took after them heroically. A boat was dropped, bearing Hearst and reporters. Before the boat reached shore Hearst jumped into the water, his trousers pulled up around his knees. Brandishing a revolver, followed by his armed crew, he called to the Spaniards to halt.

Dripping, dejected, frightened, the Spaniards weakly held up their hands. They were herded into the Hearst lifeboat and hauled aboard the *Journal's* ship, where their photographs were taken and they were interviewed. The photographs and stories were quickly rushed to New York, and the *Journal* announced an historic battle *led by the Hearst yacht*. There is a photograph extant of the Hearst party landing. It was taken from *behind* the Spaniards!

After Dewey took Manila in even easier fashion, hailed by the *Journal* with a headline saying "MANILA OURS," dispatches from Spain indicated that Admiral Manuel de la Camara intended to leave with a fleet for Manila, via the Suez Canal. Spain had no effective vessels at home, but this was not generally known. The alarming stories of another fleet were generally believed.

As soon as the dispatch entered the *Journal* office it was laid before Hearst who immediately notified Creelman (who had been transferred to London) to "buy some big English steamer at the eastern end of the Mediterranean and take her to some part of the Suez Canal where we can then sink her and obstruct the passage of the Spanish warships."[23] This act, made unnecessary by the fact that Camara had nothing to sail with, would have been in defiance of international law and might have embroiled the United States in a war with England.[24]

Was not the man capable of issuing such an order also capable of being connected with the "incident" in Havana harbor on the night of February 15, 1898?

After the war, with American troops in command of Cuba and the Philippines, three Hearst correspondents in Havana, on instructions from their office, crept about the city at night plastering walls with posters that read: "Remember the *Maine*."

A small American garrison had charge of thousands of Spanish prisoners quartered in the city. The Cuban populace, inflamed by the war, years of anti-Spanish propaganda and the sudden victory, was in an ugly mood. There had been threats of mob action against the Spanish prisoners, whom an illiterate citizenry now blamed for its misery.

The incendiary posters had no other purpose than to start a gigantic riot and produce a wonderful story for the *Journal*. Fortunately, an American patrol took the Hearst correspondents into custody. They were roughly handled. General Shafter, in command of the army of occupation, was infuriated and said "death is better than they deserve."[25] But he first communicated with Washington,

[23] *On the Great Highway*. Facsimile.
[24] Mrs. Fremont Older's authorized biography of Hearst states that the block ship was actually sent. "Hearst chartered a coaling vessel, ordered the Captain to fly English colors, and sent it to the Suez Canal. The officer was told by Hearst that should the Spanish fleet try to go through the Canal to attack Dewey, a hole in the ship should be opened and the vessel sunk in the canal to delay the Spaniards."
[25] *The Martial Spirit*, by Walter Millis.

which declined to approve execution. Thereafter no Hearst man was allowed in Cuba while Shafter was in command.

The *Journal* office immediately got busy. Shafter was bombarded with supplications from Secretary of War Alger, saying: "The New York *Journal* people are in great trouble", "The *Journal* has been doing good work," and "The New York *Journal* is in terrible distress."[26]

The deportation order *did* hurt the *Journal*, for it had to copy the *World* on Cuban news and rely on the imaginations of the office "dope-slingers." Shafter was adamant. The deported correspondents were not fired by the *Journal*, which made no attempt to disavow their provocative work.

Might not the directing intelligence behind the posting of provocative placards in post-war Havana be considered in connection with the "incident" in Havana Harbor on the night of February 15, 1898?

Echoes of the war came up in the *Journal* for a long time afterward. Admiral Sampson had been absent, in consultation with Shafter, from the battle of Santiago. The *Journal* worked up a controversy over whether Rear Admiral Schley or Sampson was entitled to the honor of having defeated Cervera. The *Journal* called Sampson a "tea-going admiral," and suggested that he had been away from the battle on purpose. In short, it impugned his courage.

The *Journal* "scooped" the world on the terms of the Spanish-American peace treaty, which it published in full on January 1, 1899. Editorials pronounced this act "a journalistic achievement believed to be entirely without precedent. Such enterprise makes Senatorial secrecy an absurdity."

It was understood in newspaper circles that the treaty had been procured in Paris by bribing a Spanish diplomatic secretary.

At the unveiling of the *Maine* Memorial in New York in 1912, Hearst was a guest and speaker.

[26] *Ibid.*

IV

HEARST and Chamberlain sponsored William Jennings Bryan primarily for circulation purposes. Bryan was Punch and McKinley became Judy in the *Journal's* bid for readers.

In July, 1896, Bryan told a perspiring Democratic convention that humanity was no longer to be crucified on a cross of gold. He was cheered and nominated for the Presidency. Because of his plan for issuing more money, he became a threatening apparition of the class struggle to the moneyed East. The campaign of 1896 was basically a duel between debt-ridden farmers and Wall Street money lenders.

In 1896 the *Journal* could have created no greater sensation in New York than by supporting Bryan. All the newspapers had been depicting him as a revolutionist, an anarchist, a corrupter of the young, a crack-pot, a fool, an idiot, a nihilist, a four-flusher, a confidence man and a menace to home, religion and public morals. And then the *Journal* solemnly announced that it was its patriotic duty to support Bryan, the opponent of that arch-friend of the trusts, William McKinley. The effect was tremendous. Where nothing but denunciation had been heard before there now ensued a wild, continuous debate. Quarrels took place in saloons, pool rooms, clubs and churches all over the country, and Hearst and the *Journal* were mentioned quite as often as Bryan. The stock market slipped down a peg and the dollar became very weak abroad.

The *Journal's* explanation of why Bryan was denounced was direct, simple and (marvelous to relate) true. The trusts were against him and the trusts controlled the newspapers. This explanation automatically drew many new supporters to Bryan, and the only paper in which these Bryanites could read sympathetic accounts about their candidate was the *Journal*. Its circulation soared.

Hearst obtained reams of free publicity from the New York papers, who linked him with Bryan as an anarchist, despoiler, evil goblin from the West. This brought still more new readers to the *Journal*.

But, looking for news about Bryan, these new readers encountered Goddard's fantasies about two-headed virgins and female Siamese twins planning marriage. Those attracted to the *Journal* by its stand for Bryan, were diverted by the photograph of an actress, "who was once Mrs. Al Weber. While the pretty actress amuses theater-goers nightly, her former husband, wrecked mentally and financially, raves in the insane pavilion of Bellevue Hospital." The *Journal* pretended that this was a great moral issue:

> Has Public Taste Sunk to This Degrading Level?
> If the New York Theater-Goers Unblushingly Flock to See a Vulgar Young Woman Undress Herself on the Stage, What May We Expect Next?
> Should Be Suppressed, Says Dr. Parkhurst
> Lewd and Indecent, Says Charlotte Smith
> Alan Dale Says: "They Are the Limit"
> The Shocking Performance
> of Miss Leona Barrison at
> a New York Theater

Under all this was a full page of sketches showing the young lady *stripped to her bloomers.*

The new Bryan readers were also enthralled with "The Suicide of a Horse"; "Cutting a Hole in a Man's Chest to Look at His Intestines and Leaving a Flap That Works as if on a Hinge"; "Experimenting With an Electric Needle on an Ape's Brain"; and "Science Can Wash Your Heart."

In the advertising sections they saw insertions similar to the ones run in the San Francisco *Examiner.* One of these said: "Ladies: Dr. Conrad's Globules, only safe, successful and painless system of 'home treatment' for female complaints and irregularities known to science; swallow no more Tansy and Pennyroyal to ruin your system."

Hearst retainers have often pointed to Hearst's "sacrifice" for the sake of principle and have claimed that because he supported Bryan the *Journal* stood at a net loss of $158,000 by October, 1896. But the *Journal* had been carrying few commercial department store advertisements. Those withdrawn were not missed, nor did they remain away for long. Even if it were a true figure, $158,000 was small change; in 1898 Hearst spent $500,000 reporting the war with Spain.

More than offsetting any advertising loss, was the tremendous circulation gain that paved the way for future advertising contracts. During the Bryan campaign the *Journal* had the biggest circulation of any paper, and the day after election it soared to 995,000 copies, until then the record in the United States. Within a year Hearst had pushed the *Journal's* circulation up more than ten times. A good part of the gain came from rural regions deficient in pro-Bryan papers. Special out-of-town editions of the *Journal, predated by three days,* were placed on sale throughout the country. The *Journal* had, by default, become the standard-bearer of the oldest political party in the nation.

Two juicy sources of revenue were opened by this campaign. Because workmen were attracted to the paper by the anti-trust hullabaloo, the *Journal* for nearly two decades thereafter was the leading paper for "help wanted" advertising. Employers had to advertise in the *Journal* to gain access to the New York labor market. Before long the *Journal* published page after page of help-wanted and situation-wanted ads, and for many years carried *more of this material than all the other New York papers combined*. Advertising of this type bore the highest rate, was on a cash basis, and attracted a multitude of new readers.

The second rich financial vein opened by the Bryan campaign was patent medicine and fake stock advertising. For many years after the first Bryan campaign the *Journal* enjoyed the dubious distinction of printing more advertisements for fake cures and bogus stock *than all the other New York papers put together*. After the political campaign ended, the "respectable" advertising also returned to the *Journal*, because of its increased circulation.

When Bryan spoke in New York Hearst sat on the platform. In the Bryan parades he rode in a carriage with the "Great Commoner." Hearst advertised Bryan, but Bryan also advertised Hearst, and Hearst turned the campaign into immediate as well as future profit. Ten years after the campaign, sleuths for James Gordon Bennett's

Herald, aided by Wall Street insiders who wanted to injure Hearst politically, revealed that the Hearst Estate, during the Bryan campaign, *had been playing the stock market on the side of the decline.* It was the *Journal* that made Bryan seem like a possible victor, and thereby depressed the mercurial stock market. What the Hearst Estate's profit was has never been revealed. The *Herald* also uncovered the fact that the Hearst Estate, prior to the dramatic announcement of the *Journal* in support of Bryan, *had gone short on the dollar in London.* Hearst, the arch-patriot of his age, hammered his own national currency for a profit!

Hearst did not sue the *Herald*.

The *Journal* found Bryan so profitable that it undertook to finance his campaign. The Republicans had a tremendous slush fund gathered by Mark Hanna from banks and corporations. Bryan had nothing—until Hearst put up some of his profits. The *Journal* offered to match all contributions to the Bryan campaign, dollar for dollar. A total of $40,000 was collected from readers. Hearst doubled the ante.

The bitterness of the campaign, the most intense in the history of American politics, with the possible exception of the campaign of 1860, was intensified by the *Journal*. Davenport's facile pencil turned out a caricature of Hanna, bulky, flesh-necked, bulbous-nosed, with a low beetling brow, decked out like a Bowery tough in a rough suit splotched with dollar signs. By his side was a midget—McKinley. Throughout the campaign those two images went through many poses: McKinley tugging at Hanna's coat-tails, McKinley shouting up at a Hanna who was too tall to hear, McKinley dangling like a ventriloquist's dummy on Hanna's fat knee.

The cartoons almost elected Bryan. The popular vote was close, but in the Electoral College the Boy Orator of the Platte was snowed under. The cartoons reduced McKinley to saddened tearfulness. It was said that after he was elected President, he knelt in the White House study and prayed for relief from this scourge.

Hanna's biographer described the effect these corrosive pictures had on the Republican chieftain.[1] "In a letter to the owner of the

---

[1] *Marcus Alonzo Hanna*, by Herbert Croly, Macmillan Co., New York, 1919.

Journal, Mr. Hanna protested vigorously against the misrepresentation, but without effect. Later the personal attack upon him was reduced to a system . . . He was depicted as a monster of sordid and ruthless selfishness, who fattened himself and other men on the flesh and blood of the common people . . . Day after day he was portrayed with perverted ability and ingenuity as a Beast of Greed, until little by little a certain section of public opinion became infected by the poison . . . Mr. Hanna was strongly tempted to bring suit for libel . . . but after consulting with friends decided that Lewis and Hearst were aiming at precisely this result—with the expectation of profiting more from notoriety and the appearance of persecution than they would lose in damages. So he decided to disregard the attacks, libellous as they probably were . . . But he was very much wounded by them and suffered severely from the vindictive and grotesque misrepresentation . . . The practice of attaching to a few conspicuous individuals a sort of criminal responsibility for widely diffused political and economic abuses has, of course, persisted."

And while Hanna was being depicted as a capitalist vampire the Hearst Estate was profiting heavily in the international speculative markets. In a speech at Atlanta years later Hearst admitted that he had not approved of free silver while supporting Bryan.

In 1900 the *Journal* again supported Bryan, more blatantly than before, even though the return of a perceptible amount of well-being for farmers and workmen had made his following less hysterical. Hearst tried to secure the Vice-Presidential nomination, but Bryan dodged cleverly (so he thought) by making Hearst president of the National Association of Democratic Clubs. Here Hearst found himself in a strategic position.

There was one difficulty about the 1900 campaign, but it did not bother the facile Hearst. Bryan opposed the Republicans chiefly on the issue of "imperialism," denouncing them for the seizure of the Spanish colonies and for the war against Spain. Hearst, as we have seen, was the instigator of that war. The *Journal* as recently as 1899 had announced itself in favor of annexation of the Philippines, the enlargement of West Point and Annapolis, the construction of the Nicaraguan Canal, and a much larger navy.

It seemed therefore somewhat odd (to those unacquainted with the infinite duplicity of Hearst) to find him supporting Bryan, the anti-imperialist. But in 1896 Hearst had supported him although he did not believe in free silver! It might have been supposed that Hearst would soft-pedal the issue of "imperialism." But the *Journal* emerged, for the purposes of the election, *as the arch-foe of imperialism, which was represented by Hanna and other shady Republicans.* Hanna was again trotted out in his dollar-checked suit, with McKinley trailing as the half-witted gnome.

During the first McKinley régime, Hearst, despite his vicious personal attacks on McKinley in 1896, sent Alfred Henry Lewis to the White House to assure the President that the *Journal* really thought of him in the highest terms. McKinley responded that he was very glad to learn this and said he bore the *Journal* no ill will. Lewis then asked the President for some favor Hearst wanted. McKinley refused, smiling. The *Journal* immediately renewed its attacks.

Hearst, for reasons we shall soon see, actually needed to exert power in Washington, and after Bryan's defeat he continued the fight. "McKinley's fat, white hand," the *Journal* declared, "has tossed to the starving American the answer out of the White House window: 'A trust can do no wrong.' "

Brisbane wrote even more ominous editorials, *and the* JOURNAL *came out as the virtual exponent of political assassination,* saying:

"Napoleon gradually developed into a pretty strong man, and nobody bothered him. If Marat had been living when Napoleon returned from Italy and he retained his populistic pull, it is quite likely that he would have got hold of Napoleon and cut his head off. He had a passion for cutting off the heads of those who made themselves conspicuous. His murder might have changed the world's history.

"Was not the history of the world changed when Philip, the father of Alexander the Great, was murdered in the midst of festivals and rejoicing? Left unmurdered he might have reigned until long past the day that Alexander the Great died and went under the ground.

"Philip's ambition was really modest. He simply wanted to rule over all Greece.

"Compared to his son Alexander, he was like the humble president of the Stove Trust compared to John D. Rockefeller. If Alexander had died before his father, who would have known how to thrash and coax the Greeks into line? Who would have conquered Persia and provided such fine historic reading?

"If Cromwell had not decided to remove the head of Charles I from his lace collar, would England be what she is today—a really free nation and genuine republic?[2]

"Did not the murder of Lincoln, uniting in sympathy and regret all good people in the North and South, hasten the era of American good feeling and perhaps prevent the renewal of fighting between brothers?

"The murder of Caesar certainly changed the history of Europe, besides preventing that great man from ultimately displaying vanity as great as his ability.

"When wise old sayings, such as that of Disraeli about assassination are taken up, it is worth while, instead of swallowing them whole, to analyze them. WE INVITE OUR READERS TO THINK OVER THIS QUESTION. [Capitals by Brisbane.] The time devoted to it will not be wasted. Any kind of harmless exercise is good for the brain as any kind of harmless exercise is good for the muscles."

In an editorial on McKinley's second victory the *Journal* said: "If bad men cannot be got rid of except by killing, then the killing must be done."

There it was: to the point, terse, specific.

But this line scared Hearst—for killing can be done on both sides. He hastily expunged the passage, which ran for only one edition. It had not escaped notice however, and was quietly filed away in the other newspaper offices.

When Governor Goebels of Kentucky was assassinated in 1901

[2] This was just before England fell afoul of Hearst's wrath.—F. L.

Ambrose Bierce wrote a political quatrain for the *Journal*, containing the deadly lines:

> *The bullet that pierced Goebel's breast*
> *Can not be found in all the West;*
> *Good reason, it is speeding here*
> *To stretch McKinley on his bier.*

This was *not* deleted after the first edition.

The increasing bitterness of the attacks in 1901 on the McKinley Administration by the *Journal*, the San Francisco *Examiner* and the Chicago *American* (founded on July 2, 1900, synchronously with the nomination of Bryan), had more behind it than circulation, as did the clamor for the war with Spain. Hearst's final savage turn against the Administration was induced by its pro-British policy. For twenty-eight years afterward Hearst was to be violently anti-British. He has been consistently pro-German since 1895, even during the World War, and today he is pro-Hitler.

These two lines of Hearst's foreign policy have had a cash basis. When the *Journal* was acquired, it included a German edition, *Das Morgen Journal,* later converted into the *Deutsches Journal* and suppressed by the Department of Justice in 1917. By owning this German paper, inadvertently acquired, Hearst came into intimate association with that part of German-American business which advertised. The big brewing interests were among his early backers, and put up the money for some of his enterprises.[3] These German-Americans, of course, did what they could to stimulate an anti-British bias in Hearst. But Hearst would have been anti-British without their promptings and without the invitations from Kaiser Wilhelm, whose guest Hearst often was before the World War, as he has been the guest of Hitler since the advent of National Socialism.

In the early years of this century and in the eighteen-nineties, Wall Street was pro-British because it received most of its financial inspiration from London, the United States then being a debtor nation. The anti-British stand of the Cleveland Administration in the

---

[3] *U. S. Brewing and Liquor Interests and German and Bolshevik Propaganda:* Senate Judiciary Comm., Sixty-sixth Congress, First Session, 3 vols., 1918-19.

Venezuelan boundary dispute had upset Wall Street and the amicable settlement of the controversy had pleased it. But in 1901 the British rapprochement with Wall Street was complete, for in that year the British government allowed J. P. Morgan & Co. the profitable job of floating a $50,000,000 loan in the United States to help finance the Boer War.

The origin of Hearst's monumental anti-British bias goes back to an expedition sent to Peru in 1899 by the University of California. It was financed by Hearst's mother as an archaeological venture, but the firm of Hearst, Haggin, Tevis and Company sent geologists and metallurgists along. The geologists surveyed the lofty and remote Cerro de Pasco region, the locale of old Inca and Spanish silver and gold mines. The geologists located the mines (sunk to levels of only a few hundred feet), and decided they were rich in copper. Ownership was acquired cheaply and secretly, and preparations were made for financing the Cerro de Pasco Investment Company.

Peru, however, had been under rigorous financial domination by London bankers since 1890, and continued to be until the World War, at which time Hearst, the Irving Trust Company, the Bankers Trust Company, J. P. Morgan & Co. and the National City Bank of New York became the financial overlords of Peru. But from the inception of the Cerro de Pasco Investment Co. the Hearst managers found that the British branch banks in Peru put every sort of obstacle in the way, and continuously intrigued in an effort to get the British taken into the Cerro de Pasco development.

In this atmosphere the McKinley Administration negotiated the Hay-Pauncefote treaty.

Washington probably knew nothing about Cerro de Pasco. The greatest secrecy surrounded the negotiation of the treaty, which merely provided that the projected Isthmian Canal would be unfortified and unmilitarized, an international water highway of the same status as the Suez Canal. It was a valuable concession for the British Foreign Office to obtain, as it made future domination of South America by the United States difficult. So secretly had the negotiations proceeded, and popular interest in the canal project was so small, that only a few lines about the British signing appeared in

English newspapers. None appeared in American papers, for the trans-Atlantic cables and news services were then still under British control. Only approval by the American State Department and the Senate was lacking, and this seemed virtually assured.

Hearst, on one of his periodic trips to Egypt, was sunning himself on the deck of a Nile river steamer, scanning the English papers that had come on board. As he later told an associate, he was electrified at what he saw. He reread the modest notice and notified the captain to put back to the nearest telegraph station.

Edward Hardy Clark had apprised Hearst of the value of the proposed canal to Cerro de Pasco, and the Hearst papers had boomed the idea of the canal at every opportunity. But Clark and Hearst had no idea that the British, their opponents in Peru, would have a string tied to the canal. It was at once obvious to Hearst that the British wanted the canal unfortified for some very well disguised reason. Hearst, therefore, wanted it fortified. He suddenly wanted Panama to be an American Gibraltar.

He cabled Chamberlain to spare no energy or expense in an attack on the McKinley Administration and the Hay-Pauncefote treaty. The *Journal* was also to inaugurate a general protest movement, with petitions. Hearst could not get back from Egypt fast enough. He took the most rapid available steamers and trains, and while touching at ports dispatched cablegrams and demanded full reports of what was being done.

It was in this period that the *Journal's* endorsement of terroristic violence became loudest. McKinley and Hanna were depicted as footmen bowing to Pauncefote and addressing him as "M'Lud." Every stray bit of anti-British sentiment in American history was seized upon to stir up anti-British feelings. McKinley and the Administration were flatly denounced as treasonable, seditious, and unpatriotic tools of Great Britain. From this time date the vast Hearst campaigns of succeeding decades for the annexation of Canada, the liberation of Ireland and the support of Germany.

Naturally, other groups opposed to this concession to Britain were galvanized into action by Hearst. In the end the treaty was rejected by the Senate. The Panama Canal Zone today is one of the most heavily fortified areas of the world.

When England, soon after the rejection of the Hay-Pauncefote treaty, concluded its alliance with Japan, it was more grist for the Hearst mill, for Hearst had a Pacific Coast capitalist's bias against the Japanese.

The denunciations of McKinley and his régime continued in the *Journal* until the fateful September, 1901. Never before in American history, or since, has a President of the United States been subjected to such merciless excoriation, unless it be Wilson, who also felt the sting of Hearst's whiplash to the full.

In 1901 it had become clear to Hearst that the policies prompted by his economic interests would make an excellent political platform for him to stand on, provided it was suitably disguised with promises to labor and the farmers. It had been rumored in 1900 that he had made a deal with Bryan for the Presidential nomination in 1904. He was violently against Japan, which was a popular stand both with labor and capital on the Pacific Coast. He was against England, which pleased German and Irish voters. He "endorsed" the aspirations of labor. If he could achieve the Democratic nomination he would have the Solid South without any effort at all.

The future seemed bright for Hearst when, on September 6, 1901, President McKinley, while attending the Pan-American Exposition at Buffalo, was shot by Leon Czolgosz, a fanatical anarchist. As McKinley lay dying, other newspapers, glad for a chance at Hearst, exhumed all the *Journal's* exhortations to personal violence against McKinley.

Hearst was immediately the target of public rage. He was hanged in effigy in scores of cities. The circulation of his three papers fell. Clubs, schools and societies barred his publications. Public speakers denounced him as the foulest person in American life.

James Creelman later wrote,[4] in an attempt to absolve Hearst from connection with the assassination, that he had been sent some months earlier to the White House by Hearst to patch things up. "Mr. Hearst

[4] *Pearson's Magazine*, September, 1906.

offered to exclude from his pages anything that the President might find personally offensive. Also he pledged the President hearty support in all things on which Mr. Hearst did not differ with him politically. The President seemed deeply touched by this wholly voluntary offer and sent a message of sincere thanks. These facts are given as an explanation of the actual terms upon which Mr. Hearst and Mr. McKinley were living when Czolgosz fired the fatal shot."

The point is that McKinley was unable to grant whatever Creelman had asked for Hearst, probably the rescinding of the Hay-Pauncefote Treaty. The bitter attacks continued down to the eve of the day on which McKinley was shot. The New York newspapers, Hearst's excluded, reported that Czolgosz had on his person a copy of the *Journal* in which McKinley was assailed, and clippings about McKinley that were inflammatory.

Hearst was now on the defensive for the first time since he became a publisher. His competitors eagerly dredged up every particle of evidence they could find against him.

The boycott against Hearst also became personal. Whereas a short while before he had been seen around Broadway with prominent men, he was reduced to consorting with his own hired men. He still appeared at night in the midtown section, but he had suddenly become grave of mien. The fury of the campaign appalled and frightened him. He was everywhere accused of responsibility for the assassination. It was even hinted that there had been a Hearst plot to "get" McKinley.

His panic was reflected in an editorial he wrote for the *Journal* as McKinley lay dying:

"The thoughts and hopes of every American mind are fixed upon the President battling courageously, patiently for life. Earnestly he longs to live.

"First, and above all, that he may not leave his much beloved wife alone behind him.

"Second, that he may devote his days and his strength to the programme of national duty and national prosperity which his latest speech outlined. A worker from his boyhood, he still longs to work for the people that trust him.

"He sees clearly the natural lines of American development:
"Peace.
"A great navy.
"The Isthmian Canal.
"Expansion.
"Energetic, peaceful development of America's greatest possibilities."

This was the man the *Journal* had characterized as "a coward," "an abject, weak, incompetent poltroon," and "the most despised and hated creature in the hemisphere."

Vice-President Theodore Roosevelt, talking to Senator Henry Cabot Lodge after McKinley was shot, said: "Every scoundrel like Hearst and his satellites who for whatever purposes appeals to evil human passion has made himself accessory before the fact to crimes of this nature."

Lodge added that the *Journal* was "an efficient cause in breeding anarchists and murder."

Hearst had to move swiftly to offset the crusade against him, which was not only depleting his circulation but also his advertising. In answer to the charge that he was "un-American," a charge he has ever since trotted out against his opponents, Hearst changed the name of his New York paper to the *American and Journal*. Later the title was divided, the morning edition taking the name of *American*. In Chicago the Hearst paper was already known as the *American*.

In desperate need of influential friends, Hearst sought out Richard Croker and Charles F. Murphy, the leaders of Tammany Hall. As recently as 1900 the *Journal* had called Murphy the worst type of political boodler (in connection with the "ice trust" scandal; Murphy, then dock commissioner, was involved in the conspiracy that forced New York's poor to pay an extra high price for ice).

Hearst wanted a political job to give himself social status. He sent Brisbane to see Murphy. Brisbane had somehow gotten the impression that Hearst merely wanted the political job in his organization. Hearst had modestly mentioned the post of Congressman. Brisbane therefore approached Murphy in such a way that the Tammany sachem thought Brisbane was the man Hearst had picked for the job. Murphy promised his support, provided Hearst put up a sizable amount of cash for the 1902 campaign managers. Brisbane immediately agreed, and hurried back to Hearst with the news that Murphy and Croker were quite willing that Brisbane should be a Congressman. Hearst quickly disabused Brisbane of this notion. Hearst was to be the Congressman.[5] Brisbane, and the other Hearst men, Chamberlain included, were astounded, for privately they did not see how a person with Hearst's reputation could pass muster before the voters. Also, there was always the danger that Hearst's personal life would be exploited.

Their fears were unfounded. On November 4, 1902, Hearst was elected to Congress from the Tenth New York Assembly District, which was safely under Tammany's thumb. Hearst made elaborate preparations to see that the event was properly impressed upon the public consciousness. He personally attended to all the details of the big election-night celebration. It was to be an *American-Journal* and Hearst-Tammany "bust" that would reduce to insignificance all previous political celebrations. He made arrangements with the owners of the Flatiron Building to have a display of fireworks from its roof, but the building's managers forbade the bringing of fireworks to the top of New York's proudest building. The display was moved at the last minute to Madison Avenue, facing Madison Square and near the old Madison Square Garden where a monster election shivaree was taking place.

The square was packed with people by ten o'clock. Suddenly there was an ominous detonation. It was followed by another, and yet another. In a moment the ground shook with one gigantic explosion after the other. Clouds of smoke completely covered a panic of human beings.

The next day every paper except the *American* had its front page filled with the news of the disaster. On page five the *American* carried an inconspicuous story under the headline: "Twelve Killed by

[5] *Collier's,* October 6, 1906. As it is put by Mrs. Fremont Older: "Arthur Brisbane was about to be nominated as Congressman from the Eleventh District of New York City, but Brisbane and his friends thought that Hearst would be more effective in Washington. At the last minute, a change in nominees was made."

Fireworks Explosion." Hearst's connection with the affair was not mentioned.

District Attorney Jerome declared, and thereby incurred Hearst's undying animosity: "In the matter of the Park Avenue explosion, the dynamite was stored for a useful purpose, but in this case the collecting together of such a quantity was only for celebration purposes and for the amusement of the people." He might have added: "and for the advertising of Hearst."

For nearly twenty years Hearst was to fight, by every conceivable means, the law suits of the injured and the survivors of the deceased. The final death toll was seventeen, with an equal number crippled for life. The suits resulting from the case at one time exceeded $3,000,000.

Hearst became inconspicuous, temporarily, after the explosion. The New York papers did not take undue advantage of it at his expense.

Hearst's entry into politics had immediately brought stories about his personal life to the fore. He was nearly forty years old, and unmarried.

So Congressman Hearst married Millicent Willson, a member of the chorus of *The Girl from Paris* which was playing at the Herald Square Theater. She was the daughter of George Willson ("George Leslie"), a vaudeville hoofer of an earlier day, and had won the *Morning Telegraph's* popularity contest because Hearst bought enough papers to swamp the ballot box. They were married on April 28, 1903, in Grace Episcopal Church, by Bishop Henry C. Potter. There was a wedding breakfast at the Waldorf-Astoria, and in the afternoon the couple boarded the North German Lloyd liner *Kaiser Wilhelm II*.

When Mr. and Mrs. Hearst landed in England Hearst was handed this cablegram:

THE CITY OF NEW YORK HAS BEEN SUED FOR $25,000 IN NEW YORK COUNTY SUPREME COURT BY SOLOMON LANDAU, ADMINISTRATOR, FOR DAMAGES FOR THE DEATH OF GEORGE LANDAU, BY YOUR FIREWORKS EXPLOSION IN MADISON SQUARE ON ELECTION NIGHT, NOVEMBER 4, LAST, AND

NOTIFIES YOU TO DEFEND THIS ACTION. GEORGE L. RIVES, CORPORATION COUNSEL.

The tragedy of the explosion, his election and his marriage wrought a curious change. He completely altered his mode of attire, and affected black frock coats and black slouch hats, the traditional uniform of the American "statesman" and bucolic politician. Said Frederick Palmer in *Collier's*: "The outsiders who saw him did not meet a man in a check suit, accompanied by two or three girls, but a silent, listening man in that inevitable frock coat."

Hearst used his Congressional seat to create publicity for himself and his newspapers. Like his father in the Senate before him, he also introduced a number of measures which would primarily benefit the Hearst organization.

The New York *Times*[6] has left us a general picture of Hearst's Congressional activity: "He was on hand when labor bills were up; any chance to advance his socialistic [sic!] principles did not find him idle . . . He is not a mixer, and the majority of Democrats were as aloof from him as he from them." Whenever Hearst swung into action "the Democratic Party in the House was smitten and frozen with a torpidity like that of the Sleeping Beauty's court, as if Hearst had been a political fairy godmother weaving a spell of lethargy; and on their motionless ranks there sat a silence so ostentatious that it was fairly blatant."

One of the first things Hearst did after he was elected was to editorialize against John Sharp Williams, Democratic minority leader. He made speeches on the floor in defense of his papers against Congressman Sullivan's (Massachusetts) criticisms of them, in which the Southern Pacific deal had been mentioned. Hearst attempted to vilify Sullivan by saying he had been convicted of manslaughter, a charge from which Sullivan had been exonerated. Nonetheless, Hearst did not hesitate to say that one of the persons who made the Southern Pacific charge was a convicted criminal.

Hearst lawyers and reporters swarmed into Washington to assist

[6] April 8, 1904.

in these publicity campaigns. Many of the Hearst proposals in Congress were drawn by Clarence J. Shearn, his lawyer.

Speaker Cannon once said he did not know Hearst by sight, implying that he was seldom in the House. This was true.

The type of legislation Hearst sponsored fell into three classes: that introduced for favorable publicity, that introduced to frighten enemies of his papers or those who refused to advertise in them, and that introduced for the private benefit of himself and his papers.

In the first class of legislation was his "Product of Labor Bill," designed to except organized labor from the operation of the anti-trust laws. In the same category was a bill to spend $50,000,000 for rural roads. Hearst once attached a rider, providing for a national eight-hour law for labor, to a naval appropriations bill. Labor and the farmers were being cozened with these measures, which the *Journal*, Hearst's new *Farm and Home* and *Cosmopolitan* publicized.

In the second category, was a measure to permit the Interstate Commerce Commission to fix railroad rates; another was designed to bring the Standard Oil pipe-lines under the jurisdiction of the I. C. C.; and another would have authorized United States District Attorneys to proceed under the anti-trust laws without authorization of the Attorney General, which would have made it easier to get at the big corporations and would have taken control of anti-trust prosecution away from Washington. Had the bill passed, the trusts would have had to "see" men like Hearst.

Hearst introduced a bill that would enable the government to acquire, operate and maintain electric telegraphs, paying for them with a public bond issue. For this he was called "socialistic." But Hearst was merely striving to get lower telegraph rates for his newspapers. He so frightened the telegraph companies that they gave him a ridiculously low press rate. When other papers learned of this they clamored for, and obtained, preferential treatment, too.

But another, and far more lucrative, result of Hearst's 1902 alliance with Tammany was the *exclusive* contract for printing the New York City Board of Elections notices, and contracts for much of the city and county job printing. He had done this in San Francisco. Later he did it in Chicago and other cities.

Hearst's marriage occupied a central position in his political affairs before the World War. Hearst agents could and did point out that he was a respectable married man. His wife does not appear to have influenced him, but she was his constant companion in the first decade of their union and accompanied him on political tours and spent evenings with him at the office of the *Journal*.

Hearst has seldom done meaningless things and his marriage, coming when it did, appears to have been significant. His henchmen were already going around the country picking up delegates to the 1904 convention which would nominate a President. His political advisers had pointed out that few bachelors have resided in the White House.

Mrs. Hearst bore him five sons, two of them twins. Twins run in the Hearst family.

During the World War she was publicly active, doing what she could to remove the stigma incurred by the pro-German Hearst policy. For a time after the war she also functioned in public life, but after 1922 she and her husband were estranged.

Mrs. Hearst, having become a devout Catholic, refused to give Hearst the divorce he sought, and he was forced to accept the decision. As a marriage settlement Hearst gave her $15,000,000, consisting of stock in *Cosmopolitan, Good Housekeeping* and *Harper's Bazaar* magazines. This she later exchanged with her husband for New York real estate. She was also given the St. Joan estate, at Sands Point, L. I., formerly the Belmont showplace.

On the surface relations are still maintained by Hearst and his wife, and she figures in political matters on his behalf and in the management of various charitable benefits which give the Hearst name "humanitarian" publicity.

It was laughable to many that Hearst aspired to the White House. But there was method in the Hearst madness. Merely the Presidential *nomination* would be a feather in his cap. He would be the Democratic Party's acknowledged leader, and the nomination would give his papers and magazines wide publicity. Under the cloak of a Presidential nominee Hearst could smuggle his utterances into the papers of his rivals.

At that time Hearst was the only man in the United States, except the President, who was quoted in full by newspapers. It was in his own newspapers, but they were located in four leading cities—New York, Chicago, San Francisco and Los Angeles. Other newspaper proprietors had never spread their most trivial remarks in full over their pages.

Charles Edward Russell, later a distinguished Socialist but then city editor of the *Journal*, wrote a puff for Hearst in *Harper's Weekly* of May 21, 1904. "I once saw this even-poised self-contained man thrash a Naples' cabman for beating a horse," Russell wrote, "and once, with a dangerous glitter in his eyes, face down a crowd of Apulian peasants that he thought were maltreating an unfortunate man. Often I have seen him stop in the street and turn to watch out of sight a limping horse, a stray dog, or a man in trouble. . . ."

Russell lauded Hearst's "humanitarianism" after the Galveston flood. Hearst sent "relief trains" from New York, Chicago and San Francisco. The trains were covered with Hearst signs and finally arrived at their destination. It would have been easier to order the relief materials from New Orleans, Nashville, Houston and Dallas. But Hearst had no papers in those cities.

Hearst personally went to Samuel Gompers, head of the American Federation of Labor, to ask his support. Gompers withheld it, and the A. F. of L. has never endorsed any of the Hearst candidacies, even under the later Green-Woll-Hearst rapprochement.

It was conservatively estimated that Hearst spent $1,400,000 of his own money to get the nomination. He entered the convention with 104 instructed delegates. His name was put in for nomination and seconded by Clarence Darrow. On one ballot he got 263 votes. The St. Louis convention finally compromised on Judge Alton B. Parker, of New York, a harmless nobody.

The Hearst papers were "regular"—and quiet—during the 1904 campaign. Hearst, immediately on his return from St. Louis, asked

Charles Murphy for the New York mayoralty nomination in 1905. Tammany had elected George B. McClellan in 1903 for the last two-year mayoralty term. In 1905 the first four-year mayor would be elected. Hearst wanted McClellan pushed aside. Murphy could not readily acquiesce, for McClellan eminently suited Tammany's needs. Tammany, moreover, had become somewhat alarmed at Hearst's ambitions and wilfulness at St. Louis. Murphy finally refused the request. Hearst, so out of control that he kicked objects of furniture about, announced himself as an "independent" candidate, formed the Municipal Ownership League and cut loose from Murphy. The first plank in Hearst's platform was that he was against the corrupt Tammany "boodlers."

Hearst obtained his municipal ownership theme from a book published early in 1905 by Municipal Court Judge Samuel Seabury, who really believed in it. Seabury's book was entitled *Public Ownership and Operation of Public Utilities in New York*. Hearst immediately sent for Seabury and appropriated the idea. It was Seabury who placed Hearst's name in nomination for the Mayoralty. In 1906 Seabury received Hearst's support for the New York Supreme Court judgeship and obtained the office. Seabury's relations with Hearst were amicable until 1909, when Seabury supported Judge William Gaynor for the Mayoralty against Hearst's wishes. After 1909 Seabury, disillusioned with Hearst, associated with other liberal "reformers" like Woodrow Wilson and Al Smith. In 1922 he placed himself on record with a biting denunciation of Hearst.[7]

It was an unhappy day in Murphy's life when the *Journal* came off the presses with the famous cartoon depicting him as a thug in prison stripes. The ward-heelers on Fourteenth Street laughed, but they obeyed the word that went out from the Wigwam: Hearst was not to win *under any circumstance.*

Hearst himself spent $150,000 on the campaign. He was still president of the National Association of Democratic Clubs and secured financial support from out of town even though he was not running as a Democrat. A patchwork of supporters gathered around him,

[7] *Samuel Seabury—A Challenge*, by Walter Chambers, Century Co., New York, 1932.

IMPERIAL HEARST

including Irish, Germans, and liberalistic reformers duped by blarney about municipal ownership. Ward and precinct workers were recruited from the staff of his morning and afternoon papers, whose reporters, rewrite men, copy-readers and editors were forced to get out and ring door-bells and make speeches on street-corners. Hearst himself made speeches on street-corners, standing in a dray.

The Hearst organization soon had New York by the ears. Billboards and electric poles were covered with full length photographs of Hearst. By the side of the candidate in these posters was Hearst's young son, George, barely able to stand up. He held his father's index finger, and it made an appealing tableau. The Hearst papers also laid down a barrage of photographs of Hearst with his wife and child *en famille*.

Every once in a while *Journal* readers found the benign visage of the Pope himself, with a complimentary reference inscribed to William Randolph Hearst on the front page. Credulous Irish, Italian, German and Slavic Catholics believed the Pope had endorsed Hearst's candidacy. Tammany frothed at the mouth to see this photograph which *had been sent to Hearst when he organized one of his publicity expeditions to help the sufferers after the eruption of Vesuvius in 1904.*[8]

To corral Protestant votes, Hearst spread the sanctimonious Rev. Charles H. Parkhurst over the front page, where he wrote about home, mother, public morals and the good life. Anthony Comstock was given a benediction by Arthur Brisbane.

So effective was the hullabaloo, so demoralized was Tammany by the novelty of the attack, that *Hearst won the election*. He was the victor by several thousand votes, it has since been established, but the Tammany bruisers, heeding their instructions from Murphy, went berserk. Hearst's campaign people were assaulted and ballot boxes were stolen from the Hearst wards and dumped into the East River. A Hearst man set out in a rowboat and scooped up a mess of filthy, water-soaked ballots. He transferred his burden to a hansom cab and repaired to Hearst headquarters.

[8] Mrs. Fremont Older, in her authorized biography, considers it significant that Hearst "has received the blessing of every Pope since Pius IX." Hearst's favorite Pope, she says, "was Leo XIII, who appealed to his aesthetic sense."

The sodden ballots were retained as evidence.

The *World*, reporting the wild election, said: "Men battered and bruised were helped by friends into the Municipal-Ownership headquarters. One man had a broken arm dangling in his sleeve. Another's head was cut and the blood was trickling through his bandages. Tammany thugs in the lower East Side district had all but killed him. From many parts of Manhattan reports poured in of the greatest violence and crimes at the polls that New York has ever known."

Hearst demanded a recount, which threw Tammany into a momentary panic. The resourceful Murphy had fresh ballots printed, however, to replace those missing, and set his men to work marking them for McClellan. When the final tally was checked by the Board of Elections it appeared that Hearst had failed of election by 3500 votes.

Hearst wasted no time in mourning or recriminations. The election was hardly over when he sought out Murphy again. He modestly asked for the Democratic gubernatorial nomination. Murphy agreed—for a price that was later generally set by political commentators at $500,000 in cash, part in down payment.

Hearst's return to Murphy, and his apparent belief that Murphy was now with him, showed how obtuse he could be. Hearst had no idea how deeply he had wounded Murphy. The Tammany leader, of course, was plainly a crook, but no man likes to have the fact published so graphically that the *meanest* intelligence can grasp it.

Hearst was preoccupied with other political matters besides elections. The Federal Pure Food and Drug Act was passed by Congress on February 15, 1906, effective June 30, 1906. The hearings on the bill terminated February 13, 1906. Hearst, as the biggest publisher of patent medicine advertising, has always had an abnormal interest in legislation affecting it. Although the *American* was cluttered with wild stuff about the insurance scandals, the coal trust, the gas monopoly, the ice boodlers, the railroad barons and John D. Rockefeller, it did not report the sensational hearings on the Pure Food and Drug Bill which extended through 1906.

In Chicago, for a while, Hearst went after the stockyard packers hammer and tongs, for earlier campaigns in New York had shown the profit to be derived from such exposures. Ella Reeve Bloor, later to achieve fame as a revolutionary, had exposed conditions in the slaughter houses for the New York *Journal*. Nothing was done about the conditions, but the *Journal's* advertising increased.

The procedure in Chicago was similar, but more spectacular. In 1905, as a result of the work of Hearst investigators, the Federal grand jury indicted Louis Swift, Edward C. Swift, Ogden Armour, Charles Armour, Edward Cudahy, R. N. Morris and Edward Morris. Nothing came of this, except publicity for Hearst. Levy Mayer, counsel of the Illinois Manufacturers Association and packers, and a Democratic politician, was not involved. Hearst and Mayer had struck an alliance behind the scenes which resulted in the elevation of Carter H. Harrison to the Chicago Mayoralty and Edward F. Dunne to the Governorship of Illinois. The Mayer-Hearst alliance continued down to the death of the former, with Roger Sullivan, the local Democratic boss, as their instrument.

When the uproar about the packers subsequently became great, largely as a result of the publication of *The Jungle* by Upton Sinclair, the Hearst papers blew hot and cold and were silent. Sinclair was engaged in exposing the unsanitary conditions within the packing plants, and about these conditions the Hearst papers had never said anything. Hearst's attack on the packers was based on the allegation that they had combined in "restraint of trade" and were illegally tapping the city's water mains.

During previous agitation for Federal supervision of the patent medicine and food poisoners, Hearst had been conspicuously reticent on the subject, although forced from time to time to print something about it. He did not make an issue of it. His pocketbook was directly affected and he openly defended the patent medicine manufacturers' motives.

When the Food and Drug Act was before the Senate for final debate, the *American* commented briefly and tepidly on the subject through the Washington correspondence of Julian Hawthorne, who alternated as Washington correspondent and sporting editor. In his dispatch of February 21st, Hawthorne inserted this tearful line: "Even vendors of patent medicines and preserved foods might do things not wholly incompatible with decency and integrity."

On February 22nd the bill was passed and the *American* reported the subject factually for half a column on page seven under the headline: AFTER 15 YEARS THE SENATE PASSES A PURE FOOD BILL.

Hawthorne had a separate section of Washington "gossip" under the misleading headline:

HAWTHORNE FINDS THAT CONGRESS
JUST NOW IS LIKE A VAUDEVILLE

*Author Describes the "Pure Food Bill" Playing
Before the Curtain While the "Rate Bill"
Transformation Scene is Being Set*

". . . At this point Mr. Bailey, of Texas, arose and immediately lifted the discussion from the level of dictionary definitions to that of statesmanship," Hawthorne wrote. "He challenged the right of the Federal Government to interfere in what should (as he contended) be a matter proper to the State police."

Note how the *American* elevated Senator Bailey's dissenting remarks to the level of "statesmanship." *At this very time Hearst possessed proof that Senator Bailey was in the pay of the Standard Oil Company.* This information, which Hearst did not release until 1912, forced Senator Bailey's resignation from the Senate in 1913.

The Pure Food and Drug Act of 1906 did not affect advertising. Although it governed what might be claimed on the label, it left publishers free to print what they liked in newspapers. It was not until the Tugwell Bill of 1934 that a real attempt was made to regulate misleading and fraudulent advertising. Hearst and other publishers, as we shall see, scuttled the effective Tugwell measure.

Before the World War the Hearst papers printed anything in the way of patent medicine advertising, just as they printed full-page ads for fly-by-night mining stocks in which price increases were "guaranteed" to gullible buyers. *Editorials palpably written by patent medicine interests against regulating patent medicines were printed by the Hearst papers wholesale. Advertising matter that made the most arrantly false claims of cures was printed as news, under news heads, with no indication that it was advertising.*

The whole Hearst patent medicine fraud was revealed by *Collier's* magazine under the editorship of Norman Hapgood.

Said *Collier's* for May 12, 1906:

" 'Canned editorials,' to employ the 'Druggist's Circular's' apt phrase, are being sent broadcast to the newspaper offices by the Proprietary Association of America. The medical profession is accused of being a huge trust, warring upon patent medicines in its own interests. Since doctors give enslaving and dangerous poisons, argues the Proprietary Press Bureau, nostrum makers should be allowed to. Verily, a remarkable plea for immunity, this! 'It's true that I'm in a murderous business, but so is Dr. Blank across the street.' . . . To the honor of daily journalism, be it said that the prepared editorial arguments of the Proprietary Association have either been totally disregarded by the more important newspapers or received with derision. One conspicuous recent exception comes to our notice. The most distinguished recruit to the editorial forces of the Associated Disciples of Ananias is Mr. William Randolph Hearst.

"Mr. Hearst defends the patent medicine people, as should be expected. He (or Mr. Brisbane for him) repeats the stereotyped and ready-made arguments of the Proprietary Association . . . Mr. Hearst (or Mr. Brisbane) is able to explain why he publishes gambling tips while attacking gambling; he is able to explain why the doctors are the real villains, not the Proprietary Association of America."

In *Printers' Ink* for February 8, 1912, appeared the following small notice: "The New York *American*, the *Evening Journal* and *Das Morgen Journal*, owned by W. R. Hearst, have given notice that on and after February 1 no so-called objectionable medical advertising will be accepted. It is believed that the loss of income resulting from this action will more than be offset by the increase of business which will result from the cleaning up of the columns."

This reflected one of the periodical and purely rhetorical reforms of the Hearst papers, made necessary by the unceasing clamor of militant journals like *Collier's* and, later, *Harper's Weekly*. *Collier's* watched to see what would become of this new "reform." As Hapgood had suspected, it meant precisely nothing.

Collier's pointed out the ambiguity of the phrase "so-called objectionable" and in a page of reproductions showed that the Hearst papers, in New York and elsewhere, continued to publish advertisements of "health belts," "rupture cures," gonorrhea, syphilis, tuberculosis, cancer, rheumatism and lumbago "specifics," as well as the traditional ads for recapturing "lost manhood" and avoiding "women's ailments."

Concluding a long and documented exposition of Hearst's continued acceptance of unethical advertising and his use of signed articles by quack medicine-men, *Collier's* for June 22, 1912, said:

"It may be claimed for Mr. Hearst that he is compelled to carry advertising, which he would fain discard, under contracts antedating his avowed intention of 'cleaning up.' The claim won't hold water. More than once the courts have held that contracts involving deals in secret nostrums—just such quackeries as Mr. Hearst derives a fat revenue from—are unenforceable as being contrary to the public weal. If Mr. Hearst should wish to clean up his columns, he need fear no trouble from his quack advertisers.

"But the plain and painful fact is that Mr. Hearst doesn't want to clean up. He only wants to get the credit for cleaning up. When it comes to the issue, it isn't the principle that sways Mr. Hearst. It is the profits. So long as medical fraud pays, it will hardly be found objectionable (so-called) by William Randolph Hearst."

Collier's grappled with Hearst on many other matters, but it had little to say about the fraudulent stock advertising in the Hearst pages.

Will Irwin charged, in the *Collier's* of June 3, 1911, that the *Journal* sold favorable theatrical notices under the name of Arthur Brisbane for $1,000 each, and cartoons by "Tad" and others and writings by Beatrice Fairfax about theatrical people and events for $500 each.[9] Hearst immediately filed a libel suit for $500,000. Hapgood knew Hearst's penchant for blustering with libel actions that his attorneys never pressed to a conclusion. Said *Collier's*: "As William Randolph Hearst is suing us for $500,000, perhaps we ought not to discuss his political affairs, but as he or his attorneys seem reluctant to press the suit toward trial (perhaps for the same reason they changed their minds about bringing a criminal action) we take our courage in both hands and say 'boo.' "

The 1906 campaign for the Governorship of New York was even more furious than the fight for the Mayoralty in 1905. In fact, it was probably the foulest of any important political campaign in American history. *The Bookman* for December, 1908, said, retrospectively, that owing to the elevation of Hearst as a serious candidate for the New York Governorship "no case of moral destitution can now be regarded as altogether hopeless; nor need we discourage any aspiring young man by telling him he must have brains."

The Republicans named Charles Evans Hughes, now Chief Justice of the United States Supreme Court. During the campaign he appeared as something of a knight in shining armor exposing Hearst; he was one of the group of New York Republicans around Theodore Roosevelt and Elihu Root. This Republican group, before, during and after this campaign represented a different clique of capitalists. Where Hearst had the support of gentry like Thomas Fortune Ryan, August Belmont and E. H. Harriman, the Roosevelt Republican faction acted in New York politics for the Rockefellers, Vanderbilts, J. P. Morgan and George F. Baker. The latter group was solidly ensconced, and it was because the former tried to make a place for themselves in the political control-room that the fight became bitter. None of this appeared in the newspaper accounts,

---

[9] Mr. Irwin declared that these transactions were "arranged" by C. F. Zittell, who became business manager of the *Journal* in 1917, succeeding Carvalho, and was discharged when he participated in an almost successful attempt to saddle Hearst with an unprofitable paper company. Hearst stopped the deal by charging in Court that Zittell had taken a $125,000 bribe.

however. Hearst revealed his political tenets in the election by villifying Hughes, whom he had praised a year earlier for his work. After the election Hearst again found Hughes splendid.

Throughout the campaign the Hearst papers cartooned Hughes as a dowdy old maid of Victorian vintage, busily running about doing errands and ringing door-bells for the "trusts," who grinned fiendishly from behind the fence. Hughes was fresh from his successes in exposing the malpractices of the insurance companies and had popular support.

Opposing Hearst for the Democratic nomination were William Travers Jerome, Mayor Adam of Buffalo and Mayor Thomas Mott Osborne of Auburn, who later became the distinguished penologist. Getting Hearst the Democratic nomination involved the seating of his delegations, and there was some doubt about the legality of their credentials because, as Osborne charged, they had been named by "snap caucuses." Convention control was vested in the Committee on Credentials, of which Tammany State Senator Thomas F. Grady was chairman. Murphy, biding his time, told him to get Hearst nominated. Hearst was pouring cash into Tammany's campaign coffers.

Grady seated the bribed Hearst delegations, picked up in the pool rooms, saloons and brothels of the up-state Republican counties. Grady performed reluctantly and at the end of his work spoke a line celebrated in the annals of New York politics: "Boys, this is the dirtiest day's work I have ever done in my life."

The Credentials Committee refused to seat sixty anti-Hearst delegates, including the entire Queens delegation, which had been elected by a popular majority of more than three thousand citizens. Osborne and Jerome bolted and called a convention of their own in Albany, and Osborne declared: "We have seen hired agents parade over the State, shouting out, in terms rising from extravagance to blasphemy, the merits of their millionaire employer; we have seen snap caucuses, as in Broome, Chautauqua, Cortland, and other counties; proxies forged, as in Orleans County; conventions purchased, as in Wayne County; delegates openly bribed for riot and disorder, as in Jefferson County; an attempt to deceive a whole community by a muzzled press, as in Erie County; newspapers blackmailed, as in Monroe and Onondaga Counties—and who can estimate the amount of lying, blackmail, bribery, and corrupt promises necessary to make such a kind of campaign even partially successful?"

Osborne incurred Hearst's undying enmity. For years the Hearst agents dogged him until they finally wove around him, by political and journalistic means, a deadly noose. When he was warden of Sing Sing, ex-convicts suddenly appeared and swore before a Westchester County grand jury that Osborne, famed for his humane handling of felons, had indulged in homosexual relations with them. The Hearst papers screamed it on the front pages. It is a favorite Hearst charge against political enemies.

Osborne was acquitted, despite jury tampering and framing of evidence by the prosecution, but he had to resign. The charges were so palpably trumped-up by the Hearst press that they did not prevent Osborne from later being made head of the Federal military penitentiary at Portsmouth.

Osborne's reference to the "muzzled press" in Erie County was literal. Hearst mobilized the three Buffalo newspapers on his side by flatly threatening to start a paper of his own in that city.

Hearst was nominated by the Democratic convention at Buffalo and also by the Independence League. This latter was a Hearst-created body to succeed the Hearst Municipal Ownership League.

In September, 1906, the Independence League held its "convention" in Carnegie Hall and endorsed a declaration of independence from the trusts.

In his letter of acceptance Hearst said, "The Democracy, denouncing bribery and its accompanying campaign of falsehood and vilification, has wrested control of the party machine from the grip of the corporations." Of Alton B. Parker, Democratic Presidential nominee of 1904, he said: "I am glad we have driven this political cockroach from under the sink." And of the New York City District Attorney: "Jerome is another political Croton bug that is trying to crawl into the corporation establishment across the way. . . . No sooner had the Democratic Rough-on-Rats begun to have its effects than Charles A. Towne scurried across the floor and out of the Democratic door . . . and now is blinking beadily back in the Republican rat-hole where he belongs."

Hearst in 1906 again managed to smuggle favorable accounts of himself into some of the magazines. Creelman, by that time editor of *Pearson's*, wrote a blurb for him in the September, 1906, issue. Lincoln Steffens, assigned by the *American* magazine to expose Hearst, was completely taken in by him and came back and wrote of him as "A Man of Mystery." Steffens' article caused a quarrel on the editorial board. He was sharply criticized by Miss Ida Tarbell and Finley Peter Dunne, among others. Dunne, the creator of "Mr. Dooley," had worked for Hearst and wanted Steffens to write about him as he would have written about a criminal malefactor. Steffens balked, and it was with great difficulty that the editors were able to get Steffens to change even the more obvious puerilities. An anonymous inspired article appeared in the *Overland Monthly* on the Pacific Coast, which showed Hearst as a model employer of labor.

The campaign itself was indescribably wild. Hearst had political "wrecking crews" in various parts of the state whose main object seemed to be to stir up so much commotion that the press had to print news about them.

Although Hearst had not secured the endorsement of the A. F. of L., nor any of the large constituted unions, the Hearst papers faked labor endorsements, hoping that the denials would not be noticed in the general turmoil. Morris Brown, secretary of the Cigarmakers' Union, Local 144, in a letter to the newspapers, protested against the "prostitution" of the name of his organization by the Hearst papers, which falsely claimed the union had endorsed Hearst. Bogus laboring men in the pay of Hearst invaded a meeting of the Central Federated Union with their banners and were booed and hissed.

At a Hearst meeting in New York City resolutions purporting to come from laborers' organizations were read and a worker created pandemonium by standing up and demanding, "Who paid for those?" He was clubbed and dragged from the hall.

IMPERIAL HEARST

The New York *Tribune* for April 26, 1906, contains an account of five hundred Hearst men appearing at Albany to demand the passage of the Raines-Murphy recount bill, which Hearst wanted passed. The crowd of five hundred jeered Governor Higgins because he would not receive it and tried to force its way into the Senate Chamber. It was halted by armed guards in the Senate reception room. Cries of "Smash in the doors" and "Tear down the whole Capitol" were instantly set up.

Senator Brackett, of the Judiciary Committee, which had charge of the bill, had to make a speech before the Hearst horde, which was in the charge of Clarence J. Shearn, Hearst's attorney. In 1916 Hearst helped to place Shearn on the New York State Supreme Court; later he was made Counsel for the New York City Transit Commission, and now is president of the New York State Bar Association.

These tactics continued throughout the campaign, although when Hearst men invaded the Hughes' rallies the audiences rose almost to a man and threatened to tear them limb from limb.

One thing that made Hearst so anxious to attain the Governorship was the accumulation of damage suits left over from the 1902 explosion, and libel suits aggregating $1,500,000. Hearst promised in his speeches that if elected he would dismiss Mayor McClellan and District Attorney Jerome for "malfeasance." Said the New York *Tribune* of September 11, 1906: "A Corporation Counsel friendly to Mr. Hearst unquestionably could load the entire damage verdict on the city." The Appellate Division had already ruled in favor of the city's contention that the fireworks display was an advertising stunt for the *American*.

Mr. Hughes campaigned vigorously against Hearst. In a speech at Mount Vernon, reported in the *Tribune* of October 9, 1906, he analyzed the Hearst corporate structure, showing that Hearst himself was addicted to practices that made those of the gas, coal, oil and steel trusts seem picayune. Mr. Hughes told of a Mrs. Mille S. Werner, a lecturer in the Law School of New York University, who had been run over by a Hearst delivery wagon and had sued Hearst, who fought her just claim (she was invalided for two years) all the way up to the Appellate division. Hearst was finally forced to settle for $20,000.[10]

Mr. Hughes termed Hearst a "tax dodger," and analyzed the Hearst corporate set-up to show how taxes were evaded. The Star Company, a Hearst holding company, Mr. Hughes showed to be simply a "paper" device to avoid service in suits and payment of taxes. It had a nominal capital of $100,000 and its officers were Hearst, Clark, Carvalho and Shearn. Its reports showed it had no accounts receivable, no inventory, no cash, no machinery, no investments and no accounts payable. Its liabilities exceeded assets by $30,000. Liabilities of Hearst's Das Morgen Journal Association exceeded assets by $40,000.

"There does not seem to be anything to tax," Mr. Hughes said. "You cannot sue my opponent. If the *Journal* wagon runs over you, he is not personally liable. It is the property of a corporation . . . it apparently does not pay taxes . . . its assessment was removed."

In another speech Mr. Hughes pointed out that Hearst, brought to court to testify in a damage action, had denied that he owned the *Journal*. This denial was technically correct. Hearst, *apparently,* owned nothing and was legally irresponsible.

Hughes also attacked Murphy, pointing out what Hearst had said of him a year before. The Republicans made a Roman holiday out of Murphy. All the non-Hearst papers pictured him in stripes, some merely reproducing the old Hearst cartoons. A clever wag in the Republican organization thought of printing thousands of posters containing a photograph of Murphy in a suit of stripes with the caption: "Wanted: $5,000 Reward." These were pasted up all over New York. Murphy writhed and his family sorrowed, but he was waiting with his knife for election day.

"Murphy, I hope," said Hearst during the campaign to Julius Harburger, a Murphy friend, "won't be offended at these cartoons.

---

[10] See the New York *Times* of October 20, 1906, for a full account of the technicalities whereby Hearst tried to escape indemnifying Mrs. Werner. The New York papers of 1906 carried many accounts of similar actions, in which the plaintiffs, not being law students, were easily routed, some even having Hearst's legal costs assessed against them.

IMPERIAL HEARST

They aren't meant, and anyhow they are only one of the penalties of being politically prominent."

Hearst's biggest mistake, after the Murphy entanglement, was that he ever locked horns with James Gordon Bennett. When Hearst was first entering New York he telegraphed Bennett in Paris to know if the *Herald* was for sale. Bennett replied tartly: PRICE OF HERALD THREE CENTS DAILY. FIVE CENTS SUNDAY. BENNETT. Hearst had never forgiven this snub and he had set out early in 1906 to expose the *Herald's* "Agony Column," containing advertising for and by prostitutes and brothels. Hearst secured the conviction of Bennett for sending indecent matter through the mails. Hearst had been in New York for eleven years and Bennett had been printing these advertisements right along, without a chiding word from Hearst. It was only when Bennett became dangerous to Hearst's aspirations that Hearst attacked him.

But Bennett more than evened the score. Instructions were given to the *Herald* executives to delve to the core of the Hearst enterprises, even if it was necessary to commit grand larceny. The *Herald* men responded gloriously. The *Herald's* big "smash" came on October 27, 1906, on the eve of election. Over the *Herald's* front page was spread the following:

HEARST ESTATE IN
PLUNDERING DEALS
IN WALL STREET

MANY SYNDICATES PARTICIPATED
IN AND "EXPOSED" WHEN
THE MONEY WAS MADE

PUBLIC THE LOSER
TO "PLUNDERBUND"

TRANSACTIONS REVEALED WITH SHIPYARD
TRUST, TOBACCO TRUST AND THIRD
AVENUE ROAD WRECK

NOW ABUSES THOMAS F. RYAN

ASSOCIATED WITH HIM THROUGH TRUSTEE AND OTHER FINANCIAL INTERESTS IN MANY PLANS TO GAIN LARGELY

The detailed account began: "One of the most notorious episodes in Wall Street history, filled with disreputable details, was the wrecking of the Third Avenue Railroad, through the assistance of the municipal government's bosses, for the benefit of the Metropolitan Street Railway. When the debris was cleared away a bond issue was brought out in which the Hearst Estate appeared as a syndicate participator through the trustee, Edward H. Clark. Kuhn, Loeb, & Co., bankers, of Wall Street, were the syndicate managers, and a mortgage created in 1900 for $50,000,000 was brought out."

The *Herald* also revealed Hearst's speculative activities during the Bryan campaign.

On October 29, 1906, the *Herald* said: "Incidentally, it became known that the managers of the Hearst campaign had resorted to forgery by writing letters to the local newspapers in Plattsburg signed with Farley's [James 'Strikebreaker' Farley] name and stating that he would vote for Hughes, with the request that they be published."

The *Tribune* thoroughly investigated the tax evasion charges and reported on October 14, 1906, that, although Hearst owned one of the biggest newspapers in the city, he had never paid any New York State taxes. The *Tribune* further related that one "James F. Hayden, the plaintiff in a libel suit, was thrown out of court because he didn't happen to sue the right corporation, and costs were charged against him."

In a speech in Brooklyn on October 27, 1906, Hearst attempted to dispose of all his rival publishers with specious irrelevancies.

". . . When he [Pulitzer] was court-martialed by the army and indicted for attempted murder in St. Louis he experienced some part of American justice," said Hearst, neglecting to point out that Pulitzer had been exonerated. "His career," he continued, "is that of a coward, a traitor and a sycophant."

Hearst recalled that during the Civil War, forty years before, the

New York *Herald* had called Abraham Lincoln "an imbecile railsplitter," "a smutty-joker," and "the same kind of traitor that was hung at Charleston."

"You know the character of the men that own the newspapers of New York," Hearst shouted in high falsetto. "You know that Villard, the editor of the *Post*, was sued by his own sister, who alleged that he tried to rob her of her share in her father's estate.

"You know that Bennett, the editor of the *Herald*, has lately been indicted by the United States Grand Jury for printing obscene and indecent advertising in his papers, and sending them through the mails and into the homes of American citizens.

"You know that Laffan, of the *Sun*, is the mortgaged menial of Morgan, and that the tame Ochs, of the *Times*, is indebted to the traction trust and the big life insurance companies even for the building that he prints his paper in.

"You know that Pulitzer, of the *World*, has his money invested in coal stocks and in the Vanderbilt roads that I have attacked, and follows the tips of Wall Street speculators more than he does the interests of the people."

Perhaps the highest, and most somber, point of the campaign arrived when the distinguished Elihu Root made a speech for Mr. Hughes on behalf of President Roosevelt. "In President Roosevelt's first message to Congress, in speaking of the assassin of McKinley, he spoke of him as inflamed 'by the reckless utterances of those who, on the stump and in the public press, appealed to the dark and evil spirits of malice and greed, envy and sullen hatred. The wind is sowed by the men who preach such doctrines, and they cannot escape their share of responsibility for the whirlwind that is reaped. This applies alike to the deliberate demagogue, to the exploiter of sensationalism, and to the crude and foolish visionary who, for whatever reason, apologizes for crime or excites aimless discontent.' I say by the President's authority, that in speaking these words, with the horror of President McKinley's murder fresh before him, he had Mr. Hearst specifically in mind. And I say, by his authority, that what he thought of Mr. Hearst then he thinks of Mr. Hearst now."

On election day instructions went out from Tammany that Hearst was not to win under any circumstance. The returns showed that, even though Tammany might again have stolen Hearst votes, Hearst could not have won. The whole Democratic ticket, state, city and judicial, was elected—except Hearst. Hughes was the only Republican victor. Rarely have the voters in any American election shown such perfect discrimination. Murphy had his revenge. The damage suits went on.

During the 1906 campaign Congressman James S. Sherman approached E. H. Harriman for Republican campaign funds. He dwelt on the dangers of a socialistic régime should Hearst be elected. Harriman snorted. "These fellows are crooks and I can buy them," he replied.[11]

Hearst had been firmly under the control of Harriman for many years. Don Seitz, in his biography of Joseph Pulitzer, tells of a certain Harriman letter that had been offered to the New York *American* and rejected. It was offered to the *World*, which joyfully printed it on April 21, 1907. The letter was addressed to Sidney Webster, 245 East 17th Street, New York. Webster was Harriman's political adviser, had been secretary to President Franklin Pierce, and was the brother-in-law of Stuyvesant Fish. Inasmuch as the letter concerned Harriman payments to the Republican party and Hearst was a Democrat, one might suppose Hearst would have wanted to print it, just as he printed other purloined letters. But Hearst refused it.

In 1909 Hearst was a candidate on the "Civic Alliance" ticket for Mayor of New York and was defeated much more decisively than in 1905. His opponent was Judge William Gaynor, who had received Murphy's endorsement. The Hearst press rose to its usual heights of invective against Gaynor. The tirades continued long after Gaynor's election, well into 1910 when Hearst, the perennial candidate, was modestly seeking the office of Lieutenant Governor as an "independent."

After many months of violent Hearst editorializing Mayor Gaynor

---

[11] *Letters of Theodore Roosevelt to Henry Cabot Lodge*, C. Scribner's Sons, N. Y., 1926.

IMPERIAL HEARST

was shot by James J. Gallagher, a discharged dock employee. In his pocket was found an editorial from Hearst's New York *Evening Journal* denouncing Gaynor.[12]

Mayor Gaynor, on September 3rd, lying in the hospital, wrote a letter to his sister describing his sensations after he was shot on the morning of August 9th and dwelling on the savage campaign in the Hearst press against him because he permitted the showing of Jeffries-Johnson prize-fight motion pictures. He had not the power to stop the showing of these films, he said, and pointed out that both the *American* and the *Journal* had secured exclusive rights to pictures and stories from the ringside on July 4th, 1910, and had exploited the affair to the limit.

"I had no way as Mayor to stop the theaters from showing them . . ." Gaynor wrote. "But the Hearst newspapers kept on denouncing me for not stopping them. I suppose you know the way they had belied me ever since I became Mayor. Finally, one day they printed in large type that an officer of the Christian Endeavor Society named Lowande had called on me at the Mayor's office and asked me on behalf of that society to stop the pictures, and that I told him he was 'a fool and was sent by fools.'

"I had never said such a thing, as you may well know. It was made up. I learned that Lowande was a process server for lawyers. The officers of the Christian Endeavor Society put forth a statement of their own motion that it was untrue that they had sent Lowande or anyone else to me, and that he did not represent them. But it made no difference. These newspapers went on repeating the falsehood, and even tried to get up a public meeting denouncing me.

"Meanwhile people of wicked or disordered minds, of whom there are a large number in New York City, would cut these articles out and send them to me with abuse and threats written on the margin, or else with anonymous letters threatening me . . . Finally they printed that terrible cartoon of me entitled 'The Barker.' I was dressed up as a ruffian and standing outside of a prize-fight ring twirling a cane and barking for people to go in and see the sport.

[12] *Collier's*, October 8, 1910.

Two men slugging each other, one of them down and bleeding, were exposed in the ring.

"Think of one who has been more of a library student than anything else all his life, and who never even saw a boxing match, being pictured like that."[13]

Hearst reacted with characteristic bravado and callousness when asked by the New York papers to comment on the attempted assassination. Hearst could afford to be bold, for Gaynor was of comparatively slight importance and had not been killed; there was no need for Hearst to fall on his knees this time, as he had after the fatal bullet hit McKinley. Hearst's telegram to the New York papers said:

"I am exceedingly sorry that Mayor Gaynor was shot, and if Mayor Gaynor has said what you tell me, I can only add that I am exceedingly sorry that his injuries have affected his mind . . . His experience did not abate his evil temper nor his lying tongue. The criticism of Mayor Gaynor's public acts by the Hearst papers has been temperate and truthful, dignified and deserved, unprejudiced and in the public interest . . . I personally will not take advantage of your columns to criticize Mayor Gaynor politically, first, because of his illness, and second because his mental as well as moral condition has eliminated him from political consideration."

When Gaynor's term expired Hearst and a Fusion group elected John Purroy Mitchel. Mitchel denounced Hearst two weeks after the election for seeking corrupt favors. Hearst then vilified for four years what proved to be New York's best administration and Mitchel lost to Hylan in 1917.

Hearst and the Tammanyites clashed from time to time between 1909 and 1917. While Murphy was taking a rest cure at a resort in Mount Clemens, Michigan, a Hearst agent bribed the chambermaid to bring him the contents of the Murphy waste-basket, in which were torn letters that had passed between Murphy and the hapless Gaynor on patronage matters. The *Journal* printed these letters, but did not mention how they had been obtained.

On October 22, 1909, Murphy and Arthur Brisbane nearly came

[13] Published in the New York *Post*, September 19, 1910.

to blows in public at Delmonico's. Brisbane had offered to shake hands with Murphy, who spoke harshly and refused to accept the editor's hand. Asked by reporters later what had happened, Murphy said: "A fellow who seemed intoxicated or under the influence of a drug spoke to me. I turned away from him."

Speaking at a dinner of the Genesee Society at the Waldorf-Astoria Hotel on January 22, 1910, Brisbane alluded to "that medley of corruption, Tammany Hall" and "those rascals with the red faces, and thick necks" in it. Justice James W. Gerard, later Ambassador to Germany, was the toastmaster and to him W. Bourke Cochran whispered, "For Heaven's sake stop it." For Brisbane was talking to a room full of Tammany bigwigs. Gerard had diplomatically introduced Brisbane as a "righter of wrongs" and a revealer of "scandals in the lives of mosquitoes." This occasioned reserved laughter.

Brisbane soon turned the merriment into scowls.

"The newspapers do libel people," he said, "they do say things that are not true, that hurt people and can't be helped. But it is the little fellows that are hurt by falsehoods in the press, big people are hurt by nothing except the unpleasant truth. Therefore we try to be truthful about the little people. But the harm done by libel is not commensurate with that which would be done should the newspapers be interrupted in the fearless or even hasty conduct of their business.

"The *Journal* and other papers—I am editor of the *Journal* and I hope it is the yellowest of them all—published recently some interesting letters. I don't know where they came from; I didn't know anything about them until they began to appear in print. Perhaps Mr. Hearst knows. I don't know whether he does or not.

"But do you know that the chief objection to the Hearst letters was that they were being published. And if they were stolen, as some say, was it not a plain duty to steal these records of that medley of corruption, Tammany Hall, and of those rascals with the red faces and thick necks who compose it?"

When Brisbane had finished State Senator Thomas F. Grady was introduced.

"As one of the gang of red-faced thick-necked grafters, I rise to reply," he said. "Nobody thinks that the Murphy letters were stolen;

the proceeding was much more dignified. The chambermaid was bribed to save the fragments from the waste-basket that they might be pieced together."

Patrick A. McCabe, Democratic leader of Albany County in 1909, said that Hearst personally had insisted on W. J. ("Fingey") Connors of Buffalo as chairman of the Democratic State Committee, even when it was pointed out that this choice would hardly captivate organized labor, to whom Connors was anathema.

"I know that Mr. Hearst demanded that Connors be made chairman of the State Committee," McCabe said. "He said that Connors was the only man he could trust his money with. As Mr. Hearst had promised to finance the campaign I advised letting him have his way about it and Connors was elected chairman."

A year before Murphy had been asked if Hearst had given him $500,000 in 1906. "I don't know," said Murphy, in a remarkable lapse of memory. "I do know that Connors told me after the campaign that he had sent Hearst a bill either for $16,000 or $26,000 . . . he never received a reply from him."[14]

The Hearst phase of the 1908 Presidential campaign had its beginning really in 1904 and its end in a Senate committee hearing room in 1913. This campaign involved the famous Standard Oil letters.

At the Standard Oil offices at 26 Broadway in 1904 three young men, reading about the machinations of the trusts in the *Journal* and the *World*, thought it would be profitable to try to sell some of the Standard Oil records to a newspaper. The idea originated with Willie W. Winfield, a Negro doorman who was the stepson of John D. Archbold's trusted butler. Archbold was the directing officer of the Standard Oil Company. Winfield broached the idea to Charles Stump, a porter, who had access to Archbold's office. Stump took Frank Morrell, Archbold's office boy, into the conspiracy.

Winfield had Stump telephone the *World*, where the proposition was weighed and rejected. So Stump telephoned the *Journal*.

There he was told to call again. A conference was held with Hearst.

[14] New York *Tribune*, October 23, 1909.

It was decided that one of the sub-editors was to confer with Stump, and the meeting took place one evening in a Thirty-Fifth Street restaurant. Hearst denied before the Senate that he paid anything for the letters. Admitting it would have made him party to a theft. The fact is, however, that sudden prosperity came to Stump and Winfield, who abruptly flowered as characters of affluence in the "Tenderloin" and eventually opened an uptown saloon and gambling house with apparently ample sources of revenue. *Collier's* later discovered that they received and split $12,000, although Winfield claimed years afterward that he had received only $1,200, implying that Stump, then dead from his excesses, had pocketed the lion's share.

It was arranged by the Hearst editor that Stump should do business with John L. Eddy, a Hearst reporter in the offices of the *American*.

For several years thereafter all of Archbold's correspondence, including the duplicate impressions of his outgoing letters, was abstracted piece-meal from the files and taken every evening to the offices of the *American*, where it was photographed. Then it was surreptitiously returned. The letters showed, in the main, that Standard Oil was making direct payments of substantial sums in cash to Senators, Congressmen and politicians, among them Senator Foraker of Ohio, Senator Bailey of Texas, Senator Boise Penrose of Pennsylvania, Senator J. W. McLaurin of South Carolina and others. Standard Oil was putting up the cash for campaigns, for lobbying activities, and for personal uses. To reproduce all the letters would fill many volumes. Some of them may be found in *Hearst's Magazine* for 1908 and 1912 and others are in *God's Gold*, a biography of John D. Rockefeller by John T. Flynn.

These letters, about which no outsider knew anything, placed an enormous power in the hands of Hearst. He could see Archbold and tell him what he had; he could immediately publish the letters and inform the American people of the prostitution of its highest legislative body; or he could "see" the individuals mentioned in the letters.

Hearst chose the latter course as the one giving him the greatest political strength. Nothing was said in public about the letters until

1908. In short, Hearst allowed the corruption of the Congress by Standard Oil to continue with his knowledge for four years. He thereby gathered in more letters and documents, which meant more power for him over a greater number of influential people.

During the Presidential campaign of 1908, while speaking for the Independence League in support of himself and his candidates,[15] Hearst disclosed letters which implicated Senator Foraker alone. These letters were published by the Hearst papers and magazines. *Not the real letters, but only parts of them,* retyped so as to seem to be complete letters, were given.

Why should Hearst publish forged letters when he had the real ones?

Publishing the full original text would implicate malefactors whom Hearst, for private reasons, did not want implicated.

The Standard Oil letters created a sensation, but did not influence the election because both major parties were involved. Senator Foraker was broken immediately. There were rumors of other disclosures to come. Archbold said nothing, apparently afraid to stir.

The Rockefellers really had nothing to fear from Hearst who, not long afterward, began to receive Rockefeller advertising. Hearst had tapped a rich vein.

Hearst's behavior in this matter reveals a despicable character more saliently than do any other of the many dark episodes in his exceptionally dark career. For at this time Hearst was still posing as the champion of the common people, as a militant radical. He possessed the letters and made use of them for private gain through political blackmail precisely in his most "liberal" period, when men like Lincoln Steffens and Samuel Seabury were lauding him.

---

[15] Hearst's candidates were Thomas Hisgen of Massachusetts for President and John Temple Graves of Georgia for Vice-President. Graves was a Hearst writer who had achieved notoriety by upholding lynchings of Negroes in the South and in generally traducing the Negro people. These candidates were chosen at a convention in Orchestra Hall in 1908. Of the 500 delegates "two-thirds were printers and other employees of Hearst papers," according to Walter Chambers in *Samuel Seabury—A Challenge.* The "other employees" were Hearst gunmen and casual riffraff recruited from the West Side saloons at $1 each by Andrew M. Lawrence, Hearst's Chicago manager. This fact was generally commented upon by the non-Hearst Chicago newspapers. Hearst's address to the assemblage contained typical references to Thomas Jefferson, independence and corporate evil-doers.

In these letters Hearst had the power to do more than any other man in recent American history to stimulate public opinion to demand drastic political reforms. Had the full letters been published in the Hearst papers, both the Republican and the Democratic parties would unquestionably have been smashed and the reactionary financial interests would have been exposed just before their hey-day, before they became as entrenched as they are today. Many fresh, vital political principles below the surface of American public life might have had an opportunity to blossom and grow. Hearst had it in his power to shake the United States to its foundations. He elected instead to sell it back to the money-changers.

Agitation over these letters was always present, sometimes above the political surface, sometimes below, during the next five years. How had Hearst obtained them? Were they real? Who else was implicated? Why did not Archbold say something?

Norman Hapgood did the most significant work in ascertaining facts about the letters. In its issue of October 5, 1912, *Collier's* created a nine-day sensation with an article which proved that many of the letters Hearst had already published were forgeries.

Said *Collier's*:

"Certain of the facsimile 'Standard Oil' letters which are being published in *Hearst's Magazine* are forgeries. The famous note to Boise Penrose, telling of $25,000 deposited to his credit, is a forgery. The signature of John D. Archbold, attached to that letter is a forgery. . . .

"The long letter of John D. Archbold to Senator Hanna, carrying the date of January 19, 1900, is a forgery. The signature of Archbold at the bottom of that letter is a forgery. . . .

"The letter of General Grosvenor to Mr. Archbold, with the date of September 26, 1904, is a forgery. . . .

"The writer in *Hearst's Magazine*, in introducing the forgery into his column, says: 'General Grosvenor's subtlety and delicacy is shown not only in his use of the official paper of his committee but—etc.'

"An examination of the forged facsimile on the next page will show that the letterhead of the 'Committee on the Merchant Marine and Fisheries, House of Representatives, U. S., Charles H. Grosvenor, Chairman,' is pasted on top of another sheet of paper on which is typewritten the forged letter of General Grosvenor. The sheet had on it numerals—'250'—and more figures. The last loop of the other numerals is still visible under the pasted-on letter-head. A clumsy job. There are other proofs of forgery in this letter which we shall expose in a moment.

"The letter of Mr. Archbold to Senator Quay, under the date of July 18, 1898, is a forgery. . . .

"These five letters (dated, one of them 1898, two of them 1900, two of them 1904) are written on a typewriting machine of which the first instrument did not reach the market until the middle of 1905, and of which the particular letters and characters used in writing the five documents were not in existence till 1907. . . .

"The facsimile letters were taken to Syracuse and shown to W. L. Smith, president of the company. He did not concern himself with the authorship or the destination of the letters, but solely with the typewriting in the body of the letters. At the first glance he noted many of the characteristics of his machine. He summoned a conference of his superintendents and of the expert engraver who from the beginning has carved the Smith letters and characters. Naturally the expert recognized the children of his skilled fingers and brain . . . and the following statement was drawn up:

"'These letters, namely, letter alleged to have been written by Mr. John D. Archbold to Hon. M. S. Quay, February 13, 1900; letter alleged to have been written by General Grosvenor to Mr. Archbold, September 27, 1904; letter alleged to have been written by Mr. Archbold to Senator Quay, July 18, 1898; letter alleged to have been written by Mr. Archbold to Senator Hanna on January 19, 1900; letter alleged to have been written by Mr. Archbold to Senator Penrose, October 13, 1904, are all of them unmistakably written on the L. C. Smith and Bros. typewriter containing élite type, or known to us as No. 6 type. No L. C. Smith and Bros. typewriting machine equipped with élite or No. 6 type was placed upon the market or manufactured earlier than June 15, 1905.'

"The Archbold signature to the Boise Penrose letter, photographed on these pages, and the Archbold signature to the Senator Hanna letter, are identical. When the two letters are brought to their original size and then superimposed, the two 'Jno. D. Archbolds' become a single 'Jno. D. Archbold' (as shown by the small photograph below). The three periods are at precisely the same distance from each other. The middle period has the same defect of being a trifle large and a little over-inked. A few of the many other duplications are the hump over the o, the white spot in the capital J, the notch in the lower part of the h, the hump at the bottom of the C, and the square end to the final d. Think of a man writing a second signature four years after the first, and duplicating at least forty peculiarities of detail, and reproducing the exact size for his total signature, so that when superimposed the two signatures become exactly and perfectly one signature. Of course, Mr. Archbold signed neither of these fraudulent documents. What is given as his signature is merely an identical reproduction of an engraver's block.

"Eight letters published in *Hearst's Magazine*, in addition to the five we have just analyzed, are signed with a 'Jno. D. Archbold' signature which is identical. No man ever wrote his signature alike eight times running. There is just one way of obtaining the identity revealed in these eight signatures, and that is by tracing them from the same model.

"But almost the prettiest touch of all is in the Grosvenor forgery. For that letter, dated at 'Athens, Ohio,' is written on the identical individual typewriter that wrote the so-called Archbold letter to Senator Penrose. Mr. Hearst asks us to believe that General Grosvenor was using the faithful, hardworking typewriter at Athens, Ohio, on September 27, 1904, and then boxed and shipped the machine by express to Mr. Archbold, who banged out his letter to Senator Penrose on it on October 13, 1904. The identities are innumerable. . . .

"That the creator of these articles . . . was well aware of his criminality and the need of trying to hide it is proved by the different degrees of reduction and enlargement used on the facsimiles in order to disguise the identity of the signatures and of the typewriting. . . .

"One further point, and this the most damaging. Mr. Hearst in his own person has tripped up and contributed the largest item in the volume of internal evidence of fraud which these Standard Oil articles carry. In his own introduction to the series in *Hearst's Magazine* on the Standard Oil letters William Randolph Hearst says:

" 'On the afternoon of the day on which I was to speak at Columbus, *a gentleman called on me at my hotel* [italics by *Collier's*] and submitted to me a number of letters which have since become known as the Standard Oil Letters. There appeared to be no doubt about the genuineness of the letters. I will not discuss further, however, the letters as they appeared in the campaign, but will allow Mr. ——, *the writer of this series of articles,* to take them on consecutively and chronologically and completely.'

"And the editor of *Hearst's Magazine,* in introducing 'J. E——,' (the 'gentleman') says:

" 'Editor's Note: Nearly four years have passed since the *author of the series of articles* made public, through Mr. Hearst's speeches, some remarkable letters written by John D. Archbold. These letters revealed the Standard Oil Company in the definite act of corrupting America's public servants. In the series of articles of which this is the first *the author, who must still remain anonymous,* makes public new and even more important letters.'

"The author of the series, then, appearing in *Hearst's Magazine,* is the mysterious 'gentleman' who brought the batch of facsimiles to Mr. Hearst at Columbus in 1908. Now listen to Mr. Hearst again, still speaking in the May *Hearst's:*

" 'The Standard Oil letters have become famous. *A President of the United States once said to me* that the value of the Standard Oil letters was not so much that they revealed anything new, but that they proved what everybody suspected but had not before been able to establish.'

"May to September is a long time when you are carrying out a fraud. Mr. Hearst's memory is short. For in the September *Hearst's Magazine* we read in 'J. E.'s' article:

" '*As a President of the United States once said to the writer,* these letters are vitally important, not because they indicate the existence of conditions which we did not suspect, but because they absolutely prove the existence of conditions which we only suspected before, but which we now know to be actualities.'

"Mr. Hearst, then, is the writer of the *Hearst Magazine* articles. Of course he is—Mr. Hearst, carrying out his series through his editorial staff. There is no unknown mysterious 'gentleman.' J. E—— was part of the plot. The mask is pulled off by the same blundering hands that used the 1907 machine to write an 1898 letter, that pasted on a letter-head, that used the same individual machine to write letters alleged to have been written a thousand miles away from each other within a few days of each other. The man of mystery is Mr. Hearst himself. But we already knew this. We knew it four years ago.

"*Collier's* knew it, and in the issue of October 24, 1908, told how the colored employee of Standard Oil . . . stole the files and notebooks, the records of correspondence to and from Mr. Archbold . . . The two thieves received just over $12,000 from the Hearst office for their dexterity. . . .

"Mr. Hearst has many genuine facsimiles in his possession. Photographs were made in his *American* office of genuine original documents. Why is he using forgeries? In particular, why has he used forged documents in the Penrose exposure? . . .

"Mr. Hearst must now produce the numerous genuine facsimiles which he actually has, and he must impart the correct information built up from notes and similar leakages, and he must tell the sources of his correct information, which he is now imparting by means of forged documents. His sources were insiders located at Standard Oil headquarters. It will not be necessary for him to explain to the Senate Investigating Committee, meeting this week in Washington, just what the rich kernel of truth is about which he has built his rotten shell. How foolish of him to pull a real leak on the invisible relationship of Standard Oil with the Government, and then create a series of forgeries *in order to exploit that secret accurate information!*"

The reason for the forgeries emerges in the last line. The italics have been added by the present writer.

Hearst had to appear before the Senate investigating committee and his testimony under oath is preserved.[16]

Hearst, in response to a question about Hanna-Archbold correspondence from Chairman Moses E. Clapp, of Minnesota, said, "I have all the letters which I think are relevant to the inquiry . . . These are photographic facsimiles . . . I have not got the original letters."

Hearst told the committee he did not know when or how the correspondence was obtained or photographed. Under oath he swore that the letters were first given to him in Columbus, Ohio, in September, 1908, by Mr. John L. Eddy, then managing editor of Hearst's Boston paper. Although in his employ, Mr. Eddy would not tell Mr. Hearst how he acquired the letters. Nor did he ask, Hearst told the Senators. Hearst declared that a brief glance convinced him the facsimiles were genuine, and that he had fearlessly quoted from them in a speech almost immediately.

"Have not most of these letters been pronounced genuine . . . ?" Hearst demanded.

"Some; very few," responded Chairman Clapp.

Hearst disavowed any knowledge whatever about the way the letters had been acquired, saying that Mr. Eddy knew all about that. And where was Mr. Eddy? In London. Was he employed by Hearst? No, by a company in which Hearst had a controlling interest, the London Budget Company. Could the committee reach him for his testimony? Hearst waved vaguely—perhaps, he did not know. The committee members seemed loath to annoy the publisher with questions.

"Have you any additional copies of letters with you?" asked the chairman.

"Not with me," said Hearst calmly. "And none that I think come under the scope of this inquiry."

After some polite fencing about the scope of the inquiry and about Hearst's competence to pass on the relevance of evidence,

---

[16] Hearings of the Senate Privileges and Election Committee pursuant to Senate resolutions 79 and 386 on campaign contributions (1912-13); parts 1 to 45, Sixty-second Congress, Second Seession, pp. 1251 to 1267.

during which it became obvious that Hearst was withholding some letters, the publisher said wearily: "Well, I have produced all the letters that I think come within the scope of the investigation...."

The committee seemed reluctant to break the ensuing deadlock. Senator George T. Oliver[17] remonstrated mildly with the publisher, saying, "But you must be aware, Mr. Hearst, that in producing and making public some correspondence which perhaps does not come strictly within the scope of the investigation, in justice to the parties named as well as yourself, it seems to me that the committee ought at least to have the chance of seeing the whole correspondence."

"I think, Mr. Hearst, that is so," said Chairman Clapp regretfully.

"I do not agree with you, Senator," said Hearst, and that ended the matter.

How many of the *committee members'* political fortunes Hearst then held in the hollow of his hand, one cannot say. There must have been quite a few.

Senator Atlee Pomerene asked what explanation Hearst had for the forgery story published by *Collier's* and Hearst responded bluntly: "I haven't any explanation to make."

Hearst said the text of the facsimiles had been retyped because they were poorly photographed.

Senator Pomerene: "For the purpose of—"

Mr. Hearst: "Making it clear."

But the committee did not inquire into the reasons for alleging the forgeries were the actual facsimiles, nor why passages had been omitted. Finally, it did not insist that Hearst produce, even for private scrutiny by the committee, all the vast Standard Oil correspondence he possessed.

The committee made no effort at all to reach Eddy or any others mentioned as having been involved in buying the letters.

Though the Senate Committee sidestepped the issue, *Collier's* did not. And Hearst did not sue.

The reader will remember how the *American*, in 1906, called

---

[17] Oliver himself was the owner of two newspapers in Pittsburgh and was financed by the Frick steel and iron interests. His properties are now Hearst's. See *Freedom of the Press*, by George Seldes, Bobbs-Merrill Co., Indianapolis and New York, 1935.

Senator Bailey of Texas a "statesman" for his defense of the patent medicine people. And back in 1906, subsequent testimony showed, Hearst had Standard Oil letters implicating Bailey. These letters came out and Bailey resigned from the Senate in 1913, bitterly denouncing Hearst, who had protected him until the last minute.

Former Senator Foraker, stirred into action by the queerness of the Senate committee proceedings and by *Collier's* revelations, determined to do some investigating on his own account, to show, apparently, that Hearst had perjured himself before the Senate.

Stories were going around *that Winfield had not returned to the Standard Oil files all of the letters Hearst photographed* but had retained some of them for future use.

This was a very dangerous thing for Winfield to say. If Winfield should produce letters and testify that Hearst had photographed them, and the Hearst "facsimiles" did not agree with originals in Winfield's possession, the Senate Committee might be forced against its will to cite Hearst for perjury.

Late in 1912 Foraker retained a Negro member of the New York bar, Gilchrist Stewart, who engaged mainly in investigating for law firms, to find Winfield and get any letters he might have. Winfield was somewhere in Chicago's Black Belt.

The Senate Committee reconvened in January, 1913, with Stewart as the star witness.

Stewart told the Senators[18] he had found Winfield in Chicago. Winfield told him that he had first talked with Fred Eldridge, Hearst night editor in 1904, in the Café Savoy on Thirty-fifth Street, New York, and had thereafter done business with John L. Eddy, the Hearst reporter.

Stewart then showed Winfield a copy of a statement Foraker had prepared, in order to check on the correctness of Foraker's facts, and asked Winfield if he had any Standard Oil letters. This was in December, 1912.

Winfield lived at 3232 South State Street, Chicago. Stewart had headquarters at the Keystone Hotel, Thirty-first and State Streets, Chicago, and slept in a nearby rooming house. On the night of

[18] Hearings of the Senate Privileges and Elections Committee (1912-13), *op. cit.*

December 21, 1912, "detectives" searched Winfield's house in his absence and also went through Stewart's rooms in the Keystone Hotel. They were looking for Stewart and Winfield, and were directed to Gumb's Café, at Twenty-ninth and State Streets, in the heart of the Black Belt. There they found Stewart, who was waiting for Winfield.

"Are you Gilchrist Stewart?" the chief "detective" asked. [All quotations are from the Senate record.]

"Yes."

"Consider yourself under arrest."

"Let me see your credentials," said Stewart.

The "detectives" showed badges which the head-waiter told Stewart were Chicago police department insignia.

"Let me see your warrants," Stewart demanded.

Papers purporting to be warrants were shown. While questioning the validity of the warrants, he was suddenly blackjacked and dragged out to a taxicab.

"If it is papers and documents that you are looking for," Stewart said to his captors, "I have some very important ones at home." He wanted to be taken somewhere where he could attract attention.

But the "detectives" were omniscient.

"Oh, no, you haven't," said the leader, "because we have searched the house."

Nonetheless the cabs drew up before Stewart's boarding house on Rhodes Avenue. By this time the cavalcade comprised six taxicabs. The "detectives" entered the house and Stewart was told they had been there before, rummaging for papers. He whispered to the taxi driver to call his lawyer.

The cabman got Edward S. Morris, an attorney and former member of the Illinois Legislature, on the telephone, told him that Stewart had been arrested and needed bail and a lawyer.

The "detectives" reappeared and reentered the taxicabs. Stewart, noticing that they were going downtown, asked what police station they were going to, and was told "to headquarters." The taxis stopped at a downtown building before which people imperturbably passed.

"As we entered the rotunda of this building," Stewart told the

Senate committee, "I saw that it was an office building, and I said to the elevator man: 'Isn't this an office building?' With that these gangsters just tossed me into the elevator, and we shot up to a floor very quickly.

"We got out there, and as I was ushered, or about to be ushered, into a large room, I saw some rubber mats on the outside in the hall, and 'Hearst' was on those rubber mats.

"Of course, then I knew just what was up—that it was not any police station. They forgot to take away those rubber mats. So they ushered me into a room, and there was a gentleman sitting, as you are sitting, Senator, at a table, and he got up and in a very stern voice said:

"'Officers, have you searched the prisoner?' ... I said to the gentleman as he was going out that I recognized him as Mr. [Andrew] Lawrence of the Chicago *Examiner*. I said: 'Mr. Lawrence, this is rather a high-handed performance to have a lot of gangsters and gunmen kidnap me in this manner,' and he seemed surprised that I recognized him so readily. And he went out, accompanied by a gentleman whom I afterward found out was Mr. Victor H. Polachek ... They came back later and they returned some of my letters. Then Mr. Lawrence started to ask a series of questions. He started out by asking me: 'When did you see Winfield last?' and I said: 'Now, Mr. Lawrence, you ought to know that I know, and am sufficiently intelligent to know, that I do not have to answer any questions that you desire to ask, and that it is ridiculous to attempt to try to hold a mock court for me in the editorial rooms of the Hearst Building.'"

"I said to him," Stewart continued, "if you were going to do that you ought to have taken up those rubber mats in the hall."

"So he told me he desired to get some information, and I would not get out until he got it, or something of that character, as I remember. I told him I did not have any information to give him. He then went out again, and Mr. Polachek asked me a few questions regarding whether I had got any letters from Winfield; if I had met a man at a train, and a few questions of that character.

"He then went out, and they left me in there, I presume, for at

IMPERIAL HEARST

least an hour and a half. Then they came back. I wanted to find out just why all this kidnapping and breaking into people's houses had gone on, so I asked them why they had broken into people's houses and kidnapped me in this manner, and if they did not know they would be liable for very heavy damages.

"Mr. Polachek jokingly spoke to Mr. Lawrence about some man who had been suing them for the past four years for $100,000, or some amount like that. They knew this man. They joked with each other about it.

"Mr. Lawrence finally said, 'You may go.'

"I said: 'Do I go to the police station or home?'

"He said: 'No, you can go home.' So they showed me out and I went down the elevator and out."

Upon his release, Stewart found that Attorney Frank A. Dennison, retained by Mr. Morris, had tried to locate him in the hands of the police with a writ of habeas corpus. Dennison and Stewart called upon Chief Justice Harry Olson, of the Municipal Court, to determine what could be done about the kidnapping. Lawrence and Polachek were summoned.

"They came over and in the office of the Chief of Police of Chicago Mr. Lawrence and Mr. Polachek—"

At this point the Senators stopped Stewart. And here the inquiry ended as far as Hearst is concerned. The Chief of Police of Chicago and Mayor Carter Harrison were under the thumb of Hearst. It was simply a joke to Lawrence and Polachek to be "summoned."

All subsequent investigations of Hearst had this peculiar, inconclusive ending, whether the charges were kidnapping, murder, treason, robbery, forgery or mayhem, whether they were preferred against Hearst himself or against his agents.

Government has never functioned against Hearst.

Willie Winfield testified before the Senate on January 15, 1913.[19] He declared, under oath, that the letters had been delivered to Hearst's office between 1904 and 1906, and he had been paid through Stump.

---

[19] Hearings: Senate Privileges and Elections Committee pursuant to Senate Resolutions 79 and 386 on campaign contributions (1912-13), parts 1 to 45, Sixty-second Congress, Second Session. Government Printing Office, 1913.

Winfield was also "arrested" in Gumb's Café the night Stewart was seized. He was taken to his home, which was ransacked from top to bottom by Hearst "detectives."

Although the Senate Committee did not recall Hearst or make any effort to summon Eddy, Eldridge, Lawrence, Polachek or anyone else from the Hearst organization, it did recall both Winfield and Stewart and attempt to discredit their testimony. Someone had discovered many "errors" in Stewart's testimony. These errors concerned dates, street names and the initials in people's names, and were manifestly so trivial as to deserve no mention.

Replacing Stewart on the witness stand proved to be a mistake, for he had a harrowing tale to tell. Because Assistant States Attorney Louis B. Anderson of Cook County, a Negro friend, had used his good offices for Stewart, Anderson's home in Chicago had been ransacked in his absence and Anderson himself was being shadowed every hour of the day.

The committee vigorously demanded of Stewart the names of all people in Chicago who had helped him with his investigation, and despite his protests forced the names from him, thus placing these persons in the bad graces of Hearst. But the committee did not force any information from Hearst which *he* thought "irrelevant." On January 13, 1913, Stewart eloquently said to the committee: "There are a number of friends in Chicago helping me with this matter and I do not want to subject them to the persecution of the *Examiner*. These people [at the *Examiner*] are getting very vicious about the matter. They threatened to ruin my character if I came here and testified. They have admitted so in their subsequent publications. . . ."

But the committee refused to entertain Stewart's plea for his friends in Chicago. He had to name them!

Although no testimony had been introduced against Stewart, the committee, *on the basis of "information" privately furnished it,* proceeded to do all in its power to ruin his character. He was asked if he had ever told one "Brown" (who was not identified) at the Keystone Hotel that he was "working on the biggest proposition a Negro ever handled" and expected to "clean up." Stewart said "No."

IMPERIAL HEARST

This "Brown" never appeared before the committee. Morris, the attorney who had acted for Stewart, had been constantly bothered in his Chicago offices by Hearst representatives, and all who had any connection with the case were subjected to persecution in print and by "detectives" who followed them at all times and frightened them and their families.

Stewart pointed out that the Hearst papers had wilfully falsified his testimony and drew attention to the fact that even the record of the hearings had, through some mysterious influence, been falsified. The name of Andrew Lawrence appeared throughout the record as "Mr. Reynolds" and numerous things that Stewart had never said had been inserted. He asked the committee to inquire into these changes, but it never did. After Winfield and Stewart had appeared the second time the hearings ended.

There was no Senate investigation into the Hearst forgeries. Yet possession of the original letters gave Hearst power over individuals which is undoubtedly still effective among those politicians who survive from the post-war period.

All investigations of Hearst, and there have been three of major proportions, have been turned against the people who brought the charges.

Until the Coolidge Administration was installed in Washington Hearst had been happiest under Taft. President Taft, after his quarrel with Theodore Roosevelt, needed friends, and he invited Hearst to the White House, where he had been received by Roosevelt only because he was a member of Congress.[20] Yet it was through Hearst that Taft, by a blunder of his own, experienced the severest set-back of his régime.

The Taft Administration was trying to bring about, as its greatest accomplishment, a reciprocal tariff agreement with Canada. Congress approved the measure, for which the Hearst papers, among

[20] Except when Hearst began publishing the Standard Oil letters in 1908 Roosevelt hastily summoned him to the White House to discover if there had been any "loose" references to him. Hearst laughingly reassured him that, if there were such references, they would not be published. There were, and they were published, but not at that time.

others, had been campaigning. To the Tories in England this was cause for alarm. It was felt that an economic interlocking of Canada and the United States, made possible by the tariff agreement, would lead, in time, to political union.

In the Canadian Parliament, however, the forces favoring reciprocity were in the ascendancy—until Taft sent Hearst an open letter congratulating him on his part in the victorious fight to get Congress to approve reciprocity. This letter doomed reciprocity, for Hearst was hated and feared in Canada as the man who had agitated for more than a decade to have Canada forcibly annexed by the United States. The idea of annexation was not nearly as silly as it may sound. Theodore Roosevelt had been quoted as saying, in one of his bellicose moods, that if the British fleet ever bombarded American coastal cities in a war the United States would simply swallow Canada.

As soon as the Taft letter to Hearst was published in Canada, the Canadian Parliament defeated the measure, and mutually profitable economic relations between the neighboring democracies were made impossible for twenty-five years thereafter.

V

THE vicious, anti-social influence of Hearst was more thoroughly exposed in Chicago than in San Francisco or New York.

The Chicago *American* first appeared with a morning and an evening edition on July 2, 1900.

The Chicago *American* has shown a steadily increasing profit since the World War. Its circulation is the largest in the evening field, which it divides with the *Daily News*, organ of the local bankers.[1] But the *Examiner*, even today, with a circulation of about 500,000 copies daily, shows a loss that eats like a cancer into the *American's* profits. Morning paper advertisers prefer the Chicago *Tribune*.

Hearst entered Chicago as the champion of free silver, the eight-hour day, the full dinner pail and God Almighty. The publishers of the other Chicago papers—the *Daily News*, the *Tribune*, the *Chronicle*, the *Inter-Ocean*, the *Herald*, the *Record*, the *Post* and the *Journal*—were aware of the death grapple going on in New York between Pulitzer and Hearst. They knew they were pitted against a gold mine and a thoroughly unscrupulous opponent. Most of them were to succumb in the gargantuan war, a classic example of capitalistic competition. This war had a great deal to do with shattering the finances and political morale of the second largest city in the United States.

"Among reporters in Chicago," says William Salisbury,[2] "the *American* office was commonly referred to as 'the madhouse' . . . noise and confusion reigned . . . Mingled with the clatter of telegraph instruments and typewriters, and the sounds of hurrying feet, were voices talking, shouting, sometimes cursing.

---

[1] Before Frank Knox, former Hearst general manager and its present owner, could purchase it, the transaction had to be approved by Chicago bankers, among them Charles G. Dawes. *Time*, October 14, 1935.

[2] *The Career of a Journalist*, by William Salisbury, B. W. Dodge & Co., New York, 1908.

"'It's a continuous performance over at the *American*,' I had been told, and so I found it. Editions were published about every hour of the day, and often there were 'extras' as late as midnight, or later. The *American* was the only Chicago paper with regular morning, evening and Sunday editions. It was also the only evening paper that printed a four o'clock edition at noon, and a five o'clock edition at one p.m."

Salisbury's first assignment was to write the story of the sinking of a tugboat on Lake Michigan. The crew of four had swum ashore without difficulty. He could find nothing unusual about the event and "wrote a careful report."

"I didn't recognize my story, at first," he says of its appearance in the paper. "It had so many features undreamed of by me. I was told that one of the 'prize dope-slingers' in the office had rewritten it. The rescue of a cat, the boat's mascot, at the risk of all the sailors' lives, was described with convincing detail. This made me feel small. . . .

"Changes in the staff took place so often that it was hard to keep track of them all. Not a fortnight passed that two or three to half a dozen were not discharged, and as many more hired, 'Just to keep things moving'. . . .

"I was separated from the payroll because another paper had printed a better story than I had written for the *American* about a North Side fire," Salisbury continues. "The rescue of several persons by means of a human ladder, formed by the firemen, had been described. No such rescue had taken place. The building was a story and a half high, and there could have been no use for a human ladder or any other kind of ladder. But I was told that I should never allow any of the old, conservative newspapers to outdo the *American* in 'features.'

"Upon my return to duty I was made a rewriter," Salisbury remarks, failing to observe that his temporary lay-off made him more willing to see events as the managing editor, and Hearst behind the scenes, wanted them viewed. "The second night the account of a street-car hold-up was telephoned from South Chicago. At a lonely part of the road two masked men had leaped from behind a clump of bushes [the bushes were supplied by Salisbury] and, flourishing revolvers, caused the motorman to stop. As they were about to board the car the motorman turned on full speed again, and the desperadoes were left behind.

"I told the night city editor the facts. He looked thoughtful for a moment. 'We need a first-page head,' he said. 'Better have 'em fire a couple of shots—and put in a panic among the passengers, too.'

"At another time the accidental killing of a Negro was telephoned in. The incident wasn't worth mentioning. When I told the city editor about it he bowed his head in thought for a moment, and then asked for the classified business telephone directory. After looking through it he beckoned for a reporter.

" 'You know these undertakers pretty well,' he said. 'Take this list and pick out the niggers. Then telephone each one in turn that he is specially wanted by the family of the deceased, and not to allow any other undertakers to get the body. Time the calls so that each man will get to the house at about the same minute. Then there'll be something doing, or I'm a poor guesser.' There was."

The ensuing riot made a good story and, what is more, it was true! The Hearst men were making news as Hearst had instructed them to.

After detailing other falsifications and chicaneries practiced by the Hearst executives, Salisbury tells about the introduction to Chicago of the signed-statement racket, with results similar to those obtained in New York with "signed" statements of the Pope, the Kaiser et al. The *American* brought Mrs. Carry Nation to Chicago to turn her loose on the saloons.

Pulitzer had sent Nellie Bly around the world in seventy-two days to show the trip could be made faster than Jules Verne had imagined. The Hearst general staff decided to have three high school boys, selected from San Francisco, Chicago and New York, race around the world by different routes. The "contestants" were selected arbitrarily without the expense of a genuine contest. It was arranged in advance that the Chicago boy would win—because the *American* needed the publicity more than the New York *Journal* or the San Francisco *Examiner*. It was also foreseen that the winner should be Irish, for the country was filling up with Irish immigrants who would be pleased to have a Celt win any sort of contest and who would think kindly of the man who sponsored it.

Before relating the culminating incident in his Hearst career, Salisbury tells how the *American* stole its news, how the Hearst management smashed a reporters' union, and how it campaigned against the local gas company—until it put money for Hearst on the line.

"It seemed that Mr. Hearst was truly devoted to labor unionism," Salisbury says. "But the unions which he specially favored were those whose members were paid by other employers. Those he himself dealt with as an employer, such as the printers', the pressmen's, and the stereotypers', were strongly organized and generally recognized long before he owned a newspaper. . . .

"A reporters' union was organized in Chicago. Most of the *American's* reportorial staff joined. More members, in fact, were from the *American* office than from any other newspaper.

"But suddenly the *American* reporters began to quit the union. Within a week all but one had left it, and a little while afterward he was discharged. . . . Strong hints had been given . . . that Mr. Hearst disapproved. . . . Those wise enough to take the hint saved their positions . . . it was the hostility of Mr. Hearst that made certain the speedy end of the Chicago union."

As to the outright theft of news, Salisbury says: "I was surprised to see only half a dozen reporters on the morning paper . . . because the night report of the City Press Bureau wasn't being served to the *American* then. . . . At least twenty-five reporters were needed. I soon learned how the paper got most of its news. Among the reporters was one who talked like 'Chimmie Fadden.' The first night, when I heard him remark, 'Oh, wot's de use o' woikin' hard on dis paper?' I wondered that such a person should be one of us. At 2 a. m. the reason was shown.

"I saw him run into the editorial department from the back stairway. He was breathing hard. From under his coat he pulled copies of the other Chicago morning papers, still damp from the press.

" 'Gee! I had a fierce tussle makin' a gitaway dis time,' he panted. 'Dey're gittin' onto me. It was hard woik gittin' dese foist editions from de delivery wagons. I guess I'll make Mr. Hoist raise me salary, or else buy me a armor soot.' "

Salisbury had encountered one of the earliest of the many gangsters on the Hearst payroll.

"The rest of us were given clippings from the papers he had brought in, and were told to rewrite the news from them as quickly as possible. 'Just a few lines of introduction will do—paste the balance on,' was the order. . . . I wondered why one so wealthy as the *American's* owner should employ such methods. I asked one of my new associates about it. 'Oh, Mr. Hearst would rather spend his money directly in uplifting humanity,' he replied. 'What he saves by taking news from other papers he likes to give to flood sufferers, and in purifying politics. Money used for ordinary news gathering can't be advertised to the world as Hearst funds for the benefit of the human race. Understand?' "

In the matter of the gas company, Salisbury says: ". . . for a time I was given some very important work to do—the kind that I had been hoping for. The *American* had started a war against the gas trust. It was a most popular war, for the city was at the mercy of a lawless monopoly. It was a mark of favor in the *American* office to be given anti-gas-trust stories to write. Only the best 'word-slingers' were so favored.

"I now felt that at least I was battling for the people, and making tyrants quail, in a truly heroic journalistic style. I was forging shafts of ripping, tearing words that would demolish the fort of the robber chiefs who were taking unlawful tribute from the public. I called the gas company 'the Gorgon-headed monopoly,' 'the banded infamy,' and 'a greedy gorger from the public purse.'

"I felt myself as heroic as those who had led the crusades of old. I was a lieutenant of a modern Godfrey or a Richard the Lionhearted in a holy war. Pen and typewriter, mightier than sword and cannon, were my weapons. In the press was concentrated the strength of an army, and this I directed.

"It was many months later, and long after I had left the paper's service, that the *American's* fight on the gas trust suddenly ceased. I still felt a satisfaction in having, at least once, fought the good fight in a righteous cause.

"But soon after the *American's* attacks ended, a full-page advertisement of the gas company appeared in the paper. I thought it strange that the company, being a monopoly, would need to advertise. I thought it stranger still that the *American* should be the medium. I talked about the matter with a friend. He was an old-time newspaperman, who had worked on Hearst's New York paper.

"I told him how I believed in Mr. Hearst.

" 'It's about time for you to wake up,' he said.

" 'How?'

" 'Oh, that ad must have cost the gas trust a good many thousands of dollars. Mr. Hearst will probably use the money to promote the people's interests, you know. He's getting into politics now.' "

The rapprochement of Hearst with the local public utility interests, closely following his initial violent hostility, led to Hearst's later communion with Samuel Insull and the Insull bankers, Halsey, Stuart & Co., who floated many Hearst bond issues as well as Insull issues.

"I will now tell how I failed as a yellow journalist," says Salisbury.

"Eastertide . . . was approaching. . . . The vernal hues I principally saw were on the colored supplements for an Easter Sunday edition which had been printed in the office of Mr. Hearst's New York paper, and shipped to Chicago several days in advance. It was announced to the night staff that a big Easter spread was to be made.

"Mr. Hearst himself was in town. We all looked up in awe when it was whispered about one evening that he was in the office. I saw a tall, youngish-looking man. He must have been six feet in height, and his shoulders were not broad, his frame not sinewy. His eyes were clear and penetrating, but his face was narrow, and his chin infirm. He was neither blonde nor brunette, neither handsome nor homely, neither strong nor weak. He would not have attracted attention anywhere, except in a crowd of under-sized people. . . . After a brief talk with his managing editor, he walked through the editorial room to the elevator. The night was showery, and he wore a handsome belted mackintosh which came almost to his heels, and gave him an imposing appearance. . . . Mr. Hearst must have been talking to his managing editor[3] about the special Easter edition, for after he left, the managing editor gave orders to the night city editor about it. He told him to send reporters to show copies of the colored supplement to preachers, to get favorable interviews about it, and have a page of the interviews well displayed in the next morning's issue.

"When the managing editor had retired to the 'throne room,' the city editor looked about in despair . . . and called his staff about him. 'Each of you take a bunch of those,' he said, 'and try to get interviews from the ministers whose names will be on a list I'll give you. Remember, we've got to have some interviews. Most of the skypilots are probably in bed by this time, but Mr. Hearst is in town, and a good showing must be made. If you can't rouse the preachers, why—well, we've got to have two dozen interviews indorsing this grand and beautiful and gorgeous and scintillating supplement. We've simply got to do it, you know. It would break Mr. Hearst's trusting young heart if we didn't. If you go to one of those addresses, and can't get anyone to the door, why, come back and write what you think the minister would have said—or ought to have said —about this supplement. If the minister objects to what's printed, we'll say, "Someone gave out this interview, and the reporter thought it was you. It may have been a burglar or a night watchman. The reporter was deceived, for the person represented himself as you."

[3] According to Salisbury, the name of the managing editor in question was Russell. *Who's Who* says that Charles Edward Russell, the Socialist writer who has been almost continuously in Hearst's service since 1896, was managing editor of the Chicago *American* from 1900 to 1902, when he was moved to another Hearst sector. Russell, the author of many books and city editor of the New York *Journal* for a brief period after F. L. H. "Cosey" Noble, was Socialist candidate for Governor of New York in 1910 and 1912, for Mayor of New York City in 1913 and for United States Senator from New York in 1914. In 1916 he was nominated the Presidential candidate of the Socialist Party but declined. In the post-war period he has been a frequent contributor to the Hearst magazines, writing a life of Charlemagne for *Cosmopolitan*. He was the first bona fide Socialist to be brought into Hearst's camp. Before joining Hearst he worked for Pulitzer who, according to *William Randolph Hearst: American,* by Mrs. Fremont Older, found him an asset because of the skillful "Socialist" editorials he could write.

Remember, we're up against it, and we've just got to have the interviews.' . . .

"I was pressed into this service. . . . I actually tried to get one interview, from a preacher who didn't live far out. . . . He declined to come to the door, and he wouldn't discuss the subject at such an hour. I returned downtown. At an all-night resort near the office . . . I met several fellow staff members. One of them said he had waked up a well-known West Side minister, who opened an upstairs window and asked what was wanted. The reporter had flourished a paper in the moonlight, and cried out: 'See this beautiful Easter supplement of Hearst's Chicago *American*! What do you think of it? Pretty fine, isn't it? I want an interview for tomorrow's paper. We'll run your picture along with it.'

"The preacher's head had disappeared for a moment, and when it reappeared the reporter was drenched with ice water. Another reporter said a preacher had threatened to set a bull-dog upon him. Still another had been told that he would be arrested if he didn't go away. A revolver had been pointed at a fourth journalist's head . . . Only one printable interview had been obtained . . . from a new minister, who had been working late on his Easter sermon.

"We all returned to the office and wrote four interviews apiece. We compared them before turning them in, to make sure that we hadn't quoted any two preachers alike . . . At ten o'clock the following night the managing editor came from his 'throne room' and gave out another Napoleonic order. Mr. Hearst and he himself had been so well pleased with the interviews that they wanted another page of them for the next morning. They got the interviews . . . The forthcoming Easter supplement had captivated clergymen—if what was read in the *American* was to be believed. 'The beautiful story of Christ's rise from the tomb, told by illustrations in color, made from masterpieces of art,' was praised in the highest terms by all."

The complaints came thick and fast. The Congregational Ministers' Association denounced the paper, Hearst and all his works, and the denunciation was featured by the rival newspapers.

"Someone sent a marked copy to Mr. Hearst, who had returned to New York. Mr. Hearst wired to his publisher and personal representative to discharge everyone concerned. So the night editor, four reporters, and myself, were at once separated from the payroll.

"It was the first time I had been fired by telegraph. The quickness of it was dazing. Then the monstrous injustice of it incensed me. I had been discharged for doing what I had been ordered to do. . . . And now that exposure had come, the men who had carried out this policy, not those who directed it, had to suffer. My fellow victims and I held a meeting on the sidewalk in front of the *American* office and discussed our wrongs. We had only half a week's salary apiece. We took up a collection to pay for a long telegram to Mr. Hearst, setting forth our side of the case. We received no answer.

"Then we decided to appeal to the man Hearst had made his publisher of the *American*. We would tell him just how it happened . . . I was chosen as spokesman . . . When I told how, under the stress of the moment, interviews had been written from the city directory, he threw up his hands in holy horror.

" 'Do you mean to tell me,' he cried, amazement in every line of his face, his entire being a-shudder, 'that you would write anything for the columns of Mr. Hearst's newspaper that was not absolutely true?'

" 'Well—yes—I have sometimes.'

" 'Terrible!'

" 'I—er—supposed a little exaggeration was expected once in a while.'

" 'Monstrous!'

" 'I—er—uh—I thought this was—er—understood in headquarters—'

" 'Preposterous!'

" 'In fact, I have often heard orders issued to—er—uh—doctor up a story a little to make it interesting, you know.'

" 'Outrageous.'

" 'Pictures, too, have been faked.'

" 'Horrible.'

" 'And now, sir, since I and my associates are so evidently victims of this policy, do you not think this error on our part should be overlooked, for once?'

" 'What! Do you ask me to condone such heinous conduct as you confess?'

" 'I thought you might, for once.'

" 'Never, n-n-never, sir! Anyone who becomes so far lost to a sense of right and justice—to a sense of honor—as to quote a person as saying what that person never said, deserves no consideration. Mr. Hearst and I will tolerate no deviation from the truth in any item, or from any right conduct in any feature of news-gathering—'

" 'How about the news we crib from the first editions of the other Chicago papers?'

" 'Eh—er—uh—what's that?'

" 'How about the way we get most of the news for the morning edition? Some people might call it stealing.'

" 'I decline to discuss the matter with you, sir. This incident is closed, sir. Good morning, sir.' "

Much later a celebrated and caustic city editor of the Chicago *American* was approached for a job by a moon-faced college youth who had romantic visions of entering journalism.

"Do you smoke?" said the city editor severely.

"No, sir," said the ambitious scholar.

"Do you drink?"

"No, sir."

"Would you seduce a luscious young innocent girl if she was left alone in your company?"

Flushed and shaken by the question, the young man stuttered a negative.

"Do you beat your mother?"

"No."

"Do you use drugs?"

"No."

"Would you steal to get ahead in the world?"

"No."

"Well, then you don't want to work for Hearst, you virtuous son of a bitch. Get out of here!"

Andrew M. Lawrence was placed in full command of the Hearst papers in Chicago. Brisbane was used as the nominal chief in order to flatter the Chicagoans, who had heard of his accomplishments in New York. The business office was placed in charge of the late John M. Eastman, a young Indiana Democrat. In a couple of years Eastman was able to purchase the Chicago *Daily Journal* on his own account. He had learned so much in the Hearst organization that his paper survived his death by four years, expiring in 1929, long after the *Inter-Ocean*, the *Record-Herald* and the *Chronicle* had succumbed in the furious circulation war.

Chicago saw little of Hearst. His interests had widened and his organization was so vast that Hearst could now be a general behind the scene of battle, silent, enigmatic, unseen. Shortly after 1900 Hearst had initiated the policy of refusing to hear from his executives how his desires were achieved. His lawyers had told him that many embarrassments would be averted if he pleaded ignorance of the deeds of his hirelings and merely fired them when their plans miscarried or became public.

The Hearst executives were projections of the Hearst personality —which we have seen in active operation in New York, Cuba and San Francisco. Most of them were men who stopped at literally nothing. This was especially true in Chicago.

Eastman's character did not come into full view until after he had left Hearst. Some friends of Eastman's, the story is told, advanced him additional funds with which to acquire the *Journal*. When he tendered them his note they refused to accept it. For this they were sorry later, because he refused to repay the loan.

Andrew M. Lawrence was known as "Long Green Andy." He was in charge of the editorial, business, *and circulation* departments when the circulation war began in Chicago and the personnel for Chicago's future gangs was assembled.[4]

Newspapers and magazines of the day from time to time published references to the sinister quality of Lawrence's activities.

One of Lawrence's deals is typical of the way in which he extracted money from the City of Chicago. On August 15, 1913, the New York *Times* carried the following dispatch from Chicago:

". . . Lloyd L. Duke, City Attorney of Ottumwa, Ia., in a statement in writing 'accuses Andrew M. Lawrence, publisher of Hearst's Chicago *American*, of having demanded $105,000 as his share of the profits for introducing the promoters to the city authorities.' " The promoters were the Empire Voting Machine Company of Syracuse, which had installed $1,000,000 worth of machines in Chicago.

"Later in the day Edward E. Marriott, a reporter for the Chicago *Examiner*, submitted a counter affidavit, in which he charged that H. W. Barr, agent of the Empire Voting Machine Company, had told him in the presence of witnesses 'that he had paid big money to get the contracts, but that the mistake he made was not to give $50,000 to Jim Keeley, publisher of the Chicago *Tribune*.' "

Marriott's affidavit, drawn for the purposes of implicating the *Tribune* in what Lawrence could not deny, as quoted by the New York *Times*, also said: "Keeley demanded $50,000, but we refused to pay him. If he had got that, there would not have been any of this trouble with the voting machine contracts."

The dispatch continued:

"Attorney S. C. Thomason, counsel for the Chicago *Tribune*, after the reading of Mr. Marriott's affidavit, demanded that it be placed in the record, which was done.

" 'We want the whole lid torn off this nasty scandal,' said Mr. Thomason. 'The Chicago *Tribune* is ready and willing to see that the entire voting machine deal is exposed.'

"Today's developments have created a sensation in Chicago . . . Mr. Lawrence is in California. Mr. Keeley is in Paris.

"Duke's statement charges that H. W. Barr, agent of the Empire Company, arranged through the officials of the City of Ottumwa, the home town of Charles A. Walsh, organizer of the Hearst Independence League, to meet Mr. Walsh, and through him to get into personal touch with Mr. Lawrence, thereby securing the influence of the Hearst-Harrison ring, which controlled the Chicago administration. The statement also says that Mr. Barr declared that the deal cost his company $200,000, and that Mr. Lawrence was down on the list for $105,000.

"Mr. Duke declares that Mr. Lawrence was originally to receive only $85,000 and Mr. Walsh $14,000, but that Mr. Lawrence objected to Mr. Walsh receiving this amount, and demanded that it be added to his share. . . . For some time, Barr stated, they could not get together or come to any understanding with Lawrence. Finally, Barr said, we made out a list of expenditures necessary in order to make the deal and placed it before Lawrence. It was a list of the amounts that would have to be paid to different parties for their influence to consummate the deal. Walsh was on the list for $14,000 and Lawrence for $85,000, as I remember the amounts. The list was then revised by Lawrence. He came to Walsh's name and the $14,000 and stated to Walsh that he wanted to know why Walsh was to have that amount of money; that Walsh could not deliver anything. Walsh then said, 'Put the $14,000 over in the Lawrence column.'

"When the list was finally completed Lawrence was to have $105,000, Barr said . . . he also had to fix up some matters with the Gray Wolves in order to keep them quiet."

Chicago was full of newspapers. The newsstands were crowded and all the distribution outlets had been preëmpted by Hearst's rivals. Lawrence hired, as circulation bosses, Max and Moses Annenberg, young German Jews who had been raised from infancy by Jesuits on Chicago's West Side district, although they were born in Aix-la-Chapelle.

It was the task of these young hustlers to persuade newsdealers to take the *American* and give it a favored position on the newsstands. They worked to such good effect that other papers had to hire similar men to do the same thing. When a stalemate was reached, the Annenbergs, with Lawrence directing from behind the scenes under full powers from Hearst, mingled a few well-timed punches with their gospel. The new tactics worked very well, and the *American's* circulation began to rise.

The *American* also editorially assaulted the other newspapers, choosing as special antagonists the *Daily News* and the *Tribune*, the leading papers. The *Daily News* was owned by Victor Lawson, one of the founders of the Associated Press, and the *Tribune* by the McCormicks of the International Harvester Company, one of the city's dominating industrial enterprises.

The *Tribune* family became affiliated by marriage with the Rockefellers, one of the interests against which Hearst campaigned until the Hearst papers were filled with Rockefeller oil and gasoline advertising. Additional reason for the *Tribune*-Hearst feud is found in the fact that Medill McCormick married Ruth Hanna, daughter of Mark Hanna, the man Hearst depicted in a suit covered with dollar signs.

The *American* revealed that the *Daily News* and the *Tribune* in 1895, at a "midnight session" of the Board of Education, had succeeded in leasing downtown school land at a ridiculously low annual rental for a period of ninety-nine years. A. S. Trude, head of the Board of Education, was also attorney for the *Tribune*. On this land stood the two newspaper plants.

The original lease contained a clause that called for the retrading of the lease at the end of each year. Faced by rising land values, it was advantageous to the two papers to have this retrading clause eliminated. R. W. Patterson of the *Tribune* had appeared before the Board and asked for its elimination. This was done, without the people of the city being aware of the loss of revenue to the public school system.

The Hearst bombardment was severe. The *American* wept for the taxpayers and the school children, although Lawrence at the time was involved in deals costing the taxpayers enormous sums, directly and indirectly. In 1905 Hearst's candidate, Edward F. Dunne, was elected Mayor of Chicago for a two-year term. He at once began the long series of suits, unsuccessful to date, to cancel the leases of 1895, which were and have since been enormously lucrative to Hearst's Chicago rivals. Every time a Hearst Mayor down to William Hale Thompson has been in office—and most Chicago Mayors since Dunne have been Hearst men, which explains much about that unhappy city—an attempt has been made to dislodge the two Republican papers from the school land or to obtain a better rental—which would have been of competitive advantage to Hearst. The only Chicago Mayor since 1911 not under the influence of Hearst was William Dever (1923 to 1927).

When a Republican Mayor was returned to office in 1907 in the guise of Fred Busse, the Republican newspapers decided to meet Hearst on his own basis. Stern measures were required to prevent Hearst from driving his competitors into the ground and capturing the city's political cash box. After much uneasy and fruitless sparring, the *Tribune* made the first effective move in the summer of 1910 by proceeding as Hearst had proceeded against Pulitzer in New York. It lured Max and Moses Annenberg and their whole retinue of plug-uglies onto its payroll. The *Tribune* paid Max Annenberg $20,000 a year on a guarantee to increase its circulation. The *American* sued Annenberg, holding that he was under contract to Hearst. The document was held invalid by the court *on the ground that it was a contract to commit illegal acts!*

With the departure of Annenberg and his men, Lawrence hastily assembled a new staff of gunmen for the contest now ominously brewing. Hearst himself stood aloof, as far away from the scene as is an ocean squid from the murky substance it sends forth. This was good strategy, for Hearst was preparing *to inaugurate the system of gang warfare and racketeering which was to cost the City of Chicago and the nation* billions of dollars and the death of thousands of citizens.

With the Annenbergs had gone "Mossy" Enright, "Red" Connors, Walter Stevens and others subsequently notorious in Chicago gang warfare. Lawrence's quickly assembled force comprised Vincent Altman; Gus, Dutch and Pete Gentleman; Jack Nolan; "Chicago Jack" Daly; Edward Barrett; Frank McErlane, and others. The chief editor of the *Tribune* at the time was Medill McCormick, who later became United States Senator from Illinois. The *Tribune* appropriated $1,000,000 for its campaign. Hearst matched it.

Hostilities began in October, 1910, when, said the Chicago *Daily Socialist*, "The circulation manager of the Chicago *Tribune* [Annenberg] furnished revolvers to some of these sluggers and the slugging crew of that paper rode around in a big black automobile truck."

One of the outstanding facts about the events which followed was that nothing of them was mentioned in the newspapers until a general reign of terror developed late in 1912 and 1913. Then the news stories falsified events to make it seem that union labor was causing the trouble. But even at the later stage no news of the happenings went over the Associated Press wires, which were controlled by the Chicago publishers. Nor did the New York newspapers and magazines carry an account of the Chicago terror.

The *Tribune's* truck of sluggers lay in wait at strategic points for the agents of Hearst's *Examiner*, the new name for the morning edition of the *American*. When they appeared, they were greeted with fusillades of shots that brought police and ambulances to the scene. The Hearst forces then resorted to counter-ambushes, with a delivery truck as a decoy. Newsboys, some of them crippled and unable to scamper to safety, were shot. Passing women were clipped by bullets.

In 1911 the *Daily Socialist* forced the whole issue before the Cook County Grand Jury. But nothing came of it. State's Attorney Charles Wayman was under the thumb of the *Tribune*, as was Maclay Hoyne, his successor. Chief of Police John McWeeney belonged to Hearst. All denied that anything unusual had taken place, although the exploits of the gunmen were the chief topic of conversation in the downtown bars.

Said the Chicago *Inter-Ocean* (which did not join the conflict until later) in an editorial on June 11, 1911:

"Why should not Mr. Wayman ascertain, and at least hold up to public reprobation, the men whose money nourished and sustained these bravos trained to swagger through the streets with automatic guns, in $5,000 automobiles, wounding or killing whosoever their employers dislike? But Mr. Wayman will not. He dare not. Everybody knows that."

Said Walter Stevens of the *Tribune* slugging staff to a reporter for the *Examiner*, while temporarily detained by the police, "All that

I know about slugging I learned through the people your boss employs to do slugging work."⁵

On June 13, 1911, the *Daily Socialist* said: "An interesting feature about this whole affair was that the Hearst newspapers had been the ones to develop thuggery to a fine art. The demand of the Chicago *Examiner* for a 'fearless judge' (to try labor thugs!) and the desire for the hanging of someone were shown up in all their glaring crookedness when the common talk about the city was that the other papers had hired sluggers to protect themselves against Hearst, several of whose sluggers had gotten into trouble later. From the time of the Hearst importation of Martin Gilhooley and others to the time Max Annenberg, Hearst's keeper of thugs, went to the Chicago *Tribune*, taking in his train Maurice Enright, Ragen, Stevens and Red Connors, agreeing to increase the *Tribune* circulation to a certain figure, Hearst's newspapers were the active promoters of lawless thuggery in Chicago. Nor did the Hearst interests tamely submit to the poaching on their thug preserves by James Keeley, now the publisher of the Chicago *Tribune*, who induced Max Annenberg to jump his contract with Hearst. Hearst's Chicago *American* sued Annenberg for breach of contract and the contract was held to be void as a contract to commit unlawful acts."

How Annenberg comported himself on the *Tribune* in 1911 may be shown by a few examples.

A typical newsboy slugging was that staged by Bob Holbrook, one of Annenberg's men.

On August 22, 1911, Charles Gallanty, a newsboy at Chicago Avenue and Robey Street, refused to take thirty additional *Tribunes*, which he knew he could not sell. Bob Holbrook, one of Annenberg's men, applying the Hearst method, smashed him in the face and knocked him down. When the boy rose he was knocked down again. This was repeated several times, with horrified spectators watching but deterred from interfering by Holbrook's assistants. Holbrook then tried to drag the newsboy into an alley, there to finish his work in privacy. The newsboy desperately clutched a weighing

⁵ Chicago *Daily Socialist*, June 12, 1911.

machine. He was then knocked unconscious and kicked repeatedly as he lay on the ground, blood pouring from his mouth.[6]

On June 20, 1912, C. D. Ray, a newsboy, swore out a warrant charging that Max Annenberg had jumped from a truck and knocked him to the street, there kicking him repeatedly, in the presence of two unconcerned detectives. Annenberg was exonerated.

These newspaper gunmen frequently unleashed their debauched ferocity among themselves. Two *Tribune* thugs became embroiled with each other in a saloon at Fifty-first Street and Ashland Avenue, back of the stockyards, and in the resulting affray ripped the interior to splinters. The Chicago *Tribune* paid the damages.[7] When Hearst's thugs caused similar damage, the Hearst office had to pay or have the acts reviewed in open court, possibly before a *"Tribune* judge".

During 1911 the newspaper gunmen branched out into other fields, especially into the operation of brothels and the terrorization of union workmen and officials.

Vincent Altman, of Hearst's office, was relaxing at the bar of the Briggs House at Wells and Randolph Streets when gentlemen unknown to detectives present (although they are said to have exchanged winks with them) stepped up and shot Altman full of holes. The dispute had been over profits from a chain of bawdy houses which Altman "protected" during his hours away from the *Examiner* office. In the same year another Hearst employee named Malloy was shot to death while stealing papers from a competing truck.

"Dutch" Gentleman, of Hearst's office, was standing at the bar of a State Street saloon boasting about his shooting prowess. "Mossy" Enright of the *Tribune* appeared. "Mossy" walked up to "Dutch," his own gang covering his rear, twirled "Dutch" about and eased six .44 slugs into his abdomen. As "Dutch" backed away, his entrails, which until then had been enjoying food and drink at the expense of William Randolph Hearst, came spilling out on the saw-dust floor. "Mossy" confessed this misstep to the police, but the *Tribune*

[6] Reported by the Chicago *Daily Socialist*.
[7] According to the unchallenged statement of the Chicago *Daily Socialist*.

printed neither the confession nor that he was a bona fide *Tribune* employee. After some jockeying, "Mossy" was freed.

The atmosphere around the Chicago newspaper plants at the time is indicated clearly by the following testimony of James Keeley, publisher of the Chicago *Tribune*, before the Senate committee which investigated the slush fund of Senator William Lorimer of Illinois,[8] given on July 27, 1911, before the circulation war had been turned into a general effort of all the newspapers to smash the newspaper labor unions:

"A man was beaten up, thrown down an elevator shaft [in the Tribune Building] and shot. He was on the mail-room floor, and he was thrown to the press-room floor. He had been beaten and knocked unconscious on the mailing-room floor before he was thrown down the elevator shaft. Some of the press-room men or stereotypers picked up the man and took him over to a big wash basin and started to wash the blood off him, and then the fellow who was after him came down after him with a gun and shot at him."

"He shot at the man that he had thrown down the elevator shaft?"

"Yes; as he came down."

"Did the bullet strike the man?"

"I do not think it did."

"He was never prosecuted, was he?"

"He was not."

"He was never arrested?"

"He was not."

"And never indicted?"

"He was not."

"And no prosecution of any kind was made against him, by complaint, indictment or otherwise?"

"No."

"Was the man who was thrown down the elevator shaft an employee of the *Tribune*?"

"I think he had been until that morning or the day before. My recollection of the circumstances is that he had been discharged and

---

[8] Investigation of funds used for the election of Senator William Lorimer of Illinois: Senate Document 484, Sixty-second Congress, Second Session, 1911.

that he came in there, and he had a row with this other man[3] over the amount of pay that was due him and that he first pulled a gun on this man and assaulted and shot at him, I believe."

"Do you not know that there were no shots fired until the man who threw the other man down the elevator shaft went down and fired?"

"That is right. They had a fight for the gun and they beat each other up. I think with the butts of the guns."

"Was the man who threw the other man down an employee of the *Tribune*?"

"He was."

"In what capacity?"

"In the circulation department."

Keeley admitted to the Senate committee that it was known that Enright had murdered "Dutch" Gentleman and that the *Tribune* had printed neither his confession nor the fact that he was a *Tribune* employee. In response to a question he granted that Enright was not a "literary man."

The newspaper circulation war reached the height of its fury in 1912 when the printing pressmen were locked out. The drivers for the *Daily Socialist* and the *Daily World* became the particular object of the venom of Hearst and the others, but their guns were also turned indiscriminately against the general public to create the impression that lawless union members were responsible for the deaths and injuries that followed. The circulation of the *Daily Socialist* shot up to 300,000 copies daily and that of the *Daily World*, which was also fully unionized, was close behind.

On May 6, 1912, the *Daily Socialist* carried the following account:

"Sluggers employed by the trust newspapers this morning beat up into unconsciousness Alexander Hickey, a newsdriver, who was delivering the Chicago *Daily World*, and then kidnapped him in an automobile under the pretense of taking him to a hospital. The assault and kidnapping occurred in front of the elevated station at Wilson and Evanston Avenues. Guns were used by Max Annen-

---

[3] Annenberg was circulation manager.

berg, circulation manager of the *Tribune*, who was in charge of a squad of plug-uglies who rode to the station in an automobile. . . .

"A warrant will be sworn out charging Annenberg and his accomplices with attempted murder. Annenberg was dressed as a typical tenderloin representative. He wore a flaming red sweater and over his low brow was pulled a soft cap. With a malicious leer upon his countenance he swaggered around the elevated station . . . using foul language in the presence of women . . . Carrying in his pocket a commission as a deputy sheriff he kept raging around the elevated station . . . flourishing and brandishing his revolver like a maniac."

Buyers of papers other than the *Tribune*, according to this account, were threatened and chased by Annenberg and his assistants.

On June 26, 1912, Max Annenberg was freed on the charges brought by Hickey. *But Hickey was held for the grand jury* by Judge John R. Caverley, who was the trial judge of Leopold and Loeb in 1924. There were scores of witnesses who testified against Annenberg, *but he was an authorized deputy sheriff!* Moreover, he was employed by the *Tribune*.

On June 17, 1912, the Chicago *World* carried this story:

"A pathetic scene occurred at the Eye, Ear and Nose Hospital, Franklin and Washington Streets, yesterday afternoon as Mrs. Minnie Lutz, 643 Wellington Street, stood weeping over the sick bed of her brother, Frank Witt, the street car conductor who was brutally shot down in a riot started by three hired Hearst sluggers at Fifth Avenue [now Wells Street] and Washington Street Saturday night . . . He was shot through the left side of the abdomen and through the neck while making an attempt to summon policemen to arrest the Hearst sluggers, who were then firing wildly through the car, filled with men, women and children . . . Louis Friedman, 17 years old, better known as the 'Farmer,' who lives at 3340 West 49th Street, and Edward and Charles Barrett, 840 Greenwood Terrace, were charged with the shooting of the three men, two of whom are not expected to live. Charles Barrett, who was shot in the left side of the back while resisting police, was taken to Iroquois Hospital."

The victims all died. Their families never collected a cent from Hearst. Some who tried to collect damages received ambassadors from the Hearst office who talked vaguely but alarmingly of the enormous risks people run of having "accidents."

Reviewing the public record of the Hearst men who shot up this trolley car full of passengers in order to discredit locked-out union pressmen, the Chicago *World* said:

"George Barrett, father of the Barrett brothers, was convicted in August, 1907, of killing John Burke, a waiter, in Ireland's Oyster House at North Clark and West Ohio Street, in a quarrel over a dish of clams. Barrett stabbed his victim 18 or 20 times with a butcher knife until he was almost hacked to pieces. He was sent to Joliet and served two years.

"Charles Barrett, 31 years old, one of the two brothers directly connected with the murder of Conductor Witt, was released from the Joliet Penitentiary last November after having done ten years time for criminal assault on a woman.

"Edward, the second member of the family implicated in the murder of the union conductor, is a confessed slugger and admitted to members of the family that he was hired by 'Chicago Jack' Daly to testify against Boener, the union printer, last winter. A few weeks ago he stabbed Emil Dietz, Edward McCarthy and Blanch Williams in a brawl in Henry Johnson's saloon at 3206 North Clark Street. He and Edward Masterson, who assisted in the cutting affair, were indicted for assault and battery June 8, but both were seen on Hearst delivery wagons yesterday with special police stars. The same evening Edward struck his sister-in-law a vicious blow in the face while out with a party of friends in Lincoln Park, but the police refused to arrest him for that offense.

"Three years ago Edward attacked Jack Mallory, a bosom friend, after a trivial quarrel. Nothing came of it as his friend refused to appear against him. A year ago in February he and his father stabbed former policeman Herbert Allen. Later he was arrested for assaulting a waiter in Silver's restaurant at Randolph and Clark Street. He served several sentences in the Bridewell.

"Arthur Barrett, now 20 years old, was released from the United States Penitentiary at Leavenworth last October after doing time for three years for robbing a sub-postal station at Chicago Avenue and

Sedgwick Street in conjunction with Thomas Delehanty. George Barrett, the fourth brother, is now serving an indeterminate sentence in the Joliet Penitentiary for house-breaking."

On June 29, 1912, Earl Farrell, nineteen years old, was attracted by a crowd buying union newspapers at Thirty-first and Halsted Streets. He sauntered over just in time to come into range when a Hearst man, posing for the moment as a union striker, fired into the crowd. On July 5, 1912, James Gould, employed by Hearst's *Examiner*, shot and killed John Moran, a union newsboy who had refused to sell the *Examiner* because the pressmen were locked out. In the dark hours of early morning on July 13, 1912, Max Annenberg, in person, fought a gun duel with Harold C. Whipple, a recalcitrant Annenberg lieutenant. The scene was the downtown "Loop," Chicago's Times Square. Ten shots were exchanged and Whipple was about to administer the *coup de fusil* at close range when Moe Annenberg pushed a Colt in Whipple's groin and threatened to "let him have it." Whipple threw down his gun, and was promptly arrested by the police who had been interested spectators. Annenberg was saluted by the arresting officers but waved his hand deprecatingly, a grin on his face.

On July 29, 1912, a slugger for the *American* terrorized the passengers on a Madison Street trolley by firing at random into the ceiling because the passengers were not reading Hearst's sheet. On August 15, 1912, a gang of Hearst gunmen shot up the Wellington Avenue "L" station in order to frighten an anti-Hearst woman newsdealer.

On October 26, 1912, the *Evening World* said:

"Besides the Witt murder is the case of George Hehr, a teamster, who was shot on the corner of Adams and Desplaines Streets on the night of August 8 at 7 o'clock. *Seven Chicago* AMERICAN *wagon drivers surrounded Hehr's wagon. Revolvers were drawn by the Hearst drivers. Hehr had no revolver. But Hehr was shot. He died before word could be sent to his young wife at home.*

"The seven Hearst drivers, all personally known to 'Long Green' Andy Lawrence, were named by the coroner's jury. Edward Barrett, 'the short man in the grey cap,' *was again involved.* Patrolman

O'Connor testified that Barrett admitted to pulling a gun and firing at Hehr.

"More than two months have gone since the murder of George Hehr. It was just as *coarse, brutal and indefensible murder* as that of Frank Witt.

"Three grand juries have been sitting since Frank Witt was shot to death. Two grand juries have been sitting since George Hehr was shot to death . . . *'Who is back of the gunmen?'*

"*Question: Did 'Long Green' Andy Lawrence from his office in the Hearst building reach for the telephone and give orders to the Democratic City Hall authorities to 'protect' the murderers?*

"*Question: Did Victor Lawson, president of the Publishers' Association and editor and owner of the Daily News, reach for a telephone and send word to the Republican State's attorney to 'protect' the murderers?*"

The nearest anyone came to answering before the bar of justice for the murders and terror, was when Hearst succeeded in having Max Annenberg indicted by the grand jury for shooting Alexander Belfort in the chest. Annenberg stood trial in the old Criminal Courts Building just north of the Chicago River and was defended by a battery of counsel retained by the Chicago *Tribune*. He was acquitted by the jury.

Annenberg was the tool of higher interests, first of Hearst and then of the McCormicks. Since they were not convicted, perhaps the jury was not as venal or stupid as might at first appear.

Even after these bloody and terroristic struggles were ended, the practice of keeping armed thugs on the payroll continued. From about 1917 until 1922 Dion O'Bannion, who was shot and killed in a bootleg feud in 1925, was the chief circulation agent for Hearst's *Herald-Examiner*, its name since the absorption of the *Record-Herald* in 1919. He was known among the police until his death as one of the most cold-blooded killers in Chicago. While working for Hearst he engaged in illegal activities on his own account, of course. He was apprehended, for example, in the act of blowing a downtown safe, *for which he served a week-end in jail.*

During the Negro race riots of 1919, in which 38 people were killed and 543 wounded, with incendiary fire loss at $2,000,000, no taxicab would enter the area of trouble. So the *Herald-Examiner* obtained some motorcycles to take its feature writers through the police lines.

In *Rattling the Cup on Chicago Crime*, Edward Dean Sullivan, former Hearst reporter, tells the following anecdote:

" 'How about it?' I said to my driver. 'Shall we go in there?'

" 'Sure,' he said. He lifted the end of a banner with the paper's name on it, which was attached to the motorcycle, and said, 'This will get us by. The paper's been giving the jigaboos[10] all the best of it. They won't pop off at us.' "

[The Hearst papers and the régime of William Hale Thompson posed as friends of the Negroes, who had been enticed to Chicago during the wartime demand for labor. The appearance of the Hearst papers as advocates of "Negroes' rights" pleased Chicago employers of the cheap non-union Negro labor. The Negroes were in Chicago as strikebreakers, although they did not know it. The depressing effect of their presence on wages was the real cause of the race riots.]

"So in we went . . . A shot exploded at my ear, fired by my driver, who was gazing intently at a roof above the policeman . . . On its roof was a Negro, his eyes on us, struggling with a giant Negress, dressed in white. He had a rifle, and was trying to turn it toward us . . .

" 'One side's enough to worry about,' said the driver, who, automatic in hand, eyed the buildings opposite as we drove along . . . And who was the driver of the motorcycle? He was Dion O'Bannion, at the time employed as 'circulation slugger' for the newspaper."

O'Bannion was not the first Hearst man to branch out into a private career of crime while on the Hearst payroll. In 1912 *all* the Chicago newspapers became accustomed to discovering their men in the clutches of the law for crimes committed unconnected with the newspapers. After their honorable discharge from the newspaper wars, all these gunmen and their many pupils opened shop on their own account, having acquired valuable lessons in typical corporation methods.

[10] Negroes.

News suppression in Chicago is a fine art. When unpleasant facts concern the wealthier citizens of the city, the Chicago newspapers vie with each other to keep the news out of the papers although papers outside of the city may, sometimes, give full accounts of matters that are of concern only to Chicagoans.

When Upton Sinclair wrote *The Jungle* the nation was horrified at conditions in the Chicago stockyards. For a long time not a word was printed locally about the book or about the stockyards, which were spreading disease all over the city and the nation. When a real inquiry into the Chicago stockyard situation began the Hearst papers did all they could to sabotage it.

What happened to the two grand marshals of the Great Circulation War, the brothers Annenberg? Max Annenberg was circulation manager of the *Tribune* until 1919, mightily helping it to prosper. Then he was transferred to New York by his chiefs to work on the New York *Daily News*. When the owners of the *Tribune* started *Liberty Magazine*, he had charge of that enterprise until it was sold to Bernarr Macfadden. He is reputed to be a heavy stockholder in the *Daily News* and is still its circulation boss at $120,000 a year.

Moe Annenberg has had a more varied career than his brother. After leaving the Chicago circulation wars, he went to Milwaukee where he founded a news bureau and built it into a national organization purveying sporting news. It is called the General News Bureau, the greatest wire service reporting sporting and race-track news in the country. It is, to organized professional sport, what the stock market ticker service is to Wall Street.

In 1921 Moe Annenberg, with Joe Bannon, circulation manager of the New York *Journal*, and Hugh Murray, bought the *Daily Racing Form*, and today also owns the *Daily Running Horse*, the *Racing Record* and the *Sporting Times*. The papers are held through the Walter Holding Company and the A. B. & M. Corporation. Moe Annenberg also owns the *Radio Guide*, official organ of the industry and a decided pro-Hearst publication. As the owner of *Baltimore Brevities* he had the brief and unhappy experience of being indicted on a charge of sending obscene matter through the mails.

Moe Annenberg is also in the real estate and brokerage business, a partner of Annenberg, Stern & Co., and has done much business with Hearst and Brisbane. When Hearst entered Milwaukee he made Moe the publisher of the *Sentinel*. In 1928 Brisbane, who often acts as the buying agent for new Hearst properties and subsequently "sells" them to Hearst, sold control of the Elizabeth (N. J.) *Times* to Annenberg and his associates.

The Hearst-Annenberg juxtaposition becomes more curious the more one studies it. Moe Annenberg has an estate at Sands Point, L. I., not far from Hearst's St. Joan place, and an estate in the Black Hills of South Dakota, the show place of the region, not far, coincidentally enough, from the Homestake Mining Company properties at Lead. At Miami, he owns the villa of the late Albert Russell Erskine, with heavy Hearst realty holdings not far away. In Miami, Walter Annenberg, Moe's son, is the publisher of the Miami *Daily Tribune*.

Although the General News Bureau competes with Hearst's International News Service in the sporting field, they exchange news matter reciprocally. They can therefore be regarded as semi-mutual interests. Although there are a number of facts which might lead one to suspect that Hearst has a direct interest in the Moe Annenberg properties there are contradictory indications that cannot be reconciled with this suspicion. However, in view of Hearst's penchant for having a concealed interest in publishing properties the idea should not be lightly dismissed.

The most curious juxtaposition of all in the Annenberg-Hearst career was revealed when the Federation Bank and Trust Company of New York, controlled by William Green, president of the American Federation of Labor, John Sullivan of the New York State Federation of Labor, and other labor moguls, failed in 1931. Among the assets and liabilities were loans of $50,000 to Moe Annenberg, who also endorsed a note of $12,687 for Joseph A. Moore of the New York *Morning Telegraph*, the leading sporting and theatrical sheet of the city; two *unsecured* loans of $50,000 each to Hearst's

American Weekly, Inc.; two *unsecured* loans of $50,000 each to Hearst's *International Publications* and two *unsecured* loans of $25,000 each to Hearst's New York *American*. Moe was also a borrower of $20,000 on collateral and the *Morning Telegraph* of $40,000 on collateral.[11]

Under Samuel Gompers the American Federation of Labor regularly castigated Hearst for his anti-union policies. The principal industrial properties owned by Hearst—Homestake Mining Company and the Cerro de Pasco Copper Company—drove the unions out at the points of guns. Only reluctantly did Hearst submit to unionization of his mechanical employees on the newspapers. More recently he has resisted unionization of his editorial employees, enjoying even the assistance of the President of the United States to sustain the illegal discharge of a member of the American Newspaper Guild.

The measure of Hearst influence over the American Federation of Labor must be left to a later chapter. But at this point we may note that Matthew Woll, vice-president of the American Federation of Labor and until recently a leading official of the reactionary National Security League, is a frequent contributor to the Hearst publications, especially on the inexhaustible subject of the "Red Menace." But, this apart, the revelations in connection with the Federation Bank and Trust Co. of New York, which did not receive the press attention they deserved, establish beyond doubt that labor funds are at the disposal of William Randolph Hearst, the arch-enemy of union labor.

Hearst's labor policy has been simple. Whatever he professed, he has been against labor at all times. His attitude toward labor in the newspaper business was never exemplified better than in Chicago, where he tried to smash the printing pressmen's union and rallied all the Chicago publishers to do the same. Salisbury has informed us how an early editorial union in Chicago was smashed by Hearst. He did the same thing in Boston in 1920, and has tried to scuttle the American Newspaper Guild ever since it was founded.

In March, 1912, the Chicago Publishers' Association offered the

[11] Annual report New York State Banking and Insurance Department for 1931.

Web Pressmen's Union, No. 7, A. F. of L., a new contract to cover all newspapers in the city, present and future. The proffered contract was binding for five years, which was contrary to the by-laws of the international union. Another feature of the proposed contract was that non-union labor could be used at the discretion of the employer.

Under the new contract there was to be no overtime pay, a ten-hour day on Saturdays, lunch-time to be granted at the discretion of the foreman, who was to be non-union. The proposal was rejected. On April 20, 1912, the secretary of the Chicago Publishers' Association wrote to publishers in other cities advocating that the new president of the American Newspaper Publishers' Association be someone who operated a non-union shop. The change in presidents, from one satisfactory to union labor to an anti-union man, was made later in the year, with the Hearst representatives voting for the non-union employer as president of the A. N. P. A.

In April, 1912, the American Newspaper Publishers Association, meeting in New York, proposed to raise an "educational" fund of $1,000,000. This fund was to finance the collection of statistics about wages paid to typographical workers throughout the country, the rules and regulations of the typographical unions and other information. These data were to be supplied to employers from a central headquarters.

On May 1, 1912, Andrew M. Lawrence, publisher of the *American* and the *Examiner*, notified George Haight, president of Local No. 7, that the Hearst papers would act under the general contract of the union with the Chicago papers instead of under the Hearst contracts, which were separate. Under the Hearst contracts more union men were required to handle the big octuple presses.

The union men accepted the proposal to transfer to the general city contract, but the *American* and the *Examiner* then notified the union that Lawrence would determine the number of men to be employed. The union men accepted this also.

The Chicago Publishers' Association then served the following notice on the union:

"Under the circumstances the Chicago Local of the American Newspaper Publishers' Association now declares the contract between it and the Chicago Web Pressmen's Union No. 7 broken by the union and therefore terminated. The press-rooms of all the members of the Chicago Local of the American Newspaper Publishers' Association will therefore hereafter be conducted without recognition of the jurisdiction of the Chicago Newspaper Web Pressmen's Union No. 7."

This notice indicated a general plot on the part of all the publishers to hamstring the union. On May 4, 1912, the union pressmen were locked out, *but the Chicago Publishers' Association broadcast the news that a strike had been called in violation of the contract.*

Participating in this scheme, Hearst caused the following advertisement to be inserted in newspapers all over the country:

"Young and energetic men to learn the web pressmen's trade. Also experienced web pressmen. Wages $24 to $30 per week when competent. Good pay and board and lodging free while learning. Best references as to character required. Apply publisher Chicago *Examiner,* Chicago, Illinois."

Hearst and the other publishers soon flooded the city with the worst riff-raff of the country. F. H. Sullivan, a professional strike-breaker, was placed in charge, after many of the scabs had turned out to be ex-convicts who took to highway banditry in Chicago in their off hours. Sullivan, in circularizing newspaper proprietors in other cities, described the Chicago situation before he took charge as follows:

"I will not now call your attention to the work done by certain famous detective agencies for Chicago publishers. I prefer that you get information on that subject from the publishers themselves, who will inform you that a large majority of the alleged experienced pressmen and stereotypers shipped to this city from New York, at great expense, were entirely ignorant of newspaper work and that many of them had never been in a pressroom or a stereotype room, and that *many were criminals* . . ."[12]

While this lockout was under way, the subject came up on the floor of the American Federation of Labor convention, where Hearst was

---

[12] Reprinted by the *American Pressman,* organ of the pressmen's union, January-March, 1913.

not without supporters, although he was trying to smash the union of pressmen in Chicago. W. C. Phillips, composing-room foreman of the *Examiner* and head of the Chicago local of the International Typographical Union, defended Hearst. The Typographical Union refused to support the locked-out pressmen. The Chicago Stereotypers Union walked out in sympathy with the pressmen, *but were ordered back to work by their officials*. At the annual convention of the stereotypers in San Francisco on June 14, 1912, the proposal to change the charter of the Chicago local so that it could go out on strike of its own volition resulted in a tie vote. President Freel of the stereotypers took with him to San Francisco *the chairman of the American Newspaper Publishers' Association to supply information that would offset anything said by delegates from the Chicago pressmen.* George L. Berry, president of the Web Pressmen's Union, in reviewing the case later, said:

"Can there by any question as to the absolute understanding between the presidents of the International Typographical Union, the International Stereotypers' Union and the American Newspaper Publishers' Association representatives?"

In reviewing the bitter struggle in the *American Pressman* for March, 1913, Mr. Berry declared:

"Where is the justice that will permit of a municipality's police department and entire official staff being used for the purpose of protecting criminals and fostering crime? In the Newspapers Publishers' Association fight against the Web Pressmen's Union in Chicago, 1,480 arrests of union men were made and less than a dozen convictions were effected, because the union secured a jury trial. Less than two dozen were charged with a crime, yet they were arrested, thrown in jail and kept there for sixty and seventy hours, endeavoring to destroy the spirit of the men who were protesting against the tyranny of a newspaper trust. Moreover, union men were murdered and the murderers have been protected in their acts. An independent newspaper, responsible for its utterances, printed this statement: 'The shameful conduct of the courts and the public officials in releasing the Barrett brothers and Art Friedman, Hearst's gun-men, who brutally murdered George Hehr and Frank Witt, both union men, has aroused the federated newspaper trades, who plan to hold a mammoth parade in protest while mass meetings will be held later.'

"These gun-men referred to above as Hearst's gun-men were indicted for murder, yet their release was secured by the newspaper trust and they are turned loose again on the citizens of Chicago to do additional murder.

"Under date of February 11, the Chicago *Day Book*, an independent publication of responsibility, member of the Scripps-McRae League of Newspapers, announced that Hearst's murderer, Barrett, had been held for another murder, making three times in eight months. Webb and McErlane, the Chicago bandits, were arrested for murder and it was declared by the *Day Book* of Chicago that they were taught to use guns on Hearst's *Examiner*. [McErlane subsequently became one of the city's worst killers, during the bootleg period on Chicago's South Side, being held responsible for scores of murders without ever being convicted. He shot and killed a prominent Indiana attorney on a dare near Crown Point, Indiana, but was acquitted by a thoroughly frightened jury of farmers. He died of pneumonia after Prohibition was repealed, raving in fear of the supposed enemies lying in wait for him.]

"The *Examiner* is owned by Hearst. The Hearst newspapers in Chicago control the administration of that city, and the administration is run to the advantage of Hearst's newspapers, regardless of the opinions of the citizenship of Chicago . . . Many of the workers are blinded to the hypocrisy and the demagoguery of his peculiar class of sensationalism by the color of the ink[13] he uses."

On August 18, 1912, the Chicago Federation of Labor passed a long resolution that exposed Hearst's political skullduggery in the city and denounced him for the murderous assaults on union men.

The city officials had to take *some* action. Prompted by the publishers, they began to hold union officials responsible for every murder perpetrated by the newspaper gunmen. The newspapers were hypocritically demanding that the "higher ups" be held responsible.

"We found," said the A. F. of L. report, "that in every department

[13] Red.

of governmental activity involved in this lockout the hand of the newspaper trust was in full control; that it dictated apparently to the mayor, the chief of police, to the sheriff, to the coroner, to the state's attorney and to the city prosecutor, and in a large measure to the judges on the bench."

The Federation ordered distributed 500,000 copies of its long resolution containing a multitude of charges of illegality against Hearst and the other publishers. All union members were urged to refrain from buying the non-union papers, which at the time included all Chicago papers except the *Daily Socialist*, Chicago *World* and the *Day Book*.

In order to discredit union labor, the former circulation department assassins were sent about the city to shoot indiscriminately, killing innocent citizens. Faked stories that union men had perpetrated the crimes were then printed. The Hearst office sent men out to street-corners to simulate union men attacking the police while photographers took pictures. The dispatches going out from Chicago to the country told of a reign of terror fomented by the unions. The assault on the unions was very costly to the publishers.

The controversy ended late in 1913 with a victory for union labor, whose branches all over the country had been contributing funds for the struggle. In San Francisco Hearst locked the pressmen out on the *Examiner*, but they eventually returned on their own terms.

"Long Green Andy" Lawrence's successor as the Chicago publisher of the Hearst papers is Roy D. Keehn, a Chicago lawyer who is also the commander of the Illinois National Guard. The Hearst organization throughout is staffed with executives who are officers of the State National Guards or Reserve Officers. Hearst has an affinity for the armed forces.

The views on public affairs of Major General Keehn[14] were strikingly illustrated in 1932 when, in a pamphlet issued to Illinois Guardsmen, Mr. Hearst's Chicago publisher instructed the Illinois Guardsmen that in the event of riots (the Chicago school teachers were staging protest meetings, the unemployed were eating from the

---

[14] *The New Republic*, January 27, 1932, and August 3, 1932.

Chicago garbage dumps, the downstate miners were becoming restive and people in general were wondering what was to happen)—in the event of riots the Guard was not to fire with blank cartridges! There was to be no amateurishness, *for that merely infuriated people*. Nor was the Guard to fire over the heads of protesting citizens! That, too, was futile. The Guard was strictly instructed to use ball cartridges and to fire point blank into the front ranks of Illinois citizens. But here Major General Keehn's instructions pointed out a danger. In the back of a crowd people press forward even though those in front are willing to retreat. To prevent such an unfortunate development the Guard was instructed to post riflemen and machine-gunners on the upper stories of buildings, in order to mow down the rear rows of "rioters."

Commenting in its issue of August 3, 1932, *The New Republic* said: "It seems to us only fair that Mr. Hearst should ask General Keehn whether he is prepared to replace those readers of his papers who happen to be shot down by the Illinois National Guard in the course of riotous disturbances by people who prefer to starve in public rather than privately."

The instructions to the Illinois National Guard were not printed in the Chicago newspapers, it is needless to say, nor were they given attention by other newspapers. In 1934 General Keehn was elected president of the United States National Guard Association, an integrating instrument for all the State National Guards.

During the Insull trial the Hearst papers sprang to the defense of this stalwart American citizen who had patronized their advertising columns for so many years. For that matter, all the Chicago papers eventually depicted Samuel Insull as a martyr. Among the defendants in the Insull trial was Charles Halsey, a member of the banking firm of Halsey, Stuart & Co., which had floated many securities issues for the Hearst newspapers during the 1920's.

Matters have not changed fundamentally among the Chicago newspapers. This was clearly brought out after the murder of Jake Lingle. Hearst and the other Chicago publishers called for a thorough investigation of Lingle and the Chicago *Tribune*, hoping to embarrass the latter. The investigation was started—but speedily stopped. A reporter for the distant St. Louis *Star* uncovered general corruption among many of the newspaper men. A police reporter for the *Journal* was the downtown partner in a speakeasy, another reporter received a rake-off of one cent on every bag of cement brought into the city, Lingle had had criminal affiliations; the interlocking of the city's gangs and the newspapers was quite complete.

In the ensuing uproar it was brought out that Harry Reid, city editor of Hearst's *American*, was aligned with the Capone mob. When Jack Zuta, a gangster, was killed, his safety deposit box disclosed cancelled checks which had been cashed by local judges, politicians, city officials—and the city editor of the Chicago *Daily News!* The lid was hastily clamped down on this reeking business. Hearst fired Reid, announcing the fact. But several months later Reid was unostentatiously rehired! Lingle was the "front man" with the police department for Annenberg's General News Bureau.

Today Hearst is firmly ensconced in the political and economic life of Chicago, levying an enormous tribute from the people through advertising and through his political affiliations. The plight of Chicago today cannot be understood without a knowledge of this background of its newspapers, which have been in direct alliance with crime, politics and Big Business.

Today the Governor of Illinois is Henry Horner, Democrat, with a long record of Hearst association. The Mayor of Chicago is Edward F. Kelly, Democrat, also an old member of the Hearst political group, as was the late Mayor Anton Cermak. Senator James Hamilton Lewis of Illinois is one of the Hearst men in Washington. As long ago as 1920 he boomed Hearst for President of the United States! In the 1932 Democratic Convention Hearst and Mayor Cermak's machine had an agreement that Illinois and California would vote together. They did.[15]

[15] *William Randolph Hearst: American*, by Mrs. Fremont Older.

VI

THE labor relations of Hearst, our most influential publicist, are of exceptional significance in revealing his character and in estimating his position in society.

Hearst's financial interests, from the very beginning, have made him an implacable enemy of labor. His own employees, even in that period before 1912 when he was publicly professing the utmost sympathy with labor, have been treated with a harshness that can only be compared with that of the early nineteenth century English factory owners. Hearst employees have not merely had to cope with sweatshop conditions: they have, in many instances, been literally enslaved, indentured for long periods, and kept in employment against their will, under the muzzles of guns.

Since 1895 the Hearst industrial holdings have been concentrated in the mining and publishing industries. There have been, as well, important ventures into real estate, ranching, and the film and radio industries, with investments in paper companies and the like.

The two basic underlying Hearst properties since 1895 have been the Cerro de Pasco Copper Company of Peru and the Homestake Mining Company of Lead, S. D. Working conditions at both these properties have consistently been of the very worst. Unless one goes to the mines of French Indo-China and South Africa one cannot find a parallel. Conditions on the Hearst ranching and newspaper properties have been slightly better, owing to their accessibility to public scrutiny. Where public inspection has been difficult, however, the Hearst rule over labor has been draconic.

Cerro de Pasco Copper is the farthest removed outpost of the Hearst industrial empire. For years after its discovery by a disguised archaeological expedition to Peru, nothing was heard of it. A strict censorship was maintained through corrupt Peruvian officials. Hearst has succeeded in securing the appointment of personal friends as consuls and ambassadors to Peru, and these American government functionaries have become legal cogs in the Hearst politico-economic machine.

The mines of Cerro de Pasco Copper are spread through the Department of Junín, 220 miles northeast of Lima by rail and at an altitude of 14,000 feet above sea-level. Within an area of more than 100 miles Cerro owns the railway lines, ore properties, refining plants, stores and the workers' dwellings. The population of the town of Cerro de Pasco, the only population center in the region, is 20,000. In this place men, women and children live in unbelievable squalor. Their city is undermined by shafts which collapse and cause loss of life, unreported to the outside world. According to the *Encyclopædia Britannica*, it is a "cold, desolate region" having "no trees or shrubs." Man's inhumanity has been added.

All the Peruvian officials in the region are subservient to the company; their jobs depend upon it. In Lima the influence of Cerro de Pasco and the banks behind it—the Bankers Trust Company (Morgan) and the Irving Trust Company—is omnipotent. The company has no difficulty in obtaining just what it wants, especially since the British politico-economic influence waned after 1914. If the company encounters difficulties with Peruvian officialdom, results are obtained through "dollar diplomacy" in Washington.

Conditions at Cerro de Pasco under the Hearst aegis have been described, although obscurely. *The Survey* for February 12, 1916, one of whose editors was the late Jane Addams, told the full story of Cerro de Pasco, quoting as authority Dora Mayer, an investigating sociologist resident in Lima, Peru, who conducted an investigation of her own on the spot and also consulted a detailed government report.[1]

The Survey, however, did not link the property with Hearst. In those days it was known only that Cerro's owners were American. Who the actual owners were was known only in a few Wall Street offices. The editors of *The Survey*, had they known how to proceed, could have ascertained the identity of the owners by consulting the *Financial and Commercial Chronicle* of New York for November

---

[1] Report on labor conditions at Cerro de Pasco made by the Societa Pro-Indigena of Peru (1909).

20, 1916. There they would have learned that "About ten years ago J. B. Haggin, D. O. Mills, Henry C. Frick, J. P. Morgan, F. W. Vanderbilt, H. McK. Twombly, the Estate of George Hearst and W. D. Sloane undertook to develop the property[2] . . . The new corporation [it had just succeeded the Cerro de Pasco Investment Company] will be handled, as in the past, by L. T. Haggin, as President, and by an executive committee consisting of Mr. Haggin [Senator Hearst's old partner], E. H. Clark of the Hearst Estate, and J. Horace Harding of Charles D. Barney & Co." The latter is a Stock Exchange house through which the Hearst group has done business.

The occasion for this first trickle of official information about the mine's ownership was the flotation of a $10,000,000 Cerro de Pasco bond issue by J. P. Morgan & Co., with whom the relations of Hearst have been close, although as recently as 1932 Hearst again publicly called Morgan "John Plunderbund Morgan." These aspersions, as the reader must understand, are meant merely for public consumption. They do not disturb the essentially identical interests of the two.

"By owning the railroad the company controls the supplies for the whole region," *The Survey* article said, "and it took care also to monopolize the two essential elements of life, water and salt; it does not monopolize the air because it cannot."

These two basic monopolies have been established by the Hearst interests at the Homestake mine as well. If one is not an obedient Hearst vassal one simply does not drink water at these properties, and woe betide the man who shares his supply with someone who has lost the favor of the authorities!

Miss Mayer revealed that the company obtained its necessary labor supply by methods which make the schemes of the early nineteenth century English factories seem genteel.

"The company needed 5,000 laborers to operate the mines," said *The Survey*. "These were recruited from the Andes region. The inhabitants were originally peasant farmers sufficiently content with their small holdings and leading an undisturbed life. They had to

---

[2] This places the Hearst association with this financial clique back in 1906, when the Hearst papers were denouncing Morgan, Vanderbilt and Frick as dishonest varlets and when Hearst was campaigning for the governorship on an "anti-trust" platform.—F. L.

be baited away from their mountain lands into the drudgery of the mines.

"A method of recruiting called the *enganch*[3] was adopted by the company. Its agent, knowing that some creditor was pressing the Indian, comes to him with a loan of from $25 to $150 and by inducing him to sign a contract, deprives him of his personal liberty until the debt is paid.

"Petty fines, mistakes in reckoning, expenses here and there, serve," says Miss Mayer, "to prolong his obligations to the company until sometimes the case is not rare that workmen who have been contracted for a couple of weeks cannot get away from the mine for a couple of years . . .

"Labor is cheap and treated so. The workmen are forced to trade at the *Mercantile*, as the company's supply store has been named, where prices are often 30 per cent higher than those current in neighboring stores.

"A few years ago a number of inhabitants of Cerro de Pasco built a new settlement in the vicinity of the village of Smelter, and called it Alto Peru . . . The company immediately grew alarmed, thinking that the merchants of Alto Peru might be dangerous competitors to the *Mercantile*, and therefore, it 'resolved to isolate this settlement from its own dependencies, by erecting a wall between the two, of eight feet in height, totally closed in all its extent and with a deep moat at its bottom, which would effectually impede any access in that direction.'

"Besides the wall, a high wire fence with points was run all around the village of Smelter, the indispensable outlets being severely guarded, so that not an employee or workman of the mining company, of whom there are more than 2,000, could buy a cent of bread at Alto Peru.

"The hospital of the company is sadly deficient and yet the common laborer's tribute to it is $1 a month. For him the railroad service out of the mining district is slow, unsafe and unhealthy . . . The workmen who bring forth the copper for North American com-

[3] Still generally in use in Peru, and particularly by Cerro de Pasco. See *Fire on the Andes*, by Carleton Beals, Lippincott Co., Philadelphia, 1934.

merce and in a body pay $350 for hospital dues, have to travel when sick, without receiving food or assistance, in a train which crawls miserably to its place of destination in perhaps twelve hours' time."

Miss Mayer pointed out that company officials and their families were given swift and efficient train service when bound for some social event in Lima or elsewhere, while ill workmen jogged along at a snail's pace in antiquated freight cars. She did not allude to the fact, for which medical sources are responsible, that if pneumonia is to be prevented in cases of common cold, rapid train service to bring the patient to a lower altitude is essential.

Before Cerro de Pasco entered the region in quest of copper, the Indians were healthy, inured to the rigorous climate and the rare atmosphere. But labor at long hours in the mines, coating the lungs with stone dust, has brought the common cold, which at the high altitude is the precursor of pneumonia. The death rate among the workers has been enormous, and the company has taken few precautions because labor has been cheap. Care has been taken, however, to see that vital statistics for the region are inadequate.

"Miss Mayer reviews a report made on March 12, 1909, to the director of public works in Peru," *The Survey's* article continues. "She says this report declared 'that the mining enterprises give no notice to the authorities of the people who are wounded in the operation of their industry; that the number of accidents is at least three or four times higher than that which becomes known to the public; that the work of perforation and the management of explosives is performed without precaution of any kind; that preliminary tests are never made in the dangerous places of excavation; that explosives are accumulated within the interior of the mines, as though it were the same as depositing wood; that the dynamite is transported together with the detonators; that too many shots are fired at one time, without employing special matches; that the explosives are heated without taking precaution, these substances being handed out as if they were inert ones; that the mines have only one outlet,' etc.

"Naturally strikes are rare since the change from agriculture to industry is sudden for the laborer, and he is 'so submissive and accustomed to all kinds of privation.' After a terrible explosion in

1908, the report relates, the workmen for very fear would not return to the mine, despite their contracts and the contracting agents who had the power of withholding water, salt and food.

" 'The company will take pride,' writes Miss Mayer, 'in being able to say some day, when it returns to the United States laden with fabulous treasures of the Cerro de Pasco, that it did not leave a cent in the country to which it owes its fortune. All that it leaves behind will be ruin, desolation, misery, and the remembrance of ill treatment.' "

This was in 1916.

Have conditions improved at Cerro de Pasco in the intervening twenty years? They have, the truth is, become worse. During the war Cerro de Pasco ran at a deficit, rate of operation was decreased, and there was much suffering among the natives, who were thrown out of employment. It will be only in the event of a war in the Pacific that Cerro de Pasco will be able to participate in wartime "prosperity," which, in part, accounts for Hearst's desire for a war with Japan.

After the war economic conditions in Peru, where all properties were owned either by London or New York interests, went from bad to worse. There have been successive revolutionary upheavals by various Peruvian political parties, and the bloodshed has been great. Although no official reports have emanated from the Cerro de Pasco region, the natives there have lost much of their submissiveness, and for a general picture of Peruvian conditions reference should be made to *Fire on the Andes* by Carleton Beals. In the heavily censored Cerro de Pasco region there have been sanguinary encounters between the workers and company and government officials, with many natives killed. Alexander P. Moore, American Minister, induced the Peruvian government to have troops shoot Cerro workers, according to the Federated Press, November 13-15, 1930.

The president of Cerro de Pasco Copper is Edward Hardy Clark, a director in the top Hearst publishing companies, and of the Irving Trust Company, the Bankers Trust Company, the National Surety Company and various other financial institutions. On the executive committee of Cerro de Pasco with Mr. Clark is Mr. Ogden Mills, former Secretary of the Treasury in the Hoover Administration and a recipient of Hearst's political support. When Mills ran for Governor of New York in 1926 he had the endorsement of every Hearst paper in New York State. These men all have a political as well as an economic stake in Peru.

Hearst's influence has been so potent in Washington Administrations since 1920 that he has had no difficulty in dictating the diplomatic appointments in Peru. The Coolidge Administration in 1928 appointed Alexander P. Moore, former Ambassador to Spain, as the American Minister to Peru, where he served until 1930. *In the year of his appointment* Moore purchased from Hearst the New York *Daily Mirror*, a tabloid in which Hearst had lost heavily, and the Boston *Advertiser*. This transaction incidentally enabled Hearst to compute losses in his income tax report. Upon Moore's death these two papers were resold to Hearst by Moore's estate.

Moore had published the Pittsburgh *Leader*, absorbed in Hearst's Pittsburgh *Post-Gazette* combination. As a Pittsburgh publisher Moore was infinitely venal, working hand-in-glove with the Mellon-Frick industrial interests, and suppressing news in the interests of the Pittsburgh industrialists. He was financed by William Flinn, corrupt political boss, and an errand boy for the Mellons.[4]

Hearst was introduced to Pittsburgh by Andrew Mellon, then Secretary of the Treasury, with whom Hearst had established an alliance in the post-war years, and by Frick, a collaborator in Cerro de Pasco. By means of bank loans the Mellon and Frick banks had established a stranglehold over the city's newspapers, with the exception of the Scripps-Howard *Press* and the possible exception of the independent *Dispatch*. The *Gazette-Times* and *Chronicle-Telegraph*, while under the nominal ownership of Senator Oliver, were in fact in hock to the Mellon and Frick banks. The *Post* and *Sun* were in the same plight, and were involved in city graft scandals through the Farmers National Bank.[5] The banks turned these properties over to Hearst, with Paul Block acting as Hearst's purchasing agent.

[4] *Freedom of the Press* by George Seldes.
[5] *Ibid.*

IMPERIAL HEARST 181

The *Gazette-Times* was joined with the *Leader* and the *Post* as the present Hearst *Post-Gazette*.

Moore went to Peru as the Hearst Minister, appointed by Coolidge at the instance of Mr. Mellon. There was every reason for Hearst to have the late Mr. Moore in Peru at this time. In 1927 the National City Bank, in which Hearst is influential (John Francis Neylan, his chief counsel, is on the board of directors), was engaged in bribing Peruvian officials to float a public loan in the United States and there were many diplomatic details that still demanded attention. And the workers had to be kept enslaved.

That the National City syndicate bribed the son of President Augusto Leguia was developed in the Senate Wall Street investigation of 1933. It was also brought out that the bank's own experts on the ground advised that Peru was economically unsound, and could probably not repay a loan. This loan was nevertheless sold to American investors, and quickly went into default.[6] In the financial sections of the Hearst papers the loan was given big "puffs" from time to time.

When Moore was no longer needed in Peru he was transferred to Poland, in 1931.

Edward Hardy Clark is also president of the Homestake Mine at Lead, S. D. In 1906, the very year in which Hearst was running for Governor of New York on a pro-labor and anti-trust platform, the workers at the Homestake Mine threatened to strike. The New York *World* sent a reporter into the region (it is difficult for a stranger to penetrate to the town) and on October 22, 1906, published his findings. The ten-hour day prevailed at Homestake, while at the property of Amalgamated Copper, owned by Colonel H. H. Rogers, who at the time was being publicly attacked by Hearst, there was an eight-hour day.[7] At the Homestake, the *World* investigator found, there was no remuneration for injuries and a general terror reigned over the workers. Land tenure was limited to ninety days, a guarantee against anyone taking root in the region and securing inde-

---

[6] *Stock Market Practices:* Senate Banking and Currency Committee, Seventy-second Congress, First and Second Sessions, 1933.

[7] The reporter neglected to ascertain that the seven-day week was also in force at Homestake.

pendence from the company, which controlled every department of life. Hearst's mother, who indulged in well-meaning but futile charities, later installed a library and recreation center, which was something not to be seen at the Cerro de Pasco.

Much has been written in criticism of the labor policies at Anaconda since the Hearst forces cleared out in 1895, but in remarking that in comparison with Hearst's, Anaconda's labor policies have been enlightened, not much is said for Anaconda, which is ruled by the National City Bank of New York.

From 1906 onward workers became increasingly restive at the Homestake. Violent encounters with company guards and the killing of workers became a matter of common occurrence. The Western Federation of Miners had secured a foothold in the mine and was struggling for more humane working conditions. The Hearst interests countered with a reign of terror which exists to this day, triumphant.

At two o'clock in the morning of June 1, 1910, a mob, inspired by company officials and composed mainly of foremen and the town constabulary, raided the plant of the Lead *Register*, local organ of the Western Federation of Miners, smashed the presses and demolished the plant.

Freeman Knowles, editor and proprietor of the independent Lead *Lantern*, was proceeded against by the Hearst forces in a subtler fashion. For his criticism of the Homestake officials he was deliberately involved in a network of libel suits from which a corrupted local judiciary took care he did not escape. The biggest newspaper proprietor in the country drove out of business a newspaper which opposed him. Hearst's fights for "freedom of the press" are hypocritical when they are not Machiavellian.

Today the newspapers in South Dakota, in towns as far away as Deadwood, are silent under the hand of Hearst, who either owns, controls or influences them all. They have nothing to say against conditions at Homestake. Indeed, they constantly attempt to show that conditions are really excellent.

From time to time the reports of bloody clashes at Lead seeped into the outside world, and at last *Harper's Weekly* sent George

Creel, the future wartime press censor, to survey conditions. Creel, in his 1934 candidacy for the Democratic Gubernatorial nomination in California against Upton Sinclair, was supported by Hearst. But in 1914 Creel was of another temper, and he wrote in the December 19, 1914, issue of *Harper's Weekly*:

"The general superintendent of the mine is president of the bank, president of the Hearst Mercantile Company and sole dictator; mine employees dominate the local government; mine detectives and guards are also deputy sheriffs with power to carry arms and to arrest; the company owns the water works and the lighting system, and the carefully directed votes of the 3,000-odd employees of the company elect the public officials in town, county and legislative district."

Creel noted that the recreation center was not built until 1914, and really came into existence as a result of the discontent among the workers, who were also forced to pay $1 monthly dues to maintain the inadequate local hospital, and continued:

"In commencing a study of Lead, the first thing that strikes one is the remarkable care and precision with which every detail of autocracy is worked out. Nowhere may be found the haphazard, hit-or-miss defects that mar the feudalisms of Colorado, West Virginia or Michigan. In the whole town of Lead it is doubtful if there are more than one hundred lots owned outright by the people living on them. The company, when allowing surface rights, issues permits that are terminable on sixty days' notice, all improvements being forfeited unless removed in ninety days ... Of the 2,500 Homestake employees, 2,000 belonged to the union, and of the remaining 500, only ten or twenty were eligible to membership, the majority being shift bosses, guards, clerks, etc. Confident in its strength, the union issued a statement to all miners in the district stating that they must become members by November 25, 1909, or be branded as 'unfair.'

"The Homestake, without bothering about conciliation or arbitration, promptly locked out every union man, and commenced the importation of labor under the protection of one hundred armed guards. The union, aghast, tried to arrange conferences, and even dispatched two men to California to beg the mercy of the Hearst interests, but their efforts were unavailing.

"By March 3, the Homestake was running as usual. One thousand of the union men had returned to work, tearing up their membership cards, and the other thousand had been driven out of the community. In consideration of the bloodshed and turmoil that attended similar action in Colorado, there must come a certain admiration for the efficiency of the Lead methods.

"Having crushed the miners' union, the Homestake did not sit down in idle complacence, for it knew that as long as any kind of unionism was left there would be unrest. So, quickly organizing all the mining companies of the district into an informal union, this warning was served upon the community:

" 'To Whom It May Concern:

" 'In view of the fact that the mining industry in the Black Hills district is the source from which all the other business interests in the said district derive their main support and that said industry intends to establish permanently in said district what are commonly called non-union labor conditions, it is respectfully suggested to all other business interests that their actions should be vigorously in support of the aforesaid expressed intention.'

". . . Nor are precautions lacking to maintain this condition. One central agency employs all men for the Homestake, and applicants are made to fill out blanks relative to their politics, religion and past records. Socialists are banned, and every worker, when accepted, signs an agreement not to become a member of any labor union. In order to see that he keeps this agreement, a very thorough system of espionage is maintained, not only by the detectives, but through a 'spy system.'

"To maintain its rule the Homestake saw to it that 'the miners are split into 26 nationalities, many illiterate.' This insured a continuation of petty bickering about trivial issues, usually the result of language misunderstandings, among the men.

"At the recent hearing conducted in Lead by the Commission on Industrial Relations, the political activities of the Homestake were also described in detail. The shift bosses are used as precinct captains, the attorney for the company gives the orders, and in this manner the election is assured of such vital officials as sheriff, coroner and circuit judges. . . ." The office of coroner was "vital" because that official formally recorded the cause of death. Suits for damages by miners' families against the company could be hamstringed by the coroner before they were even instituted.

"The matter of religion is equally safeguarded against revolt," Mr. Creel found. "The Homestake grants $200 a year to each church, regardless of denomination, and in the majority of cases, the churches occupy company ground by virtue of a revocable permit. There is no such thing as Sunday observance in Lead, the mine and all other industries working as on week-days. Up to date there has been only one case of clerical rebellion, a Catholic bishop so far disregarding the company's power as to agitate the question of Sunday observance.

"Had he succeeded, the company's output would have been lessened by about $70,000 a month, nor would it have been able to make such a good showing in the matter of wages, since the pay for the four Sundays adds materially to the total monthly compensation. Owing to its perfect control of the situation, however, Bishop Joseph F. Busch was driven from the community, and the town of Lead still labors seven days a week without interruption."

Bishop Busch had come to Lead in 1909 as the first Catholic Bishop in western South Dakota. He was horrified by the condition of the miners and came to the accurate conclusion that "the mine owns, and has owned for years, not only the individual employees, but the city, the county, the state representatives, and even the men that represent that section of the country in Washington."[8]

Inspired by the bishop's statement, the Deadwood *Daily Telegram*, then free and independent, on September 8, 1913, declared:

"It is extremely difficult for anyone to be elected to office, or to make a success of any business, or run anything in Lead, from a saloon to a church, who dares to show hostility to the Homestake or what it does."

Bishop Busch appealed directly to Hearst's mother. She, who upon

---

[8] From a report by Monsignor John A. Ryan of the Catholic University, *The Survey*, November 1, 1913.

her death in 1919 was eulogized as a great philanthropist, washed her hands of the whole affair, saying she left everything to the mine's managers. This has also been the way in which her son has evaded similar responsibility.

Before the American Federation of Catholic Societies in Milwaukee, in August, 1913, Bishop Busch issued a scathing denunciation of the Homestake. Immediately the Mayor of Lead called a mass meeting of cowed Homestake workers to "protest this slander on the fair name of the city." Bishop Busch, seeing that he was getting nowhere, called upon the Catholic hierarchy and the Federal Commission on Industrial Relations for support. The American Federation of Catholic Societies appealed to Mrs. William Randolph Hearst, herself a devout Catholic. But nothing happened. Catholics in Lead, prodded by the Homestake managers, wrote to Archbishop Bonzano, the apostolic delegate to the United States, denouncing Bishop Busch as a "trouble-maker." Bonzano replied in reproval of the "spineless" Catholics of Lead. All that happened was that Bishop Busch was removed from the scene; his subsequent career has been marked by significant silence.

"Wherever one turns in Lead," George Creel also said, "there is evidence of this shrewd foresight on the part of the company. Nothing has been left undone to perfect and bulwark the Hearst autocracy, nor, on the other hand, has anything been omitted to make for the content and well-being of the people."

Mr. Creel, in this passing attempt to walk the critical tight rope, immediately contradicted himself by saying: "It must be admitted, however, that there is rebellion in Lead, well-developed even though deep and very secret."

He continues: "Not only does the Homestake system of espionage keep track of all the miners, but of all citizens and of every person who visits the town. This feeling of being watched every minute, together with the company's political coercion and control of the churches, is the basis for a bitter charge that in Lead there is no such thing as freedom in business, movement, thought, religion or politics.

"These malcontents are kept well in hand, however. The fact that the general superintendent of the Homestake is also president of the Hearst Mercantile Company and the First National Bank is a club of exceptional size and weight. Merchants asking a loan from the bank must file a statement of assets and liabilities and a discussion of their business in its most intimate details. Any business man who offended, therefore, could not only be deprived of credit, but might also find the Hearst Mercantile Company engaging him in competition based upon his own figures and disclosures. This course has been followed out in a good many cases.

"A very interesting witness before the Commission was S. R. Smith, at one time a merchant, furniture dealer, bank director, undertaker and liveryman, but who has been forced out of business by the enmity of the Homestake company.

"Mr. Smith contends that this hostility was incurred because, as member of the school board, he tried to make the company pay up taxes to the amount of $6,000, and did succeed in forcing a compromise on $3,000; also that he held a certain mining claim, bought by the school board, at a future value of $40,000. After being forced off the board, this claim was turned over to the Homestake for $600.

"The general superintendent, Mr. Grier, admitted the facts, but insisted that his opposition to Mr. Smith was based upon the fact that Smith charged $50 for embalming.

"There is also a feeling in Lead that while the Aid Society and hospitals are very nice, a good, strong Workmen's Compensation Law would be vastly preferable. The $50,000 given to the hospital by the Homestake, and the $12,000 donated by the Aid Society, make a total of $62,000, which, when figured on the payroll of $2,700,000, amounts to $2.41 per $100, a very low premium indeed.

"The allowance of $1 a day for sickness or accident, and $1,000 for death from injuries received in the mine, are bitterly attacked as rank swindles. It is pointed out that in the twenty-five states where workmen's compensation laws have been adopted, the compensation for disability averages 65 per cent of the man's wages, while in event of death, the dependents receive 65 per cent of the earnings of the deceased for three years. In many other states, death damages are assessed at $5,000 by law, and where the dead man is the support of a family, the amount is even higher.

". . . not only does $1,000 look little by comparison, but there is the added fact that the 3,000 employees pay $36,000 each year to the fund from which this limited compensation comes . . . No human being in Lead has any civil, religious, industrial and political rights except by consent of the Hearst interests."

Creel's account, while just on the whole, omitted some of the more nauseating details which were spread on the record of the Walsh Commission on Industrial Relations.[9]

With Professor John R. Commons acting as chairman, the Commission began its hearing in Lead on August 3, 1914. Among the witnesses were Bishop Busch; Dr. F. E. Clough, first assistant surgeon of the Homestake hospital; Thomas J. Grier, the Homestake superintendent; E. F. Irvin, employment chief; Chambers Keller, attorney for the mine and political control officer; J. L. Neary, the mine's credit man; G. A. Northam, detective for the mine; Thomas Ryan, a member of the Western Federation of Miners; Dr. D. C. Warren, Methodist minister; and various others, including Mayor H. L. Howard; S. R. Smith, furniture dealer, and Thomas D. Murrin of the Hearst Mercantile Company. This report was never publicized.

Dr. Clough testified that since 1909 conditions had greatly improved. Prior to that time the environment, he admitted, had not been good. Dry drilling in the mine produced many tubercular casualties. In 1913, the best year of record, the mine accounted for 800 accidents, of which 30 were serious and 4 were fatal. The local hospital had 1,109 surgical cases in the year for a population of 8,000, with 27 per cent of the cases involving members of the miners' families. Most of these were confinements. In 1909 there were 783 surgical cases, in 1910 there were 918, in 1911 there were 1,276, and in 1912 there were 1,228.

Most of these cases involved mashed fingers or broken legs, the surgeon said. In the preceding eight years only two legs and two hands

---

[9] *U. S. Industrial Relations Commission (The Walsh Commission)*: Final Report, 1916, Sixty-fourth Congress, First Session, Senate Document, 415, pp. 3539-3679, Vol. IV.

had been amputated and only three men had lost their sight. "There have been quite a few who have lost the sight of one eye," he admitted, but said he had no records on this point.

"We have on hand right now twenty cases of pulmonary tuberculosis," Dr. Clough said, and admitted this was a vast improvement over earlier years when dry drilling had been general in the mine.

"I feel that the conditions in Lead are away beyond anything that exist in any similar industrial center," Bishop Busch said after careful consideration. This remark was made in the face of revelations about conditions at the Colorado Fuel and Iron Company and in the Eastern steel plants and coal mines.

A clipping from the Milwaukee *Leader* of August 12, 1913, was introduced into the record, giving the speech of Bishop Busch which brought about the unpublicized investigation of Homestake. The headline over the news account was:

BISHOP DRIVEN OUT BY GREED OF GOLD APPEALS TO FEDERATION

CATHOLIC BISHOP SAYS CAPITALISM DROVE HIM OUT —HAD TO ABANDON SEE AT LEAD, S. D., WHEN MINE WORKERS FLED FROM INTOLERABLE CONDITIONS

"In the early days of Lead as a mining camp," the *Leader* said, "wages were at the subsistence point, the miners were not permitted to own any land, houses cost an average of $5 each, and (according to the Bishop) the 'cemetery was filled with the bodies of those who died premature deaths. . . .' "

The mine was founded in 1877 by Senator George Hearst and the Hearst family had been dominant in its management ever since.

The Bishop had also told his Milwaukee audience that a fire in the mine once caused an exodus from the town. Thereupon, in 1906, the Western Federation of Miners tried unsuccessfully to establish decent living conditions. The miners were locked out and, according to the Bishop, were replaced by scabs and guards, the "riffraff of the world, who were given fine furniture, better houses, and wages higher than the old employees had ever received."

As to the Hearst Mercantile Company, the Bishop told the commission that the women were induced to exceed their credit so that the families would be tied to the company. He said he had written several times to Mrs. Phoebe Hearst, who had merely sent the letters on to the superintendent. The superintendent in turn instituted reprisals against the Bishop's communicants, forcing them to desert him.

"There is no free press nor free speech here?" the commission asked.

"Hardly," the Bishop replied. "Everybody is afraid to say a word against this great company."

The Rev. D. C. Warren of the Methodist Episcopal Church, who said he had been resident in Lead for twenty-nine years, asserted that the seven-day week and ten-hour day had been in force ever since he had arrived.

E. F. Irwin of the employment office testified that the pay scale ran from $3.50 per day to $4.50, with most of the workers receiving the smaller rate even though they were highly skilled. But very few men were given full employment.

Bishop Busch explained that the lay-off system was entirely unnecessary, and was the result of the seven-day week. The Bishop estimated that the company had ore reserves sufficient to keep the smelters going for several months. The fact that many of the men failed to receive full-time employment each month made it difficult for them to keep themselves and their families out of debt at the company's store. Sixty-five per cent of the men were married. For the entire month of July, 1914, the *highest* paid worker received only $117.

Nevertheless, the populace paid 50 per cent of the local tax bill of $136,000 each year. This, the Mayor explained, did not include the school appropriation. He refused to attempt an estimate of the yearly school appropriation, contenting himself with saying it was larger than the town's budget.

No political parties were allowed to compete in the local election. Local officials were nominated by petition and then were voted upon. These local officials were all company executives. It was brought out, when the attorney for the company was being questioned, that the district usually voted for those state and national candidates which the company favored.

This, then, is Hearst the industrialist, the "friend of labor." The conditions described by Creel at the Homestake in 1914 are essentially unchanged today. Lead is a non-union open-shop town, under the complete domination of the company. It is, furthermore, quite inaccessible, and must be reached by bus from Deadwood. Strangers are not welcome and, unless they can show cogent reasons for traveling in this zone, they are turned back. The vicinity around Lead is like certain sections of the Balkans.

The Homestake is the biggest gold producer in the United States. During and after the war its earnings were down, and the earnings of the town's inhabitants were correspondingly low. With the era of low prices inaugurated by the depression of 1929-36 the cost of producing gold was reduced, and consequently production increased. When the Roosevelt régime increased the official price of gold from $20.67 to $35 an ounce, unprecedented prosperity dawned for the company, but without commensurate improvement for the dwellers in the miserable hovels of Lead, all of which are undermined by shafts and are in constant danger of caving in. Whole rows of rickety houses have had to be razed to lessen the public danger.

The latest "survey" of Homestake was published in *Fortune* Magazine for June, 1934. It was a highly idealized picture of current conditions that does not square with private reports from people in the region nor with the internal evidence. This report, depicting a benignant paternalism holding sway over a prosperous community, is so at variance with all other descriptions of Homestake that it necessitates a later close analysis of *Fortune* in relation to Hearst.

"There is a rare atmosphere of tranquillity about Lead, South Dakota," said *Fortune*. "It has never known a depression and disease bothers it little.

"There is, of course, some miners' phthisis, the disease they get from dust in their lungs, but this mine is at least well ventilated," the magazine said cheerfully. "Yet the fine, clear, dry air above ground must be given its share of credit." *Fortune* said nothing about the acid fumes from the gold refining process that swirl about the town in the shifting winds. "Stand on the crest of the mountain beside the big open cut and you will wonder how anybody could get sick in such a place. Enter the hospital down at the other end of Main Street and you will understand why they do not stay sick long. There are five physicians, seven graduate nurses; rooms are broad, light, airy; medicine is free." And here comes the priceless clue which reveals everything: "The Homestake Mining Co. spends $65,000 a year on its hospital. It can afford to: last year it made $5,000,000 net."

In short, the company spends 1.35 per cent of its net earnings for hospitalization, the amount being deducted, of course, before net earnings are computed and half being contributed by the employees themselves. Creel and the Federal Commission in 1914 considered $62,000, or $2.41 per $100 of net income, too low for hospitalization charges. The expenditure for the hospital in 1933, on the basis given by *Fortune*, was only $1.15 for $100 of income, a reduction of 50 per cent below the amount thought wholly inadequate by Creel and others in 1914, when all costs were much lower than they were in 1933 or are now.

Lead today harbors 8,000 persons, all dependent on the company in one or another of its many ramifications. The hospital expense allotment therefore figures down to $8.12½ per inhabitant annually. Either the people of Lead are unusually healthy or the expense of maintaining a staff of five physicians and seven graduate nurses, plus a building with its necessary attendants, such as janitor, porter, cook and laundress, is very low. Leaving aside the cost of medicines, surgical instruments and appliances, it is clear that a hospital budget of $65,000, in a locality where industrial accidents and tuberculosis are prevalent, is wholly inadequate, and we must conclude that either this staff is not maintained, that it does not consist of five accredited physicians and seven graduate nurses, or that the medical staff is underpaid.

Fortune admitted that there was tuberculosis in the locality, as there is in all mining communities. It cannot be cured, or even properly treated, by week-end hospitalization. Its victims require a long and expensive period of treatment. An annual hospital budget of

$65,000 is not adequate to handle the tuberculars among 3,000 miners and their dependents.

"There are no pool rooms," the article continued, "no saloons, no loafers standing out in front of the drugstores. People in Lead have the preoccupied look of inmates of a well-run sanitarium—but they are all busy. They do not gape at visitors; the visitors gape at them."

The people of Lead are afraid to look at visitors. The casual traveler who secures entry into Lead upon one pretext or another is immediately enmeshed in a network of spies. He must stay at a Hearst hotel (no resident is allowed to take in boarders or lodgers); shop at the Hearst Mercantile Company; be entertained at the Recreation Center, where there is a movie theater, billiard and pool rooms, card rooms, bowling alleys and a gymnasium and swimming tank. All the services are "free," except the movies, which cost 10 cents. The visitor moves about among suspicious people who studiously take no interest in him. They are all quiet, well-behaved, completely lacking in initiative. Here, in microcosm, is the totalitarian state, a citizenry contented with what it has because it is afraid of something worse.

Although Hearst's influence in the state legislature is strong, it is not strong enough to stifle unrest in other parts of the state. Between 1932 and 1935 "radical" farmers sought to compel Homestake to pay taxes in proportion to the amount of wealth it takes out of the state every year. They did not succeed; neither did they stop agitating.

Hearst, as Charles Evans Hughes charged in 1906, dislikes to pay taxes. For years Hearst has always agitated against taxes on himself and on wealth in general. When he has not agitated in the open he has intrigued with national, state and municipal political machines. Reductions and abatements of his taxes are political plums for which Hearst is constantly, and, on the whole, successfully conniving.

In the Eighteen Nineties the Hearst ranches were the largest employers of Chinese labor in California. Hearst's father employed Chinese and the son and mother continued to do so until political critics forced them to cease. The Hearst ranches today hire Mexican and other foreign migratory workers at exceedingly low wages.

Hearst denied that he employed Chinese, or had ever employed them. In 1906 W. H. Driscoll, formerly employed on Hearst's Pleasanton Ranch in California, declared that in 1892 and 1893, while he was there, the ranch employed two hundred to three hundred Chinese to pick apples. The ranch manager, Joe Costello, used to telephone to San Francisco whenever he needed more.

In the same year C. A. Hitchcock, part owner of the Hermit Mine near Oroville, California, close to Hearst's Palermo Ranch, said Chinese labor was even then employed on the ranch. The plight of the Chinese was terrible: the average pay was 50 cents a day, plus a meager diet and housing in temporary shacks.

On his newspaper properties Hearst early acquired the reputation of being very generous to his employees. It is a fact that up to 1906 he paid his editorial workers in New York better salaries than the other papers paid. This was not true after 1906. High salaries still went to the Hearst executives to insure their loyalty but low salaries became the rule for the average rank-and-file worker. Hearst has saved money by dividing his newspaper workers into the haves and have-nots. Outside New York the Hearst papers never paid above the editorial market, and often paid below. The pay of editorial workers in the Hearst organization, after three 10 per cent cuts and individual reductions in the years 1929-35, is the lowest of any large organization in the newspaper business.

Hearst came into conflict with his mechanical workers, printers, stereotypers, pressmen, mailers and delivery men early in his newspaper career. He refused to operate a union shop until after 1900 when, seduced by political ambition, he decided to give in. Despite Carvalho's remonstrance, Hearst recognized the powerful pressmen's union, but refused to deal with the other unions outside New York.[10] In Chicago, as we have seen, the typographical and stereotyping unions were *being fought from within* by pro-Hearst officials.

Though Hearst in New York recognized the Typographical Union, he soon turned against it. In New York and in other localities the Typographical Union continued to extend its influence in the Hearst organization, however. It was slow, uphill work for all the mechanical unions, marked by many incidents similar to those in

---

[10] "Hearst and Hearstism," by Frederick Palmer, *Collier's,* September 22, 1906, *et seq.*

Chicago and San Francisco in 1912 when the pressmen were locked out. Today the mechanical portions of the Hearst papers are fully unionized. While Hearst has unmercifully slashed the wages of his editorial workers, he has been unable to touch the unionized mechanical workers.

Hearst has campaigned against the newsboys in every city in which there is a Hearst paper. In Chicago the Hearst managers induced all the newspaper proprietors, soon after Hearst came to the city, to raise the prices to carriers from 50 cents to 60 cents per 100. The price of the papers to the public was 1 cent in those days. Whenever any newsboys, or union of newsboys, protested, they were answered by gangsters and left with smashed faces, broken skulls or severe internal injuries.

When Hearst, in 1906, raised the price of his papers 20 per cent to the New York newsboys, the *Tribune* accused him of financing his gubernatorial campaign with the pennies of children. At the same time Hearst was accusing Rockefeller of raising the price of oil to finance benefactions to the University of Chicago.

In Boston in 1908 the newly-arrived Hearst managers so treated the newsboys' union that Hearst was placed on the "unfair list" by the Central Labor Union of Boston. The newsboys had gone on strike against the Hearst exactions, and were beaten by armed thugs imported from New York. This union was broken up. Hearst has succeeded in either forcibly breaking other newsboys' unions or in running them himself. The Chicago newsboys' union had a brief existence from 1910 to 1913, but the members could not afford to risk sudden death for a few pennies. It was manifestly the better part of wisdom to choose slow death from malnutrition.

Hearst and the American Newspaper Publishers' Association have prevented government "interference" with the "right" to exploit child labor. The newspaper industry today is the greatest employer of child labor in the country, with 500,000 children on its roster. When the NRA was drafting a newspaper code, the newspaper publishers, with Hearst and his representatives actively in the forefront, successfully kept out any provision against child labor. Why do Hearst and other publishers insist on exploiting children? Why do they not permit adults to handle the papers as they do in Europe, where only adult news-dealers are licensed? Would not adult employment be increased if 500,000 boys were kept in school and their jobless elders placed at work? The answer is that if adults were exclusively employed they would have to be paid more than children.

Hearst is the biggest employer of child labor in the United States, and one of the biggest foes of a Child Labor Amendment to the Constitution.

Hearst smothered a budding union of editorial workers in Chicago in 1901. A union of news-writers was formed in Boston after the war; Hearst fired all the union men and brought in workers from California and Chicago. Sporadic attempts to form a union of editorial workers in San Francisco and other localities also failed because of the hostility of Hearst.

But in 1933 the American Newspaper Guild was launched. The issue of organization had been raised by Heywood Broun, noted columnist, who became the president of the organization. Under the inspiration of the professed ideals of the National Industrial Recovery Act, newspaper workers coalesced in New York, Cleveland and elsewhere. The movement spread rapidly and was especially strong among workers on the Hearst papers. The average pay on the New York *Journal* copy desk was under $40 weekly. The *Journal* publishes eight to ten editions daily. Copy-readers edit all copy and write the headlines. Changes must be made for every edition and the tempo of work on the *Journal* is furious. The *Journal* had and has fewer copy-readers than the *Daily News*, which publishes only three main editions and which pays its copy readers about $80 a week. The *Journal*, although it has the greatest evening circulation in New York, pays its editorial workers the least of any of the big metropolitan dailies.

Hearst immediately became the Guild's biggest foe. Other newspaper publishers either disguised their hostility, professed themselves indifferent to it (as did the owners of the New York *Daily News*), or else "welcomed" it as did J. David Stern, publisher of the New York *Post* and the Philadelphia *Record*. Hearst set about pulling political wires to break the Guild, whose well-being promises the American public the possibility of at last getting fairly honest news.

Interviewed by a Guild member on shipboard on his arrival from Europe, Hearst said he was opposed to editorial organizations because it would take the "romance" out of the newspaper business.

On the New York *American*, William Randolph Hearst, Jr., a chip off the old block, prompted the city editor to "induce" some Guild members to announce their resignation from the Guild on the office bulletin board. Twenty-three resignations were obtained. But a new spirit was abroad in the land, for many of the resignations were later cancelled and some who did not feel they could afford to stand up against the "front office," reëstablished their membership under assumed names so that they might support the Guild and its members.

In Chicago the *Guild* flared into existence and quickly died when Hearst applied pressure. An original branch of more than one hundred was reduced to fewer than ten. The Chicago *Times*, which supported the Roosevelt Administration, was the only paper not hostile to the Guild. But in 1935 the Chicago branch of the Guild revived, and now has more than seventy-five members, a good percentage of whom work for Hearst.

The anti-Guild terror launched by Hearst was most severe in San Francisco. Louis Burgess, an editorial writer for many years, had been elected chairman of the *Examiner* chapter. He was abruptly discharged as soon as the Guild attempted to negotiate about working conditions. It was made plain to the whole office that Hearst would stand for no "nonsense" in San Francisco, where he felt exceptionally strong. Dean Jennings, a rewrite man, was also fired. In New York Hearst proceeded more obliquely against the Guild. The *Journal*, engaged in stiff competition with the Scripps-Howard *Telegram* and Stern's *Post*, both pro-labor, could not afford a labor boycott. The *Mirror* and the *American* also are pitted against strong competition and would suffer from being placed on a labor "blacklist."

Hearst dominates the newspaper field in San Francisco and he proceeded against the Guild without hesitation. After Jennings was fired, renewed pressure was placed on the Guild. Redfern Mason, music critic of the *Examiner* for more than twenty years, and favorably known to musical celebrities who have performed on the Pacific Coast, a man of acute sensibilities, was suddenly transferred from music to reporting hotel arrivals! He resigned after a period of this work, which is usually assigned to novices. Despite the reign of terror, the *Examiner* chapter has remained in existence. There is also a chapter in Hearst's *Call-Bulletin*.

The Jennings Case, as it came to be called, reveals a great deal about Hearst's power today. After being shunted between various Federal labor boards in San Francisco, the members of which were too frightened of Hearst to proceed with a hearing on this flagrant violation of a worker's right to join an organization, the matter was brought to Washington, there to be engulfed in all the varieties of red tape. The Guild pushed the case, however, and at last succeeded in bringing it before the National Labor Relations Board, headed by Francis Biddle of Philadelphia. The Board held that Jennings had been illegally discharged and should be reinstated. Donald Richberg, then Administrator of the NRA, secretly demanded that the case be reopened, however. His order was complied with, but the first decision was reaffirmed by a Board which apparently did not understand higher politics.

Thereupon President Roosevelt personally interceded, and in a public letter to the Labor Relations Board requested it not to take jurisdiction in labor disputes but to refer all questions to the various Code Authorities, which consisted of a majority of employers or their lawyers. The Guild subsequently withdrew its outnumbered representatives from the code authority. No denial was ever made of the charge that President Roosevelt acted on the prompting of Hearst.

Paul Ward, Washington correspondent of the Baltimore *Sun*, has told a bit of the "inside" about this episode.[11] The President, importuned by Hearst, asked Stephen Early, his press officer, whether any of the White House correspondents belonged to the Guild. Early said none of the correspondents belonged, but the men he had in mind were the chiefs of the various Washington bureaus of out-of-

---

[11] *The Nation,* September 25, 1935.

town papers—executives who never stir out of their offices, leaving the news to be gathered by humble "legmen."

It was a quiet and tensely dramatic scene as the President announced to the correspondents assembled at the White House—80 per cent of whom were Guild members—the evasion he was about to endorse.

Ward characterized this as one of the colossal "inside" blunders of the present Administration. That one action was an education to the newspaper men present.

In February, 1936, Hearst's hounded editorial workers in Milwaukee, at bay, turned in a body against him. After seven weeks of attempts at collective bargaining with John Black, publisher of Hearst's *Wisconsin News*, the editorial staff walked out on strike under the auspices of the American Newspaper Guild. It was the first strike of Hearst editorial workers and the first strike of American newspaper editorial workers on a large newspaper.

Reporters' salaries were as low as $15 a week and editors were paid $18.50, the American Newspaper Guild announced.

The paper issued a typically misleading statement pointing to the "satisfactory relations" with 655 employees who did not strike. It was not explained that the union employees who did not walk out had union contracts and could not leave without breaking their agreement.

Hearst is heavily interested in the film industry. Until quite recently he was a heavy stockholder in Metro-Goldwyn-Mayer, but withdrew in 1934. It was said that M. G. M. had refused to cast Marion Davies as Elizabeth Barrett in *The Barretts of Wimpole Street*. Hearst took over a block of stock in Warner Bros. Pictures and Miss Davies was soon under contract with that firm.

Hearst has carried on a ceaseless campaign against organized labor in the film industry. When Actors Equity called a strike of film actors in Hollywood in 1929, the Los Angeles *Examiner*, a Hearst paper, bristled with angry, untrue accusations. The strike was broken. In Los Angeles, an open-shop town partly because of the activities of Hearst, the *Examiner* has never missed an opportunity to put the organized mechanical workers of the film industry in a false light before the public and to prevent the organization of non-union scene shifters, electricians and technicians.

A union in any form within a Hearst organization will not be tolerated if it can be kept out. Hearst, with his own employees, and in his newspapers' campaigns, has been a constant scourge to organized labor. Under the late Sam Gompers the American Federation of Labor never endorsed a Hearst candidacy or campaign, and Gompers went to his grave publicly denouncing Hearst. It has been left to the later régime of William Green and Matthew Woll to allow Hearst the use of labor's hard won funds for the promotion of Hearst enterprises.

VII

HEARST'S systematized theft of news finally embroiled him in court with the Associated Press. There had been numerous bickerings between Hearst and the Associated Press down through the years. Competition from Hearst's International News Service at last became so severe that the Associated Press, which had apparently been deterred by fear of Hearst, was forced to protect itself. It cannily chose the war period, when Hearst was under general fire, to launch its attack in the courts.

International News Service fed the Hearst papers, but also sold its service to independent papers. Some of these independents, finding INS adequate, discontinued the more expensive AP service. This weakened the Associated Press news-gathering organization, for all who took its service were pledged to supply it with the news gathered locally.

After careful preparation, the Associated Press applied, late in 1916, to the United States District Court, Southern District of New York, for an injunction which would restrain Hearst's INS from the wholesale filching of its news. Hearst elected to defend the action without denying the facts. A battery of lawyers, led by Samuel Untermyer, who had distinguished himself shortly before as counsel for the Congressional Pujo Committee which investigated the New York bankers, was retained by Hearst.

After hearing the evidence, and reading voluminous briefs from both sides, the court entered an order dated July 7, 1917, permanently enjoining the Hearst organization from ever again stealing the news of the Associated Press. Hearst appealed up to the United States Supreme Court, but lost all along the way. The final injunction was signed by Federal Judge M. T. Manton on May 19, 1919.

The body of the complaint by the Associated Press,[1] which the Federal courts sustained, was:[2]

---

[1] *Property in the News* carries a complete record of all the documents in the case.
[2] The italics are mine.—F. L.

"Complainant has made careful investigation of the matter and has found ... that the defendant, a profit-making corporation, *by corruption of employees* of members and *by other wrongful and illegal methods*, has in many cases obtained the news gathered by the complainant and sold it to its clients at a cost less than that to the members of The Associated Press, which the defendant was able to do because its cost of *corruptly and otherwise illegally and wrongfully getting* the complainant's budget of news was trifling in comparison with the cost to complainant of gathering the same from the various fields in which the separated events occurred.

"As a result of this practice a number of the members of The Associated Press, finding that they could get the news at less than their equitable proportion of the cost of gathering the same, have quit The Associated Press and are now buying the news reports of the defendant.

"That as deponent is informed and believes the defendant gets the news which makes up the daily reports, and especially important foreign news, in large part by *bribing and corrupting* employees of members of The Associated Press, inducing them by such bribery and corruption to secretly and furtively furnish to the defendant the current news of the day as supplied by The Associated Press to its members. This has been done, as deponent is informed and believes, in the City of New York, in Detroit, San Francisco, Los Angeles and Cleveland, and no doubt elsewhere; but for some time as deponent believes, the principal and most flagrant case of such corrupt arrangement, and the principal source of such leakage of news, has been through an arrangement between the Cleveland office of the International News Service and employees of the Cleveland *News* which receives the service of The Associated Press. For a considerable time heretofore the Cleveland office of the International News Service has had and it still has, an arrangement with the telegraph editors of the Cleveland *News* by which for a consideration regularly paid, such telegraph editors have telephoned or otherwise communicated to such Cleveland office of the defendant important news received by the Cleveland *News* from The Associated Press promptly as the same was received. . . .

"It appears from the affidavit of F. W. Agnew, submitted herewith, that this arrangement has continued at least from January 17, 1914, to the present time, and under it important news gathered by The Associated Press at heavy cost has been appropriated by defendant and sold by it at a great profit to its clients and customers throughout the United States, and has been so sold and distributed by defendant as if properly gathered by itself from the original sources of information, with all the labor and expense involved, when in fact, the same was obtained at the trifling cost of ten dollars per week paid to employees of the Cleveland *News* for betraying the interests of their employer and of The Associated Press, whose reports thus appropriated were sent to the Cleveland *News* under seal of confidence and under the obligation to use it only for publication in its own columns. . . .

"News furnished by The Associated Press to the New York *American* is sent in part by a printing telegraph process which runs into the office of the New York *American*, and although such service is confidential, and under the by-laws the member representing the New York *American* has no right to permit such news to be delivered to unauthorized persons, it has been customary, this deponent is informed and believes, for representatives of the International News Service to copy regularly from the report as received in the office of the New York *American* such news as it has thus obtained from The Associated Press, and to sell and transmit the same to its clients or customers.

"In addition to this *system of piracy*, the defendant has also obtained news furnished by The Associated Press to its members, from early bulletins and editions of newspapers represented by membership in The Associated Press, and has sold and transmitted such news to its clients throughout the United States, as if the same had been gathered by its own efforts, at great expense and from original sources of information.

"Not only has the International News Service been engaged, *by surreptitious and corrupt means,* in securing the news of The Associated Press in advance of publication, but upon the appearance of an edition of an afternoon or morning paper of The Associated

Press, it has been its practice as deponent is informed and believes to take from such edition such news as was available and send it out to its clients as its own news, either textually following the despatches of The Associated Press or rephrasing them.

"Thus, despatches received during a given day or during the early hours of the succeeding night, as deponent is informed and believes, have systematically been, and are sent to the clients of the International News Service for immediate publication in their newspapers. Such newspapers are in direct competition with The Associated Press newspapers, and thus are able to print much of the news simultaneously with the newspapers of The Associated Press.

"By reason of the rapidity of telegraphic transmission, it frequently happens that these papers are able to publish the news of The Associated Press before it is possible for The Associated Press to deliver it to its own members. Telegraphic communication frequently is interrupted by storms or other causes. In such cases it is possible for the International News Service to send Associated Press despatches, taken from the editions of Eastern papers, on their wires, if such wires are not interrupted, and those of The Associated Press are, and not infrequently these despatches are printed in the papers of their clients before it is possible for The Associated Press papers to use them.

"Again, as the news despatches are being transmitted continuously and are sent out to the papers upon their receipt, it often happens that an editor sending service in a given order over The Associated Press wires will be forced to delay a comparatively unimportant despatch, while meantime this relatively unimportant despatch has been published in some edition of an Eastern paper, and, the order of transmission being different, has gone to the client of the International News Service in some other city, and has been printed before it has reached The Associated Press in the same city.

"Such is the situation in respect of the newspapers served by direct telegraph wires. But a majority of the members of The Associated Press are supplied with their news service by despatches or telephone messages in limited measure and sent from numerous relay offices at fixed hours. In these cases, it is even more difficult to prevent the pirated telegrams from reaching their destination before or simultaneously with those of The Associated Press.

"Thus for the reasons already stated and also on account of the difference in time between New York and the cities farther west, the defendant can copy the despatches of The Associated Press from bulletin boards or early editions of the newspapers represented by membership in The Associated Press, and transmit the same to its clients throughout the West in time to be published in their current newspapers; and as deponent believes, *this has been a common and continuous practice on the part of the defendant,* and the defendant has thus been able, without substantial expense or cost to itself, to obtain and sell to its clients at a large profit news which The Associated Press has obtained for its members at very great cost.

"That the news obtained from The Associated Press by the defendant has been sold to its clients as its own, and as if obtained from original independent sources, and has been credited in the newspapers of such clients to the International News Service.

"These practices, as deponent is informed and believes, *have been constant and continuous ever since the organization of the defendant,* but they have been particularly flagrant and noticeable during the latter part of the present year, since the International News Service has been cut off in large measure from obtaining foreign news.

"As deponent is informed and believes, on October 10, 1916, the International News Service was forbidden by an Act of the British Government from securing any news in Great Britain, or from using any of the cable lines running from Great Britain. On November 8, 1916, a like prohibition was established in France. On or about November 11, 1916, a similar prohibition was established in Canada and on or about November 17, 1916, a similar prohibition was established in Portugal and Japan. From and after these dates it was not possible for the International News Service to obtain or receive news by telegraph or cable from any of the countries indicated, and yet day by day it has regularly sent out news to its clients as if received from these countries by the cables connecting them with the United States. As deponent believes it has taken the news of The Associated Press wherever and however it could get it, regardless of means and of the rights of The Associated Press, and has sent it out, in some cases with slight verbal alterations, in many cases *verbatim*, as if it had obtained the same independently from its own sources of information abroad. . . .

"Similar misappropriations will, as deponent verily believes, be made until defendant is enjoined, and it is of the greatest importance to the complainant, in order to save it and its members from irreparable loss, that defendant be enjoined forthwith.

"Especially at this time, when the affairs of the world are at an epochal crisis and events of the greatest public importance and of incalculable news value are happening, every hour of the day, it is essential to the complainant that its rights as aforesaid should be protected against the *unjust, unconscionable, and corrupt piracies of the defendant.* . . .

"As the deponent is advised, nothing but the interposition of an immediate injunction can prevent similar piracies in the immediate ensuing days, to the irreparable loss of the complainant.

"Melville E. Stone."

[January 3, 1917]

One of the Associated Press' supporting affidavits follows:

"Fred W. Agnew, being duly sworn, deposes and says that he is and has been since Jan. 17, 1914, in the employ of International News Service at Cleveland, Ohio. That from that time to about January, 1915, he was in the position of telegraph operator; from about January, 1915, to November 20, 1916, he was manager of the Bureau of the International News Service at Cleveland; and since that time has acted as telegraph operator in their employ at Cleveland. . . .

"That during the entire time that this deponent has been connected with the International News Service, the International News Service has had an arrangement with B. F. Cushing, telegraph editor of the said Cleveland *News*, by which for a consideration regularly paid to the said Cushing by the International News Service, the said Cushing has delivered to the representative of International News Service at Cleveland information in respect to important items of news which have been received by the Cleveland *News* from The Associated Press and that during the time between about November 1, 1916, and the present time the said International News Service has had a similar arrangement with T. J. Thomas, the assistant telegraph editor of the said Cleveland *News*. That under this arrangement such information has been telephoned by the said Cushing or by the said Thomas to the manager of the International News Service immediately upon the receipt of such dispatches from The Associated Press, and thereupon the manager of the International News Service has written out the same and transmitted it at once by wire to the main office of the International News Service and the same has been sent out over the wires of the International News Service to their clients and customers. . . ."

Counsel for the Associated Press, by affidavit and deposition, introduced into the record hundreds of examples of news theft by the Hearst organization, both in America and abroad. Hearst excused himself to the profession, at any rate, by indicating that the anti-Hearst censorship abroad had made his depredations on the Associated Press necessary. But Hearst also raided the Associated Press for domestic news, and had been stealing foreign news before there was a war in Europe.

There was no doubt whatever about the evidence. The Associated Press showed that where it had misspelled names, International News Service followed the misspellings. All the Associated Press mistakes had been faithfully reproduced by International News Service in stories which it pretended it had gathered on its own initiative.

"Deponent further says," the affidavit continued, "that he has personal knowledge of the facts hereinbefore stated; that the despatches hereinbefore quoted sent or received by the Cleveland office of the International News Service were either actually sent or received by him or the original despatches have been seen by him; that during the time when he was the manager of the Bureau of the International News Service at Cleveland he actually received by telephone such information as that hereinbefore referred to from the telegraph editor of the Cleveland *News*, and since he ceased to be such manager he, as telegraph operator of the International News Service, has occupied the same room as Frank H. Ward, who was then the manager of the Cleveland office of the International News Service, and daily heard the said Ward communicating over the telephone with the telegraph editor of the Cleveland *News*.

"And deponent further says that at about 1 p. m. daily the messenger of the International News Service in Cleveland goes to the composing room of the Cleveland *News* and obtains proof of the Cincinnati Livestock Market, which are delivered by The Associated Press daily to the Cleveland *News* for its exclusive use.

"Fred W. Agnew."

Another affidavit:

"Kent Cooper, being duly sworn, deposes and says: that to the best of his information and belief Frank H. Ward became manager of the International News Service office at Cleveland, Ohio, in November, 1916; that upon instructions from the headquarters of the International News Service in New York said Ward took up the work formerly carried on by one Fred W. Agnew in respect to the piracy of Associated Press dispatches in the office of the Cleveland *News*. . . ."

The restraining order of the court stated "that in the particulars aforesaid, and each of them, the defendant has greatly injured and is injuring the complainant and its members, and has been, and is, depriving them of the just benefits of their labors and expenditures, and has been and is causing them irreparable damage, for which they are without adequate or substantial relief except by the interposition of this Court by its order of restraint and injunction."

This litigation had a revealing sequel. One might suppose that Hearst and the Associated Press would continue at loggerheads, and that the Associated Press would feel itself unable to afford further dealings with such an individual and his organization. But this did not turn out to be the case.

There was talk among the Associated Press directors of depriving Hearst of those valuable Associated Press franchises which he held, but the talk came to nothing, nor did the Associated Press either sue for damages or try to make out a criminal case against Hearst, although it had charged corruption and bribery in its plea for an injunction. Oswald Garrison Villard, then publisher of the New York *Evening Post*, was also a director of the Associated Press, and he has since written that the suspension of Hearst was merely deferred. When the time arrived for the consideration of the Hearst case, Villard, Hearst's only critic in the Associated Press, was no longer a director.

With minor exceptions, relations between Hearst and the Associated Press since this court decision have been cordial. The Associated Press has not found it expedient to part company with him. In fact, it has found association useful, for Hearst owns twenty-eight newspapers and a number of others through "dummy" control. Hearst is a valuable cog in the Associated Press organization, if he can be made to follow the rules, and there is a permanent court order that guarantees this. In subsequent minor squabbles the Associated Press prevailed upon Hearst to limit the news-dispensing of Universal Service, the morning division of International News Service, to papers under direct or remote control of Hearst. This was necessary because Universal Service was able to pick up the previous evening's news sent out by the Associated Press.

Commenting on the failure of the Associated Press to follow up its court victory, Oswald Garrison Villard wrote:[3]

"The Associated Press was afraid of Mr. Hearst's power, and the growing number of newspapers brought into his chain of dailies. . . . The dark journalistic shadow of Mr. Hearst is over the Associated Press."

Although Hearst lost his fight to break down property rights in the news in the United States, he continued the struggle in international press associations. To one with a vast organization such as Hearst dominates, the free and ready access to all information, whether printed or not, is vitally important. Therefore Hearst men fight at the annual conventions of international news-gathering organizations against any mutual limitation on the reprinting of news which others have gone to great expense to obtain. It is less expensive for the Hearst organization if it can, as it did in the old days in

[3] *The Press Today*, by Oswald Garrison Villard, The Nation Press, New York, 1930.

this country, purchase all its news for a penny or two in the local papers of cities all over the world.

Literary rights in general have from time to time been under assault from the Hearst organization. After the war Hearst was accused by writers of preëmpting the film rights, without compensation, to stories sold to the Hearst newspapers and magazines. These publications had valuable arrangements with various film companies and with Hearst's Cosmopolitan Film Corporation. Hearst denied it through his newspapers, but he was publicly contradicted by Louis Joseph Vance, the author, then head of the Author's League. The attendant publicity and agitation over this issue secured for writers some portion of their legitimate rights in stories which were filmed.

VIII

Hearst began the stormiest period of his life, and his rise to first-rank power, in 1912. His personal political defeats have obscured his real power throughout, however, as a political boss and international imperialist behind the scenes.

The change in Hearst in 1912 had an outward manifestation. His political uniform of frock coat and slouch hat was discarded and he dressed in the garb of an ordinary businessman.

This, Hearst's third phase, is the Conference Phase, for he now became a personage moving from one conference to another. And between conferences, Hearst was to be busy for the rest of his life endlessly dictating and reading telegrams.

In search of relaxation he also became, in this final phase, a large-scale purchaser of antiques and objects of art, the suzerain of many private estates, and the patron of the Hollywood cinema and its pretty ladies.

Until 1912 he had cherished some lingering notion that he might be able to seize the Democratic Presidential nomination and his personal life was, during the period of this aspiration, outwardly decorous. His hopes were finally dispelled. He appeared at the Jackson Day Dinner in Washington on January 8, 1912, an ominous enigma to the Wilson managers.

Ray Stannard Baker, Wilson's biographer, makes a point of this:[1] "The attitude of William Randolph Hearst, a problem in every Democratic campaign, required peremptory attention. One of Hearst's right-hand men, John Temple Graves, was on the ground asking embarrassing questions. Hearst's chain of newspapers might prove a formidable factor in the campaign ... The Hearst situation came up at the luncheon which followed, raised by Wilson's old college friend, Frank P. Glass, then editor of a newspaper in

---

[1] *Woodrow Wilson: Life and Letters,* by Ray Stannard Baker, Doubleday, Doran & Co., 1931.

Alabama. Glass reported that John Temple Graves was opposed to Wilson, saying that Wilson had refused to accept Hearst's invitation to dinner or even to meet him. Wilson told his friends that he would make no terms with Hearst.

" 'I want the Democratic Presidential nomination and I am going to do everything I can, legitimately, to get it, but if I am to grovel at Hearst's feet, I will never have it,' said Wilson."

Boss Murphy was also at the Jackson Day dinner, once more on good terms with Hearst.

Wilson was a strong candidate for the nomination early in 1912 and Hearst, who favored Senator Champ Clark of Missouri, ordered his papers to attack Wilson without restraint. Mayor Gaynor of New York wrote to Wilson about these editorials and received the following reply dated March 11, 1912:

"Misrepresentation is the penalty which men in public life must expect in the course of their efforts to render public service."

Wilson went to Chicago during the pre-nomination campaign. Illinois, firmly in the grasp of Hearst and the Roger Sullivan machine financed in part by the late Levy Mayer, was anti-Wilson.

In March, 1912, a curious incident occurred in Woodrow Wilson's Chicago hotel room. His luggage was rifled and a suitcase, containing only letters, was taken. Nothing of intrinsic value was disturbed.

Those who knew about the theft of the Murphy-Gaynor correspondence, the rifling of the Standard Oil office files, the stealing of the Spanish Ambassador's letter in 1898, the procurement by bribery of the British-American Venezuela boundary dispute treaty and the text of the Spanish-American peace treaty, and other Hearst exploits, had no doubt that Hearst wanted to discover something incriminating in Wilson's correspondence.

Nothing was found, or the course of American and world history in the next eight years might have been altered.

Alfred Henry Lewis was assigned by Hearst to editorialize against Wilson before the Democratic convention met in Baltimore. Wilson was difficult material; he had never been closely allied with Big Business nor, apparently, departed from the straight and narrow moral path.

Lewis depicted him as a snob. Wilson, according to Lewis, had dropped his name of Thomas but retained Woodrow. This, said Lewis, was sheer pose. Also, Wilson had gone to Davidson College and therefore, according to Lewis, was guilty of "Presbyterian piety." He was only forty-first in his class of 122 at Princeton and therefore he was "neither distinguished nor extinguished."

Hearst had been ejected from Harvard.

In college Wilson had read "The Gentleman's Magazine," Lewis wrote, implying that it was a high-brow publication, whereas it contained the best political thought available in its day and was read by Wilson for that reason. In school Wilson read and recited the speeches of Burke, and hence was "pro-English." This was an attempt to trade on Irish-American and German-American prejudices, just as the allusion to Presbyterianism was an attempt to plant distrust in the minds of lowly Southern Baptist and Methodist voters to whom Presbyterianism meant wealth and snobbishness.

For Southern consumption, Lewis also observed that although Wilson's father had upheld the Confederate cause, he did not exchange his farm for Confederate currency. Why he should have done so, or what the son had to do with this, was not explained. But the point was meant to be telling in the South, and at the same time, telling in the North, since it emphasized for Northerners that here was a son of the unregenerate Confederacy brazenly seeking the Presidential chair.

His college days, Lewis found, composed Wilson's "mocking bird period," for he sang tenor in the college glee club and serenaded girls "who wished he would go away and let them sleep." Lewis did not refer to the dissolute brawls and dissipations indulged in by his own master at Harvard. Lewis made much of the fact that Undergraduate Wilson had a tenor voice, but he tactfully omitted pointing out that Undergraduate Hearst's voice had been mezzo-soprano.

Again introducing a sexual undercurrent, Lewis wrote that, while teaching at Bryn Mawr College, Wilson had shaved off his mustache and had thereby shaken the hearts of his feminine pupils. While adorned with the mustache he had captivated the girls, Lewis said, implying that the young college professor may have been engaged in surreptitious seduction.

As president of Princeton University, Wilson was paid $8,000 a year, Lewis wrote, as though this was excessive, and to thousands of readers of the Hearst papers the sum undoubtedly seemed like a fortune. Hearst's annual income was not mentioned. Wilson had a "row" with the authorities at Princeton, Lewis truthfully noted, and was obliged to leave. He did not explain that the "row" was occasioned by Wilson's insistence upon the dissolution of the aristocratic fraternities and his plans for making Princeton a vital center of democratic learning rather than a collegiate "country club" for rich men's sons.

In horror Lewis related that Wilson willingly accepted a Carnegie academic pension. "I confess that I cannot see how he brought himself to do it," wrote the hypocritical Lewis.

Said *Collier's*: "This from Hearst, who takes money from quacks, gamblers, defrauders of the poor; and from Lewis, who takes money from Hearst."

Wilson had changed his views on direct government by the electorate, Lewis charged in a final flourish.

After Lewis had completed his "analysis," Hearst, in a public ukase, said:

"The constant intrusion of certain pieces of silver into the career of our modern convert is more suggestive of a Judas than a St. Paul."

This made Hapgood write in *Collier's*:

"He loves the word 'Judas'—he of the Hughes overnight change,[2] the Harriman deal in California, the sale of editorials, the poisoning and defrauding of the poor, the tricky and dishonorable methods of the Star Corporation . . . Hearst is a snob for money, a defamer for profit."

The assaults on Wilson's character caused the pro-Wilson *Collier's* to bestir itself further to uncover Hearst activities. It was found that Champ Clark, no less than Hearst, was a supporter of the patent

---

[2] Alluding to Hearst's change to antagonism toward Hughes, and then back to friendliness.—F. L.

medicine trust, had issued endorsements for its nostrums and had worked in Congress for the patent medicine interests.

Hearst and his allies entered the Democratic Convention at Baltimore to nominate Champ Clark or to wreck the meeting. They very nearly succeeded in doing the latter.

On May 1, 1912, E. M. House wrote to Senator Culberson:

"It looks to me as if the opposing candidates might again be Bryan and Roosevelt . . . Wilson's best chance now, I think, is the fear of many people that Bryan will be nominated and the further fear that Hearst may succeed in landing Champ Clark and then dominate the Administration."

Hearst's delegates on the convention floor were allied with representatives of the Ryan-Belmont-Murphy machine, and constituted a large minority. On the tenth ballot Clark had 556 votes, Wilson 350½, Underwood 117½ and there was a scattering of lesser totals for others. Clark had the support of all the big Democratic machine politicians, who distrusted Wilson.

In the course of the bitter struggle Wilson sent a note to Bryan. In it he said:

". . . It is the imperative duty of each candidate for the nomination to see to it that his own independence is beyond question. I can see no other way to do this than to declare that he will not accept the nomination if it cannot be secured without the aid of that delegation (the Ryan-Murphy-Belmont delegation from New York with which Hearst was allied). For myself, I have no hesitation in making that declaration."

After the fourteenth ballot, Bryan, long since abandoned by Hearst, took the floor as "pandemonium broke loose." Bryan secured passage of a resolution pledging the convention not to support anyone backed by the New York delegation, which was teamed with the Hearst-Sullivan delegation from Illinois. In his speech Bryan linked Champ Clark with the Ryan-Murphy-Belmont-Hearst coalition. Then he said: "I cast my vote for Nebraska's second choice, Governor Wilson."

Clark hurried from Washington in "a rage," according to Baker. He had been certain of the nomination. When he arrived in Baltimore he "was in an ugly mood," according to Baker, "and after long talks with his managers and with Hearst gave out a statement declaring that the 'outrageous aspersion' put upon him by Bryan was 'utterly and absolutely false.'"

Hearst sat with Murphy on the convention floor in the New York delegation, and with Thomas Fortune Ryan, the stock market manipulator with whom the Hearst Estate had been associated since the turn of the century. August Belmont, with whose banking house Hearst then had close relations and whose estate at Sands Point, Long Island, he later bought, sat on the floor in the Virginia delegation. The Illinois delegation was led by the late Roger Sullivan, a Hearst tool.

On July 1, 1912, Frank I. Cobb wrote in an editorial in the New York *World*: "Compromise was possible until it became apparent to every intelligent man that the Ryan-Murphy-Belmont-Hearst coalition had set out to strangle progressive Democracy, destroy Mr. Bryan politically and prevent the nomination of Woodrow Wilson at any cost."

On the forty-third ballot Sullivan, unable to hold out against the now certain victory of Wilson and fearful of being excluded from the patronage plans of the new Administration, delivered fifty-eight votes to Wilson. Virginia soon followed, and Wilson was nominated.

It was a sharp blow to Hearst. The Hearst papers nominally supported Wilson during the election.

Hearst, it is true, as a practical capitalist, could not cooperate with Wilson. His financial interests lay in directions wholly different from those served by the Wilson policies.

The first opportunity for the Hearst-Clark cohorts to crack down on the Administration came early in 1914 when Wilson asked Congress to repeal the measure under which American-flag vessels received preferential treatment in the Panama Canal, a matter about which England had been making strong representations. Burton J. Hendrick summed up the episode:

"The Hearst organs, in cartoon and editorial page, shrieked against the ancient enemy. All the well-known episodes and characters in American history—Lexington, Bunker Hill, John Paul Jones, Washington and Franklin were paraded as arguments against the repeal of an illegal discrimination. Petitions from the Ancient Order of Hibernians and other Irish societies were showered upon Congress."[3]

Hearst was merely using the Irish for his own purposes. Wilson had, in the Panama Canal, touched a vital Hearst nerve. Champ Clark and other anti-Wilsonians rallied behind Hearst for the fight.

American vessels passed through the Suez Canal for the same rates as British and French vessels, but Hearst was not concerned with the Suez Canal, nor with the palpable impossibility of continuing to charge higher rates for foreign vessels than for American vessels at the Panama Canal. What concerned Hearst was the desire to establish himself as the supreme arbiter of the Panama Canal administration. As such he could force the British to grant the Cerro de Pasco various concessions in Peru.

The Hearst forces lost on the canal toll issue, and Hearst gathered his strength for the next lunge at Wilson.

This opportunity came with the World War. Notwithstanding the economic character of the struggle, Hearst left no stone unturned to impede and embarrass the Wilson Administration. Hearst's course during the World War, both before and after the entrance of America, delineates the extent of his power—which had grown enormously with the establishment of more newspapers. He was in intimate association with German interests, and he got away with it. He was pro-German before the United States declared war, having been financially allied with German-American business interests since his acquisition of the *Morgen Journal*, renamed the *Deutsches Journal*.

Opposition newspapers during the war attempted to explain Hearst's pro-Germanism, which, after his imperialism, has been the most consistent thing about his policies since 1895, by tracing it to personal friendship with von Bernstorff, the German Ambassador, and the Kaiser. But these friendships were merely the surface reflections of deeper, material ties. Hearst's expansion, as it later developed, was financed by German-American bankers and brewers. In

---

[3] *The Life and Letters of Walter Hines Page,* by Burton J. Hendrick, Doubleday, Page & Co., New York, 1922.

addition to the advertising his papers received from German-American business houses, he had every reason for aiding the German imperialists. Moreover, Hearst was anti-British, as we have seen. His Anglophobia was advantageous because German-American and Irish-American readers were drawn by it to his papers. The native Americans did not mind until Wall Street sponsored the pro-Ally propaganda. Hearst has since discontinued his demands for Irish independence, having obtained his *quid pro quo* from the British in Peru.

Hearst was aided, and possibly inspired, by the German imperialist propaganda bureau in the United States and by the German espionage service, with both of which the Hearst organization became intimately linked.[4] Hearst correspondents in Europe were German secret agents, paid under contract by the German government.[5] Hearst himself engaged, before American participation, in anti-Ally intrigue with von Bernstorff and the egregious Franz von Papen, later to become Chancellor of Germany and Ambassador to Austria.[6] After the United States entered the war Hearst exerted every effort, with cooperation from some members of Congress, to prevent the government from participating more than passively. Hearst was eventually successful in undermining the prestige of the Wilson Administration at home.

Despite the startling revelations in the Senate inquiry, convoked to choke off all protest against the war, no action was taken against Hearst. The Hearst phase of the Senate hearings ended in discrediting the persons who uncovered evidence against Hearst, a climax in which Senator James A. Reed of Missouri participated.

It was amazing that Hearst should have stood against the will of the powerful Wall Street banks during the World War. The whole imperialist drift of the American economy was toward participation on the side of the Allies.

The war was actually bringing black ruin to Hearst, or so he thought. A survey of the Hearst economic domain during the war

---

[4] *U. S. Brewing and Liquor Interests*, etc.: *Op. cit.*
[5] *Ibid.*
[6] *Ibid.*

explains Hearst's trepidation over American participation on the side of the Allies. Throughout the war Cerro de Pasco and Homestake operated at a loss. Although Cerro produced copper, its mines were too far out of the channel of the war trade. Rising costs made production unprofitable. The wartime derangement of the international currency systems caused Homestake, the richest gold mine in the United States, to show a loss. The London gold market was closed, the world was off the gold standard. International gold movements virtually ceased. The price of gold had been fixed by act of Congress ever since Grant's Administration, and was not changed during the World War. All commodity prices advanced many hundred per cent, and with them the price of labor. This made gold production unprofitable.

The defeat of England would have left Hearst in a strong position in Peru. This was unquestionably a basic consideration in shaping his imperialist attitude for a German victory.

Aside from all this, Hearst in 1914 had been driven to the banks. This was not unusual because for fifteen years he had a credit line with the Wells Fargo Bank. However, this avenue was now closed and he was over-extended. He had bought the Atlanta *Georgian* in 1912 and *Harper's Bazaar* in 1914, and *Good Housekeeping*, acquired in 1909, had not stopped losing money. In Atlanta, moreover, he had offended a city of conservative tastes with a wildly sensational paper. Hearst tried to reingratiate himself by supporting locally the murder case framed against Leo Frank, a wealthy young Jew, but he created additional resentment. The other Hearst publications were forced, for circulation's sake, to campaign for Frank's exoneration.

There were predictions of Hearst's imminent fall. But Joseph Moore, a bright young man who had founded the Good Housekeeping Institute, saved the day by obtaining a bank loan of $500,000 in Wall Street.[7]

Seeking supporters for his wartime policies, Hearst had Andrew Lawrence write under date of August 13, 1914, to Chester M. Wright, managing editor of the Socialist *Call* of New York, inviting the *Call*

[7] *W. R. Hearst*, by John K. Winkler.

to join the *Examiner* in "this great movement for peace." Wright sent a stinging reply. He recalled Hearst's attempts to involve the United States in war with Mexico and Japan, and added: "It cannot be that you have forgotten the assaults and the murders of Ed Barrett and his men. There was a war in which you stood for war . . . your plea for peace is too ridiculous . . . There are too many wavering lines in the record of your newspaper. There have been too many convolutions in its career."

Although rebuffed by Wright, Hearst, the imperialist, drew close to many Socialists during the war. His newspapers fought against the ejection of the Socialist bloc from the New York State Assembly, supporting the position of Governor Smith. This fight and his wooing of Victor Berger in Milwaukee with cash paid through Brisbane pulled many influential Socialists into his sphere, among them the late Morris Hillquit.

Shortly after the flight of the tyrant Porfirio Diaz from Mexico, the Hearst papers began propagandizing for American intervention "to restore law and order." Hearst was among the forces that impelled Wilson to send an expeditionary army under Pershing and Funston to invade Mexico and part of the fleet to bombard Vera Cruz and Tampico. Other Americans, with heavy interests in Mexico, of course, also directly prompted Wilson to interfere with the attempt of the Mexicans to force the large foreign interests to disgorge.

The Babicora ranch had been greatly enlarged by Hearst, who was, and still is, one of Mexico's biggest absentee landlords.

Late in 1915 General Pancho Villa and his irregulars raided the Hearst ranch near Madera, Mexico, and held all the employees prisoners; five were Americans; one was British, and the rest were Mexicans. The Villistas helped themselves to food and whatever else was of value, and cantered away to add a footnote to history.

Hearst raged over this act of "vandalism," and his papers became more draconic in their demands for war with Mexico. But as early as 1913 Hearst had not scrupled to fake news and photographs in the effort to involve the American people in conflict with the republic below the Rio Grande.

IMPERIAL HEARST

Max Sherover writes:[8]

"On the 22nd of December, 1913, the New York *American* published a picture where seven children holding up their hands can be seen on the shore of the ocean. The paper said in black type: 'As proof of an almost unbelievable state of barbarity existing in Mexico Mr. Russell, an English traveller, fellow of the Royal Geographical Society of London, sends the photograph shown here to the New York *American*. The children were driven into the water, forced to hold their hands above their heads and shot in the back. The tide carried their bodies away. Note the terror in the face of the one child who partly faces the shore.'

"Mr. Russell was very indignant when he saw the inscription under the picture published in the *American*. He immediately sent a communication to the New York *World* in which he said in part: 'The representative of the New York *American* manifested special interest in a picture taken by me in February, 1912, and published in the New York *Tribune* of September 1, 1912. This picture, as I explained to him, showed a number of Carib children bathing. As I told him, I had asked the children to raise their hands, so that the picture would afford a view of their remarkably fine physical equipment.

"'By way of refreshing this sadly deficient memory of my caller, let me repeat here the information I gave him with the picture, that it is not, and never was, a Mexican picture, having been taken in British Honduras long before the outbreak of the present disorders in Mexico, that the unfortunate child looking over its shoulder, for whose unhappy state the sympathies of readers of the *American* are demanded, was animated by no motive stronger than curiosity, and that if the reporter desires to accompany me to Honduras I hope to be able to introduce him to several of the originals of the picture, still enjoying the most robust health.'"

In January, 1916, the Villistas paid a return visit to the Babicora ranch. This time they encountered resistance. A ranch employee, an American, was killed, others were wounded. Two weeks later the Villistas again returned and drove away live-stock.

[8] *Fakes in American Journalism* (pamphlet).

On July 11th a battle raged over the Hearst property and the Carranzistas captured it. J. C. Hayes, a Hearst agent, asserted that Carranza had confiscated the ranch and its property, but on July 18th the Governor of Chihuahua stated that it had not been confiscated, that the cattle had been simply detained to prevent transfer across the border without the payment of duty.

As far as Hearst was concerned all became quiet below the Rio Grande until February 15, 1917, when two Mexican cowboys employed on the ranch of Mrs. Phoebe Apperson Hearst at Naherachic, were killed by roving insurrectos. Hearst, as a matter of routine, was still demanding a full-fledged war against Mexico, but he was also busy with anti-Ally intrigue.

The events on the Hearst properties in Mexico were not reflected solely in Hearst's interventionist policy. He tried by falsified news to smash the Mexican-American peace conference at Niagara Falls in 1914. Roscoe Conklin Mitchell was assigned to report this meeting. All other Hearst men were barred. When Wilson sent battleships to Vera Cruz all Hearst men except Mitchell were refused passage; Mitchell was taken along only because of his personal integrity. He was vouched for at Niagara Falls by Robert F. Rose, State Department attaché.

The first story Mitchell sent to the New York *American* was not printed. In its place appeared something which *Harper's Weekly* of July 25, 1914, said "simmered with insinuations that President Wilson was backing down and yielding in a humiliating manner to each demand upon him." It was essentially identical with the campaign instituted against McKinley before the war with Spain.

Subsequent dispatches were Mitchell's in part only. Interpolations indicated there was "trouble" in the conferences, and that "shameful" concessions were being proposed by Wilson and Secretary of State William Jennings Bryan. Mitchell protested. He was assured by telegraph that it was all a "mistake," and would not occur again. Thereafter none of Mitchell's dispatches was printed; instead, "inspired" stories, written in New York by Alfred Henry Lewis, were published. A reporter was sent to "help" Mitchell, but he was really a scapegoat designed to take the blame for all complaints from the

American negotiators, Justice Frederick W. Lehmann, former Solicitor General, and Supreme Court Justice Joseph R. Lamar.

After this scapegoat appeared, the *American* "broke" a big sensation—a message from Carranza to the Mexican negotiators which indicated that Mexico was double-dealing. Mitchell called upon Justice Lehmann at the Hotel Prospect and said: "I do not want to ask you, Judge, if this Carranza message is genuine or not. I merely want to notify you and the others who gave me their confidence when I came here, that this part of my dispatch did not go out over the wire from Niagara, and was not part of my dispatch. I never saw it until I found it in my dispatch upon reading the paper."[9]

The "message from Carranza" was a fake, concocted in the Hearst New York office. Mitchell asked his office to be recalled and received the following telegram:[10] "ALL RIGHT. PLEASE COME HOME TONIGHT. ALWAYS SEND THE NEWS FACTS AND LEAVE POLICY TO EDITORS. SHOW MR. JOHNSON AROUND. BRADFORD MERRILL."

Mitchell replied that he would introduce the new man to the other reporters but not to the delegates, and added his resignation. He received the following telegram:[11] "WHY RESIGN WITHOUT CAUSE? WE SHOULD GREATLY REGRET IT. PLEASE BE GOOD SOLDIER AND GOOD BOY. BRADFORD MERRILL."

Mitchell insisted upon resigning by return telegram, recalling his continual protests about the mutilation of dispatches. He received the following telegram:[12] "COME HOME COMFORTABLY. BE PHILOSOPHICAL. MR. HEARST SENT JOHNSON. NO REFLECTION ON YOU. GOOD SOLDIERS ARE PATIENT EVEN IF SUPERIOR OFFICERS MAKE MISTAKES. BE RESIGNED WITHOUT RESIGNING. MERRILL."

Mitchell, however, left the Hearst organization, although he was back before long. Ten days after the *American's* fake, the actual message Carranza had sent was released for general publication. It showed, contrary to Hearst's invention, that Mexico was extremely conciliatory.

Hearst used both Japan and the Philippines in 1915 to distract at-

[9] *Harper's Weekly,* July 25, 1914.
[10] *Ibid.*
[11] *Ibid.*
[12] *Ibid.*

tention from Europe. He published a pamphlet entitled *Our Obligations and Opportunities in Mexico and the Philippines*.

He also published a spurious translation of a Japanese melodrama about an imaginary Japanese attack on the United States.

The *American*—on Sunday, September 26, 1915, and October 3, 1915—carried in its magazine section two double-page articles on the Japanese book, the first of which was entitled "Japan's Plans to Invade and Conquer the United States, Revealed by Its Own Bernhardi." The book, said the *American*, "is cunningly devised to fan hatred against the United States," and is written "not by one author but by a very powerful society known as the National Defense Association." This society, according to the *American*, consists of "naval officers, cabinet and government officers" and "its president is now Count Okuma, the Premier of Japan, and its last president was the ex-Premier, Count Yamamoto."

This was a lie. Investigation of the "National Defense Association" revealed it to be the device of the Japanese publisher. It was a "paper" society.

The translation itself was deliberately falsified. The real title in Japanese was *The Dream Story of the War Between Japan and America*. It had been published in July, 1913, and was written by a sensational Japanese newspaper man who was capitalizing on agitation against the California anti-alien land law. The title, according to Hearst, was "The War Between Japan and America." The book was never popular in Japan, but the *American* said "more than a million copies have already been sold and distributed."

"The translation," the *American* declared, "is a strictly literal one by the well-known American writer, Lawrence Mott,[18] in collaboration with Mr. Han Jou Kia, a distinguished Chinese writer and scholar."

The second chapter, *in the original Japanese,* began: "The beginning of the anti-Japanese question in California, U.S.A., is not of today. Therefore, it is necessary to speak of the land and affairs of California."

The Hearst "translation" read: "The problem of California is so

[18] Who was not known to exist at all.—F. L.

much in the mind of the Japanese at present and also in view of the fact that we intend to colonize it shortly that we give its description."

The original read: "On the south it is bounded by Mexico and on the north it touches Oregon."

Hearst's "translation" read: "On the north, California is side by side with another small state—Oregon—and is bounded on the south by the territory of our great and powerful ally—Mexico, who will help us against the U.S. when the time comes."

The "translation" was falsified throughout. The second article was entitled: "Japan Plans to Destroy Canal," and contained this statement: "The Americans boast of their Panama Canal, but it is only too ridiculously simple for us to dynamite it *effectively*—at the cost of an old ship full of powder."

There was no mention of the Panama Canal in the whole book!

The article was illustrated by pictures said to be drawn from the Japanese book. One illustration showed Japanese seamen landing from warships on the American coast. Investigators for *Harper's Weekly* discovered that these were actually posters left over from the Sino-Japanese War of 1895, and had not been used in the Japanese book. The Japanese sailors shown were landing on the coast of China!

As soon as the war began in Europe, the *American* printed the following photograph caption: "This is the type of English soldier who is doing such fine work on the battlefront in France."

Hearst's *Deutsches Journal* captioned the photograph as follows: "British troops who are able to sprint so fast that German soldiers cannot catch up with them."

The *New Yorker Herold*, German paper owned by the Ridder brothers, commented on another Hearst story:

"In yesterday's *American* we read the following big heading: 'Germans Burn Village. Women and Children Shot.' In the body of the article it was asserted that German soldiers had saturated mattresses with oil, lit them, and thrown them into cellars where women and children sought refuge. They shot those that fled. This brutal slander of German soldiers was made on the authority of Frenchmen in Chalons and the 'Special War Correspondent' of the *London Daily*

Telegraph, and the New York *American* telegraphed it. Why is it that Mr. Hearst fails to publish these reports in his German edition? He must implicitly believe them, otherwise he would not run them under a positive heading as above."

But this was before a $500,000 fund was raised for Brisbane by German-American banking and brewing interests,[14] and it was also before Edward Hardy Clark had analyzed the position of the Hearst industries with respect to the war.

Soon afterward the Hearst papers editorialized about Germany's economic need for "peaceful expansion in Europe." Some weeks after war began a Hearst editorial said the issue was "whether the luminous German thought should be victorious or not in Europe."

Until America's entry into the war, the Hearst papers editorialized against the first Anglo-French loan and urged the Administration to forbid it; called on Congress for a munitions embargo; extenuated the sinking of the *Lusitania*; applauded the position of Secretary of State Bryan and denounced Wilson for dismissing him; charged that Greece had been mistreated by England and France as Belgium had been mistreated by Germany; stressed the suffering in Germany caused by the illegal British blockade; insinuated in January, 1917, that France was preparing to violate Swiss neutrality; opposed the arming of American merchant vessels and the passage of Americans through the war zone; pictured the "invincible" strength of Germany; tried to deflect attention to the "menace" of Japan and Mexico; stressed American unpreparedness for war; at the last minute before war called on Congress for *armed neutrality*; and, as soon as war *was* declared, said that the United States must prepare at home to endure "the furious and terrible onslaught of a victorious Germany."

Throughout the duration of the war the Hearst papers struck many correct attitudes. Almost everything they said about the nature of the war as a gigantic slaughter for the benefit of financial and industrial groups was literally true. But Hearst's whole war policy illustrated again, in a highly dramatic fashion, how it is possible to render hypocritical lip-service to correct ideas, *for private profit.*

[14] *U. S. Brewing and Liquor Interests,* etc.: *Op. cit.*

IMPERIAL HEARST

Hearst's cries for peace were echoed discreetly in Berlin, where the authorities were appalled by the imposing array of world imperialist interests mobilized by London and Paris against the German expansionists. Peace on Hearst's terms, abstention of the United States from the war as he demanded, would have been only a victory for the imperialists of Berlin as against the imperialists of London, Paris and New York.

Hearst proved the fact that the demand for peace in the modern capitalist economy can be raised with as reactionary and selfish intent as the demand for war. His maneuverings for "peace" were identical in aim with the pre-war maneuverings of the diplomats for alliances.

After war was declared by the United States, Hearst's editorial line was shifted to demand the defense of America; retention of the army at home to fight Mexico; abstention from loans to the Allies; building a huge aerial and submarine fleet to attack Germany—projects which, military men pointed out, would be equivalent to not fighting Germany at all; the arrest of "alien slackers" (which spread internal dissension by splitting the populace); the non-shipment of food to the Allies, etc.

The Hearst papers at first disparaged the Liberty Loan, but, under popular pressure, supported it; demanded that the fleet be concentrated in the Pacific to "repel" Japan; insisted on food being sent to neutrals adjacent to Germany to "prevent" them from going over to the German side; alluded to the war repeatedly as "starvation," "devastation," "militarism" and "autocracy." Periodically the Hearst papers demanded that the United States secure a separate peace with Germany, and said that revolutions and a food shortage would soon force peace on the Allies.

Hearst cannot be censured any more for maintaining close financial and business relations with Germany than J. P. Morgan & Co. and other Wall Street bankers (as fiscal agents for the British Treasury) for assisting in the spread of pro-Ally propaganda in the United States. Both Hearst and his temporary domestic opponents were identical in that they sought to have the American people rake profits out of the European conflagration for themselves. Hearst was merely on the losing side.

The uniquely significant thing is that Hearst then, and always since 1895, has been an agent of propaganda for the German Foreign Office in the United States. The Hearst papers are American organs in the orbit of the German Foreign Office today,[15] and are more aggressive about it than they ever were before.

Hearst's efforts to embarrass the United States government after war was declared in 1917 cast a curious light on his *own* definition of patriotism, which is, the unquestioning support of the government and its policies by all citizens no matter what those policies may be. Hearst himself has subscribed to but never acted in accordance with this idea. When the government's policy has been opposed to his interests, as it was during 1914-18, he has done everything in his power to sabotage that policy. Had Germany won the war, even against the United States, Hearst could probably have been solaced because England would have been smashed in Peru and the international gold market would have been moved to Berlin, where he had friends. In the post-war readjustment, on the basis of a German peace, Hearst, as a confidant of the German imperialists, would have been in a favored position to obtain concessions for himself.

Samples of Hearst editorials after the *Lusitania* was torpedoed in 1915 follow:

"The President's letter is undeniably vigorous, *but it is possibly dangerous as well*. The nation desired that its rightful demands should be laid before the German government, but it did not anticipate that the President would go so far beyond the plainly and soundly rightful scope of those demands as to invite a rebuff." (*American,* May 14, 1915.)

"Whether the Lusitania was armed or not, it was properly a spoil of war, subject to attack and destruction under the accepted rules of civilized warfare . . . The Lusitania incident is, of course, no cause for a declaration of war." (*American,* June 6, 1915.)

Harper's Weekly, in its issue of October 9, 1915, showed how war news was being faked by the Hearst papers. *Harper's* revealed that Hearst "staff men" in leading European cities were wholly fictional

---

[15] See Chapter XI.

characters whose false stories were appearing under the following headlines (September 11, 1915):

GIANT TEUTON DRIVE BEGUN IN WEST

CABINET OF THE CZAR RESIGNS OFFICE

This last story, woven out of the whole cloth, was given "spot news" space. Its purpose was to foreshadow the collapse of the Allies. The official denial a few days later was printed obscurely under the heading: "Russian Cabinet Holds On."

"Who has not heard of Frederick Werner, Berlin staff correspondent of the International News Service?" said *Harper's Weekly*. "Who has not read with awe the news from London, revealed by no less a person than Herbert Temple himself—Herbert Temple, the European manager of the International News Service!

"*Herbert Temple, European manager of the International News Service, does not exist. If there is any press correspondent in London named Herbert Temple, he is not known there.*

"*There is no Frederick Werner working in Berlin as correspondent for International News Service.*"

Other fictitious Hearst correspondents uncovered by *Harper's* were John C. Foster, London; Lawrence Elston, London; Brixton D. Allaire, Rome; and Franklin P. Merrick, Paris.

"Brixton D. Allaire, dear reader," said *Harper's*, "is not a romantic figure in khaki, braving untold dangers in the field of battle, but simply a common, ordinary contemptible Hearst fake."

Harper's had sent letters to all the capitals of Europe. The letters to the Hearst "correspondents" came back marked "no party" and "not found." Responsible authorities indicated that the correspondents in question did not exist.

Hearst was alarming the English, and on June 10, 1915; Sir Cecil Spring Rice, British Ambassador at Washington, wrote to Sir Edward Grey, Foreign Secretary.

"Hearst, who has spent more venom upon Bryan[16] than upon any other politician, now espouses his side warmly. We may expect to

---

[16] Who had just resigned as Secretary of State when his demand for a strong tone against England was rejected by Wilson.—F. L.

find him a very serious factor in the movement for prohibiting the export of ammunition to the Allies. This is, of course, the most serious question of all. . . ."

On April 13, 1917, Spring Rice again wrote to Lord Robert Cecil:
"One of the favourite lines of attack on the President by the pacifists and pro-Germans is that Great Britain for her own purposes has inveigled the United States into the war and is going to make use of this country for her selfish objects. It will be said, especially in the Hearst papers, that, in order to carry out this object, the British mission is sent here to induce the United States to take action best fitted to promote British purposes, and is sending specialists to teach the United States how to raise an army and conduct the war. . . ."

British imperialism continued to oppose Hearst after the war. Stanley Baldwin, Prime Minister of England, during the campaign on the issue of Empire Free Trade of 1929-30, said:[17]

"'There is nothing more curious in modern evolution than the effect of an enormous fortune rapidly made, and the control of newspapers of your own. The three most striking cases are Mr. Hearst in America, Lord Rothermere in England, and Lord Beaverbrook. It seems to destroy the balance: the power of being able to suppress everything that a man says that you do not like, the power of attacking all the time without there being any possibility of being hit back; it goes to the head like wine, and you find in all these cases attempts have been made outside the province of journalism to dictate, to domineer, to blackmail (Cheers).'" The esteemed Viscount James Bryce alluded similarly to Hearst after the war in a letter to A. Lawrence Lowell.

It was exacerbating to the pro-Ally faction to read in the New York *American* of June 6, 1915, an editorial over the signature of Hearst himself, declaring that the United States had no right to insist that Germany refrain from submarine warfare. It was little less than maddening to have him write over his signature on April 11, 1917: "Stripping our country of men, money, and food is a dangerous policy. Our earnest suggestion to the Congress is that it imperatively

---

[17] *Beaverbrook, An Authentic Biography of the Right Honorable Lord Beaverbrook,* by Frederick A. Mackenzie, Jarrolds, Ltd., London, 1931.

refuse to permit the further draining of our food supplies and our military supplies to Europe."

On April 24, 1917, the *American* said: "The painful truth is that we are being practically used as a mere re-inforcement of England's warfare and England's future aggrandizement." On May 17th it advocated spending money on the army and navy at home "and so compelling Germany, if she wants to fight, to come to us."

On May 25th the *American* said of the Liberty Loan: "If you want our food and wealth sent abroad to help suffering England, buy a Liberty Bond, furnish the sinews of war," and suggested that the purchase of a bond was for the dismemberment, not defeat, of Germany. On July 27th, the *American*, suddenly weeping for our soldiers, spoke of American troops "offered up in bloody sacrifice to the ambition of contending nations on foreign battlefields." On November 22, 1917, the paper alluded to "interfering in Europe's quarrel," and on June 11, 1918, to "killing millions of men in the trenches . . . rotting in the trenches . . . the United States must lose *five million men* in the next three years." On June 29th it referred to "these bloody shambles," and on June 30th to "the bloodiest, blackest, most brutal war in all history."

The Hearst papers serialized Ambassador James W. Gerard's *My Four Years in Germany*, which gave an impression of invincible German strength. On September 12, 1917, the *American* and other Hearst papers *exclusively* carried "Kaiser's Message to President Wilson. Full Text of Secret Cablegram to President Wilson in this Edition of the Sunday *American*."

Plans were made to publish serially Henri Barbusse's *Under Fire*, the first of the realistic war novels. In a panic, the arrangements were cancelled at the last moment, but not until the Hearst papers, now grown to seventeen, had advertised it as follows:

"No such tales of the terrible life of the trenches was ever written before . . . Barbusse . . . tells the story of his squad day by day, as they take part in the fighting, wallow in the mud, shiver and freeze and are wounded. It is all there. For the first time we are shown the truth. The details that other writers have skimmed are here set forth clearly, vividly, nakedly. There is a message in it for Americans.

Barbusse tells us what our boys in France would write—if they were allowed."

A few days before the United States' declaration of war the Hearst papers declared: "Wall Street wants to . . . send American boys over to fight in the trenches . . . It may be taken for granted that any American boys sent over on that errand would be accommodated with places in the *front trenches*. Now, we propose to fight this business right now and clear through to the end. Let the Allies fight their own war. We did not start it, and it is none of our business to prosecute it for them."

Kenneth Macgowan, of the New York *Tribune*, in 1918 counted seventy-four Hearst attacks on the Allies, seventeen defenses of Germany, sixty-three pieces of anti-war propaganda and one significant excision from a Presidential proclamation—after the United States was at war.

The deletion was of Wilson's prayer for victory in the 1918 Memorial Day proclamation. The Hearst managers alleged the censoring of the Presidential remarks, unheard of in the annals of American journalism, had simply been a typographical error. It was then asked why the prayer had been excluded in *all* the Hearst papers?

The public reaction to Hearst's anti-war policies late in 1918 became hysterical. Hearst had already been roundly assailed by all of the nation's newspapers and magazines and public figures. Theodore Roosevelt had pontificated: "Since we entered the war Mr. Hearst has at various times issued editorials professing great patriotic zeal, at the very time when in other editorials he was attacking the Allies of America, England and Japan, in the most offensive way, and thereby doing his best to weaken the effect of our war against Germany." On November 12, 1917, James M. Beck, former Solicitor General of the United States, declared before a large audience in Carnegie Hall that treason's "chief source is to be found in the journalistic enterprises of one man, and his name is William Randolph Hearst. His power for evil is immeasurable. He is said to own seventeen newspapers and magazines . . . No single influence is comparable with the Hearst influence in its potency for evil . . .

His adherents do not greatly exaggerate when they claim for Mr. Hearst a daily audience of five millions of people. It is thus within Mr. Hearst's power to convey to these millions the subtle poison of insidiously disloyal utterances, and it may be said without exaggeration that the great menace to the part which America is destined to play in the struggle comes from the Hearst press."

By the middle of 1918 there was a widespread public boycott. His publications and correspondents were already banned in Canada, Japan, England, France, Italy and the possessions of the Allied nations. Organizations throughout the United States went on record against the Hearst papers, the circulations went down precipitately and advertising was cancelled.

Reinforcements were needed and were commandeered. James A. Reed, of Missouri (the old bailiwick of Champ Clark, the center of the German-American city of St. Louis and the home state of Edward Hardy Clark), spoke vigorously in the Senate on behalf of Hearst. Senator James Hamilton Lewis, of Illinois, the political creation of Roger Sullivan, Levy Mayer and Hearst himself, also spoke in his defense. Senator Hiram Johnson of California similarly bestirred himself. Mayor John S. Hylan of New York, elected in 1917 by Tammany at Hearst's instigation, and Mayor William Hale Thompson of Chicago, both outspokenly pro-German, pro-Irish and anti-English, orated on Hearst's behalf.

As Hearst cracked the whip even influential Cabinet members jumped. Secretary of the Treasury William Gibbs McAdoo congratulated Arthur Brisbane on his war work in Chicago. Postmaster General Burleson warned government officials against over-zealousness toward "friendly" newspapers whose policies they might not completely understand.

The opposition press pointed to publishers who, for doing much less than Hearst, had been forbidden to do business. One of these was Tom Taggart, Indiana politician and newspaper owner. The government did refuse to renew the foreign language license of the *Deutsches Journal* soon after the United States entered the war. Amid great difficulty, with the New York *Tribune* questioning Hearst's "singular and sinister immunity," a Senate investigation was launched in the fall of 1918, from the records of which one can obtain a fairly complete record of Hearst's wartime activities.

The government's case against Hearst was presented in the testimony of Bruce Bielaski and Captain George B. Lester of the United States Secret Service. Their statements were supplemented by Alfred L. Becker, Deputy Attorney General of New York State, who was a candidate for the Attorney Generalship on the Republican ticket in 1918. Becker conducted an independent investigation of his own.

Hearst was not called to testify, but Brisbane, Roy Keehn and Walter Howey of the Chicago *Examiner* appeared, and Bradford Merrill sent a long, irrelevant written denial of various charges. The testimony of Brisbane was the most revealing.

Brisbane was forced to admit that a group of German-American brewers had given him $500,000 to purchase the Washington *Times* from Frank Munsey *after* the United States declared war on Germany. This fact came to light only when the Alien Property Custodian found a memorandum in the possession of Christian W. Feigenspan, New Jersey brewer, showing that the contribution was made jointly—and secretly—by George Ehret, Julius Liebman, G. C. W. Hupfel, Jacob Ruppert, Reuter & Co., William Hamm, A. J. Houghton Company, Gustave Pabst, Fred Miller Brewing Company, C. Schmidt and Sons, F. A. Poth & Sons, and Bergner and Engel.[18]

Brisbane claimed it was because he was friendly to light wines and beers and hostile to whiskey that Feigenspan and the others had put up this money. He denied these men gave the money for the purchase of the Milwaukee *Wisconsin News* (created by merging the *Evening Wisconsin* with the *Press*), or had advanced the funds which enabled him to lend $8,000 to Victor Berger and to buy $5,000 of stock in the Milwaukee *Leader*,[19] which was published under Berger's name. Berger was a Socialist.

According to Brisbane, Hearst had nothing to do with the sudden

[18] *U. S. Brewing and Liquor Interests,* etc.: *Op. cit.*
[19] Recall that the *Leader* in 1913 had published Bishop Busch's exposure of conditions at Homestake. After 1917 Berger had nothing to say against Hearst.

purchase of these two newspapers, although Brisbane remained on Hearst's payroll at $104,000 a year. As to Hearst's attitude toward his chief lieutenant becoming an independent publisher, Brisbane informed the committee that Hearst had said, "I am paying you to look after my papers. Now you will look after your own and neglect mine."

"I think I will not," Brisbane said he had replied. "Because what I write for your papers will be in my own, and as it goes in my paper I shall be interested in making it good. However, if you feel that my ownership of the paper would probably interfere with your work, I will agree that you can take the paper at any time you like for what it cost me."

Later Brisbane testified under oath that he told Hearst, "As long as I made that agreement with you I think you should say that if I find that I have undertaken too much you will buy the paper. And he said he would do that."

"Does he not offer any objection to your using material that you were writing for him, at $2,000 a week, in other newspapers of your own?" Brisbane was asked.

"Not the slightest."

Brisbane also denied that he had a concealed interest in the Chicago *Herald*, which had been purchased by Hearst from Levy Mayer, the Chicago corporation lawyer and politician.

Brisbane told the Committee that he had, in fact, tried to acquire the Newark *Star-Eagle* before he bought the Washington *Times*. Feigenspan was closely questioned as to whether his group had not financed Paul Block in the purchase of the *Star-Eagle* shortly afterward. Feigenspan said he had never heard of Paul Block.

Now, although Hearst was shielded from direct connection with these German-financed papers in Washington and Milwaukee in 1918, the fact is that Brisbane later "sold" them to Hearst, who now owns them. The passing mention of Paul Block, an advertising man, is interesting. Paul Block, as we shall see, later emerges as a Hearst "dummy."

The foregoing makes it obvious that Hearst and Brisbane had an agreement whereby Hearst was given an option to take over the papers bought with the money of men sympathetic to the imperialist aspirations of Berlin and antagonistic to the imperialist aspirations of Wall Street, London and Paris. Mrs. Older's *"authorized"* biography makes Hearst's rôle even more definite. She says Hearst acquired the Washington *Times* in 1917.[20]

The revealing letter written by Feigenspan to Brisbane on June 29, 1917, and uncovered by the Alien Property Custodian, reads: "The money, which we gladly contribute to your enterprise . . . It is understood that, after a period of five years, you will repay to me and my associates, at your discretion and convenience, on account of principal, so much of the profits as may be derived from such newspaper as may, in your judgment, be taken out of the business without interfering with its proper operation and development, and that you shall be under no liability whatever for repayment of the sums contributed other than out of such profits. It is understood no interest shall be paid upon this money. . . ."

Brisbane was not subjected to the embarrassment of being asked about this letter and was permitted to tell about the arrangement in his own way. This he very cautiously did:

". . . I went to Mr. Feigenspan, and I said: 'I want to borrow this money. I shall pay it back and pay you interest. I can not borrow it from a bank.' And he was glad to lend it. He said: 'I may not lend it all to you, but I will guarantee, among my friends, that I will let you have this money.' And he agreed to lend me $500,000. . . ."

Brisbane denied knowing that Feigenspan got the money from a German-American committee.

"You gave no collateral?" asked Senator Lee S. Overman, the Committee's chairman.

"No, Senator," said Brisbane, "for this reason. I asked Mr. Feigenspan to take a mortgage on my real estate, and he declined, because he said, 'I do not want to go on record as trying to influence the press.'"

"Do you regard that transaction as a loan, strictly, Mr. Brisbane, or does it not come pretty close to being a gift?" asked Senator Josiah O. Wolcott.

[20] *William Randolph Hearst: American,* by Mrs. Fremont Older.

"It is absolutely a loan, Senator," said Brisbane.

"But from their point of view it is tantamount to a gift?" continued Wolcott. "That is to say, they can not collect it."

"Yes, they can; because Mr. Feigenspan has my note *at the present time.*"[21]

Senator Wolcott: But the terms of that note, as I recall, briefly stated, are about as follows: You are given an unlimited time in which to repay the loan.

Senator Knute Nelson: Without interest.

Senator Wolcott: And there is no interest. You are to repay the loan; you are obligated to repay the loan; you are obligated to repay it only out of the profits that the paper makes; and then it is left entirely in your discretion as to how much of those profits, and when, out of those profits, you shall make payment?

Brisbane: Yes. That was the idea. . . .

Senator Wolcott: But I say, from the viewpoint of the lenders of the money, it really was a gift; that is to say, the money had gone out of their reach and they could not force you to repay. They would have to trust entirely to your disposition to repay or not?

Mr. Brisbane: They could have taken over the property here. They had a claim against me for $375,000.

Senator Overman: Suppose you had died. There would be no claim then?

Mr. Brisbane: They would have had the property in which their money was invested—a lien on the Washington *Times.*

Senator Overman: There is no arrangement in this note giving them a lien on the *Times.*

Mr. Brisbane: No: they did not want it. I wanted them to take a mortgage on my real estate, and I asked Mr. Feigenspan to do that, and he said he did not want to do it.

Senator Overman: But there is no lien on the paper?

Contradicting his previous assertion, Brisbane said, "No; there is absolutely no lien on the paper. I could not run a paper with any liens on the paper itself. This was a personal loan made to me, which I agreed to repay."

[21] My italics.—F. L.

Brisbane pointed out that he had paid interest to Feigenspan in the amount of $22,000 the preceding August, despite the fact that the arrangement was that no interest was to be paid. But it was not brought out that the interest payment was made only when it was certain Brisbane and Hearst would have their affairs examined by the Senate.

Further questioning revealed that in the spring of 1918 Brisbane had resold his stock in the Milwaukee *Leader* to Berger, thereby clearing himself and Berger of that connection in time for the investigation.

Brisbane denied that the Washington *Times* had pursued a policy of emphasizing the horrors of war and deprecating the Allies, despite clippings introduced to this effect. Quotations from the Washington *Times* introduced in evidence showed that it was following Hearst's general war policies.

The Hearst organization was more deeply implicated in the strategy of the Imperial German Government than even the questioning of Brisbane revealed.

Bruce Bielaski, on behalf of the United States Secret Service, testified that William Bayard Hale, Hearst correspondent in Berlin, was on the German payroll at $15,000 a year, that he acted as a confidential messenger for the German Embassy in Washington, and that he was moved about in response to promptings of the German Ambassador, Count von Bernstorff.

Bielaski produced a wireless telegram dated June 2, 1916, routed through Buenos Aires and Stockholm to the German Foreign Office from Bernstorff, as follows:

"In conformity with Your Excellency's wish I suggest that the present is a favorable time to get Hearst to send a first rate journalist to Berlin. The man selected, W. B. Hale, has been, as Your Excellency knows, since the beginning of the war, a confidential agent of the Embassy, and as such he has been bound by contract until June 23, 1918. In making this arrangement the main idea was that Hale would be the most suitable man to start the reorganization of the news service after peace on the right lines. I request that full confidence may be accorded to Hale, who will bring with him a letter of recommendation from me to Dr. Hamman. Hearst is not aware that Hale is our agent, but knows him only as a Germanophile journalist who has contributed leading articles to his papers."

Bielaski also introduced a complaint from Bernstorff to his superiors that the New York *World* was obtaining exclusive news in Berlin and demanding that Hearst be given preference "as Hearst organs have during the course of the war always placed themselves outspokenly on our side."

Bielaski placed into the record the minutes of a meeting in New York of German agents, including Meyer Gerhard, Dr. Heinrich Albert (who was subsequently deported for his activities), Hale, George Sylvester Viereck, Dr. Carl A. Fuehr, former German commercial attaché at Tokyo, and agents Meyer, Cronemeyer, Claussen, and Hecker, on May 24, 1915. The minutes showed that Hale advised on counter-propaganda to offset sentiment evoked by the torpedoing of the *Lusitania*.

This meeting concerned the activities of Edward Lyell Fox, a newspaper man, who was on the payroll of the German Imperial Government, and under agreement to send articles from Europe to the Hearst papers. Bielaski introduced a letter from Fox to Captain Franz von Papen, then German military attaché. This letter was purloined from the German Club in New York by United States Secret Service agents. It indicated that the flow of munitions from the United States to the Allies could be hampered "by fomenting a war scare between the United States and Japan; at the present time this is not dangerous, for the United States Army and Navy men believe that war between America and Japan is inevitable."

Fox informed Papen that he had learned from Naval officers in Washington that the United States had come close to going to war with Japan in 1913. "The source of that situation was California. Cleverly handled," the letter continued, "California can be used to create the same situation today . . . The public mind must be diverted from Europe to the Orient. Pro-German publicity is futile . . . The Hearst papers will lead in the attack on the Japs."

Hearst's anti-Japanese campaign was synchronized so that it accorded perfectly with the desires of the German agents.

Bielaski said that "our records show that Mr. Hearst went to the office of Dr. Albert, 45 Broadway, on June 24, 1915."

Fox and Hale were not the only German agents on Hearst's payroll. The office of Hearst's *Deutsches Journal* was, in fact, a nest of German secret agents and propagandists.

Captain Lester, in his testimony, said the *Deutsches Journal* was edited by Gustav Schweppendick, who, after the paper was suppressed, "turned up in Berlin as the manager of the Hearst Bureau."

"Another writer for the *Deutsches Journal*," he testified, "was Albert O. Sander, the man who was convicted of sending spies to England."

The business manager of the paper was Albert Schoenstadt, "who ran between the *Deutsches Journal* and the Albert Bureau, and in order to facilitate this means of communication there was a private wire between Dr. Albert's office and the *Deutsches Journal* . . . Schoenstadt was an admitted German propagandist."

Captain Lester told of a mysterious character named Marshall Kelly whose existence the Hearst organization subsequently denied. Marshall Kelly was either an imaginary creation of the United States Secret Service or an important Hearst-Bernstorff go-between functioning under an alias. The Secret Service could not produce him, and yet Captain Lester gave such a circumstantial account of his activities that there was every reason for the Hearst organization to deny the existence of such a personality.

"Marshall Kelly is reported as being the man who was representing the Hearst publications in the [Albert] Bureau," said Captain Lester. "He was the messenger, the man who came to discuss matters."

"Mr. Marshall Kelly was sent to Baltimore some time in 1915, in behalf of Dr. Albert and Dr. [Bernard] Dernburg [German propaganda chief in the United States], to negotiate the purchase of the Baltimore *Sun* for the Germans. This mission, apparently, came to nothing. We next find that Marshall Kelly is connected with the Chicago *Herald-Examiner* in 1917, and in the fall of 1918 he is sent to Milwaukee, Wis., to take charge of the *Wisconsin*, the paper purchased by Mr. Brisbane. [Brisbane denied ever having heard of Kelly.]"

Captain Lester also told of the production in 1915, by the Hearst interests, of an anti-Japanese serial film called *Patria*, with Mrs. Vernon Castle in the leading rôle. This film excited popular feeling against Japan and was drastically changed at the solicitation of President Wilson, who wrote to a Hearst executive:

"Several times in attending Keith's theater here I have seen portions of the film entitled *Patria*, which has been exhibited there and I think in a great many other theaters in the country. May I not say to you that the character of the story disturbed me very much. It is extremely unfair to the Japanese and I fear that it is calculated to stir up a great deal of hostility which will be far from beneficial to the country, indeed will, particularly in the present circumstances, be extremely hurtful. I take the liberty, therefore, of asking whether the company would not be willing to withdraw it if it is still being exhibited."

Alfred L. Becker, Deputy Attorney General of New York, who was summoned before the Senate Committee, linked Hearst intimately with Ambassador Bernstorff and with Bolo Pacha, the Paris publisher who was executed as a traitor by the French government. Bolo Pacha came to the United States in 1916 with credentials addressed to J. P. Morgan & Co. and the Royal Bank of Canada. He was ostensibly interested in procuring newsprint supplies, but his paper, *Le Journal,* was subsidized by the Germans and he made contact with German agents in New York. Bolo Pacha gave a dinner for Hearst at Sherry's and Hearst tendered him a farewell supper.

Becker introduced the affidavits of taxi drivers, private chauffeurs, and hall attendants in Hearst's apartment building, declaring that Count von Bernstorff and Bolo Pacha had been frequent callers, both together and singly, and that the German Ambassador had frequently tried to avoid giving his name. At Bolo Pacha's trial in France the name of Hearst was frequently mentioned and Hearst was depicted by the French prosecutors as a German go-between.

Roy D. Keehn, in his testimony, showed that Hearst had succeeded in obtaining strong support from within the Cabinet. He read a letter from Secretary of the Treasury McAdoo, written to Keehn on October 1, 1918, just as the inquiry was gathering headway, as follows:

"Extremely sorry I did not have the pleasure of seeing you in Chicago. Many thanks for the kind support the *Examiner* is giving the Liberty Loan and for its generous treatment of me. You are rendering a genuine service to the country, and I want you to know how deeply I appreciate it. Warm regards."

Keehn also produced the following letter from Samuel Insull, the utilities magnate, who had been appointed by Governor Frank O. Lowden as chairman of the Illinois State Council of Defense. Its text shows it to have been written after the investigation began. "If I were called to testify I would have to say that I had something to do, in a semi-official capacity, in directing the work of the British Government in this country prior to the entry of the United States into the war. At that time I believed Mr. Hearst's newspapers to be anti-British—not pro-German, but anti-British.

"After America's entry into the war, as chairman of the State Council of Defense, I had occasion to watch the Hearst papers and I know that they gave my committee full and complete support, and I know them to have been truly American and very patriotic."

Hearst's rapprochement with Insull had taken place much earlier. When Insull was under fire for financial legerdemain in 1932 and 1933 the Hearst papers favored him and cheered when he was acquitted in Federal court.

Senator James A. Reed, of Missouri, although not a member of the investigating committee, claimed the privilege of interrogating Mr. Becker. He violently accused Becker of gathering evidence against Hearst for political reasons (Becker was obviously acting on behalf of the pro-Ally bloc centered around J. P. Morgan & Co.). Becker accused Reed of appearing as counsel for Hearst. Reed charged that Becker had used ex-convicts in gathering evidence against Hearst, to which Becker blandly replied that all prosecutors make use of ex-convicts as stool-pigeons and spies. Reed failed to break down the substantial nature of Becker's allegations.

This phase of Hearst's career has contemporary significance: it gives a clue to the inner workings of the Hearst organization in its recent rapprochement with the Hitler government of Germany.

IMPERIAL HEARST

Many of the threads of the period 1914-18, seemingly unconnected, have since come together around William Randolph Hearst. Brisbane, financed by a group which included enemy aliens, turned the newspapers they financed over to Hearst. Paul Block, whose purchase of the Newark *Star-Eagle* was a subject of Senate suspicion and inquiry, has recently become known as a more or less open Hearst lieutenant. A person apparently remote from Hearst in 1917—Edward A. Rumely, who was sentenced to a Federal penitentiary for failing to notify the government after the United States entered the war that the money for the purchase of the New York *Evening Mail* had come from Dr. Albert—has in recent years operated in close association with Hearst. Rumely came to light in 1933 as the executive secretary of the Committee for the Nation, an inflationary group whose effusions were printed in bulk by Hearst from 1931 to 1934, and were broadcast by Father Charles E. Coughlin, a Hearst political ally. Rumely has also been publicized as a Nazi connection in the United States.

As will be shown in the final chapter, Hearst has received since 1934 much more money from the Hitler government than Brisbane received from the German-American Committee in 1917.

Another example of Hearst espousing causes for the good of humanity, but from unworthy motives (and later abandoning them) is provided in the early support of the Bolshevik revolution in Russia. Hearst heralded it as a sign of the weakening of the Allied strength.

On June 3, 1918, the New York *American* and other Hearst papers said:

"It is the part of statesmanship, wisdom and justice for the American people to inform themselves concerning the real character of the Bolsheviki, and to understand that the Bolsheviki have committed no act of treason or disloyalty to their allies; that they have done nothing that we in their circumstances would not have done; that they are today working out the problems of democracy as they never can be worked out by war in Russia; that considering the suspicion of the Russian people toward a war which their tyrants had begun, and their positive determination not to continue it under any circumstances, the Bolsheviki took the only course open to them in abandoning a conflict which they could not, under any circumstances, continue, and the abandonment of which appeared to be the best way of giving Russia a breathing spell in which to settle her internal conditions upon the firm, deep foundations of true democracy."

Hearst at that time opposed American participation in the Allied interventionist adventure in Russia.

On July 16, 1917, Brisbane had written under his signature:

"Anarchy rules in Russia—somebody must do something. The natural somebody is Germany, right next door to Russia." He went on to say that Europe might later be grateful if the war ended and found Germany "with enough strength left to undertake the maintaining of order in Russia—developing the resources there and making a few billion of rubles in the process."

Again it was Germany that Hearst was really worried about! Why?

The Bolshevik revolution was hailed in Germany as well, for it signalized the breakdown of the Russian military effort. The German General Staff had facilitated the passage of V. I. Lenin from Switzerland to Russia early in 1917, not out of sympathy with Lenin's cause, but to break the Czarist Russian military machine.

As sentiment against Russia in high American circles became more bitter, owing to the confiscation of Russian properties owned by the Singer Sewing Machine, the International Harvester Company and others, and the default on Czarist bonds owned by enterprises like the Metropolitan Life Insurance Company among others, Hearst became more and more pro-Soviet. The Hearst papers published one glowing article after the other about Russia and the Bolsheviks.

The Weimar Republic of Germany established close economic and military relations with Bolshevik Russia. Germany purchased raw materials from the Soviet Union and sold heavy machinery, all on the basis of large credits arranged by Germany through bank loans obtained in London and New York. The Soviet Union was the only big nation friendly to the Weimar Republic, and Germany made the most of it, both from the economic as well as the diplomatic standpoints, as a threat to France, England and others who upheld the post-war status quo. Germany and the Soviet Union were barred from the League of Nations.

The League of Nations, proposed by President Wilson although probably indirectly inspired by Foreign Secretary Edward Grey of England, was accepted by England and France as a means of holding Germany in a vise. The League was immediately denounced in the United States by all the Hearst papers and by such Hearst political adherents as Senators James A. Reed and Hiram Johnson. *The United States was kept out of the League and the World Court largely through the opposition of Hearst.* Hearst opposed the League on the purely "American" ground of non-entanglement in European affairs.

The "non-entanglement" line of the Hearst press was spurious, impractical, without concrete motive. But the opposition to the League on behalf of German interests, with which Hearst was deeply entangled, was concretely motivated. German-American business interests revived after the war, and once more grew to tremendous proportions. Hearst continued a close and profitable relationship with them. He again obtained revenue from German sources. Furthermore, alliance with the German party in international politics continued to be useful in forcing concessions from the British in Peru. As soon as a free hand in Peru was obtained, around 1928, Hearst veered to a friendly view of England's problems. But England, by that time, because of post-war loans, had a large economic interest in Germany. Hearst's continued German orientation was therefore not contradictory to his new attitude toward England.

As soon as Hitler rose to power in Germany in 1933, occasioning a profound change in German foreign policy toward the Soviet Union, *Hearst changed his Russian policy,* and began falsifying facts about the Soviet Union just as he had falsified facts about Spain, Mexico, Japan and England.

Samuel Gompers charged after the war that Hearst was friendly toward the Soviet Union because he was seeking mining concessions. Gompers' accusation was based on the fact that Hearst was part of a syndicate of concession hunters headed by Colonel William Boyce Thompson, mining magnate and former chairman of the Republican National Committee, which was dickering for mineral rights in the Soviet. Thompson propagandized for an "understanding" with the Bolsheviks, but was nonetheless unsuccessful in getting concessions. Gompers was wrong in supposing that this abortive mining deal, in which Hearst was undoubtedly interested, lay at the root of Hearst's pro-Soviet policy. Hearst was merely trying to cash in on a Russian policy instigated by acquaintances in Berlin and German business interests in the United States.

Hearst, with German agents in his own organization during the war, succeeded in placing one of his men in the British intelligence service. Ariel Varges, a Hearst camera man, was recruited into the British army during the war, detailed on photographic and intelligence work.[22]

As early as 1914 Hearst had dealt British prestige a tremendous blow by publishing the photograph of the sinking of the torpedoed H. M. S. *Vindictive* after the British admiralty had denied the big man-of-war had been sunk. This advertisement of the German submarine was of enormous value to the imperialists of Germany in their struggle against the imperialists of France and Britain. It was this smuggled photograph which caused the officials of Great Britain and France to ban all Hearst operations in the Allied countries. "Varges eluded the restrictions by becoming a captain in the British army."[23]

One of Varges' major wartime assignments as a captain in the British Intelligence was to track down "'The Cruise of the Moewe,' a veracious camera record of the captures and sinkings of that famous sea-wolf. For more than three years spies, diplomatic agents and secret service men sought a print of this amazing picture. It had been made by deliberate plan of the Germans for use in internal propaganda, to give their own people courage through seeing Ger-

[22] *A Million and One Nights: A History of the Motion Picture*, by Terry Ramsaye, Simon and Schuster, New York, 1926.
[23] *Ibid.*

IMPERIAL HEARST

man triumphs at sea. The showing in Geneva proved to be a mistaken unpopular confession of *Schrecklichkeit*. The film was hastily recalled and secreted."[24] Varges finally obtained a print of the film from a German secret agent through the agency of his "inamorata," fair but approachable... Captain Varges bought a lot of wine and displayed gold money.

"One day in May, 1920, the diplomatic pouch received at the British consulate in New York, included a considerable package under seal of Captain Ariel Varges, addressed to Edgar B. Hatrick, general manager of the International Newsreel Corporation, 228 William Street, New York. The Cruise of the Moewe had arrived."

The Hearst organization released the film for display throughout the country as a journalistic scoop. By that time the war was over.

A revealing fact about Hearst's character is related in connection with this film by Silas Bent.[25] "At an editorial conference once, for instance, it was mentioned that the pictures of the German raider Moewe had been obtained for Hearst by bribing a minor official. Hearst repressed a smile. 'Don't you know,' he said, 'that you must never tell me things like that?'"

"But at another conference," Bent continues, "when a business manager was urging, on the ground that honesty was the best policy, a truth-in-advertising campaign, Hearst said, dryly, 'I have observed that principles are the impediments of small men.'"

Hearst's enterprises are so varied and some of them so disguised that even the British government did not realize he owned one of the biggest periodicals in England. Clarence W. Barron, late editor of *The Wall Street Journal*, says in his memoirs[26] that F. W. Kellogg, organizer of Kellogg Newspapers, Inc., told him that "Hearst got £30,000 from *Nash's Magazine* in London during the war most unexpectedly.[27] The Nash manager had raised the price from sixpence to a shilling. It became the largest magazine in Europe ... The English government never stopped it. Probably never knew that the money came to Hearst."

---
[24] *Ibid.*
[25] *Strange Bedfellows*, by Silas Bent, Liveright Pub. Co., New York, 1928.
[26] *They Told Barron.*
[27] Hearst had bought the publication before the war and still owns it.

IX

Does Hearst understand the objective significance of his own rôle? Has he merely been an improviser, without any sense of social responsibility, as romantic journalists have supposed, taking what each day brings and drifting capriciously? Or has he been the realistic master of his affairs?

Clarence W. Barron says that Hearst said to George Whelan, the president of the United Cigar Stores Company, who was close to Hearst in a number of real estate deals:[1] "You know I believe in property, and you know where I stand on personal fortunes, but isn't it better that I should represent in this country the dissatisfied, than have somebody else do it, who might not have the same property relations that I may have?"

The end of the war found Hearst in a strong position in New York. Clarence J. Shearn, his attorney, had been placed on the New York Supreme Court bench in 1916. Tammany elected Hylan New York's Mayor in 1917. The agreement between Hearst and Tammany stipulated that Tammany was to have full control of Hylan's patronage while Hearst dictated city policies. A Grand Jury even went so far as to investigate Hearst's influence upon Hylan, but the move came to nothing when the District Attorney's office backed water.

Hearst's liaison officer with Hylan was Victor Watson, later managing editor of the Chicago *Herald-Examiner*, but then a Hearst "trouble-shooter." Hearst himself has said the organization could "stand only one Watson." Watson laid the trap that caught James Gordon Bennett in 1906; Watson handled the case of the forged Mexican documents in 1928. The Hearst papers from time to time printed letters from Hylan on the traction situation, taxes and real estate, written by Watson. Many of the speeches and statements made by the Mayor were written by Watson.

[1] *They Told Barron.*

IMPERIAL HEARST

Mayor Hylan was frequently in the company of Hearst himself. He went to Florida in the winter to confer with Hearst, and while there declared: "I want the people to know Mr. Hearst as I know him. I had an entirely different impression of him until I knew him. We were on the beach yesterday and a jellyfish had closed about a little toad. Mr. Hearst flicked it away with the end of his cane and said: 'Why let the poor little thing suffer?' I think that typifies what I like in Hearst."

As soon as Hylan was installed in office, Hearst and Brisbane commenced their extensive New York City real estate operations. The first property Hearst owned in New York was the mansion of former President Arthur on Lexington Avenue at Twenty-eighth Street. In 1912 he bought the Clarendon, a big apartment building on Riverside Drive at Eighty-sixth Street, and began a long and costly litigation with the New York Central Railroad to have it remove trains from along the river front. Years later the railroad tracks were covered.

The Hearst real estate façade extended mainly along Fifty-seventh Street. There were definite reasons why this thoroughfare and regions adjacent to it were chosen by Hearst, who has come to be viewed, erroneously, as an unsuccessful real estate speculator. In 1898 the plan was first broached for a Fifty-seventh Street bridge over the Hudson River, connecting Manhattan with New Jersey. When and if such a bridge is built, Fifty-seventh Street will constitute a great highway between New Jersey and Long Island across the middle of Manhattan, for at the eastern end it leads into the Queensborough Bridge over the East River. The War Department still opposes the project.

Ever since their owner became a big real estate operator the Hearst papers approve any municipal expenditures, however large, which improve real estate values in the midtown section. The Thirty-eighth Street Tunnel to New Jersey is being completed and the Thirty-eighth Street Tunnel to Long Island is about to be bored. These tunnels greatly enhance the value of Hearst's real estate along Forty-second Street and the East River and are blatantly cheered by the Hearst press.

The first center of the Hearst real estate domain in New York was Columbus Circle, at Fifty-ninth Street and Broadway. From here the holdings were extended along Fifty-seventh and Fifty-ninth Streets to the east, and then southward down the East River.

Most of this expansion took place under Hylan, but some during the subsequent administration of James J. Walker, whose closest adviser was Paul Block. During both régimes Hearst was successful in securing minimum tax assessments and favorable zoning rulings. The question of transportation was, however, crucial.

Plans for the city-owned Independent subway system were drawn during Hylan's régime. A casual study of the present Independent system shows that Hearst's special interests were considered. Hearst was mistaken when he assumed the Times Square section would gradually move up around Columbus Circle, which he planned to have renamed Hearst Plaza. Columbus Circle, with Central Park abutting on one of its corners, contributing no increase to its population, has remained a relatively quiet section. Nevertheless, the Hylan-planned subway system placed a gigantic express station under Columbus Circle, at great expense. It is little used. Express stops on the preëxisting West Side Subway line were at Forty-second and at Seventy-second Streets, with only local stops at the intervening quiet points. Hearst saw to it that the new subway line had express stops at Forty-second Street, at Fifty-ninth Street—and next at One Hundred Twenty-fifth Street!

After the passing of Hylan and Walker (supported by Hearst in 1925 after Hylan was beaten in the primaries), Hearst continued to boost the value of his properties by taking a direct hand in contiguous civic improvements. When the great Tri-Borough Bridge was projected as a means of linking Manhattan, Queens and the Bronx, the Hearst agents, advised in advance of the plans, were reported to have taken options on desirable sites near the approaches. The city was unable to finance the project, and the Roosevelt Administration had to come to the rescue with public works funds. But the funds were withheld owing to a local political dispute. The Hearst papers thereupon began a denunciation of Secretary of the

IMPERIAL HEARST

Interior Harold Ickes, who had charge of Federal public works, and did not stop until the original schedule was resumed.[2]

As soon as Hearst heard of plans for an East River Drive between Fourteenth Street and downtown Manhattan, his agents swung into action and took options on various properties nearby. The Hearst papers then began beating the drum. The beginning of work was reflected in the editorial satisfaction of the Hearst newspapers in New York.

Both the Hylan and Walker Administrations were among the most corrupt in the annals of New York, and compare with the Ruef-Schmitz-Hearst Administration of San Francisco from 1901 to 1907, and the Thompson-Hearst Administration of Chicago from 1915 to 1923 and from 1927 to 1931.

It is not denied that these municipal projects represent improvement and progress. Hearst is always for improvement—when he can make a profit.

Although Hearst achieved his heart's desire in controlling the policies of New York City, he was partially rebuffed in his statewide ambitions. He appeared again toward the end of 1918 as a Democratic aspirant for the Governorship. Hearst petitions were circulated at great expense, but were withdrawn at the last minute because the convention had passed a resolution repudiating "every truckler with our country's enemies who strives or has striven to extenuate or excuse such crimes against humanity as the rape of Belgium, the sinking of the *Lusitania* and the German policy of assassination by submarines."

Al Smith was nominated, supported by Hearst, and elected. Friction developed. Hearst did not know it, but he was losing his grip on the New York State political machine. In the previous administrations of Governors Charles S. Whitman and William Sulzer, Hearst had exercised enormous influence in Albany. He maintained close and friendly relations with Whitman, and Sulzer

---

[2] See New York *Journal* editorials, January 7, 12, 16, 23, *et seq.*, through February and March, 1933.

was a Hearst puppet, with Hearst financing his campaigns and receiving appropriately valuable favors.

Smith was President of the Board of Aldermen before he was elected Governor and he sat on the Board of Estimate and Apportionment. Here he could scrutinize the Hearst-Hylan maneuvers without hindrance. "Smith, during his contact with Hylan on the Board of Estimate, made up his mind quite firmly that Hylan was entirely lacking in intelligence," Norman Hapgood observed in his biography of Smith.[3]

The Hearst-Smith feud, according to Hapgood, "had its origin far back in the history of the Fourth Ward. In its earlier stages it had nothing to do primarily with either Smith or Hearst, but was a conflict for local power between Tom Foley and some of Hearst's employees. After Smith's election, in 1918 with a certain amount of support from the Hearst papers, Mr. Hearst felt that he had a right to ask for recognition, to the extent of having either himself or his wife on the State committee to receive the returning soldiers. This desire was the stronger in that Hearst's efforts to keep us out of the war had greatly increased the amount of hostility to him. Smith felt he could not make the appointment on account of the feeling of many who would have to be on the committee."

Rebuffed, Hearst organized a special welcoming committee, with tugboats, bands and appropriate decorations.

There were other clashes behind the scenes. Clarence J. Shearn planned to resign from the New York Supreme Court and a Hearst emissary asked Governor Smith if he would appoint a Hearst-chosen man to replace Shearn. Smith refused, and when Shearn resigned Hearst lost control of this strategic post. Hylan made Shearn counsel for the Transit Commission. When Shearn eventually left this post he was replaced by Samuel Untermyer, Hearst's counsel in the Associated Press litigation.

Hearst made other futile attempts to obtain favors from Governor Smith. At last he ordered the big editorial guns unlimbered. Notice was privately passed to Smith that a certain day was the "zero

[3] *Up from the City Streets: Alfred E. Smith,* by Norman Hapgood and Henry Moskowitz, Harcourt, Brace & Co., New York, 1927.

hour" to accede to Hearst's demands. A salvo of silence came from the Executive Mansion in Albany. The Hearst papers opened with a broadside. It was charged that Smith had spoken confidentially on taxes to a meeting of trust magnates at the Metropolitan Club, an organization of plutocrats founded by J. Pierpont Morgan. The Hearst papers did not point out that Edward Hardy Clark, Hearst's financial adviser, was a member of this club. Other oblique assaults were made on Governor Smith.

Then the Hearst papers charged that the New York milk supply was contaminated and that Governor Smith was responsible. Hearst cartoons showed emaciated children dying for lack of clean milk, captioned:

"Mr. Governor, What Are You Going to Do About It?"

The *Journal* and the *American* accused Governor Smith of being in league with the "milk barons," who were alleged to be conspiring to starve the children of the poor. The fact is the Governor had no power or direct control and could not be held responsible. The milk situation had been intolerable under both Governors Sulzer and Whitman, but Hearst had said nothing about it then.

As the campaign against Smith continued, copies of the Hearst newspapers were mailed to the Governor's mother, an aged woman who was ill in her old home on the East Side. She was horrified by what she saw and, according to the later testimony of Governor Smith himself,[4] she raved on her death bed over the charges.

It is a curious coincidence that whenever the Hearst newspapers make accusations against any individual, relatives and friends mysteriously receive free copies in the mails.

Back in 1896 Hearst published the fact that, thirty-three years before, Congressman Grove L. Johnson, father of the present Senator Hiram Johnson and a former Hearst attorney then at odds with him, had been indicted for embezzlement in Syracuse, N. Y., although the charges were dropped. In subsequent years Johnson's conduct had been irreproachable. Johnson, speaking in the House of Representatives of the United States on January 12, 1897, declared that "while my wife lay sick upon her bed during the campaign,

[4] *Ibid.*

from which sickness the doctors said she might not perhaps recover, this infamous wretch sent copies of his paper to my wife; and in order that she might be given the agony of reading this abuse of her husband, he cut out the editorials and the caricatures from his paper, put them in envelopes, sealed them, and sent them to her as correspondence, until the doctor directed my daughter never to give my wife a letter until they had first read it themselves to know what was in it."

Smith challenged Hearst to a public debate in Carnegie Hall on the milk situation, and appeared before a packed auditorium, but Hearst did not appear. Smith characterized Hearst as a "man as low and as mean as I can picture him," who has "not got one drop of good clean pure red blood in his body" and who is "a pestilence that walks in the dark." Applause and cheers filled Carnegie Hall.

Hearst later complained that Smith had made an "indelicate" and "personal" attack.

Smith was defeated for reëlection in 1920. According to Hearst, Al Smith came "hat in hand" to the Riverside Drive apartment to ask his support. There *was* a conversation, at any rate, and Hearst came out for Smith. Nathan L. Miller, Republican, was elected for the next two-year term.

Smith was again a candidate for the nomination in 1922, with Hearst as his Democratic opponent. Hearst made a deal with Boss Murphy in which Murphy assured Hearst of support for the Governorship. It was Murphy's plan to kick Al Smith upstairs to a Senatorship, in Villard's phrase, and to give Hearst the support of Tammany for the Governorship a second time.

Boss John H. McCooey of Brooklyn came to Al Smith's smoke-filled hotel room in Syracuse during the convention and informed him of Murphy's plan.

"Nothing doing," Smith replied. "Say, do you think I haven't any self-respect? You can tell Murphy I won't run with Hearst on the ticket, and that goes."

Murphy, too, was stubborn, and a stampede was beginning for Hearst on the convention floor. When reporters apprised Smith of the situation he replied enigmatically: "They don't vote until tomorrow night."

When Hearst learned of this remark he became fearful of a repetition of the Carnegie Hall speech on the convention floor. He sought out Murphy and offered to take the United States Senatorship in order to keep Smith appeased. Several Tammany emissaries, seeking party harmony, came to Smith and urged him to compromise.

His reply to all was simply, "Nothing doing, they don't vote until tomorrow night."

Boss Foley pushed his head into the hotel-room door and uttered one word, "Stick!"

Smith nodded.

To another emissary Smith said bitterly, "My mother was delirious in her illness in 1919. As she raved she said, 'My boy did not do it. He was a poor boy. He loves children. He would not feed them poison milk. He did not do it.' You can go back and tell those who sent you that no matter what happened, and no matter how long I live, you will never find my name on the ticket with that ——"[5]

Hearst capitulated. He withdrew his candidacy and timidly suggested the name of Dr. Royal S. Copeland for United States Senator. Murphy snatched at the peace offering and told Smith it was Copeland or nothing. Murphy did not think Smith could win without the support of the Hearst papers. There were now five in New York State alone.

"All right," Smith growled. As a result, Dr. Royal S. Copeland sits in the United States Senate.

In 1924 Hearst collaborated with William Gibbs McAdoo at the Democratic National Convention in New York in stopping the Smith Presidential boom. After a deadlock developed between McAdoo and Smith, John W. Davis, the leading counsel for J. P. Morgan & Co., was nominated. Smith, despite the continuing Hearst opposition, won the Democratic Presidential nomination in 1928, however, and placed Franklin D. Roosevelt in office as Governor of New York.

In 1926 Hearst supported the reactionary Republican Ogden L.

[5] *Ibid.*

Mills for the Governorship. There was a logical interlocking of economic interests here, for Mills, next to Hearst, is the largest stockholder of the Cerro de Pasco Copper Company. Mills was ignominiously defeated by Smith.

In California Senator Hiram Johnson, head of the Republican machine, was endorsed by Hearst in his campaign for reëlection in 1926. The New York *Times* on September 12, 1926, published an analysis showing that Hearst would control the political apparatus of California through Johnson.

The San Francisco law firm of Sullivan, Johnson, Barry and Roache is the switchboard of Hearst's control in California. This firm is closely allied with the political machines and the leading California banks and bankers, including Herbert Fleishacker and Amadeo P. Giannini. The senior partner is Matt J. Sullivan, former Chief Justice of the Supreme Court of California and subsequently adviser to the late James Rolph, Mayor of San Francisco and Governor of California. Sullivan composed Rolph's report which rejected Tom Mooney's plea for a pardon. Theodore Roache, the junior partner of the firm, was Director of the State Motor Vehicle Department under Rolph, the man who shocked the world by approving the San Jose lynchings of 1933. Roache is considered in San Francisco to be the intelligence behind Mayor Rossi's régime.

Although Hearst and Johnson had a temporary falling out in 1934, there is no reason to suppose that the Hearst-Johnson dictatorship over unhappy California is terminated. All the evidence indicates that Hearst's influence, especially since the San Francisco general strike of 1934, has been increasing. Senator McAdoo's election gave Hearst a stranglehold on the state.

Hearst became doubly active in the national political arena after the war. He correctly assumed that only the Republicans had a chance to win the Presidential election of 1920. Hence he took little interest in the Democratic candidate, and confined himself to serving notice on James M. Cox, the Democratic nominee, that the American people would not stand for the League of Nations or "entangle-

IMPERIAL HEARST

ment" in European affairs. Cox and other Democrats were properly impressed.

The Hearst papers boomed Hiram Johnson for the Republican nomination. Hearst closely followed developments at the Republican convention in Chicago where General Leonard Wood, Governor Frank O. Lowden and a number of others, including Johnson, were candidates. All ran afoul of the delegates controlled by the Doheny-Sinclair oil faction. After fruitless jockeying, Warren G. Harding of Ohio was agreed upon as the "compromise" most acceptable to the oil clique, whose tools later became known as the "Ohio Gang."

Johnson was asked in his hotel room to accept the Vice-Presidential nomination but refused it as beneath his dignity, thereby losing the chance to become President. The nondescript Calvin Coolidge of Massachusetts agreed to run and the record shows that Coolidge did everything for Hearst that Johnson could have done.

The Hearst papers warned Harding against "meddling" in European affairs, the League of Nations or the World Court. Until the day of his early death Harding did or said nothing of which Hearst disapproved.

Hearst was very close to the Doheny-Sinclair gang responsible for the theft of the American Navy's Teapot Dome oil supply. An entry in Barron's memoirs, written after having had lunch at the Boston Algonquin Club with Frederick C. Dumaine, Hearst's Boston manager, reads:

"Mr. Hearst wants to support Coolidge if he can. He was in favor of Mellon's tax bill. There never would have been any oil scandal in Washington if Doheny had kept still. Mr. Hearst looked over certain private papers of citizens and then sent word to [Senator] La Follette to hold off on the oil investigation as they would never get anywhere going into private records of certain people. And you may remember the oil investigation was held up for two or three days. It was to proceed on Monday, but was postponed from day to day and the private records were never shown. There was nothing in them and Mr. Hearst stopped it by influence with La Follette just at that time."[6]

[6] Entry of June 17, 1924.

Barron was the best posted man in Wall Street and, as publisher of *The Wall Street Journal,* was not one to whom false information could lightly be given. The authenticity of the material in his published memoirs has never been challenged.

There is important supporting confirmation of Hearst's important rôle in the Teapot Dome affair from Norman Hapgood. Hapgood, in *The Changing Years,* tells how he became a Hearst employee. From 1912 on Hearst had been after him to work for him, and he had refused, Hapgood declared. "In view of the sharpness of some of my attacks on him his consideration for my attitude was remarkable."

It was not at all remarkable. Hapgood had built up a reputation for honesty and Hearst wanted to purchase that reputation.

After the war Hapgood became editor of *Hearst's International Magazine,* with the understanding that he was to have a free hand. Hapgood tells in his memoirs that Hearst never interfered with what he wanted to publish, and points out that when Hearst advocated the post-war sales tax, which Wall Street wanted to saddle on the American people, Hapgood was allowed to campaign against it.

Unfortunately, Hapgood contradicts himself by telling how Hearst prevented the *International Magazine* from disclosing the Teapot Dome scandal. "It was through him[7] also that the same magazine [*International*] published indications of the crookedness of Secretary [Albert B.] Fall many months before the papers took it up; we were kept from a world-wide sensation only by the unfortunate accident that Mr. Hearst knew Secretary Fall, liked him, and believed in him. . . ."

This is not the old Hapgood writing. Did the heavy advertising budgets of the Sinclair and Doheny companies influence Hearst? Or was it only because Fall had been a member of the Hearst-Thompson foreign mining concession group and, as a Mexican landowner, had joined in earlier campaigns for military intervention below the Rio Grande?

H. W. Ballard, California oil man, testified before the Senate

[7] Glavis, government investigator who had precipitated the Ballinger scandal in the Taft administration and had done much work for Hapgood in the past. Glavis is now with the Department of the Interior.

Committee (in the Teapot Dome case) that a Presidential nominee suitable to the oil interests was being sought at the Chicago Republican convention in 1920, and named Hearst, Doheny, and Harry Chandler, publisher of the Los Angeles *Times,* as being aware of the importance of the Teapot Dome leases *at the Chicago convention*

The committee sent Hearst a telegram, addressed to the Ritz Towers, in New York, and signed by Senator Robert N. Stanfield, asking him to explain Ballard's testimony.

Hearst's telegraphed reply, dated April 20, 1924, and part of the record of the investigation by the Senate Public Lands Committee[8] into the Teapot Dome situation, was:

"I appreciate fully the duty of every citizen to contribute whatever he can to the remedying of the conditions revealed by this oil investigation, and it is a matter of real regret to me that I have absolutely no information to offer your committee. I think you are justified in your 'grave doubts as to the responsibility of Mr. Ballard as a witness.' If I had ever possessed any knowledge of any such oil scandal as Mr. Ballard says was in circulation at the Chicago convention, I would, as a newspaper man, both as a matter of duty and as a matter of public interest, have printed the facts and scooped both Mr. Chandler and him. I know that as a competent and conscientious newspaper man if he had been aware of any such conditions he would have printed the facts and scooped me. I really think that Mr. Ballard's assertion that this Teapot Dome scandal was a matter of general knowledge at the Republican convention in Chicago and that every schoolboy in Texas knows of it, or has known of it all along, is supremely silly. If your committee were to give any credence to such a nonsensical statement as that, you would be summoning before the committee every schoolboy in Texas and every member of that Republican committee. It is unfortunate that a man giving such irresponsible testimony can not be disciplined in some way for wasting the valuable time of your committee in this important investigation."

The committee did not ask Hearst to appear.

[8] U. S.: Public Lands Committee (Senate) Leases upon Public Lands: **Hearings,** Sixty-seventh Congress, Second Session, 1923-24.

Hearst publicly defended Attorney General Harry M. Daugherty from the charges made against him, and the Hearst papers denounced all who demanded during February and March, 1924, that Daugherty resign.

Hearst permitted the *International Magazine* to support La Follette for President on the Progressive ticket in 1924 (the Hearst chain of newspapers supported Coolidge). Hapgood, of course, thought the choice lay with him, whereas Hearst had very close connections with the "progressive" La Follette,[9] who, after all, was a practical Wisconsin politician before he was anything else, and Hearst was an important publisher in Milwaukee, Wisconsin's largest city.

Hearst used Hapgood to gain friends in other quarters as well. Brisbane suggested that Hapgood lead the campaign for freeing the Socialist Eugene V. Debs from Atlanta by publishing interviews with Debs and sympathetic stories about him. Since 1914 Hearst has been on friendly and even intimate terms with the Socialist "Old Guard" leaders. Hearst's "contact man" with the Socialists is Arthur Brisbane, son of the old Socialist, Albert Brisbane. In 1917, when Hearst was backing Hylan, Brisbane telegraphed to him as follows:[10]

"THERE IS ACTUAL POSSIBILITY OF HILLQUIT'S ELECTION IN FOUR-CORNERED FIGHT [Hillquit was a Socialist, and after the war became a member of the conservative "Old Guard" faction]. CONDITIONS OUGHT TO DISTURB THE CORPORATIONS WORKING FOR MITCHEL. THEY WILL SWEAT AND PAY TAXES ON THEIR PERSONAL PROPERTY IF HILLQUIT IS ELECTED. SHALL I WRITE EDITORIAL WARNING CORPORATIONS THAT THEIR EFFORT TO GET EVERYTHING FROM MITCHEL MAY COST THEM DEAR THROUGH HILLQUIT'S VICTORY? IF THEY UNDERSTOOD SITUATION AND DANGER THEY WOULD DROP MITCHEL AND VOTE FOR HYLAN. EDITORIAL WOULD DESCRIBE HILLQUIT'S ABILITY AND SINCERITY. REMARKABLY ABLE LAWYER. ROSENWALD, WHO ASKS ME INTRODUCE HIM TO HILLQUIT, SAYS LATTER ONE OF ABLEST MEN IN COUNTRY. CAN WRITE EDITORIAL IN SUCH WAY AS TO TRANSFER MANY VOTES FROM MITCHEL TO HILLQUIT. PLEASE REPLY."

[10] *W. R. Hearst*, by John K. Winkler.
* *They Told Barron.*

Hearst telegraphed to Carvalho:[11]

"BRISBANE WANTS TO WRITE EDITORIAL PRAISING HILLQUIT. BRISBANE THINKS HILLQUIT MAY BE ELECTED. OF COURSE HILLQUIT WILL NOT BE ELECTED ALTHOUGH GOVERNMENT'S POLICY WILL MAKE SOCIALISTS VERY STRONG. EDITORIAL OF KIND BRISBANE SUGGESTS WOULD BE CONSTRUED AS DISLOYALTY TO HYLAN AND UPSET ALL OUR PLANS. PLEASE PREVENT IT."

When the *International Magazine* was merged with the *Cosmopolitan* in 1925, Hapgood was dropped. He had served his purpose.

Hapgood, searching for something good to say of Hearst, remarks in his memoirs: "It must be remembered that while he no longer fights trusts as trusts, it is still characteristic of him that he made a better showing than any other publisher against the most important recent trust evil, the control of education in schools and colleges by the power lobby."[12]

But Hearst was part and parcel of the power lobby.

Shortly after the war he began campaigning for government "regulation" of the public utilities. These campaigns continued up to 1935, when, after Congress passed the Public Utilities Holding Company Act, he vigorously defended one of the most condemned companies and one of the most condemned men in the industry— the Associated Gas and Electric Company and Howard Hopson. Hopson and Hearst exchanged a series of telegrams, Senate investigators showed,[13] wherein Hopson demanded assistance in fighting against "government interference." Hearst complied by writing and printing a long editorial which was almost identical with Hopson's telegram.

Superficially, it would appear that until 1934 the Hearst papers conducted a sincere campaign to secure Federal regulation of the public utilities. This campaign fooled many Hearst newspaper men and others. Behind the scenes of the public utilities question there has been, for years, a bitter fight among the big companies for

[11] *Ibid.*
[12] *The Changing Years,* by Norman Hapgood, Farrar & Rinehart, Inc., New York, 1930.
[13] *Investigation of Lobbying Activities:* Special Senate Committee, Seventy-fourth Congress: First Session, 1935.

control of certain properties. Hearst's campaign for government regulation was intended to frighten the biggest, most respectable and most powerful of the public utilities companies, those allied with J. P. Morgan & Co.

The Morgan group consisted of Electric Bond and Share, the United Corporation, the Consolidated Gas Company of New York and the Niagara-Hudson combine, and endeavored to absorb various properties all over the country. It came into conflict with the Cities Service Company of Henry L. Doherty, the Associated Gas and Electric Company of Howard Hopson, and the Insull companies.

The Morgan utility men in Wall Street deplored the methods under which Cities Service, Insull and Associated Gas operated, and there was, truth to tell, much to deplore, for these companies were the very worst offenders in the sale of dubious stocks and bonds to middle-class investors throughout the country. The Morgan group felt they were bringing the industry into disrepute and attracting unpleasant attention to the industry at large, *i.e.*, to their own operations.

As a matter of fact, Hearst's campaign was making it difficult for the Morgan group to expand as rapidly as it wished, and enabled the Cities Service, Insull and Associated Gas companies to expand in directions that the Morgan crowd wanted for itself. This was especially true in upper New York State, where Associated Gas was able to grab many properties while the Niagara-Hudson combine had to comport itself decorously or confront a government investigation, and where Hearst himself was interested in St. Lawrence River Valley power companies.

Hearst had his finger in several public utility pies. It might easily be pointed out that a member of the board of directors of the Pacific Gas and Electric Company was Fred T. Elsey, first vice president and a director of Hearst's Homestake Mining Company. Elsey was also a director of the American Trust Company of San Francisco throughout a period of Hearst's "anti-utilities" campaign. This bank was controlled by the Goldman Sachs Trading Company of New York through subsidiaries. Goldman Sachs was one of the biggest operators in the boom stock market to collapse in 1929, with especially heavy losses to small stockholders in Goldman Sachs, Cities Service, Associated Gas and Insull utilities. Two of Goldman Sachs' biggest operations consisted of the flotation of the Blue Ridge Corporation and the Shenandoah Corporation, investment trusts which acquired several hundred millions of dollars in public utility shares and lost hundreds of millions for small investors. The flotation of both corporations was given tremendous publicity by the Hearst press.

Hearst was also interested in Canadian power and paper properties, notably Canada Power and Paper. Part of the animus he exhibited with respect to the Morgan-controlled section of the industry stemmed from rivalry for water power and other rights in northern New York, southern Canada and northern New England, where Insull also became a big factor.

The public utility interests grouped around Hearst had the least to lose and the most to gain from the campaign in the Hearst newspapers.

The Senate proved close relations between Hopson, of Associated Gas, and Hearst.[14]

In April, 1923, Hearst himself bought control of the Union Public Service Company of Kansas. Phillip Francis, then business manager of the New York *American*, acted as his agent. In the following year the property was sold to the Cities Service Company, part of the consideration involved being Cities Service securities. This was the beginning of the close and amicable relationship between Hearst and Henry L. Doherty, who controls Cities Service.

The Hearst papers continually printed "puffs" about the securities of Cities Service, Insull and Associated Gas and Electric. To list all the "puffs" about securities which have appeared in the Hearst papers —to the ultimate distress of a gullible public—would require a separate book containing nothing else.

Hylan, "Big Bill" Thompson, Senator Copeland, Senator Reed of Missouri, and James Hamilton Lewis of Illinois, all participated in 1922 in a Hearst boom for the Presidency. Hearst repaid both Reed

[14] *Ibid.*

and Copeland in 1924 by supporting their Senatorial election campaigns. Lewis was in temporary eclipse, but eventually returned to the Senate with Hearst's support.

Thompson and Hylan demanded a third party.

The anti-English line was worked for all it was worth by both metropolitan mayors. Thompson had not yet risen to the heights of offering to "bust King George on the snoot" if he came to Chicago, but he had already launched his crusade against "pro-English" textbooks and Hylan joined him from New York. In Chicago the Thompson-controlled Board of Education singled out Superintendent of Schools William McAndrew, English-born and one of America's progressive educators, for assault. The Hearst movement to rewrite American history reached tremendous proportions. The American Historical Association soon became concerned, and denounced Hearst, Thompson, Hylan and all their temporary and permanent allies.

No one realized that the cause of it all was to be found in Peru.

The Hearst Presidential boom of 1924, of course, came to nothing. Hearst made his agreement with Coolidge, and a very satisfactory agreement it was. Hearst has since said on many occasions that Coolidge was one of the greatest Presidents the United States ever had. After Coolidge left office he was lavishly entertained by Hearst at the San Simeon showplace in California.

When Coolidge declined the Presidential candidacy in 1928, Hearst rallied his forces around Andrew W. Mellon, Secretary of the Treasury. Hoover nosed Mellon out of the Presidential nomination at the Republican convention in 1928 and Hearst never forgave him.

Why did Hearst prefer Mellon?[15] In brief, it was this: Mellon as Secretary of the Treasury gave Hearst heavy rebates on the income taxes paid during the years 1918, 1919 and 1920, and made it possible for Hearst to pay the very minimum in income taxes from 1921 to 1928. Hearst was richer by millions because a kind fate had sent

[15] The record of this phase of the Hearst career as far back as 1904, is to be found on pages 284 to 291, Part 2, of the Report of the Select Senate Committee on Investigation of the Internal Revenue Bureau, 3 parts, Senate Report 27, Sixty-ninth Congress, First Session, 1926.

Andrew Mellon of Pittsburgh to Washington. When Mellon left he was succeeded by Ogden L. Mills, another Hearst favorite and business associate.

In its investigation of the Internal Revenue Bureau, the Senate Committee uncovered Hearst's income tax story. The Senate report referred to the Star Publishing Company as taxpayer, and noted initially that the company treated borrowed money as invested capital, thereby establishing, through a bookkeeping device, a means of showing a smaller income return than it actually had. The report was drawn by George G. Box, chief auditor for the committee, of which Senator James G. Couzens, Republican, of Michigan, was chairman.

Hearst paid the Federal government $525,110 in income taxes for the years 1917-19, the report revealed, through the Star Publishing Company, a personal holding device. The Internal Revenue Bureau found that Hearst had underpaid the government by $1,506,325, but, before he could be forced to disgorge, the Republicans had taken office.

The Internal Revenue Bureau under Mellon found that Hearst should have paid the government only $294,339 for the years 1917-19, and refunded $230,771 to him. Combining the cash refund with what he would have had to pay—$1,506,325—under the Internal Revenue Bureau's ruling in the dying days of the Wilson Administration, the Mellon régime was worth to Hearst *at the very outset* $1,737,096. As time went on the cash value of the Mellon régime increased by reason of further tax concessions.

The Couzens Senate report found that Hearst had been allowed $203,964 as a "loss" resulting from the forced liquidation in 1917 of the German Journal Corporation. "This loss," said the Couzens report, "is purely inter-company and therefore not deductible in determining consolidated net income, as the consolidated surplus is not affected by such liquidation." To sustain its point, the Senate committee cited three court decisions. "It was held [by Hearst]," said the Senate report, "that the receipt of the dividend in liquidation represented a loss." The committee forebore to comment on the treatment of a dividend as a loss.

Point two of the Senate report showed how the Star Publishing Company allocated to itself $2,953,772 in "good will" of the subsidiary International Magazine Company and used it to reduce its tax liability. No less than $1,499,982 of this "good will" was acquired from Mrs. William Randolph Hearst in an inter-family transaction.

Item three in the Senate report showed that Hearst claimed, and the Mellon-directed bureau allowed, as paid-in surplus an item of $2,052,683 representing the value of tangible assets of the San Francisco *Examiner*, which was acquired in 1903 by the Examiner Printing Company from Hearst the individual. Hearst had merely shifted the property from one hand to the other.

The balance sheet of the *Examiner* at the time of the transfer showed paid-in surplus of $2,846,471. Among the assets underlying this item, subject to deductions for stock issued to Hearst, was Hearst *himself* valued at $2,295,611 and the Los Angeles *Examiner*, his personal property, valued at $326,450!

Both these items, said the report, "are properly debits of the personal account."

"In order to show a correct statement the debits of the personal account should have been offset against the credits," with the result that the final accounting would show net assets transferred of only $224,409 instead of $2,846,471.

"No contention was made on the part of the taxpayer that Mr. Hearst ever paid into the corporation" this amount, the report indicated. "It is evident that Mr. Hearst withdrew from the business [$2,622,062] but the company subsequently claims these amounts as paid-in surplus. The net assets acquired were actually valued at $224,409, as shown by the balance sheet, which was less than the par value of the stock issued in exchange therefor and therefore there was no paid-in surplus. It is inconceivable that the bureau should allow this item as invested capital in view of the facts," said the Senate report.

Yet the Mellon-directed bureau allowed this "inconceivable" transaction at the expense of the American people.

For the reader not versed in income tax procedure, the following analogy will be helpful: Let us take a man with a net income of

$2,000 a year, on which he should, according to law, pay a tax. A relative (or himself acting in a corporate capacity), purchases a vase for fifty cents. Then this relative (or his other corporate self) "sells" this vase to him for $4,000, for which he gives a promissory note in this amount. Then, before the income tax period ends, let him accidentally break this $4,000 vase. The "loss" can be deducted from the $2,000 income, leaving no taxable income. But the $4,000 note will still be outstanding. This can be liquidated by the issuance of personal stock to the willing note-holder in payment of the "debt." If the average man were to confront the Internal Revenue Bureau with such a transaction involving inflated "assets" he would probably be adjudged insane and made to pay the tax as well. Yet this was precisely the nature of the *Examiner* transaction.

Item four of the Senate report described how the Illinois Publishing and Printing Company leased land in Chicago for ninety-nine years and claimed $400,000 on this lease as invested capital. In short, what it paid in rent was termed "invested capital." However, under certain circumstances, a leasehold may be legally considered invested capital, but not under a system of valuation such as Hearst employed in this connection. The lease took effect in 1910, for which year $10,000 of rent was paid. For the next nineteen years, or until 1929, $25,000 annually was to be paid and $30,000 annually thereafter for seventy-nine years.

Up to 1917 Hearst had paid only $160,000 rent on this land. By the end of 1919 he had paid only $235,000. In short, he had not put $400,000 into it. In computing income taxes in any specific year for which the lease was to be treated as capital, not more than $25,000 should have been allowed as "invested capital."

In 1914, when the Wilson Administration was preparing to place the new Federal income tax law into effect, Hearst transferred this leasehold to the Illinois Publishing and Printing Company, receiving therefor $400,000 of its stock. This was Hearst's own stock, for he owned the Illinois Publishing and Printing Company.

"From all the evidence presented," the Couzens report said, "it appears that the acquisition of the lease by Mr. Hearst was an open transaction and that all facts then known would have been taken into consideration by the lessor. If the lease had been worth more than the stipulated annual rental, it is only reasonable to assume that such additional value would have been added to the rental charges . . . It is contended that the value of the leasehold was not established and that the bureau should not have allowed any value for the leasehold to be included in invested capital."

Let us translate this transaction into terms of a man who rents a store for $1,000 annually on a ten-year lease. The small businessman, if allowed to do as Hearst did, would call this lease invested capital of $10,000, even though he had not yet actually paid this amount in rent. The more invested capital he could show, the smaller would his income return be. He might be able to show a bookkeeping loss instead of his actual profit of, let us say, $4,000 net annually. But on this profit he would not need to pay any income tax. Needless to say, the Internal Revenue Bureau under Mellon stood for no nonsense of this kind from small storekeepers. Rent is not capital investment for the small taxpayer nor can the small taxpayer compound future rent as present capital.

Item five of the report showed that up to 1918 Hearst had lent to his corporations $6,201,556. "These amounts appear on the books as accounts payable to Mr. Hearst . . . In 1918 the taxpayer took up the matter of including this indebtedness in invested capital" although "there was no fixed time for payment of the accounts, they did not bear interest, and no written evidence of the indebtedness was presented to the bureau."

The Internal Revenue Bureau under the Wilson Administration refused to consider this vague item a capital asset, and insisted that it be treated as a liability. This reduced the amount of capital Hearst could claim in computing earnings, and necessarily made earnings larger.

Hearst protested, however, and there was a conference with Internal Revenue officials on November 18, 1921, after the Harding Administration had been installed. An Internal Revenue letter to Hearst dated August 11, 1922, allowed his claim of this item as invested capital.

The Couzens committee brought forward a quotation from the

brief which Hearst attorneys had filed at the time of the first protest, admitting that this money was "never considered as paid-in surplus." The Couzens committee cited much evidence from the Hearst books, dating back to December 31, 1903, showing that the advances had always, prior to the enactment of the Federal income tax law, been considered as liabilities rather than as assets. Hearst claimed in a later letter to the Internal Revenue Bureau that he had never authorized such entries.

"The allowance by the bureau of this borrowed money to be included in invested capital is directly contrary to the provisions of both the revenue acts above mentioned," said the Couzens report in conclusion.

C. B. Allen, Assistant Deputy Commissioner of Internal Revenue under Mellon, in reply to these findings of the Senate Committee, said:

"After careful consideration of all the items set out by the Senate committee as erroneous in principle or otherwise, I am forced to the conclusion that the closing of the case by the Income Tax Unit was proper and in accord with the law and regulations."

Hearst never had to pay.

When the estate of Hearst's mother, who died in 1919, was probated, it was disclosed that she had lent the New York *American* $1,000,000, for which she received interest-bearing notes. These notes she assigned to her son "for no apparent consideration," as the statement of Senator Couzens indicated. This transaction was an apparent loan but actually a gift constituting an anticipated inheritance on which no tax was paid.

Charles Evans Hughes, in 1906, established conclusively that one of Hearst's major preoccupations was the avoidance of tax payments. The anti-tax motif became stronger as Hearst grew older and his income increased. Tax rebates and concessions are among the political stakes for which he has constantly fought.

On December 1, 1923, Hearst publicly endorsed the plan of Secretary Mellon to reduce taxes in the high income brackets, a measure which appreciably slowed down the partial liquidation of the national debt and left the national finances less able to bear the inroads of the depression that began in 1929. The New York *Times* of May 4, 1933, reported that Hearst had demanded further tax reductions on some of his realty enterprises from New York City. The Hearst Hotels Corporation claimed it had been over-assessed by $240,000 on a valuation of $4,300,000 for the Ritz Towers, at Park Avenue and Fifty-seventh Street, and over-assessed $490,000 on a valuation of $3,700,000 for the Hotel Warwick in West Fifty-fourth Street. At the same time the International Magazine Company claimed it had been over-assessed by $700,000 on a valuation of $3,400,000 set on the block front from 951 to 959 Eighth Avenue and the W. A. R. Realty Corporation, owner of the Ziegfeld Theater, claimed it had been over-assessed $200,000 on a valuation of $1,300,000.

The story is monotonously the same in all cities where Hearst has property. When Hearst turned against the administration of Franklin D. Roosevelt in 1934, the Hearst papers immediately began decrying the "high" taxes imposed by Roosevelt, and claimed that a "soak-the-rich" program had been adopted. When this did not evoke approval from the general public, the Hearst papers called it a "soak-the-thrifty" movement. Still the public was unresponsive. The Hearst papers then further modified their characterization of the tax program by calling it a "soak-the-successful" plan. There are, obviously, more people who consider themselves successful in one way or another.

The New York *Times* of September 19, 1935, carried this dispatch from Washington: "William Randolph Hearst, newspaper publisher, petitioned the Board of Tax Appeals today for the redetermination of income tax deficiency claims of $508,466 for 1929 and $32,496 for 1930. The Bureau of Internal Revenue, the petition said, made twelve errors in computing the alleged deficiency. In one instance, the petition recited that receipts of stock of Homestake Mining Company and the Cerro de Pasco Copper Corporation from Hearst Estate, Inc., was erroneously found to constitute taxable income. The petitioner held the stock was received in exchange for stock of Hearst Estate, Inc. The petitioner further charged error in the assessment of taxable income for the free use of residential property on the San Simeon, Calif., ranch of the Piedmont Land and Cattle Company."

In November, 1935, Hearst dramatically announced that he was closing his California estates because of high taxes. He came East, vowing never to return unless his taxes were reduced and dropped a few pointed remarks about the desirability of Florida as a residence for rich tax-evaders. He soon returned to California, having widely publicized his thesis.

Hearst finally came out in opposition to all income taxes, preferring the sales taxes which he had already helped foist on the American people in twenty-four states and many cities.

Hearst reluctantly supported Hoover in 1928. A typically scurrilous campaign in the Hearst papers, by cartoon and verbal innuendo, made Al Smith appear as a boozer and tenderloin tough.

Hearst never liked Hoover, however, and delighted to harass him while he was Secretary of Commerce. Hearst's distrust of Hoover began because, as a mining engineer, he had been employed by British trusts which, at times, came into competition with Hearst's foreign mining interests. Hearst also disliked Hoover because he had been a functionary of the Wilson Administration as the United States Food Administrator, in which capacity he worked in post-war Europe in close collaboration with Allied commissions that were saddling the terms of peace upon Germany.

As Secretary of Commerce, Hoover had to bear much from the Hearst papers, which never permitted themselves to be gulled by the Hoover myth of the great engineer and humanitarian. In April, 1924, the Hearst papers charged that Secretary Hoover had turned the government fisheries in Alaska over to a friend. Hoover hotly denied it.

The Hoover Administration was one disappointment after another to Hearst.

By 1931 Hearst was calling upon Hoover for various measures that would aid his enterprises. He demanded a public works program of five billion dollars for the aid of industry, and had Merryle Stanley Rukeyser, one of his financial writers, convoke a meeting of compliant university economists who, miraculously, came to the conclusion that a five-billion-dollar works program was just what was needed. When Hoover declared the moratorium on the Allied indebtedness to the United States, Hearst, who wanted this debt paid down to the last farthing, lost all patience, and when the European default on the war debt became complete Hearst held Hoover responsible.

Hearst was sufficiently intelligent to know that this debt could be neither paid nor serviced. It was Hearst's strategy, however, to make it impossible for the former European Allies to reach an amicable working agreement with the United States, and force them to default. The Allied default suited Hearst's pro-German policy, for the prestige of England and France suffered in the popular American mind as soon as the Allies "refused" to pay. Germany, with considerable success, had sought to edge her war enemies out of favor with the American public ever since the war.

Hoover, by his promulgation of the moratorium proposal, seriously interfered with the Hearst-German program. Hearst said the moratorium was "pro-English," and so it was, as far as international political maneuverings were concerned. The moratorium, the first recognition by an American government that there was some economic merit in the contentions of its former Allies, took the edge off the subsequent default.

Hearst, moreover, had a private grudge against France. *The French had deported him in 1930.*

Certain important papers had been stolen from the French Foreign Office in 1928 and the French traced the documents to a Hearst man, Harold Horan, correspondent of the International News Service. Horan was not the principal in the affair, however. It was engineered by Hearst personally, who was then in and about Paris. But Horan was the scapegoat behind whom Hearst hid and Horan was deported in 1929.

The stolen papers concerned an agreement for coöperation of the British and French fleets in European waters. This naval rapprochement was, naturally, anathema to Germany. The British and French plans had nothing whatever to do with the United States, but the British-French agreement was very important to Germany.

The Sûreté Générale was not fooled by the appearance of Horan in the case. Agents of the Sûreté Générale arrested Hearst in Paris in 1930 and escorted him to the frontier. Hearst's humiliation was complete. He tried to bluster it out, saying his arrest was the result of his ardent "Americanism." Upon his return to the United States he was acclaimed by pro-German elements from coast to coast. Hearst made a radio address in which he implied that he had exposed a hideous anti-American plot on the part of the French. He did not link the British collaborators with the "plot," for he had now come to dollars and cents terms with London about Peru.

Toward the end of Hoover's term Hearst called on the Republicans to elect Coolidge and "save the country." Hearst's 1931 choice for the Democratic Presidential nominee was John N. Garner of Texas, Speaker of the House of Representatives. Garner's boom was begun by the Hearst papers in December, 1931, and continued until the Democratic convention in Chicago in the summer of 1932. Behind Garner the whole Hearst phalanx of the Democratic Party rallied—with Senator William Gibbs McAdoo of California as the whip. At the 1924 Democratic national convention, when Hearst and McAdoo joined forces to stop Smith, McAdoo's political manager had been Daniel C. Roper of North Carolina, who was to become Secretary of Commerce in the Roosevelt Administration. Roper joined with Hearst and McAdoo behind Garner in 1932 and enlisted other forces, all of them the most reactionary in the whole Democratic Party.

Eric P. Swenson, head of the Texas Gulf Sulphur Company and chairman of the board of the National City Bank before Charles E. Mitchell, was familiar with Garner's career in Texas, where Garner was a small town banker. Swenson acquainted various financial associates in New York, among them Hearst, with the virtues of Garner as Presidential material. An active section of the National City Bank crowd was strong for Garner before the Democratic convention opened, and Hearst, whose general counsel the following year became a director of that bank, was the strongest pro-Garner man before the public. The Roper-McAdoo-Hearst clique quickly rallied a considerable force, and entered the Chicago convention with the ninety votes of Texas and California pledged to Garner. The Illinois delegation was also pledged to go with California.

Franklin D. Roosevelt and his former friend, Alfred E. Smith, were opposed to each other at the convention. As the ballots were taken, with Roosevelt a favorite, due to the excellent preparatory work of James Farley, Roosevelt's manager and later Postmaster General, it became doubtful whether Roosevelt could capture the nomination in the face of Smith's opposition, especially as the McAdoo-Hearst bloc persisted in voting for Garner. There was even talk that Garner might be brought from behind as a compromise candidate.

Hearst had long been waiting for a chance to humble Smith decisively, and the chance had arrived, for Smith's whole avowed purpose in the convention was to "stop Roosevelt," the pupil who had dared put himself above the master. Arrangements were quietly made behind the scenes to throw the ninety Garner votes to Roosevelt. The *pourparlers* were carried out by Messrs. Farley and Roper. As soon as word of these conferences got out, Smith telephoned Garner on long distance to keep the Garner bloc from going to Roosevelt.

As McAdoo dramatically announced from the floor that the ninety California-Texas votes were being switched to the Roosevelt column, the stampede to get on the band-wagon began.

The nature of the Hearst-Roosevelt rapprochement was not entirely clear in the early days of the "New Deal." Numerous strategic appointments fell to the Hearst-McAdoo faction. Garner, of course, had secured the Vice-Presidency, a post Hiram Johnson had scorned in 1920.

The contact between Hearst and Garner in Washington has been James T. Williams, Jr., political writer for the Hearst papers, and John A. Kennedy, Hearst Washington lobbyist. Daniel C. Roper, as Secretary of Commerce, has been an aid and comfort to some of the most reactionary business interests in the nation. For his Commissioner of Air Commerce, Roper chose Eugene L. Vidal, of South Dakota, the state whose politics are virtually dominated by Hearst's Homestake Mining Company. J. F. T. O'Connor, McAdoo's law partner, was appointed Comptroller of the Currency. The job of administrator of the Newspaper Code was given to George Buckley under the title of Deputy Administrator. Buckley stepped out of a vice-presidency of the National City Bank to accept. This post could have been used to agitate against the employment of 500,000 children by the newspaper industry, but under Buckley a code was written which allowed the publishers to employ children. Buckley was later shifted to the post of Deputy Administrator of the Federal Housing Administration, a key position for all real estate interests. There he remained. Buckley was a Hearst executive in Chicago before he went to the National City Bank to take charge of its publicity. Men have shuttled frequently between the Hearst organization and the National City Bank. Lee Olwell, vice-president of the National City Bank, was made publisher of the New York *Journal* in 1932 because the bank was interested in its bonds.

The chairmanship of the Consumers' Advisory Board, after the untimely death of Mary Harriman Rumsey in 1934, was given to Mrs. Emily Newell Blair, associate editor of Hearst's *Good Housekeeping* and since 1933 a member of the Board. How the bedevilled American consumer is represented in official encounters with the manufacturers of food, drugs, clothing and other commodities has been of intense concern to the nation's biggest recipient of advertising—Hearst. Under Mrs. Blair the Consumer's Advisory Board did nothing whatever to give the slightest alarm to manufacturers and purveyors of patent food and medicine products. On the contrary, the Consumers' Advisory Board did not even attempt to stop the manufacturers and advertisers from scuttling the excellent Tugwell Pure Food and Drug Bill.

Mrs. Blair's husband, Harry Blair, of Missouri, was appointed Assistant Attorney General under Homer Cummings. Oddly enough, of all the departments in this office, he has charge of the Division of Lands.

Hearst, among his other extensive interests, owns hundreds of thousands of acres of mining, agricultural and forest lands in the West. Both the National City Bank and the Giannini Banks of California, with which Hearst is tightly interlocked, have millions of dollars outstanding in loans on mineral, forest and agricultural land. Decisions of the Division of Lands of the Attorney General's office have a direct bearing on these vast land holdings. If this is mere coincidence, it is indubitably significant coincidence. Giannini is the largest stockholder in the National City Bank of New York, owning 10 per cent of all its outstanding shares, a proportion equivalent to the Rockefeller's holdings of the Chase National Bank stock.

H. R. Tolley, director of the Giannini Foundation on furlough, was placed in charge of the marketing agreements of the Agricultural Adjustment Administration. The Tolley agreements have been shown to be monopolistic in character.[16] Many of them concern the California fruit and packing industry. Hearst has heavy investments in his own canning factories, fruit orchards and ranches. Most of the large packing and canning enterprises on the Pacific Coast are clients of the Giannini banks.

The Roosevelt monetary policy played into Hearst's hands. Many bankers and industrialists favored currency devaluation, and Hearst was one of them. Long before Roosevelt took office, a large section of the financial and industrial community wanted currency devaluation in order to boost prices and exports and salvage billions of dollars in bond and commodity holdings. As early as 1931 Hearst was intimately connected with these plans, as they began to be agitated for by the Committee for the Nation. The first head of this self-styled Committee for the Nation was Frank A. Vanderlip, former chairman of the National City Bank.

The executive secretary of the Committee for the Nation turned out to be Edward Aloysius Rumely, owner of the Advance-Rumely farm implement company, which had, since 1929, been the subject of official attention in a number of unsavory stock market manipulations. As a former German agent in charge of the New York *Mail*, Rumely had been convicted and sentenced to serve a term in Eastview Penitentiary after the war. He was, as we have seen, closely associated with the Dr. Albert who maintained a German "bureau" in New York City and direct telephonic connections with the offices of Hearst's *Deutsches Journal*. The members of the Committee for

[16] *The Nation*, May 8, 1935.

the Nation consisted of bankers, industrialists and businessmen, including such figures as Lessing Rosenwald, Vincent Bendix and Vanderlip.

The publicity it released was distasteful to most of the conservative newspapers, which were not yet committed to devaluation. The Hearst papers, and Paul Block's papers, printed all of the Committee's publicity.

As this Committee began functioning, Father Charles E. Coughlin, of Detroit and Royal Oak, Michigan, appeared on the radio. Hearst was one of Coughlin's original backers. In 1932 Coughlin was Hearst's guest at San Simeon. In the same year, on a visit to New York, he occupied a suite at Hearst's Hotel Warwick. On subsequent visits to New York Coughlin usually stayed at that hotel.

The economic and financial ideas recommended weekly over the radio by Coughlin were, without the variation of a detail, those of the Committee for the Nation. They were also the ideas of the Hearst papers. Late in 1933 the Committee for the Nation sponsored an address by Coughlin at the New York Hippodrome.

Father Coughlin received most of his publicity from the Hearst papers. His remarks were printed almost in full by Hearst's Detroit *Times* and all Hearst papers, on standing instructions from Hearst himself. From the very beginning of his radio career, Coughlin appeared to take most of his general views from Hearst editorials, and to change his views as the Hearst editorials changed. When Hearst was for Roosevelt, Coughlin was; when Hearst turned, Coughlin turned. When Hearst demanded inflation, Coughlin followed. Hearst cried for higher silver prices, and Coughlin wanted higher silver prices. Hearst endorsed Mussolini's adventure in Ethiopia, and Coughlin approved it. When Hearst simulated alarm at the "Red Menace," Coughlin also took fright. When Hearst attacked academic freedom, Coughlin immediately favored a crusade against school teachers. Almost without variation, the counterpoint between the two has been perfect. Coughlin, like Hylan and Big Bill Thompson, is obviously a Hearst puppet.

The extent to which Father Coughlin has been willing to stultify himself on behalf of Hearst, as distinguished from the Committee for the Nation, was never better illustrated than in Coughlin's frequent predictions that France would leave the gold standard in such and such a month. While gratifying to the German party in international politics, such flat predictions about an international currency frequently result in *speculative movements in the foreign exchange market*. The liaison between Coughlin and the Committee for the Nation was achieved through Wall Street speculators: George Le Blanc, an investment counsel of 1 Wall Street who was formerly vice president of the Equitable Trust Company, and Robert M. Harriss, of the Wall Street brokerage house of Harriss & Vose.

The public opinion which the Committee for the Nation created had much to do with making it possible for the Roosevelt Administration to reduce the gold value of the dollar to 59.6 cents. A number of the Administration's earliest monetary advisers were, indeed, drawn from the ranks of this Committee. One of them was Professor George E. Warren, of Cornell University, an economist whose opinions were circulated by it. All the early financial and economic measures of the Roosevelt régime were measures Hearst and his associates wanted. The five-billion-dollar public works program, for example, had been advocated by Hearst in 1931.

Toward the end of the summer of 1933, however, Hearst became alarmed, in common with most of Wall Street, over the Administration's industrial and agricultural program. Throughout the winter of 1933-34 the Hearst papers criticized the Administration with increasing bitterness. The Pure Food and Drug Bill written by Rexford Guy Tugwell, Assistant Secretary of Agriculture, struck at the heart of Hearst revenue. The moment the Tugwell Bill was introduced in the Senate (January, 1934) Hearst's Senator Copeland moved an amendment which vitiated the intent of the whole bill. As proposed by Tugwell, advertisers of patented and canned products would be compelled to be as truthful and accurate in their advertising as the present food and drug act compels them to be on their labels.

Debate on the Tugwell-Copeland Bill lasted for more than a year. The Senate hearings whittled away until the proposed legislation presented no obstacles to misleading advertising. Representatives of pharmaceutical, proprietary, canned goods and advertising associations appeared before the Senate with objections to every section designed to protect the health of the American people. The American Newspaper Publishers' Association and various magazine publishers' associations also sent representatives to protest against the bill.

Senator Copeland, who, after his arrival in Washington in 1922, became a radio speaker and writer on health in Hearst publications, has endorsed many of the nostrums and preparations advertised in the Hearst publications. Obviously, he was too vulnerable and too politically inept to handle the Tugwell Bill single-handed.

Other Hearstians were called into action, among them young Senator Bennett Clark, of Missouri. His father, Champ Clark, had been aligned with Hearst against the original Food and Drug Bill. The final Copeland Bill was characterized by Consumers' Research in its Bulletin for November, 1935, as a "betrayal of consumers." Consumers' Research noted the fulsome endorsements given the vitiated bill by such publications as *Business Week*, the New York *Times, Printers' Ink*, and the *Confectioners Journal*. It has also been endorsed by the Hearst press and the membership of the A. N. P. A.

Behind the scuttling of the vital Tugwell Bill—an excellently drawn and important piece of legislation which, if enacted, would have meant the difference between life and death, health and illness, to hundreds of thousands of Americans—there was a vast intrigue.

Of Mrs. Blair and the Consumers' Advisory Board, Consumers' Research in its Bulletin[17] of March, 1935, said:

"What may we expect of Mrs. Blair in her new post? In her capacity as a Hearst reporter, Mrs. Blair wrote the following graphic description of the famous White House Tea Party for Consumers: 'The smartly-gowned wives of Cabinet officials and administrators mingled with the heads of national women's organizations, economists, and professional defenders of consumers. More, the two hundred attendants remained for lunch, consuming fish and cucumber salad, ice cream and cake, in the interest of the consumer . . . What a superb setting it was! The stately East Room with its long yellow hangings and high mirrors. The old chairs arranged before

[17] The citations herein from CR's confidential Handbook (and confidential Bulletin) are quoted by special permission of Consumers' Research, Inc.

the wide east windows . . . George and Martha Washington. . . . still seem to hover over it in spirit.'

"Nothing noteworthy has been done for the consumer by the Roosevelt Administration since that festive occasion when two hundred doughty consumer yeomen (we said yeomen, not yesmen) ate 'fish and cucumber salad, ice cream and cake, in the interest of the consumer.' Nor has Mrs. Blair, a member of the Consumers' Advisory Board from near the beginning, been conspicuous except in her capacity of reporting the White House Tea Party for Hearst's *Good Housekeeping* (March, 1934)."

Drug Trade News in the issue of March 18, 1934, carried the following indiscreet tip-off about the gathering of the anti-Tugwell clan:

"Senator Joseph T. Robinson, of Arkansas, majority leader of the Senate, is scheduled to be the leading speaker at the tenth annual banquet of the Drug, Chemical and Allied Trades Section of the New York Board of Trade to be held at the Waldorf-Astoria on Thursday evening, March 21. Robert L. Lund, executive vice-president and general manager of the Lambert Pharmacal Company [manufacturers of Listerine. Lund was also president of the National Association of Manufacturers] will be toastmaster at the banquet and Arthur (Bugs) Baer, humorist and columnist for the Hearst papers, will also speak. . . ."

Baer, like all Hearst special writers, had to function for the business and advertising offices.

Another example of Hearst's rule that his feature writers must function in behalf of business, was reported by *Tide*, an organ of the advertising trade, in its issue of April, 1935: "Most unique and comprehensive stunt came from the Hearst organization, first of this month. The N. Y. *American* claims credit for the idea, but the other Hearst papers followed its lead. Every morning paper in the Hearst chain devoted part of almost every page to men's fashions.

"There was the regular daily column, 'Man of Manhattan' (or 'Man of San Francisco,' 'Man of Omaha,' etc., as the case might be). But what made this event was that the whole battery of Hearst feature writers—Arthur Brisbane, O. O. McIntyre, 'Bugs' Baer,

Damon Runyon, etc.—gave men's wear a play. Each one managed in some way to tie up men's styles with sports, bridge, finance, theater, radio, society, shipping news.

"It was, said the *American*, the first time that all the Hearst columnists had dealt either in whole or in part with the same subject. And it was also, said the *American*, responsible for a substantial increase in men's [advertising] lineage so far as they were concerned."

President Roosevelt publicly endorsed the original Tugwell Bill. Mrs. Roosevelt spoke in its behalf on the radio. The press, however, kept the American people from rallying behind it. Tugwell became the *bête noir* of the Hearst papers, which have depicted him as a symbol of the "communistic" and "socialistic" Brain Trust.

Good Housekeeping, one of whose editors is Mrs. Blair, is Hearst's most profitable publication, returning a net income of more than $2,500,000 annually. Its circulation is more than 2,000,000 copies a month. It has achieved this circulation by "guaranteeing" to American housewives that the products advertised in it—foods, cosmetics, clothing, drugs, pharmaceuticals—are pure and conform in every respect to the claims made for them. Details of how valueless this guarantee is may be obtained from *100,000,000 Guinea Pigs* by Arthur Kallet and F. J. Schlink; *Eat, Drink and Be Wary* by F. J. Schlink; and *Skin Deep* by M. C. Phillips.

Considerable money has been expended to build *Good Housekeeping* into a confidence-inspiring institution. People with strings of degrees from scientific schools adorn its staff. It has laboratories, to which subscribers are invited, in which all the products "guaranteed" by *Good Housekeeping* are "tested." For more than seventeen years, Dr. Harvey Wiley, the man who did most to force passage of the first Pure Food and Drug Bill, was head of the scientific and food departments of *Good Housekeeping*. Hearst saw the drift of the public mind and acquired Wiley as a "front." Dr. Wiley unconsciously so functioned while organizations like Consumers' Research and the American Medical Association have since exposed frauds perpetrated under the *Good Housekeeping* reputation created by Dr. Wiley. Since Dr. Wiley left, *Good Housekeeping* has been turned into an advertisers' paradise. It prints deceptive advertising in the old Hearst fashion, and presumes to give it "scientific" endorsement.

In the bulletins and handbooks of Consumers' Research many products approved by *Good Housekeeping* "scientists" are given inferior ratings, or found harmful, or gravely misrepresented.

Hearst has not challenged Consumers' Research in the courts, nor have the *Good Housekeeping* advertisers or degree-holders. But Consumers' Research reaches only about 55,000 informed people; *Good Housekeeping* has an audience of more than 2,000,000, few of whom even suspect that something may be wrong. It would obviously be to Hearst's disadvantage to have the uncontested fact revealed in court that the Federal Trade Commission, the American Medical Association, and various state boards and individual experts apart from those with Consumers' Research, have at one time or another found reason to differ sharply with the "scientific" findings of *Good Housekeeping*.

Hearst was publicly involved in two major post-war political scandals. One was the case of the forged Mexican documents, which concerned him alone; the other was the revelations about the munitions lobby.

Hearst, tax-dodger and secret party to the Teapot Dome Scandal, has propagandized for years in favor of a large army and navy which the small taxpayer must support. Hearst, and his collaborators among men of wealth, have succeeded, beyond question, and almost beyond their dreams. When Hearst has called for reductions in government expenditures it was not for reductions in military and naval budgets, but for reductions in those government activities concerned with unemployment, social services, education and other "frills."

William B. Shearer is the man who, on behalf of the armament and munitions makers, wrecked the international naval limitation conference of 1927. Without the help of Hearst, Shearer would never have attained sufficient stature to be sent by the leading American munitions firms to Geneva in 1927 with instructions to sabotage the conference. Shearer was in the employ of Hearst during the Washington naval conference of 1922, according to the record of the

Nye munitions investigating committee, and Hearst urged him to procure an injunction against the destruction of American warships in accordance with the Washington Treaty of 1922.

During the Geneva conference of 1927 the Hearst papers featured Shearer's propaganda which also filled all the American papers, so that more was being accomplished for the shipbuilders than by having him work for Hearst exclusively.

The Senate naval investigation of 1929[18] dropped the Hearst phase almost as soon as it was touched.

Since 1929 the increasing scandal of the munitions conspiracy became so great that the Senate, early in 1935, authorized a special committee headed by Gerald P. Nye, to investigate. Before this committee[19] Shearer, according to the summarized account of *Editor and Publisher*, organ of the leading American newspaper publishers, in its issue of March 16, 1935, was forced to admit "that William Randolph Hearst had given him financial and editorial support several times in the past when Shearer was promoting 'national defense' movements, such as the establishment of a West Coast naval base and opposition to the World Court."

Shearer denied that Hearst financed him at Geneva, explaining that the money had come directly from the shipbuilders.

Again quoting *Editor and Publisher's* summarized account:

"A booklet entitled 'The Cloak of Benedict Arnold' was introduced, as written by Shearer. President [Franklin D.] Roosevelt was attacked in this book as an advocate of the World Court, under an editorial headed: 'Knaves or Fools.'" Hearst's tool did not scruple to assail a President who *had already embarked on the greatest peacetime military program in American history.*

" 'And you linked President Roosevelt to Benedict Arnold. Is that what you mean?' asked Senator Bone of Washington.

" 'That is a Hearst editorial, I plagiarized,' replied Shearer.[20]

" 'But you published it without giving any credit?' insisted Bone.

[18] Sub-committee of Senate Naval Affairs Committee to Investigate the Alleged Activities of William B. Shearer in Behalf of Certain Shipbuilding Companies.
[19] Special Senate Committee on Investigation of the Munitions Industry, 1935-36.
[20] *Ibid.*

"Shearer replied that he had not called the President a 'knave or a fool.'

"'Are you so cowardly that you hide behind the cloak of the Hearst newspapers?' Bone shot at him."

Although the two munitions investigations pointed directly at Hearst and his organization, no move has been made to delve into the Hearst munitions intrigues. Even the Nye committee dropped the Hearst phase soon after it was broached. Hearst, as a copper magnate, is also part of the armaments trust.

In 1927 the Hearst newspapers made another attempt to involve the United States in war with Mexico, and, at the same time, to discredit American opponents of certain Hearst policies.

The case of Hearst's Mexican forgeries presents certain aspects of Hearst which have not yet been brought out.

The Hearst papers, from November 14 to December 10, 1927, published[21] a series of sensational stories under the customary scare headlines, based on alleged Mexican government documents about a Mexican plot to bribe four United States Senators with $1,215,000, and two prominent American publicists with lesser sums; a Mexican plan to subjugate Nicaragua; a Russian-Japanese-Mexican plot against the security of the United States, and other similar intrigues. (Nicaragua was included because Hearst was then promoting American intervention in Nicaragua, on behalf of certain Wall Street banks, against the "rebel" Augusto Sandino.)

"These documents are not copies," said the Hearst papers. "They are the originals in every case and they bear the recognized and attested signatures of the President and the leading representatives of the Mexican government. *There is no question of the authenticity of these documents as records of the Government in Mexico.*"

Despite the apparent gravity of the revelations, other American newspapers did not carry the story because the editors knew the "documents" were faked.

[21] Hearings Before a Special Committee to Investigate Propaganda or Money Alleged to Have Been Used by Foreign Governments to Influence United States Senators: U. S. Senate, Seventieth Congress, First Session, in response to Senate Resolution 7.

IMPERIAL HEARST

The "documents" related that Mexico had spent $1,000,000 to foment revolution in Nicaragua, had donated $100,000 to Soviet Russia, had financed radicals in China who were affecting American and British interests, had given American clergymen $210,000 for spreading Mexican propaganda, and had made a fund of $2,400,500 available in New York for buying favorable American press notices.

The four United States Senators were not named by the Hearst papers. Senator David A. Reed of Pennsylvania, a Mellon man, therefore called for an investigation to "clear" the good name of the Senate as a whole.

The Senate Committee was informed that John Page, a Hearst correspondent in Mexico, had purchased the "documents" for $20,000 from Miguel R. Avila, a person who did espionage work for various embassies, including the American, below the Rio Grande. The "documents" had been offered previously by Avila to various correspondents, and to United States Ambassador Sheffield. They had been rejected as clumsy forgeries. The Chicago *Tribune* even sent a man to Mexico City to examine the papers. Carleton Beals, the well-known expert on Latin American affairs, has since announced that he could have bought the "documents" for a few hundred dollars.

Page, on instructions from his superiors, bought the "documents," which were then studied by Hearst and Victor Watson at the San Simeon ranch and distributed to the Hearst papers for publication.

The "documents" were so obviously forged that a number of Hearst executives, for purely journalistic reasons, remonstrated against their publication.[22] Hearst ignored their advice.

What were Hearst's motives in this case? An ordinarily shrewd observer like Silas Bent attributed the publication of the documents merely to Hearst's desire for a "story" that would take the edge off the scoop of a competitor on certain rights in connection with the Dempsey-Tunney fight in 1927.[23] The motive was much more important.

Shortly before Hearst published the "documents," the Mexican government had passed new land laws requiring payment of higher

[22] *Prophets True and False*, by Oswald Garrison Villard.
[23] *Strange Bedfellows*, by Silas Bent.

taxes and relinquishment of underground mineral rights by foreign property owners. These laws were extremely distasteful to the Hearst-Doheny-Sinclair interests, as well as to others.

From the standpoint of profits Hearst unquestionably did the expedient thing in publishing the "documents." His journalistic enterprises did not really suffer, and by going to such lengths he demonstrated to the Calles government that he would stop at nothing to undermine it.

Before the documents were published it had already been decided that Dwight Morrow, Morgan partner, should replace Ambassador Sheffield in Mexico City. A reorientation of Mexican policy along Morgan lines was under way. Morrow was conciliatory. The Mexican government and the Mexican railways had floated bonds through Morgan's, and these bonds were in hopeless default. Morrow was to reëstablish Mexico so that these and other obligations might be repaid. This was a banker's program. The Hearst-Doheny-Sinclair interests, and other landholders in Mexico, stood to gain nothing from this rapprochement.

Although Avila apparently fabricated the "documents" himself, and offered them to all the other correspondents at extremely low rates before they were brought to the attention of the Hearst agents, it is a highly suspicious circumstance that Avila did not *first* offer them to Hearst, who is so well known as the highest bidder for material of this sort. Avila, the record shows, was not a dunce. Hearst paid Avila $20,000, a stupendous sum in comparison with the earlier prices Avila quoted to other correspondents. Was it Avila's own idea? Was it planned to have the documents "planted" *in the hope that some other paper would first take the responsibility of publication, after which Hearst would reprint the material in his papers?* If Hearst inspired their creation why, the question arises, could not the forgeries have been better done?

It would obviously have been difficult to bring an honorable scholar into the business. Whoever inspired the forgeries was forced to have recourse to a person who would inevitably turn out a very clumsy job.

It is exceedingly strange that *a collection* of forged documents should materialize just when Hearst, of all people, wanted to embarrass Mexico. *It is also strange that only Hearst political foes of the moment, with one exception, should be named in the documents.* Why should a forger sitting below the Rio Grande insert *only* the names of Americans whom Hearst opposed? Why should not a forger accidentally include, out of ninety-six Senators, at least one who was dear to Hearst and the Coolidge-Mellon machine? Why should the forger pick out two editors who were abhorrent to Hearst?

The Senate committee conducted the most forthright and damning inquiry on record into a Hearst intrigue. Hearst was forced to appear and testify, which in itself was unique, even though the committee was not without its protective Hearst member. Senator Johnson of California directed the questioning from time to time in such a way as to establish Avila as the confidant of Ambassadors, a valued source of news for American newspaper men in Mexico City, and a generally reliable person.

Hearst had deleted the names of the Senators. The Senate committee discovered that the Senators named in the forged documents were William E. Borah, Thomas J. Heflin, George W. Norris and Robert La Follette.

While the investigation was getting under way, *The Nation* proved that the "document" printed by Hearst purporting to show that Villard had been paid $25,000 for spreading propaganda, was also a forgery. This "document" also indicated that Dr. Ernest H. Gruening[24] of *The Nation* had been paid for "Communist" activities in developing Mexican government policies. Before its publication, *The Nation,* aware of its imminent appearance, had submitted proof that it was a forgery to the editors of the New York *American* and had been promised it would not be published. As a result of its publication, Gruening filed a $500,000 libel suit against the *American*, Hearst, Brisbane and others of the Hearst staff, and later obtained a satisfactory settlement.

In the Senate witness room Hearst was asked: "Did you investi-

[24] Now Administrator of the Puerto Rico Reconstruction Administration.

gate whether money had been actually paid to the United States Senators?
A. "No, sir, we didn't.
Q. "Did you go to the Senators mentioned and ask them?
A. "No; we could not without revealing the contents.
Q. "Have you any evidence that any Senator received any such money as mentioned here?
A. "No. In fact, I do not believe they did receive any money.
Q. "Have you ever heard of any evidence to sustain such a charge?
A. "No; I do not believe the charge."

Hearst was asked why he had deleted the Senators' names, inasmuch as the Hearst papers claimed they were satisfied of the authenticity of the "documents."
Q. "Did you consider the liabilities for the libel you might be subjected to?
A. "Yes, I guess so.
Q. "You had the liability in mind when you did not use the names?
A. "Probably."

Various members of the Hearst organization were also called to testify—Victor Watson, the Hearst undercover agent, Edmond D. Coblentz, publisher of the New York *American*, and Edward Hardy Clark. All professed to be extremely gullible and innocent men.

Document and handwriting experts pointed out that someone with a very insecure knowledge of Spanish, obviously uneducated, had written the Hearst documents. They were full of misspellings, ungrammatical locutions and minor and major errors of fact. They could not, in short, have come from a Mexican government bureau. Hearst, faced with ignominious exposure, finally had handwriting experts of his own testify. He admitted he had not submitted the documents to experts before publishing them.

According to the testimony of Hearst and Clark, an unnamed businessman had told Clark about the papers. Clark himself took the papers to President Coolidge, who was summering in South Dakota (as a result of the desire of Hearst's political friends in the state

IMPERIAL HEARST

to have him there). Coolidge refused to look at them, Hearst said. Secretary of State Kellogg also, strangely, refused to look at them. This may or may not have been true, but Coolidge and Kellogg, if we are to believe Hearst and Clark, were refusing a slight favor to powerful political figures. Hearst said that Coolidge "apparently had some knowledge of them, possibly through Ambassador Sheffield, to whom they had been submitted."

These colorings were introduced into the case to lend some respectability and to make it seem that he had made some effort in high places to establish their authenticity. Befuddled newspaper readers could not help but be impressed at the frequent mention of President Coolidge, Secretary Kellogg, President Calles and Ambassador Sheffield.

"I understand that the President said to Mr. Clark—but Mr. Clark will testify as to that matter," Hearst said, "that it was desirable to bear in mind that while certain accusations were made in these documents, there might possibly be the situation that the moneys mentioned therein had never reached the gentlemen mentioned."

When his own handwriting experts were about to testify, Hearst gave out the following remarkable statement:

"If the handwriting experts should all agree that the documents we have produced bear evidence of having been fabricated, I will not dispute that decision further than to maintain persistently, and I believe patriotically, that the logic of events gives every evidence that the essential facts contained in the documents were not fabricated, and that the facts—the political facts, the international facts—are the things which are of vital importance to the American people and to the loyal representatives of the interests of the American people."

How amazing that an obscure forger, without Hearst connections, could contrive to produce papers which, although proven false, yet would contain "facts" that Hearst continued to believe even after exposure!

Of Hearst's statement the San Francisco *Argonaut* said: "Here is true moron logic."

"The annals of yellow journalism," said the Los Angeles *Times*, "will be searched in vain for anything remotely approaching this performance by Hearst."

Senator Norris closed the case with a magnificent denunciation of the Hearst newspapers, which, he said in closing, "constitute the sewer system of American journalism."

The Hearst newspapers the next day printed this: "My papers have always been in the main supporters of the insurgent group of Senators," said Hearst. "Senator Borah I have had occasion to support and commend probably more than any other man in the Senate. I do not know that I have ever supported Senator Norris, but then I cannot recall that he's ever done anything worth supporting . . . As a matter of fact, I'm an insurgent myself. . . .

"I had these documents for five months, carefully considering what was the best course to pursue and what was the most considerate course to pursue. And it was only when the authenticity of these documents became almost overwhelmingly established, that publication began."

Here, despite the admitted falsity of the "documents," Hearst was asserting again—for wide public consumption—that they were authentic! He knew that the memories of the Hearst readers were short!

As always, although he had been caught red-handed in a false accusation against four United States Senators, one of them chairman of the powerful Foreign Relations Committee, Hearst was let off scot-free. Must it not now be admitted by the most skeptical that Hearst is stronger than the government, that Hearst is a part of the constituted government, occasionally quarreling with some other part of it and merely *appearing* in the rôle of an outsider proceeded against by the government?

The committee asked Hearst what his own personal interests in Mexico were. He grandly disclaimed knowledge of details and referred the Senators to Mr. Clark. It was the first time any investigating committee had inquired into Hearst's economic stake and the question therefore deserves special notice.

Simultaneously with political affairs, the various other activities of the Hearst papers after the war were pushed with the old savage vigor.

The first blow against Hearst in the newspaper domain after the war was struck by competitors. Colonel R. R. McCormick and Captain J. M. Patterson of the Chicago *Tribune* took an exceedingly significant step against Hearst by starting the New York *Daily News*, a picture tabloid, in 1919. Hearst regarded the *News* as directed primarily against himself, for it aimed to secure the patronage of the lower masses to which Hearst's *American* and *Journal* catered.

There is little to admire in Messrs. Patterson and McCormick, but at least they refused to be terrorized by Hearst. True, in Chicago they descended to Hearst's level, but there it was either beating him or going out of business. Patterson and McCormick knew that in founding the New York *Daily News* they would again come up against Hearst. Realistically, they brought with them their Swiss Guard, under the command of veteran Max Annenberg.

Annenberg surveyed the Hearst position. He found that the Hearst circulation manager was Joseph D. Bannon, who, in 1900, had founded the Newspaper and Mail Deliverers' Union, composed of newspaper delivery men. Hearst saw the value of having the union leader on his side and in 1902 made him circulation manager for New York. It may, at first, seem odd that the drivers and delivery men would tolerate, as their leader, the circulation manager of one who exploited them daily. Yet Bannon remained head of the union for twenty-nine years, retiring in 1929 in favor of Harry Feldman.

Bannon ruled the newspaper delivery men cleverly. They were split into two classes: those who merely delivered papers and those who were permitted to own newsstands as well. Bannon exercised a firm control, through Hearst's Tammany connections, over those permitted, upon payment of substantial fees, to own newsstands. The fees were split several ways; only a portion went to Tammany Hall.

The stand-owners became Bannon's staunch backers in the union. The union members who were merely delivery men were kept in their places by threats, cajolery and inertia. If they strung along with Bannon they might be tossed a bone in the form of a newsstand. But if they fought Bannon, they would meet with "accidents."

Hearst's competitors in New York had, by 1919, abandoned the more ignorant readers to him. Pulitzer, Whitelaw Reid, Adolph Ochs, James Gordon Bennett and Frank A. Munsey found it more profitable—and safer—to cater to the higher income strata of the population. Hearst was very upset by the *Daily News* and was not long in taking defensive steps against it. Annenberg, his former pupil, took the offensive.

Bannon had a caller one day, whom he greeted affably. Who the caller was we do not know. He was accompanied by two gentlemen who made themselves comfortable, keeping their hands in their pockets. The gist of the one-sided conversation was, "We don't want any trouble. Just keep out of our way." Bannon, ever the diplomat, is said to have indicated blandly that he had no desire for trouble.

Thereafter, in the late evening hours when the *News* and the *American* appeared on the city's newsstands, but more especially after editions of the *Times, Herald,* and *Tribune* had also arrived, alert New Yorkers witnessed such occurrences as this: An automobile stopped near a newsstand. A man emerged, followed by another man who stationed himself in a doorway. The first man, with two others watching intently from the car, approached the stand and surveyed the display of papers. If satisfied, he withdrew to the car, followed by the man in the doorway. Both had their right hands in their pockets. But if the display on the stands did not appeal to the silent visitor, he reached over and rearranged it, keeping his right hand in his pocket. When the rearrangement was completed the New York *Daily News* would be in a front position, the photograph on its front page easily visible.

New York was not a suitable place for such a fight as the *News* was clearly prepared for. The *News* was, indeed, inviting Hearst to start something, even if he did control City Hall. There was much Hearst-Tammany scandal which the *News* could have published. New York, however, was too much in the national and international limelight for such a circulation war as was staged in Chicago. Annenberg and his boys were never challenged on the streets. Annenberg's guns were to remain silent.

The *News* adopted the time-honored American journalistic

method of attracting readers by conducting contests and giving away prizes. Readers were lured, for the most part, from the *American,* and Hearst replied with a "Lady Luck" lottery for a $1,000 cash prize. The *News* also instituted a lottery, with $2,500 as the prize. The *American* responded with a $5,000 prize, the *News* raised the stake to $10,000 and Hearst gravely countered with a $15,000 prize. The *News* then offered $20,000 and the *American* outbid it with $25,000. Both papers had at that point snared a good deal of artificial circulation from their competitors.

Hearst also shifted the fight to Chicago. There the *Herald-Examiner* caused riots in the crowded downtown section by *giving* money to persons who clipped specified coupons from the paper. The *Tribune* began giving away money, too.

In New York, by the lottery device, Hearst increased the *American's* circulation by 200,000 copies. It was expensively bought. Advertising rates, determined by circulation, could not be raised as fast as the inflated circulation, and both papers were taking heavy losses. Editorial expenditures were curtailed to a minimum while the competition lasted. The writers in the city rooms paid for the fun.

Hearst won the battle, morally at least, because it was the *News* that made the first move for peace. Captain Patterson's cousin, the late Senator Medill McCormick, who was the former editor of the Chicago *Tribune,* made representations to the United States Post Office Department, which obligingly ruled that papers conducting lotteries could not be sent through the mails.

"Thus was terminated a main engagement in what was to prove a sanguinary war," observes Silas Bent in *Ballyhoo.*

Hearst had the happy idea of rehiring Moe Annenberg, who had been his Milwaukee publisher of the *Sentinel* (the ownership of which Hearst did not acknowledge), as well as one of his circulation executives in Chicago. Hearst probably reasoned that Max would not resort to the automatic pistol against his own brother, and he was correct. Moe Annenberg was made general circulation manager of *all* the Hearst papers, and Bannon became merely his New York assistant.

In 1924 Hearst, desperate because of the fallen fortunes of the

American, which has never recovered and is now known to newspaper men as *The Vanishing American*, founded the New York *Daily Mirror*, a tabloid. He hired Philip Payne, editor of the *News*, to run it, and the *Mirror*, with a circulation of more than 500,000 (in contrast with the 2,200,000 of the *Daily News*), was to treble the losses of the *American*. The *Mirror* was intended to annoy the *News*, which it never did.

In 1925 Bernarr Macfadden, publisher of *True Stories* and bogus health periodicals, started the *Evening Graphic*, which newspaper men quickly dubbed the *Porno-Graphic*. The *Graphic* ate into the *Journal's* circulation, and although the *Graphic* has since been discontinued, the *Journal* has barely been able to hold its circulation of nearly 700,000 against lively new competitors like the Scripps-Howard *World-Telegram* and J. David Stern's New York *Post*.

The brothers Annenberg meanwhile had reached the zenith of prosperity. Moe Annenberg and Bannon began to add racing papers to Moe's General News Bureau and eventually owned all the big racing and sports papers. The General News Bureau and Hearst's International News Service entered into a reciprocal agreement for the exchange of sporting news and betting quotations. Bannon, out of the new prosperity brought by Moe Annenberg, even bought the *Morning Telegraph*, New York's leading sporting paper, and later sold it. Bannon needed Moe, but Moe also needed Bannon. As we have seen, the Bannon-Annenberg enterprises and Hearst both became large borrowers of A. F. of L. funds at the same time.

Bannon, whose *Morning Telegraph* was financed by William Green's Federation Bank, was a "labor leader"—head of the delivery men's union—whose union was not affiliated with the A. F. of L. It was a company union, fiercely anti-labor.

With the Annenberg brothers employed by competitors, an agreement was made among the New York circulation managers for *all* the newspapers to arbitrate disputes and to submit to the rulings of a mutually agreeable "czar." John C. Mansfield was appointed. This solution was not advanced until there had been numerous sluggings and there was danger that they would become public knowledge.

Bannon and his successor, Feldman, directed strong-arm methods more discreetly than had Annenberg in Chicago, when he was fighting his way up and did some of the skull-crushing and body-breaking himself. The New Yorkers had this work done by persons called "punks," who were set in motion through third and fourth parties and took all the risks upon themselves. Among these "punks" were narcotic addicts, ex-convicts, dipsomaniacs and feeble-minded products of the slums, all of them ready instruments for nimbler wits.

With the circulation managers and the newspaper proprietors in agreement among themselves, the struggle for further profits took the form of exploitation of the newsstand operators. The privilege of returning unsold copies is complicated and almost always works against the dealer. It was still the Annenbergs' slogan to the newsstand dealer: "If you can't sell 'em, eat 'em." The newsstand operators and newsboys of New York quietly "ate" newspapers and are doing so today.

It is not that Hearst or other publishers who follow this practice make any money out of forcing the newsdealers to pay a few extra dollars out of their meager earnings. Hearst and other publishers are solely interested in boosting their monthly showing in the Audit Bureau of Circulation, which determines a newspaper's circulation with what passes for official exactitude and is the basis used for computing advertising rates. Although they did not know it, the big advertisers were paying for a good deal of "dead" circulation, especially in Hearst papers. If there are no returns from the newsstands, the circulation obviously seems larger, and there are no returns if the newsdealers are afraid to give back unsold papers.

The privilege of withholding licenses to newsdealers is a powerful weapon in the hands of the circulation managers. It makes a "clean" handling of recalcitrants possible. The newspapers seldom need be directly involved in punitive actions by their circulation managers and circulation "czar." The police handle their victims for them.

This arbitrary control by Tammany and the circulation managers created a lucrative new racket. It was so overworked that it flared into public notice in 1934. The law stipulated that war veterans and the blind should have first call on available newspaper stands. This provision was ignored by the Tammany License Commissioner. The stands were given only to interests which paid large sums to Tammany and certain circulation managers. During the depression there were many new bidders for stands. Some who had never paid tribute were dispossessed from locations they had developed over a long period of years. Early in 1934, Jack Beall, a reporter for the New York *Herald Tribune*, heard about it, wrote the story, and it was printed, much to the astonishment of working journalists. An investigation had to follow. The newspapers printed a good deal about the investigation, but not all. Mr. Beall, however, gave a summarized account which was placed on public record.[25] The investigation was eventually dropped. Beall wrote nothing more about it. Although conditions are not now precisely the same, they have not greatly altered.

There are about 4,000 newsstands in New York City. According to law they must be allocated to the blind and to war veterans, but only one-tenth of the stands, the evidence showed, were in their hands.

"The other nine-tenths are held by able-bodied businessmen and women who have purchased their stands, in direct contravention of law, for sums ranging from $1,000 to $18,000," said Beall.[26]

The go-betweens in these transactions, the inquiry showed, were Jake Sbar and Louis Breines, who maintained headquarters in a Harlem ice cream parlor. License applicants had first to "see" Jake or Louie, and "see" Joseph W. O'Connor, the assistant to Commissioner of Licenses James F. Geraghty, Bronx Tammany leader. Geraghty's office was being filled by Commissioner Levine at the time the investigation developed, and the record of the inquiry showed that Levine was functioning to protect Geraghty.

After "seeing" O'Connor, the applicant would get his license. But, if the applicant came to see O'Connor without first having paid Jake and Louie, he would get no license.

Geraghty was not called to testify before the Grand Jury, although he had held the office of License Commissioner for many years!

After giving this background, Beall continued:[27]

[25] *The Nation*, March 7, 1934. [26] *Ibid*. [27] *Ibid*.

"The circulation departments play a direct part in the newsstand racket in New York through the fact that they decide arbitrarily what dealers are to be supplied with papers. Thus they have the power of life and death over the individual dealer. Further, they have veto power over any move of the Commissioner of Licenses. For what good does it do a dealer to have a stand on a good corner and a license to operate it, if he can get no papers to sell? The power to withhold papers is the power to destroy. The right to withhold or to sell to whomever they like is zealously defended by circulation managers and newspaper owners. It was upheld recently in the Supreme Court of New York. Decently used, this right cannot be complained of, but when it is corruptly used, it directly implements the newsstand racketeer.

"Jake Sbar confessed once in an unguarded moment how the money paid over for the purchase of a newsstand was 'cut up.' Half of it went, he said, to the former owner of the stand, part of the remaining half went to himself and Louis Breines as their commission, part of it went to the department of licenses—whence a goodly percentage was siphoned upward to the Tammany coffers, presumably—and part of it went to the circulation departments of newspapers. Approximately the same division was made of an $8,000 'defense fund' . . . raised . . . at a secret meeting of the New York Newsdealers Protective and Benevolent Association, of which Sbar was a director . . . two shares, according to Sbar, went to certain persons in the Department of Licenses, and certain persons in the circulation departments of newspapers."

The circulation departments all coöperated, Beall wrote, by not selling papers to persons Jake and Louie ruled off the stands. This coöperation was arranged through the circulation "czar," who had the power to withhold all papers from anyone.

"How high in the circulation departments the money collected in these ways went is an extremely difficult question to answer. On only one newspaper is it known to have gone as high as the head of the department."[28]

Beall related that James Haseneck, circulation manager of the New

[28] Beall did not name the paper but the reader can guess it.

York *Sun*, told Herman M. Immelin, director of social welfare of the New York Association for the Blind, that if the license was taken from any dealer his successor would not get newspapers. Immelin, desirous of obtaining stands for blind citizens, suggested that the licenses of those who operated stands in contravention of the law be revoked. Haseneck's observation was merely meant to explain that the possession of a public license would be of no assistance.

Beall then told of a meeting of circulation managers called by Mayor-elect La Guardia a week before he took office in January, 1934. This meeting was not reported in the newspapers. La Guardia asked that Mansfield, the circulation "czar," be removed, but the circulation managers flatly rejected the request. Mayor La Guardia, Beall's account stated, accused the circulation managers of knowing what was going on. They did not deny it, Beall said, and even discussed the pros and cons of the matter with the Mayor. ". . . Seven of these same circulation managers swore on the witness stand two weeks later, that they knew nothing personally about the buying and selling of stands. In two instances they said they had never heard of it until they read the reports of the newsstand hearings."[29]

Mayor La Guardia did not volunteer to testify against the circulation managers. As a result of the exposure, the New York *Times* withdrew from its agreement with Mansfield.

There was no significant outcome to this case. Apart from the indictment of Jake and Louie, the New York newspapers ignored most of the vital points sketched by Beall in *The Nation*. But the exposure had reverberations in the Newspaper and Mail Deliverers' Union.

For some years a faction in this union (composed of the delivery men who were not Feldman-Bannon favorites and hence owned no newsstands) had been fighting against the Feldman-Bannon leadership. This faction published an occasional paper, *The Laborite,* edited by Joseph Chernow, a newspaper man who had started his career as a delivery helper. Chernow had worked for the *World* and various New York newspapers at police headquarters for more than twenty years. During most of that time he fought, sometimes single-

[29] *The Nation*, March 7, 1934.

IMPERIAL HEARST 299

handed, first against Bannon and then against Feldman. When the *World* was bought by the *Telegram* Chernow got a job with the City News Association, a coöperative news-gathering agency financed jointly by all the New York City papers.

After the exposure of the newsstand racket, previously inert members of the Newspaper and Mail Deliverers' Union rallied around the anti-Feldman faction and *The Laborite* renewed its exposure of what it termed "Feldmanism." Chernow was warned several times to desist, but refused. Then he was waylaid on his way home at night and severely beaten. But he persisted, and one evening was blackjacked in the lobby of the *World* building. His assailants escaped both times. His injuries were so serious after each assault that he had to go to a hospital at his own expense.

He was next sued for libel in a Brooklyn court by Feldman. Chernow was finally dismissed from his job with the City News Association and was unable to obtain a job with any New York paper, despite his experience. He had to take government relief work.

The Printing Worker, organ of members of Typographical Union No. 7, in its issue of April, 1935, said:

"The charge of criminal libel against Joe Chernow . . . was thrown out of court, April 2, by County Judge George W. Martin, in Brooklyn. The case had been called for trial thirteen times in as many months, but only once (upon the ninth time) was it brought to trial, after persistent and repeated efforts on the part of the [preceding] judge and prosecutor to force Chernow to retract had failed, and resulted in the jury's disagreement. . . ."

The May, 1935, issue carried another account of Feldman's activities:

"About 400 newsdealers of Newark and its suburbs have refused to handle the New York newspapers as a protest against their being forced to accept more newspapers and magazines than they can actually sell. . . .

"The dealers are well organized for a fight to the finish, which, from all indications, promises to be of long duration. Many dealers have said they didn't care if they never handled any New York papers again as they will not pay for papers they do not order and besides they will not pay extortionate delivery charges for the sake of enriching a millionaire distributor. The strike is now in its seventh week. . . .

"Harry Feldman, circulation manager of the *Evening Journal* and president of the Newspaper and Mail Deliverers' Union—a racket-ridden organization—is in command of the forces that are fighting the dealers. Unscrupulous circulation managers for the sake of showing 'increased' sales make it a practice of adding on papers to the distributor, who in turn pads the dealers' orders regardless of whether the dealer can sell the papers or not. The dealer is forced to stand the loss of all unsold copies, and often finds that his labor and investment are for naught."

Feldman began life as a newsboy in Wall Street, becoming a member of the Newspaper and Mail Deliverers' Union in 1907. He soon made himself useful to Bannon, and was lifted to the status of "circulator," a euphemistic term for slugger. He first attained public notice during the newsboys' strike of 1918 which was smashed by concerted action of the New York publishers.

In 1929, when Feldman became head of the union, Bannon sold most of his interest in sporting papers to Hugh Murray, and retired with a reported $5,000,000. He entered into partnership with Harry A. Braelow in the Newsdealers' Supply Company of New Jersey. This organization is also a part of the New York newsstand racket and unquestionably an interstate affair. The Department of Justice has carefully sidestepped all entanglement with this racket, although the facts have been put directly up to it. Bannon was received in a private audience by the Pope in 1934.

Although in New York City a special "investigation" of rackets was conducted in 1935 and 1936, the leaders of the Newspaper and Mail Deliverers' Union were not inconvenienced by it.

The Newspaper and Mail Deliverers' Union is at the very heart of the notorious racket situation in New York. It has been guided by Hearst executives for thirty-three years, and their cohorts still exercise power within the union. The upper strata of union "executives" rub elbows with New York's biggest racketeers, as the programs of the union's annual dinner-dances show.

IMPERIAL HEARST

The following appeared in the November 9, 1935, issue of *The People's Press*, a weekly picture tabloid published by Frank Palmer, head of the Federated Press, of which the associate editors are James Waterman Wise, son of Rabbi Stephen S. Wise, and Arthur Kallett, of the Consumers' Union of U. S., Inc.:

"William Randolph Hearst, who has kept his California love nest, his movie queen and their children, out of the press for years by gangdom threats . . .

"Struck back at the *People's Press* in Chicago for telling the story.

"Charles Krata, manager of the distributing agency which is handling the *People's Press* on contract, was slugged by two thugs in front of his office and severely injured.

"The next day Hearst drivers and agents told newsdealers handling the *People's Press* that they would take the Hearst publications off their stand if they did not drop the *People's Press* and would beat up the dealers in addition.

"The policeman on Van Buren street in the Loop, appealed to for protection by the newsdealer, answered that he could not promise protection if the *People's Press* is handled."

Subsequent issues told of threatening letters and telephone calls received by the editors, who also had "shadows" placed on their trail.

As a consequence of the *People's Press* story about Hearst, the Hearst Chicago office caused an ordinance to be passed by the compliant City Council, barring from the newsstands all out-of-town publications unless they were licensed by the city. This was clearly an infringement of the Constitution.

All Broadwayites are Hearst-conscious.

Hearst is a Protean fellow, unquestionably. In addition to his other activities he is a theatrical and film producer, a promoter of prize-fights, a great booster of sports.

Hearst was one of the first experimenters with the cinema. The camera was an early passion with him, and during his San Francisco days he made it a hobby. When the movies were invented Hearst men experimented with the first newsreels, and Hearst filmed the burial of the *Maine* in 1911 and the inauguration of President

Wilson in 1913. During the war Hearst became a producer of anti-Japanese and anti-Mexican films.

At the termination of the war the Hearst Cosmopolitan Film Corporation began the production of feature pictures, but later functioned solely as a stockholder in various large film companies, including the Hearst-Metrotone News, half owned by Metro-Goldwyn-Mayer. Hearst has been, at one time or another, a big stockholder in the largest film companies, and is now associated with Warner Brothers Pictures after his quarrel on Miss Davies' behalf with Metro-Goldwyn-Mayer.

In New York City Hearst has also been concerned with amusement enterprises, both as a theatrical producer and a theater owner. For many years he has owned the Cosmopolitan Theater on Columbus Circle and the Ziegfeld Theater. In his real estate dealings he has also held options and leases on theater properties.

His first theatrical venture, apart from the films, was probably when Morris Gest, just after the war, was having difficulties with *Aphrodite*, an extravaganza with music and semi-nude girls. Business was not good. Gest offered Hearst an interest at a low figure, hoping Hearst would place the weight of his papers behind the show, into which Gest had already sunk a small fortune. The offer appealed to Hearst and was accepted. The Hearst papers immediately manifested unusual interest in the show. Indeed, they began denouncing it!

According to the *American* and *Journal, Aphrodite* was salacious beyond words. The women were incredibly nude, and it was even doubtful to spectators if the personable Miss Dorothy Dalton had a stitch on. Moreover a Negro made love to the practically nude Aphrodite and the Hearst papers wondered editorially whether this should be permitted. The hullabaloo converted the show into a financial success.

Hearst has been a silent partner in other Broadway productions, and his newspapers brought the public in by one means or another, usually by extravagant praise. It has meant peremptory dismissal for a Hearst reviewer or critic to denounce a show or a film in which Hearst has an interest. The most recent Hearst theatrical venture was the last *Ziegfeld Follies* produced by Florenz Ziegfeld, who was then in financial difficulties. Instructions, it is said, were given to the Hearst theatrical reviewers to give the show a big boost. Walter Winchell, the popular columnist of Hearst's *Mirror*, was also "assigned" to the job of boosting the Follies. *Winchell virtually killed the production by overpraising it!*

It has been the Hearst ballyhoo which has mainly supported the prize-fight racket. At the time of the San Francisco earthquake Hearst began staging "benefit" fights in New York. They did not cost him a penny, brought some funds to unfortunates, and gave him much valuable advertising. The late Tex Rickard and the reigning Mike Jacobs have been Hearst's principal collaborators in this lucrative business.

It is true that the fighters get advertising from the Hearst papers. And it is true that part of the proceeds goes to charitable enterprises. The fight business, however, like the racing business, is extremely crooked, and is of principal concern to the big Broadway gambling syndicates that "fix" fights and make big killings, as the sports editors of all except the Hearst press freely relate in their columns. Both the fight and racing rackets, which sell so many newspapers for Hearst, have become such public nuisances that New York State must maintain special racing and boxing commissions in order to control the grosser forms of swindling.

But, whether "fixed" or not, 10 per cent of the proceeds of the Milk Fund fights goes to the *American* and the *Journal* charities.

It is an open secret in sporting circles, known, discussed and written about by non-Hearst sporting editors, that not all of the proceeds of these fights go to the simple poor. William Farnsworth, sporting editor of the *Journal*, and his staff have received a substantial fee after each fight for doing the publicity. A well-known sports writer complained directly to Mrs. Hearst of this, for the funds are nominally in her charge. She is said to have replied: "I don't see why Bill Farnsworth should not make something out of the fights. He works so hard to put them over."

People who wish to gamble, who are incited to gamble by the

"sporting" stories in the Hearst press, are not the only victims. The non-gambling public is victimized as well.

If a big demand for tickets develops as a result of Hearst's publicity, the management places them with its outside agent who sells $15 tickets for $25. Only $1.50 has gone to the Milk Fund from such sales. Under Rickard the custom of selling "ringside" seats grew to such an extent, and has been so developed since his death, that today purchasers of "ringside" seats may find themselves sixty rows away from the ring. Press seats were always in great demand, and Rickard decided to cash in. The newspaper men were not deprived of their seats at the ring, however. At first tickets were sold to the "working" press, and these gentry—politicians, brokers, gunmen, gamblers and the like—found themselves placed just behind the actual newspaper men. The sale was so good that new press gradations were introduced, until tickets finally came to be sold to the "working press," the "patron press" and the "donor press." After these came the "ringside" seats.

In the Hearst organization all the sports department men speak highly of him while the news department men are bitter. The explanation lies in the perquisites that fall in the way of the sporting writer, who is not hindered in collaborating with sporting promoters, especially if the name and fortunes of Hearst are given proper attention. The financial writers speak well of him for similar reasons.

Each year several theatrical "benefits" are sponsored in the name of Hearst in New York and Los Angeles, and sometimes in Chicago, San Francisco and Boston. Los Angeles and New York, as the nation's amusement centers, are the recurrent scenes of these "benefits." The proceeds go to the various Hearst philanthropic funds, after expenses have been deducted, of course. Hearst himself gives nothing.

Hearst is an important participant in the proceeds from the racetrack racket in the United States. The Hearst organization is probably more closely integrated with racing than with any other racket. This integration takes place through the International News Service, the telegraph news bureau of the Hearst organization. In addition to supplying news to publications, the International News Service is one of the greatest race-track quotation and sporting news communication systems in the country, its chief competitor being Moe Annenberg's General News Bureau. Syndicates, bookies, poolrooms, clubs and cigar stores doing a gambling business depend either on the General News Bureau or International News Service for betting quotations and track reports.

Moe Annenberg, unlike Hearst, is not given to striking moral attitudes in his papers, which deal solely with sporting "dope." Hearst, however, uses morality to assist in the promotion of his sporting interests. This was strikingly illustrated in 1935. International News Service was peacefully supplying quotations to all the principal gambling centers along the Pacific Coast by special arrangement with the syndicate heads. Moe Annenberg, no longer employed by Hearst, offered his service for a lower fee and it was accepted when Hearst refused to reduce his fees.

As General News Bureau began supplying reports of track, fight and game results—the only equipment required being a receiving ticker in each place hooked up to an A. T. & T. leased wire—all the Hearst papers began a campaign against gambling.[30] They described the suffering that resulted from gambling. Even people on relief yielded up their few dollars to unscrupulous gambling racketeers.

There was very little reaction. The bookies and General News Bureau kept on doing the lucrative business in which INS had previously shared. It was necessary for the Hearst organization to mobilize the professional moralists and clergymen of the Pacific Coast. These came trooping with their signed statements and messages of approval for the great good Hearst was doing. Never have the moralists and clergy, who know very little about the real nature of society, failed Hearst.

The Hearst-Annenberg duel was still undecided at the close of 1935, and the Hearst papers were continuing hysterical about the suffering wrought upon hard-working folk by the gambling racket-

[80] Throughout 1935 the *Pacific Weekly*, a liberal periodical, carried realistic reports of this sudden moral Hearst campaign.

eers. In New York, Boston, Chicago, Baltimore, Milwaukee, Omaha —the Hearst newspapers did not crusade against gambling racketeers. It was only gambling on the Pacific Coast that was immoral!

The ability of the Hearst papers to raise a moral storm makes the leading figures in the sporting world wary of crossing Hearst.

Hearst has turned many criminal law cases to his own private uses. Hundreds of instances of innocent people being brought to trial simply to give the Hearst papers circulation, or a Hearst prosecutor with political ambitions publicity, could be cited. Hundreds of cases could also be cited in which the Hearst papers have interfered with the operation of justice simply to embarrass a prosecutor or political administration unacceptable to Hearst.

An outstanding example of this sort of thing in the post-war period was the Hall-Mills murder case in New Jersey. The New York *Mirror*, although the case had long before been closed, caused its reopening on the basis of bogus "new" evidence and brought about the indictment of people who had been acquitted after a long and arduous trial. What the *Mirror* was after was the salacious evidence that eventually emerged, and increased circulation. All the New York papers profited from the case, but Hearst had three papers in New York which profited and more than twenty-five throughout the country.

Hearst has often financed the defense of indicted murderers, not to aid justice, but to secure the kind of story which arouses mass sadism—or masochism.

The most flagrant recent case of this nature is that of Colonel Charles A. Lindbergh. After Lindbergh made the good-will flight to Mexico in 1927 at Ambassador Morrow's behest (just at the time of Hearst's Mexican "exposé") he was pursued day in and day out by Hearst agents professedly after "news." It was really Hearst who drove Colonel Lindbergh and his family out of the United States. And it was the Hearst papers which spread doubt about the fairness of the trial given to Bruno Richard Hauptmann for the murder of the Lindbergh child.

Before the flight of the Lindbergh family to England to escape

IMPERIAL HEARST

the Hearst thugs who constantly hounded the family, George Seldes wrote as follows:[31] "When he married privately, the tabloid press felt itself insulted. When he tried to take his honeymoon without benefit of publicity, the sensational press hounded him. One tabloid called him a 'Grade A celebrity,' therefore a public commodity, like gas or electric light . . . Lindbergh had forced every reporter and photographer to sign a pledge that he would use the baby's photograph only in his own paper or his own service, making sure that the following newspapers did not receive a copy: *Graphic, News, Mirror, American* and *Journal!*"

This was before the Lindbergh baby was kidnapped.

"*Time* reported (July 21, 1930)," Seldes continued,[32] "that several days later when an airplane belonging to a company of which Lindbergh was a technical adviser ran into a crowd, the *Daily News* headline read:

LINDBERGH LINER KILLS 2

But Hearst stooped lower.

Both the New York *Post*, and the New York *Times* in its exclusive story of Lindbergh's flight from the United States, said the direct cause of the aviator's leave-taking was a certain incident involving his son Jon. Jon was being brought home from school in the family automobile by his nurse, according to the newspapers. After proceeding a short distance the car was forced to the curb by another automobile filled with men. The nurse and the chauffeur thought they were kidnappers after the second Lindbergh son.

But they were merely Hearst photographers. The photograph appeared in the Hearst newspapers and was offered for sale to other newspapers by the Hearst photographic services. The photographer assigned to the job was paid a bonus.

The actual fact is that it was the mother, daughter of the late Dwight Morrow, who was in the car and received the full force of fright at the prospect of her second child being kidnapped. She appears in the photograph, New York *American*, November 28, 1935.

[31] *Freedom of the Press*, by George Seldes.
[32] *Ibid*.

X

THE Hearst economic empire consists of newspapers and magazines, many ostensibly owned by other interests; paper companies held in association with the Rothermere yellow press of London; a radio chain; film and theater investments; cattle ranch and fruit properties; canning and packing plants; real estate, and mining enterprises centering in the Homestake Mining Company of Lead, South Dakota, and the Cerro de Pasco Copper Company of Peru.

The latter, by direct stock ownership in the American Metal Company, an international mining trust of British capitalists conjoined with the Morgan and Guggenheim groups, participates in vast properties scattered throughout the United States, Canada, Latin America, Asia and Africa. In Africa, American Metal jointly controls, with British interests, vast copper properties that exploit native Kaffir labor.†

† *The New Republic,* March 18, 1936, contains the following significant note on labor conditions in the region where the African copper properties of American Metal are located:

"The report of the Commission of Enquiry into the disturbances in the northern Rhodesian copper belt has recently been laid before the British Parliament. Last May native police killed six and wounded twenty-two African copper workers who had gone on strike. The cause of the strike was the sudden announcement that the miners' poll tax was to be raised retrospectively from 12s. 6d. to 15s. . . . The police seem to have lost their balance when confronted by the unusual spectacle of miners at rest during working hours, and charged the men, who in self-defense took to stone-throwing, and the shooting resulted. Although the strike was accompanied by the usual pandemonium of imperialism with troops arriving by airplane, etc., the occurrence itself was soon over. But the strike was notable as being the first in the internationally important Rhodesian copper belt, and there was evidence of concerted action among miners of different districts. The Commission also believes that prospects of further industrial disputes in the copper belt are increasing, and makes recommendations about greater protection, which Parliament will doubtless carry out. The average monthly wage of an African miner is 23s. 6d. [$6]. One of the companies concerned in the dispute has made profits of nearly a million pounds in the last two years. The mine authorities are somewhat opposed to educating African workers."

In February, 1936, workers of the Tererro, N. M., mine of American Metal went on strike against intolerable conditions.

ciated Press, although his influence is subject to qualification by other big publishers. *Editor and Publisher* of March 16, 1935, quoted Frank B. Noyes, publisher of the Washington, D.C., *Star* and president of the Associated Press as saying: "By virtue of the number of member papers owned by Mr. Hearst, he controls the largest number of bond votes of any individual member" of the Associated Press. Control of Associated Press is vested in the bond votes.

The individual properties owned by Hearst Consolidated are the *American Weekly*, whose Sunday circulation within Hearst newspapers exceeds 5,000,000 copies; the Chicago *American*; the Detroit *Times*; Los Angeles *Examiner*; Los Angeles *Herald-Express*; New York *Journal*; Oakland *Post-Inquirer*; Pittsburgh *Sun-Telegraph*; San Francisco *Call-Bulletin*; San Francisco *Examiner*; and Seattle *Post-Intelligencer*. Excepting the last, these are the money-makers among Hearst newspapers.

Hearst Publications, Inc., owns the losers, as follows: Albany (N. Y.) *Times-Union*; Atlanta *Georgian* and *Sunday American*; Baltimore *News and Post* and Baltimore *Sunday American*; Boston *American*; Chicago *Herald and Examiner*; Milwaukee *Wisconsin News*; New York *American*; New York *Mirror*; Omaha *Bee-News*; Rochester (N. Y.) *Journal* and Rochester *Sunday American*; San Antonio (Texas) *Light*; Syracuse *Journal* and Syracuse *Sunday American*; Washington (D. C.) *Herald* and Washington (D. C.) *Times*. Associated with this group is the Newspaper and Magazine Newsprint Company, which supplies paper. Hearst Consolidated controls the American Newsprint Company for the same purpose.

After the losses of these and a few other Hearst newspapers are subtracted from the profits of Hearst Consolidated, the "genius" of Hearst as a businessman suffers some deflation, for the net profit of *all* is only approximately $4,850,000. The 1934 net profit of the Los Angeles *Examiner, Good Housekeeping* and *American Weekly* was, combined, $5,850,000, or $1,500,000 more than for all the Hearst publications. In short, Hearst's profits would be greater if he discarded all his publishing properties except these three, his biggest moneymakers. If he discarded all the losers he could show a net profit probably in excess of $10,000,000, which could be further increased if some of the inflated salaries of executives were reduced.

Fortune listed three newspapers "ostensibly owned by others" which Hearst permitted the magazine to indicate were owned by himself. These were the Milwaukee *Sentinel*, the Pittsburgh *Post-Gazette* and the Boston *Sunday Advertiser and Record*. Moe Annenberg acquired the *Sentinel* for Hearst and Paul Block the *Post-Gazette*. It is generally understood among Hearst men that Paul Block has become a Hearst agent. Paul Block and Associates is a New York advertising firm with which Hearst has long done business. This firm nominally owns Consolidated Publishers, Inc., which operates the Pittsburgh *Post-Gazette*, the Milwaukee *Sentinel*, the Toledo *Blade*, the Newark *Star-Eagle* (which Brisbane tried to buy in 1917), and the Duluth *Herald*. Block is credited with the ownership of the Duluth *News-Tribune* and the Toledo *Times* by N. W. Ayer and Sons Directory of Newspapers for 1934, although Consolidated Publishers does not claim their ownership. They are probably held through the Paul Corporation, a holding unit.

According to Poor's Register of Directors for 1935 Paul Block is president and director of the Pittsburgh *Post-Dispatch* and the Milwaukee *Sentinel*, which *Fortune* asserted Hearst actually owned. N. W. Ayer lists Block as publisher of the *Sentinel* but notes, "see *Wisconsin News*." This is the local avowed Hearst paper. For the *Wisconsin News* N. W. Ayer says, "see Milwaukee *Sentinel*."

Consolidated Publishers, Inc., defaulted on notes of $500,000 in 1932, the remainder of an original issue of $2,333,000 issue of 1926 which was "personally guaranteed" by Paul Block. Hearst is understood to have stepped into the situation at this time, taking up the notes and becoming the controlling interest in the seven Block newspapers.

The editorial policies of the Block papers have been the policies, in the main, of the Hearst papers. Paul Block's political favorites have also, strangely enough, been Hearst's, and Hearst and Block often tour the country together. Block was the confidant and spokesman of Mayor James J. Walker of New York. Block was against Hoover when Hearst was against Hoover. Block swung to Roosevelt when Hearst did. When Hearst recently began booming Alf Landon of Kansas for the Presidency, Block joined in and, with Hearst, visited

Landon. Those details of the "New Deal" which Hearst opposes, Block also opposes; those details which meet with Hearst's approval meet with Block's.

Hearst has recently acquired an interest in Macfadden Publications, Inc., hard upon losses suffered by Bernarr Macfadden in real estate and the stock market. Since this secret Hearst ownership was acquired, *Liberty* Magazine has taken to publishing articles by all the various Hearst favorites, such as Matthew Woll, William Green, Father Charles E. Coughlin, Bainbridge Colby and others. It has also been notoriously conspicuous in publishing material impugning the fairness of Bruno Richard Hauptmann's trial. In general policy, too, *Liberty* has functioned as a Hearst unit since 1934, even down to following Hearst's fascist line. Along with *Liberty*, Macfadden Publications controls *True Stories, True Romances, True Experiences, True Detective Mysteries, Master Detective, Physical Culture, New York Investment News,* and *Radio Mirror*, all of them influential in shaping the mass mind.

There is a myth that Hearst has never been unsuccessful in the operation of a publishing property. To preserve this myth among other reasons, he has had a concealed interest in certain properties, selling out when he could not make them go. We have noticed how Brisbane, an advance Hearst agent as publisher on many occasions, bought an Elizabeth, N. J., paper and later sold it to Moe Annenberg and others. Many of the Hearst papers represent mergers of two or three papers. The *Wisconsin News*, for example, now stands where three papers stood before. The Chicago *Herald-Examiner*, the San Francisco *Call-Bulletin*, the Los Angeles *Herald-Express*, the Seattle *Post-Intelligencer*, the Pittsburgh *Sun-Telegraph* and *Post-Gazette* and others function where two or more papers stood before.

The magazine field is strewn with Hearst failures. Hearst bought both *McClure's* and *Smart Set*, with the late James Quirk as his "dummy," and was forced to discontinue both. *Puck*, the comic weekly, was acquired by Hearst and discarded when it proved unsuccessful. *Farm and Home,* a pre-war Hearst venture, was discontinued. The present *Cosmopolitan* magazine represents the merger of three unsuccessful Hearst magazine properties, *Hearst's Magazine,* the old *Cosmopolitan* and *International*.

332 IMPERIAL HEARST

It has been said that pride has kept Hearst from relinquishing a property, even if it was unprofitable. This is nonsense. He publicly acquired a Fort Worth, Texas, paper after the war and gave it up.

The currently unprofitable Hearst papers are retained for reasons having nothing to do with sentiment or pride. They are all useful. The Albany paper is located, for example, in the capital of New York State, obtaining entry for Hearst into political circles under journalistic privileges. The two Washington (D. C.) papers afford similar opportunities.

Magazines owned by Hearst other than those already mentioned in this analysis are the *American Druggist* (patent medicines), *American Architect* (real estate), *Town and Country* (real estate) and *Home and Field* (real estate). In 1935 Hearst acquired the *Pictorial Review*, a woman's magazine. In England he owns *The Connoisseur* (antiques), *Nash's (Pall Mall) Magazine* (a British version of *Cosmopolitan*), and the British *Good Housekeeping*.

Hearst Radio, Inc., is owned by Hearst Corporation. Its broadcasting stations are WINS, New York; WCAE, Pittsburgh; WSWS, Pittsburgh; WBAL, Baltimore; WISN, Milwaukee; KYA, San Francisco; KELW, Burbank, Cal., and KEHE, Santa Monica, Cal. Hearst's plans call for radio stations in each of the eighteen cities where his main newspaper properties are. The Hearst agents in Washington today are continually lobbying before the Federal Radio Commission for desirable wave lengths.[7]

Hearst's real estate and ranching empire is valued by *Fortune* at $56,000,000. The real estate is heavily mortgaged. *Fortune* listed the following as Hearst's real estate holdings:

	ACRES	ASSESSED VALUE
Ritz Tower, N. Y. C.		$3,750,000
The Warwick Hotel, N. Y. C.		3,100,000
The Lombardy Hotel, N. Y. C.		2,200,000
Sherwood Studios, N. Y. C.	27	1,050,000
471 Park Avenue, N. Y. C.		1,275,000
Ziegfeld Theater, Manhattan		1,090,000
Other New York real estate		25,595,000

[7] During 1934 and 1935 *Variety*, organ of the amusement industry, carried full reports of Hearst's various radio maneuvers.

	Acres	Assessed Value
San Simeon ranch, Cal. (land only)	270,000	2,222,000
Wyntoon estate, Cal.	50,000	300,000
Southern California land	21,000	500,000
Campeche Ranch, Mexico (chicle)	350,000	
Vera Cruz, Mexico, land (hardwood)	260,000	12,000,000
Babicora Ranch, Mexico (cattle)	900,000	
Ojinaga, Mex., land (petroleum)	70,000	
Other real estate	12,000	3,000,000
Approximate totals	2,000,000	$56,000,000

It is noteworthy that the biggest single items in the foregoing are "other New York real estate" and "other real estate." Hearst does not want to particularize. The realty holdings of the newspapers, included in their valuations, are not in the above list.

The Hearst acreage is 33 per cent more extensive than the area of the State of Delaware, about 60 per cent greater than the area of Rhode Island, about half as extensive as the State of New Jersey or Massachusetts. San Simeon alone is greater in area than the island of Puerto Rico. The above real estate summary omits the thousands of acres owned by the Homestake Mining Company of South Dakota and the Cerro de Pasco Copper Company of Peru. By assembling all the Hearst land of the publishing, mining and real estate categories (Cerro de Pasco alone controls over 200 square miles, with its own towns, railroads and public utility plants and stores), we obtain a domain exceeding in size eight or ten single states of the Union.

Vincent Astor is popularly reputed to be the largest New York realty owner, but Hearst is surely a close second and may even outstrip Astor. In Mexico, however, Hearst is the largest absentee landlord. Our enumeration up to this point does not exhaust Hearst's direct Mexican holdings, which include the Las Dimas and Guanacevi gold and silver mines, nor his indirect holdings through stock in Mexican mining companies.

Arthur Brisbane has also been active in New York real estate, and some, or the major part of his transactions, may account in part for the $25,000,000 of New York City real estate about whose location

Fortune does not particularize. Brisbane and Hearst are jointly associated in Hearst-Brisbane Properties, Inc., in which Hearst is the dominant interest.

In 1933, during Mayor O'Brien's Tammany Administration (the Hearst papers supported O'Brien for reëlection), Brisbane leased the Packard Building in Long Island City, which he owned, to the New York City fire department for $65,000 annually, or about $40,000 more than the department was paying in rent on the neighboring Brewster Building. There was a political outcry, and the city administration explained that the new quarters were larger and more efficient from the fire department's point of view. This occurred at the very time that *the city was ostensibly in the throes of an economy wave and O'Brien was surrendering to the demand of the bankers to curtail city expenditures.* The pay of school teachers and other civil servants was reduced.

In the same year Realtor Brisbane was the creditor of Don Dickerman, owner of a chain of Greenwich Village night clubs, among them the Blue Horse, the County Fair and the Four Trees. Brisbane owns the northeast corner building at Fifth Avenue and 102nd Street, mortgaged to the Metropolitan Life Insurance Company at $950,000 and therefore worth at least $2,000,000. He owns the northeast corner building at Eighty-third Street and Madison Avenue, New York, which he leases out at $100,000 annually. He owns the block within Lewis Street, the East River, Seventh and Eighth Streets, Manhattan, which he purchased from the Long Island Railroad in 1929 for $315,000. This property is of especial interest. It is located in New York's worst slum area, remote from all means of rapid transportation. Why should Brisbane want it? It so happens that the new East River Drive will run right past it, beginning downtown near the South Street newspaper properties of Hearst. The New York Hearst newspapers have boomed this project,[8] which, in 1929, was known only to a few Tammany insiders. Construction will be financed with Federal public works funds.

At 110th Street and Fifth Avenue in New York City facing Central Park, whose surrounding properties have so attracted both

[8] See New York *Journal* editorial, January 29, 1935.

tration's principal monetary adviser, had so much to do—Homestake's profits, on the upgrade for several years, soared to record high levels. The earnings of $19.94 a share in 1933, for example, compared with $4.16 for 1929. The dividend of $15 a share in 1933 was only a foretaste of what was to come, for $30 a share was paid in 1934 and $54 a share in 1935. In 1934 and 1935 most of the dividends were "extra." The book value of the common stock remains at $85 a share although the stock is quoted at more than $500 a share on the Stock Exchange.[12] The open market value of all outstanding capital stock is more than $138,000,000 compared with the asset valuation of $25,000,000 in the company's balance sheet. In 1920 Homestake common sold down to $5 a share and stayed below $100 a share until the inflationary demands of the Committee for the Nation, mainly in the Hearst papers and by Coughlin, in 1932. The tremendous increase in Homestake profits is directly due to the Administration's monetary policies, which were influenced if not determined by the Committee for the Nation.

Homestake, as the nation's largest gold producer, gives Hearst an immediate participation in the international commodity market. Thus nothing of major import in the world market leaves Hearst's pocketbook unaffected, either negatively or positively, for all commodity transactions take place in terms of gold. The wartime income figures on Homestake are eloquent in the light of Hearst's wartime policies:

1914 (deficit)	$530,653
1915 (profit)	135,338
1916 (deficit)	386,680
1917 (deficit)	763,666
1918 (deficit)	808,872

Cerro de Pasco is rated as one of the most completely equipped copper producers in the world, with assets placed, conservatively, at $40,986,757. On its executive committee sit Mr. Clark, and Ogden Mills, former Secretary of the Treasury. On the board of directors are representatives of Bankers Trust (Morgan) and Irving Trust. As with Homestake, none of the holding company obscurantism

[12] January, 1936.

of the Hearst newspaper properties envelops Cerro's crystalline balance sheets. The capital structure is simple. The company has no securities for sale, has no "opportunity" to offer to the public. Gold and silver, as well as copper, are produced. Much of its recent prosperity derives from the Roosevelt silver-buying policy.

The fortunes of Cerro de Pasco under the Hoover and Roosevelt policies are shown in the following table:

	Net Income	Dividends
1929	$4,729,113	$6,456,341
1930 (deficit)	1,986,836	6,175,631
1931 (deficit)	2,963,681	1,543,917
1932 (deficit)	3,441,890	280,710
1933 (deficit)	298,882	not paid
1934 (profit)	1,782,019	

Heavy dividends were paid despite the depression deficits, although the company laid off thousands of its workers. Homestake also paid dividends when it was losing money.

Under the Coolidge-Mellon régime Cerro's earnings showed a steady rise, as follows:

	Net Income	Dividends
1923	$2,699,866	$2,971,686
1924	3,224,327	4,413,608
1925	6,016,166	5,614,060
1926	4,550,837	5,614,210
1927	3,664,281	4,491,368
1928	5,756,328	5,052,789

The foregoing figures cover the period just before Moore was sent to Peru as Ambassador and while the National City Bank was pumping American investors' money into Peru notwithstanding the advice of its own agents that Peru was unsound, economically and socially.

The wartime record, beginning with the company's first public report, is as follows:

1916 (net income)	$3,554,216
1917 (deficit)	1,930,603
1918 (deficit)	4,157,085

The war meant only losses to Hearst.

Cerro de Pasco is a big factor in Latin American political affairs. It owns 39,000 shares in the American Metal Company, on whose board of directors Mr. Clark sits with Mr. Joseph Cotton, former Under-Secretary of State in the Coolidge-Hoover Administration, and representatives of the London mining trusts. American Metal Company's assets, conservatively valued, are $76,000,000. It owns 36 per cent of the Roan Antelope Copper Mines in Africa, controlled in London; controls the Rhodesian Selection Trust, another big African producer, with 52 per cent of the stock; shares control (with London interests) of the Bwana M'Kubwa Copper Mining Company of Africa. All these holdings were acquired by American Metal after the war, as, simultaneously, Cerro was buying its stock. As the Americans came in, certain British interests were ousted. Morgan and Guggenheim copper interests are also involved in American Metal.

American Metal also controls the American Metal Company of Canada, Ltd., the American Metal Company of Colorado, the American Metal Company of Mexico, the American Metal Company of Texas, the American Zinc and Chemical Company, the Blackwell Zinc Company, the Chanute Smelter Company, the Langeloth Coal Company, the Langeloth Mercantile Company, the Retort Metals Refining Company and the South American Metal Company. Its bankers are Irving Trust and Bankers Trust.

The Mexican subsidiary controls or participates in many operating companies in northern Mexico (on whose boards Mr. Clark sits). Some of these Mexican operating companies are: In the State of Durango, the Compania Minera de Penoles, owner of 6,318 acres of silver, lead and zinc properties; the Guanacevi mines (which Hearst personally controls); and a white arsenic plant at Mapimi. In Nuevo Leon, the Cerralva mines and Las Minas Viejas. In Zacatecas, the Eta Grande, the Avalos and the Refugio mines. In Coahuila, the Higueras mines and properties in the Sierra Mojada, Jimulco and Santa Elena and Anahuac districts. And in Chihuahua, the Santa Eulalia mines, the Naica mine and various others. Clark is a director of Santa Eulalia as well as of Hearst's neighboring Babicora Development Company.

If the profits of Hearst's mining companies had not been restored, judging from the current state of his newspaper properties, he would have faced an uncertain economic future early in 1933, and might well have gone the way of Insull and Kreuger. The recovery of real estate values since 1933, paralleling the mining recovery, has also been of great assistance to Hearst.

The question is often asked among newspaper men: What will happen to the Hearst empire when he dies, as he must before very long, since he is now seventy-three years old? There have been romantic surmises that it will disintegrate without the "demoniacal" Hearst drive behind it. But the destiny of the Hearst properties is clearly indicated by the stake of the banks in them. As long as the banks have a stake they will keep the properties afloat. Moreover, the Hearst publications are of distinct political value to the banks, providing an enormous propaganda mechanism for influencing the lower masses.

Wall Street has already picked Hearst's successor. He is John Francis Neylan, who is currently taking the kinks out of the tangled Hearst holding company structure and curbing Hearst's passion for squandering money on gaudy palaces and objects of art. The Hearst sons, whatever their native capabilities, are manifestly unable to manage this very complex and widespread domain. Indeed, it is probable that they do not realize its magnitude or its full implications.

In 1906, while campaigning for the Governorship of New York, Hearst caustically denounced rival New York newspaper proprietors for owing money to banks and insurance companies because such obligations make them puppets of Wall Street. These words were a prophecy of what the Hearst of 1920–1936 would be.

XI

IT WAS inevitable that Hearst should become the most influential American fascist, aping his friends Alfred Hugenberg, the German publisher, and Lord Rothermere, the English publisher. Today Hearst is the keystone of American fascism, the integrating point in a structure around which political reaction is attempting to develop a movement which, if it succeeds, will tragically dupe America.

In the first months of the Roosevelt Administration Hearst was a "New Dealer." The Hearst papers applauded reopening gutted banks with taxpayers' funds, lending to mismanaged railroads, devaluing the currency, raising the price of gold from $20.67 an ounce to $35, an ambitious program of public works, raising prices, allocating huge new sums to the building of an unprecedented military machine, etc.

It was only when the Roosevelt régime, confronted by 15,000,000 unemployed and a farm population on the verge of armed revolt, began to offer *them* some measure of concrete aid, that Hearst cooled toward the "New Deal." By the end of 1933 Hearst's pæans of praise for Roosevelt had changed into criticism and denunciation. Hearst was against public relief payments to the unemployed, subsidies to the farmers (he had never been against subsidies to banks, railroads, shipbuilders and munitions fabricators), the Roosevelt promises of old-age pensions and social security for the masses.

This opposition, of course, derived from the fear of higher income taxes. Hearst renewed his banker-inspired campaigns for a sales tax. Many states and municipalities, including Illinois and New York City, had passed sales tax legislation. Hearst demanded that the Federal Government follow suit.

On May 26, 1934, Hearst sailed for Europe.

After a brief visit to Spain, Hearst took a plane for Germany, where he passed the whole summer of 1934. On August 18th he was visited in Berlin by Dr. E. F. S. Hanfstaengl, Nazi foreign press chief. Four days later, Hearst was quoted in the German press as follows, according to a dispatch to the New York *Times* published on August 23, 1934:

"Dr. Hanfstaengl quoted Mr. Hearst as saying of last Sunday's plebiscite:

" 'The results represent a unanimous expression of the popular will. This overwhelming majority with which Hitler astonished the world must, as we now learn, be accepted as self-evident and in a sense must open up a new chapter in modern history.

" 'If Hitler succeeds in pointing the way of peace and order and an ethical development which has been destroyed throughout the world by war, he will have accomplished a measure of good not only for his own people but for all humanity.

" 'Germany is battling for her liberation from the mischievous provisions of the Treaty of Versailles and for her redemption from the malicious suppression and encirclement to which she has been subjected by nations which in their avarice and shortsightedness have only shown enmity and jealousy over her advancement.

" 'This battle, in fact, can only be viewed as a struggle which all liberty-loving peoples are bound to follow with understanding and sympathy.' "

Hearst's blessing upon the Hitler régime was given while the world was still aghast at the June 30th massacre of Hitler's intimate political associates.

Hearst was invited to attend the Nazi conclave at Nuremberg which confounded the world with an astounding farrago of medieval theories about politics, culture, society and biology. He was even photographed with various high Nazis, including Dr. Rosenberg, and on September 16th he was admitted to conference with Hitler.

After a summer spent in an extended series of discussions with high Nazis, including Franz von Papen, who, as German military attaché in Washington during the war, contacted German agents in

Hearst's organization, Hearst left for London late in September. From London he personally directed John Francis Neylan, his attorney, in the strategy of breaking the San Francisco general strike of sympathy for the dockworkers.

Neylan constituted himself generalissimo of the San Francisco newspapers and the members of the San Francisco Industrial Association. The Neylan-directed papers suddenly declared it was not a strike *but a revolution*. General Hugh S. Johnson, then head of the NRA and a visitor on the Pacific Coast, was induced to characterize the strike as revolution. The newspapers then introduced the strain that it was a "communistic revolution," and that children, patients in hospitals and the aged would soon be without food, milk, medicine, electric light. The striking unions had made full provisions for supplying all these needs. However, the humanitarian forethought of the unions only infuriated the forces gathered around Neylan. In order to obscure from public view the humaneness of the unions in the very midst of bitter class warfare, the San Francisco papers spoke of a "new government" having taken power, a "revolutionary government," whose permission was required for all public acts.

It was the Neylan-unified press which broke the strike, with assistance from various A. F. of L. executives. William Green, president of the A. F. of L., of course denounced the strike at a crucial moment.

Federal investigators did not find a trace of revolutionary plotting. There was not the remotest tinge of revolution about the strike. It was a simple strike for decent wages for the dockworkers. The employers won by lies and murder. Newsreels showed the police deliberately shooting into a cluster of idling dockworkers, killing two.

As soon as Neylan and the San Francisco Industrial Association raised the cry of revolution, the National Guard was sent in by the Hearst government of California. Most of Hearst's higher executives are, as has been indicated, National Guard officers and Roy D. Keehn of Chicago, Hearst's Mid-West manager, is president of the United States National Guard Association.

During the closing stages of the strike the three Hearst papers in the San Francisco area repeatedly called upon the police to take violent measures against the strikers and the police did shoot and kill. Not satisfied, though the police and Guardsmen were in full charge, the Hearst press demanded that vigilante bands be formed to proceed against the "revolutionaries." At once mobs of hoodlums under the leadership of brokers, commission merchants, straw bosses and dividend beneficiaries in general, roved through San Francisco, looting, pillaging and assaulting citizens. The police stood by inactive, *and even helped*.

The offices of *The Western Worker*, Pacific Coast organ of the Communist Party, were demolished and its staff members beaten. This invasion of the "freedom of the press" was applauded by the Hearst papers. (The Hearst cohorts of Lead, S. D., demolished the plant of an opposition newspaper and forced another paper out of business in the years 1910-13.)

The atmosphere of violence and sudden death created by the authorities and the "respectable" element of the city spurred the police to redoubled activity. A number of known radicals, including girls and young women, some of them high school and university students, were arrested on trumped-up charges. The city's jails were crammed with these young girls and boys, who were confined in cells with felons, diseased prostitutes, dope-fiends and other human débris.

After more than a score of acknowledged Communists had been arrested or beaten, the vigilante bands, unmolested by the police, applauded by the Hearst press, with other San Francisco newspapers saying nothing, broke into private homes and physically attacked well-known liberals, progressives, and Jews. They stormed about the university campus at Berkeley nearby and invaded the homes of faculty members, slugging women, locking frightened children into clothes closets, and throwing petroleum over books and household furnishings.

The vigilantes had learned from the Hearst editorials about "intellectuals." In the mob-mind all intellectuals were thought to be liberals or radicals, so that some amazing depredations occurred. In San Francisco the home of a writer of popular mystery stories, who knew little about politics and cared less, was entered and he was beaten and his wife was molested. Teachers of botany and mathematics, who had only the vaguest notions about politics, were assaulted along with historians, sociologists, political scientists, economists and anthropologists.

On all of this the San Francisco press—and the outside American press—was silent. The same sort of censorship laid down during the Hearst-*Tribune* gun-battles in Chicago obtained again. *Editor and Publisher* later carried a full account for "the trade" of how Hearst's Neylan rallied the anti-strike forces. Some faulty staff-work permitted the appearance of this story.

As yet the world did not know that Hearst, like his friend and business associate Rothermere in London, had become converted to fascism. Nor did the world yet know that Hearst was receiving a heavy annual subsidy from the Hitler government for his efforts in its behalf.

As soon as Hearst returned from Europe he defended nationalism in a letter of reply to the College Editors Association. He also financed a trip of college editors to Washington to study the government at work. Since his German trip, Hearst has been very preoccupied with students.

In November and December Hearst reporters were sent incognito into various American campuses with the express design of "framing" professors as Communists. The Nazis had convinced Hearst that communism was an intellectualistic business, as well as a social aim.

Syracuse University, situated in a Hearst town, was the scene of the opening fascist operation—for Hearst's anti-Communist campaign is part of a program to dupe the masses into an American fascism, just as the bankers and industrialists of Germany and Italy, working through Hitler and Mussolini, duped the unhappy people of those countries.

On November 22, 1934, Hearst's Syracuse *Journal* carried this banner-line:

DRIVE ALL RADICAL PROFESSORS AND STUDENTS FROM UNIVERSITY

A Hearst reporter, impersonating a student just entering the university, had interviewed Dr. John N. Washburne, head of the department of educational psychology. According to the Syracuse *Journal*, this "communistic" professor had been very outspoken with the reporter, a complete stranger, about the "coming revolution." The Syracuse *Journal* portrayed the professor as gleefully confiding revolutionary plans. Other professors were interviewed and similarly misquoted.

As anyone of ordinary perspicacity would know, revolutionists do not confide in the first person who accosts them, especially if the revolutionists occupy public jobs. But Hearst's patrons, from the beginning, have been people who read and run, unable to puzzle over such questions.

On November 26th the Syracuse paper demanded that eight professors be cashiered as "Communists." Endorsements of its stand from the local American Legion and its women's auxiliary were also printed. Hearst has never had difficulty in rounding up signed endorsements for any of his campaigns.

The attack of the Hearst press was repelled. Students and professors rallied to Professor Washburne's side and, fortunately, there were witnesses to the interview.

New York University and Columbia University in New York City were the locales of the next thrust of Hearst fascism. On November 29, 1934, Professor Sidney Hook, of New York University, was intérviewed by a reporter for the *American*. Hearst was baffled in his immediate aim because the reporter was a former student of Hook's and a member of the American Newspaper Guild. Since the Guild's formation, Hearst has had some difficulty in dispatching men on thieves' errands.

On December 2, 1934, the *American* carried a story about the merger of two political groups, with one of which Hook was associated, into an organization "so radical that even the Communists have refused to have anything to do with them."

After several weeks the assault on Professor Hook, and Associate Professor James Burnham of the philosophy department, closed as follows:

"Well! Gentlemen of the Faculty of New York University, trustees, alumni, students, and everyone else who is a friend of New York University and proud of its history—if the alleged actions of these two professors have been correctly reported, what do you say to it?

"WHAT DO YOU PROPOSE TO DO ABOUT IT?

"Is this old and respected institution of learning to be classified hereafter as a seeding-ground for disloyalty to America and its cherished institutions—as an active center for treasonable plotting for the overthrow of the American Government?"

This would be absurd in its immediate effect were it not that New York University, like other schools, receives some financial assistance from the state and depends upon alumni to some extent for endowments. A recent Hearst policy calls for a reduction in all school budgets so that taxes on millionaires, who pay very little anyhow, may be reduced. This new Hearst tactic will make it rather difficult for schools and universities to get funds, especially those schools whose teachings run counter to the concepts of Hearst.

On December 14, 1934, the attack began at Columbia University, where a reporter, posing as a student, wished to enroll in the classes of Professor George S. Counts of Teachers College. As the "student" in his letter manifested unusual interest in liberalism and communism, Counts immediately smelled Hearst, for the Hearst editors alone lump liberalism and communism together as two related things and they alone suppose students have such matters uppermost in mind. Counts and his associates prepared to greet the "student." The reporter readily and shamefacedly admitted who he was, but Professor Counts said he would submit to an interview, with a stenographer at his elbow. The reporter also interviewed Dr. William H. Kilpatrick, who then interrogated the reporter and drew from him the admission that he knew he was on a caddish assignment. Professor Jesse H. Newlon also granted an interview.

The reporter, on closing his talk with Dr. Counts, said: "You realize of course that because of my assignment I will have to select the most sensational statements from the interview in order to make out a good case. This is what Mr. Hearst is expecting."[1]

The reaction from the universities was not quite what Hearst expected. He was denounced by students and professors alike, and by liberal newspapers like the New York *Post*. Dr. Counts and his associates devoted the entire February, 1935, issue of *Social Frontier*, an educational magazine, to an exposition of Hearst's anti-social career.

At various universities and colleges in the East—Princeton, Dartmouth, Amherst, Yale, Williams, Columbia, New York University and many more—students voted to boycott the Hearst magazines, newspapers and militaristic newsreels. Alarmed by Hearst's clearly defined fascist propaganda, various liberal and radical groups began a nation-wide Hearst boycott. The students of Northwestern University, the leading Methodist institution in the country, voted to boycott the Hearst press before the Hearst *agents provocateurs* appeared on the campus.

Hearst's *Wisconsin News*, published in Milwaukee, successfully brought about a legislative investigation of "communism" at the University of Wisconsin. The university was cleared, but much filth was strewn before Hearst's readers about "communistic free love practices" and "orgies" by faculty members. These allegations were merely untrue.

Hearst's Chicago papers precipitated an Illinois legislative inquiry at the University of Chicago and the University of Illinois. The universities were unqualifiedly cleared, but the Hearst papers again poured poison into ignorant readers' minds. Professor Frederick Schuman of the political science department of the University of Chicago was singled out for special attack because he had written a scholarly book called *The Nazi Dictatorship*, which has informed many cultivated minds about the true state of affairs in Germany.

[1] *Social Frontier*, February, 1935.

In *The Nation* of April 24, 1935, Professor Schuman told what had happened: "On November 14, 1934, the Chicago *Herald-Examiner* published a report of a meeting of the University of Chicago Student Union Against War and Fascism, in which I and several other people were grossly misquoted. In a letter to the editor, Mr. [Victor] Watson, I protested against this misrepresentation and, incidentally, called attention to the fact that the alleged quotation from Lenin on the dictatorship of the proletariat which was then appearing at the top of the editorial pages of all the Hearst papers was nowhere to be found in Lenin's writings. Mr. Watson sent my protest to Mr. Hearst, who asked Mr. Charles Wheeler[2] of the *Herald-Examiner* to 'investigate.' I received Mr. Wheeler in the presence of a third person and was shown material from his files showing conclusively that I had been 'accidentally' misquoted—a fact which Mr. Wheeler blandly conceded. He also conceded that the Lenin 'quotation' was a pure invention. 'We just do what the Old Man orders. One week he orders a campaign against rats. The next week he orders a campaign against dope-peddlers. Pretty soon he's going to campaign against college professors. It's all the bunk, but orders are orders.'

"Shortly afterward a New York anti-Nazi group requested me to prepare a series of replies to the syndicated articles by Goering appearing periodically in the Sunday issues of the Hearst papers. The International News Service (Hearst) encouraged the group to believe that an opportunity would be given for such replies. Two articles were submitted. Both were refused. The Hearst press has subsequently published more articles by Goering and one by Alfred Rosenberg, all of them consisting of crude pro-Nazi propaganda of the most blatant type. When it became clear that the I. N. S. would refuse all proffered replies to these misrepresentations of the situation in Germany, the New York group abandoned negotiations, convinced that Mr. Hearst is now an authorized disseminator of Nazi propaganda in the United States."

Professor Schuman described in detail more falsifications by the

---

[2] Charles Wheeler is a veteran of the Hearst political machine around Chicago and his antagonism is enough to give independent politicians and judges nightmares.

Hearst press in Chicago. Though such falsifications were corrected in publications like *The Nation*, the corrections never reached the audience which belongs to Hearst.

Hearst's curious campaign on behalf of Bruno Richard Hauptmann was also pleasing to Berlin, where the authorities were very disturbed that the perpetrator of an internationally notorious crime should be a former German army man. Defense funds were collected for Hauptmann in New York under Nazi auspices.

The Hearst press threw itself behind the various teachers' and students' oath bills in the state legislatures, and Hearst himself is said to have dictated the Ives Law in New York. The editor of Hearst's Boston *American*[3] was responsible for the passage of the Massachusetts teachers' oath bill. By singling teachers out for a unique oath, their patriotism is manifestly called into special question, and this is the atmosphere Hearst is trying to create.

Hearst obviously would like to bring about in the United States what obtains today in Germany, where university students are limited to 50,000 persons out of a population of 65,000,000 people and are chosen from the upper social strata.

Frederick T. Birchall, former managing editor of the New York *Times* and now its roving correspondent in Europe, cabled to his paper[4] that the German propaganda division had signed a contract to purchase the Hearst news service at 1,000,000 marks annually. In American money this is $400,000.

Hearst sold his service direct to the Hitler government, and not to a private news agency. The Hitler government, through the Wolff Bureau, German news agency, was previously well supplied with American news, for the Wolff Bureau had a mutual exchange agreement with the Associated Press which did not cost Germany a penny. The daily news report of the Associated Press is much more complete than the Hearst news services, which deal merely in a few sensations and "filler" material.

[3] Alfred L. Southwick, according to *Editor and Publisher*, June 29, 1935.
[4] New York *Times*, December 31, 1934, and January 1, 1935, first edition. The details of the financial arrangements do not appear in the later editions of the *Times* for January 1, 1935.

IMPERIAL HEARST 353

Why then is Hearst receiving $400,000 each year, even though Germany is hard pressed for foreign exchange? Is it not apparent that this Hitler-Hearst contract, the most expensive news contract in the world, would establish such an obligation as might well result in favorable newspaper comment for the Hitler régime and unfavorable comment for the Soviet régime, of which Hitler has chosen to be the arch-enemy? Does not this "news agreement" have about it an even more offensive aroma than clung about the $500,000 "loan" made to Arthur Brisbane by Germans in 1917? Is it not very much like the Southern Pacific contract?

It is a fact that after Hearst entered into this contract the Hearst newspapers switched to the policy of praising the Hitler régime whenever possible and denouncing the Soviet Union in particular and communism in general. This anti-Communist line fitted in with the requirements of reactionary leaders of American business and industry, who feared that the American government might be forced to spend money to help distressed citizens.

The German fascists, however, do derive more from their $400,000 annual contribution to Hearst than the friendliness of the Hearst press. Not only do they receive the full news reports of INS and Universal Service (which they could obtain in a more readable form from the Associated Press or the United Press) but they obtain special information services from Hearst which others would not supply. Any event of special interest to the German Foreign Office is reported to Germany in much more exhaustive detail than any German newspaper could handle.

One instance will illustrate. When New York Magistrate Louis B. Brodsky freed anti-Nazi demonstrators who tore down the Nazi swastika from the German liner *Bremen*, there was, owing to the nature of Magistrate Brodsky's strictures upon the Hitlerites, a tremendous furore. From Germany the Hearst headquarters got the request to send every scrap of material on the case that could be found. Reporters were sent out to obtain comments from citizens high and low. Whole stories and editorials from non-Hearst American newspapers were placed on the wires. Several hundred thousand words were sent to Germany by INS and US; several cables were utilized for more than twenty-four hours. None of this material found its way into German newspapers, but it did enable the German Foreign Office to gauge the full significance of the court decision and the reaction to it down to the slightest shading. It is only through Hearst that Berlin can utilize a big American news-gathering organization for spying on behalf of foreign imperialism.

Many little incidents that never find their way into the American or European press are sent to Germany by the Hearst organization. Whole magazine articles bearing on Germany, Hitler and German fascists are immediately relayed to Berlin as part of this "news service."

Hearst's personal editorials in all his papers have deplored both fascism and communism as abhorrent, un-Jeffersonian forms of regimentation. Hearst's Jeffersonianism is one of the most effective blinds behind which to accomplish various political and financial purposes and to deceive the American population. But in action, Hearst praises Italy and Germany, the outstanding fascist states, approves violent assaults on organized labor and farmers, terrorization of teachers, reduction of school budgets, creation of concentration camps for radicals, and the like. Hearst has become fascist in deed, even though he is still afraid to endorse fascism explicitly.

Italian fascism had Hearst approval long before Hitler came into power. Even while Hearst was complimenting the Soviet Union he was at the same time endorsing Mussolini. The late Richard Washburn Childs, former American Ambassador to Rome, was a paid agent of Mussolini in the United States, as was publicly revealed shortly before Childs' death. As such, Childs regularly wrote signed articles in praise of fascist Italy for the Hearst papers. Childs, incidentally, had also been paid $7,500 by the "Power Trust" for condemning the Boulder Dam government project in his newspaper writings. The economic reason for Hearst's applause for Mussolini in the days when he found the Soviet acceptable lay in the fact that the Italian fascist government controlled all of Italy's foreign advertising.

Hitler wanted to mobilize world hatred against the Soviet Union, and, by war against the first socialist country, spread fascism—and, at the same time, distract the attention of the German people from the sub-human living standards to which fascism had brought them. When Hearst returned from Germany he began a campaign of vilification against the Soviet Union. The Roosevelt Administration, seeking to build up trade between the Soviet Union and the United States, had created the Export-Import Bank for the purpose of fostering and financing Russian-American trade.

As the Administration was preparing its plan for recogniton of the Soviet Union, Senator Hiram Johnson introduced in the Senate the Johnson Act, which provided that no foreign country in default on its obligations to the United States or to Americans, might borrow in the United States. Ostensibly the legislation was directed against the former Allies, which had just defaulted on their governmental debts to the United States. The Allies, however, were not at the moment seeking loans in the American market. The Soviet Union intended to seek credits.

The United States government had been foolish enough to grant a loan on the request of the short-lived Kerensky government of Russia. This loan was in default. Unless the Soviet made it good it could not get credits here under the terms of the Johnson Act. The Soviet Union had no intention of paying this loan, which had been granted to a Russian tool of the Allies solely for the continuation of war with Germany. The Johnson Act made it impossible to finance American trade with the Soviet Union.

Why did the United States recognize the Soviet Union? For sixteen years successive American governments refused recognition with the full approval of Wall Street. Who prompted the Roosevelt régime to change? Why did not the leading American capitalists forbid Roosevelt to recognize the Bolsheviks?

The Chase National Bank, which endorsed many early Roosevelt policies, wanted the Soviet Union recognized. Vincent Astor, director of the Rockefeller-controlled Chase Bank and a trusted Roosevelt adviser, was the liaison officer. The Roosevelt policies were highly beneficial to the Rockefeller oil and real estate interests. Higher commodity prices and real estate valuations were, early in 1933, essential to the Rockefellers, and the Roosevelt Administration, by its monetary policies, produced them. That section of Wall Street oriented around J. P. Morgan & Co., with the bulk of its wealth in liquid funds or fixed-interest obligations, found less to admire in these Roosevelt policies.

In pushing for recognition of the U.S.S.R., the Chase Bank, the largest individual financial institution in the United States, was merely serving its own interests. The Rockefeller Socony-Vacuum oil enterprise had a long-term contract with the Soviets for the Russian oil output, and was selling this oil throughout the Orient in competition with the British Royal Dutch interests. The Chase Bank itself was the American fiscal agent for the State Bank of the U.S.S.R., and as such handled the sale of Russian gold bonds in the United States. Strengthening American-Russian relations and creation of Russian-American trade would benefit the Chase Bank no less than the U.S.S.R.

When the United States recognized the Soviet Union, the National City crowd was disgruntled, but was busy with its own troubles. Chase had the inside track in Washington, on this question at least. But National City set about, in collaboration with Hearst, to undermine Russian-American relations, and it was in response to the clamor of the Hearst-National City clique that the Roosevelt Administration in 1935 resolved to postpone building the projected million-dollar American embassy in Moscow and recalled several American consuls from the Soviet Union. Although the United States maintained its diplomatic relations, even though protesting at the behest of Hearst and National City against "Communistic propaganda," it abandoned plans for financing Russian-American trade.

National City had reasons other than rivalry with Chase for wishing to see American-Russian relations disrupted. When Chase Bank wrote off on its books all the open bank credits to Germany which the Hitler régime refused to pay, National City became Germany's largest creditor in the United States. National City did not write this debt off. It still hoped to collect.

National City not only wanted to collect this money, but also had a personal bone to pick with the Soviets, for its Petrograd branch was confiscated by the Bolsheviks in 1917. The Russian properties of many American corporate clients of National City were also confiscated. National City, moreover, was head of the syndicate that placed the last pre-Soviet Russian loan of $50,000,000. Chase had had no significant interest in Czarist Russia.

Diplomatic, political or financial gains by the Soviet Union therefore meant more business for Chase. Diplomatic, political or financial gains by Germany meant profits for National City. The two institutions were diametrically opposed on the German-Russian issue in European politics, and Hearst was allied with National City, and Germany.

Hearst, however, had at least moral support from Chase Bank in his opposition to the Roosevelt policies of social reform, because Chase, in common with other Wall Street banks, was opposed to the continued unbalance of the budget and the consequent threat of higher income and inheritance taxes.

Hearst did not hesitate to stigmatize the various reform elements in the Administration as "Communists." The Brain Trust, Secretary of Interior Ickes and Assistant Secretary of Agriculture Rexford Guy Tugwell incurred Hearst's especial ire, which he vented in cartoons showing them as nuts with squirrels chasing them, and as inane "parlor pinks."

Through 1934 there were still vague aspersions in the Hearst press on bankers in general. But there is not even pretense any longer.

The change dates from a visit paid to Hearst at San Simeon by Thomas W. Lamont, Morgan partner, in February, 1935. The financial specialists in the Hearst organization all knew that Lamont was visiting Hearst. What it meant they did not know until, while the Hearst-Lamont visit was still in progress, the Hearst editors received a memorandum from Hearst to keep all unpleasant mention of bankers out of the papers in the future.

Hearst's anti-communistic campaign now became a way of stirring up rancor against the liberal aspect of the Roosevelt policies, earning the gratitude of Big Business in general. It was also a means of combating organized labor under the guise of anti-radicalism. And, also, the masquerade against communism was building up a force the only logical product of which would be a fascist régime in the United States.

In working to undermine Roosevelt, Hearst did not depend solely on the communistic farrago. He also maneuvered in the realm of "practical" politics. This maneuvering was plainly designed to split the Democratic Party and solidify Republican reactionaries for the campaign of 1936.

In rallying opposition to Roosevelt, Hearst received powerful assistance on the radio from the anti-Semitic and anti-Protestant Father Charles E. Coughlin. Before the death of Huey Long, who veered against Roosevelt just when Coughlin and Hearst and Wall Street veered, Coughlin and Long were exchanging compliments. Political circles anticipated that they would join publicly in opposing Roosevelt. Allied with Long was Governor Eugene Talmadge of Georgia, who, after Long's death, vowed that he would run as an independent Democrat in the Presidential election of 1936 merely to capture at least two Southern states from the Roosevelt column and thus assure Roosevelt's defeat.

Georgia is a Hearst state, with the Atlanta *Georgian*, a Hearst paper, the center of Hearst political intrigue in the region. It was therefore no coincidence that Talmadge found himself in complete agreement with Hearst. Nor is it mere coincidence that Father Coughlin has his center of activity in Detroit, where Hearst publishes the *Times*.

In the summer of 1935 Hearst encouraged Alfred E. Smith to run for President in 1936. Hearst did not declare for Smith, but in favor of his *candidacy*. Smith had joined the reactionaries of the American Liberty League. He was also the head of the Catholic Action, political instrument of the Catholic Church. Smith ignored the invitation to join the battle against Roosevelt on behalf of Hearst, although his public speeches increasingly assumed the tone and content of a Hearst editorial.

Hearst simultaneously concerned himself with developing a Republican candidate who would keep Hoover from being nominated. Hearst had two Republican possibilities—Governor Alfred Landon

IMPERIAL HEARST

of Kansas and Frank Knox, publisher of the Chicago *Daily News* and Hearst's personal creation as a metropolitan newspaper manager.

As to Knox's candidacy, Hearst spoke pleasant words, and endorsed him as fully qualified. But the full weight of Hearst's political propaganda was thrown to Alf Landon, who as Governor of Kansas had pleased all banker-minded persons by reducing the state's budget at the expense of the unemployed. The availability of William E. Borah of Idaho for the Republican nomination on an ostensibly liberal platform was scarcely mentioned by the Hearst press.

At this point Hearst had Talmadge, Smith, Landon and Knox on his knee. He counted on the Republicans, with the help of a Democratic split, to defeat Roosevelt and his mildly reformist régime. If Alf Landon was unable to get the nomination from the Republicans, Knox might.

This is Hearst, the Jeffersonian Democrat!

Within the Democratic ranks themselves there were many powerful individuals giving support to Hearst, whose influence extends into the Cabinet. Of the Cabinet, Hearst has praised War Secretary George H. Dern, whose perennial calls for a greater military machine were echoed in approving Hearst editorials; Secretary of the Navy Claude A. Swanson, approved for similar reasons; Secretary of Commerce Daniel C. Roper, a Hearst-McAdoo connection; and Vice-President John Nance Garner.

Hearst's pet aversions in the Roosevelt Cabinet have been Secretary of the Interior Harold L. Ickes; Secretary of Labor Frances Perkins; Secretary of Agriculture Henry A. Wallace and Assistant Secretary Tugwell; and Secretary of the Treasury Henry Morgenthau. As to the latter, Hearst's distaste was never very great. Hearst has seemed neutral about Secretary of State Cordell Hull, Attorney General Homer S. Cummings and Postmaster General James A. Farley, all of them stand-patters.

We find, not at all oddly, that it was precisely those Cabinet members who were not regular political wheel-horses who caused Hearst to dance with rage in his editorial pages. Whatever else one may say about Ickes, Tugwell, Perkins, Wallace, and Morgenthau, they were definitely not persons with profound experience in political intrigue. The other Roosevelt Cabinet members either fell into this dark category, or, like Dern, were bankers and mining magnates. As for President Roosevelt himself, Hearst soon found his mild reformism and tentative humanitarianism a manifestation of weakness, even of illness.

In his campaign against the latter phases of the "New Deal," Hearst did not scruple to use Communist slogans himself, slogans which the Communists used against Roosevelt in the earlier stages of the "New Deal" but which they discarded in favor of coöperating with the more democratic factions in a struggle against political reaction and fascism. Where the Communists used these slogans for Leftist reasons, Hearst employed them for the benefit of the predatory class. Thus, the Communist designation of the "New Deal" as the "Raw Deal" became a regular feature of the Hearst press. The National Recovery Act was characterized by the Communists as the "National Run Around" because of certain features, and Hearst took up this slogan in 1934 to mobilize Right-wing opposition to the Act.

While Hearst sought to intimidate President Roosevelt, the conservative Cabinet members, by adroitly placed advice, tried to steer the "New Deal" itself to the extreme Right.

Hearst's ballyhoo about communism did not fool organized labor nor, indeed, did it fool any intelligent individual. The country, however, is not populated solely by intelligent people. There is an extensive element in the electorate which is clay in the hands of an unscrupulous and sinister character like Hearst. It is unquestionably true that Hearst can swing millions of these voters one way or the other. Some of them do not even know that their subconscious thoughts are being shaped by Hearst. Some, though they read the Hearst papers, even speak scornfully of their proprietor, but are nonetheless infected by what they ridicule.

In October, 1935, Hearst was formally denounced at the annual convention of the American Federation of Labor in Atlantic City as an enemy of organized labor. Nonetheless, it was very difficult for an aroused membership to get a resolution against Hearst passed.

Years ago Gompers himself sponsored such resolutions, but today both William Green, president, and Matthew Woll, vice-president, are Hearst friends, lending labor bank funds behind the backs of the members even while the A. F. of L. is formally on record as opposed to him. The policy of the A. F. of L. since 1917 has been anti-Communist and anti-Socialist. When Hearst used to speak in favor of the Bolsheviks, the A. F. of L. denounced him for it.

Woll and Green remained in charge of the A. F. of L., however. Woll, judged by his writings and by his truly Hearst magnification of the "Red Menace," is himself little more than a fascist, as were a number of German and Italian labor leaders before fascism took power in those countries. There is slight difference between the public pronouncements of Woll and those of Hearst. Hearst, incidentally, refers to Woll and Green as the "legitimate," "honest" and "reliable" leaders of American labor.

Individual trade unions have passed hundreds of denunciations of Hearst since 1934 and, while these resolutions seldom see the light of day in the established commercial press, they are reported in the labor papers which circulate among millions. Trade unions endorsed boycotts of Hearst films and publications.

The Hearst pro-fascist campaign had five facets:

1. Hostility toward the Soviet Union.
2. Friendliness toward Italy and Germany, both of which were sources of profit.
3. Antagonism toward the "New Deal" at home because of its mild reformism, abhorrent to the Wall Street banks.
4. Enmity toward domestic labor unions and their liberal sympathizers, under the cloak of anti-communism.
5. Persistent polemics against communism and the Communist Party as a means of creating fascist formations around organizations like the American Liberty League, the American Legion, the National Security League, the Navy League, the Crusaders, the Committee for the Nation, the D. A. R., the Veterans of Foreign Wars, the National Economy League, etc.

Hearst's raising of the Communist "issue" had nothing at all to do with communism as such. Hearst had other aims, of which crushing of the Communist Party in the U. S. A. for theatrical effect was incidental. Hearst was actually after the labor unions and independent teachers and professors not on the payrolls of the banks and electric light companies. It is characteristic of the Hearst pro-fascist political campaign that none of the labor leaders and professors who has been involved in graft scandals was singled out for attack. The Hearst campaign was directed solely against people of integrity, in the labor unions, in the universities, in the Roosevelt Administration and in municipal and state governments. Only those trying to do something for an impoverished people were "dangerous" and "subversive" influences. All grafters, labor racketeers, political chiselers and academic frauds were exempt from Hearst attack; many were praised.

The familiar Hearst fabrications and bogus documents have been utilized in Hearst's attack on the Soviet Union and communism. When Hearst falsified about university professors and the Roosevelt régime, he had to tread more carefully, employ innuendo, because there were many newspapers and magazines willing to defend the Administration and academic freedom. He also had to tread cautiously when dealing with the trade unions. But the cry of "red communism" is an unspecific mob appeal, a kind of voodoo which the owning class is only too glad to have him intone. The Communists, of course, quickly exposed his faked charges. For this they were denounced, by such informed and disinterested persons as Frank Belgrano, a Giannini vice-president who was the head of the American Legion, 1934-35.

The result was that, although millions of people might be apprised of the Hearst crimes against the universities, the Labor unions and the "New Deal," comparatively few were enlightened about his lies concerning communism. This is very dangerous, for Hearst has popularized the trick of branding anyone who opposes him as "communistic."

If communism can be made to seem terrible to the mass mind, it follows that whomever Hearst stigmatizes as communistic is, *ipso facto,* unworthy, and can be singled out for false arrest, entanglement with the law, physical assault, and other forms of fascist terror.

To open its "anti-communistic" campaign late in 1934, the Hearst papers published photographs of "conditions in Russia," showing terrain strewn with dead men, women and children, and soldiers shooting down an obviously starving populace. According to Hearst, these were scenes from the Russian "famine" of 1932-33.

The photographs were taken neither in Russia nor in 1932-33. They were war photographs of 1918, taken in Rumania and Bulgaria. They were photographs *which had been published by Hearst and non-Hearst papers in 1918, 1919 and 1922.*

Most of the perpetrators of the horror stories about the Soviet Union have been exposed as American or Russian ex-convicts. One was an escaped convict remanded to jail after a short career as a Hearst journalist. Some of the Hearst Russian "experts" had never seen Russia. Not a few have been expelled from Russia as thieves, saboteurs and military and industrial spies.

Harry Lang, a member of the Socialist "Old Guard," contributed a series to the Hearst chamber of Soviet horrors after returning from a trip to Russia. Hearst's collaboration with the Socialist "Old Guard" continues down to the end. In July, 1935, Thomas Walker, who had contributed a series to the Hearst newspapers on "terrible conditions" in Russia and "the Stalin dictatorship," returned to the United States from England. He was immediately arrested. It developed that Walker was really Robert Green, sentenced in 1919 to Colorado State Prison for forgery. Green escaped in 1921. He had also once served a year in a Texas penitentiary.

Said the *New Republic* of July 24, 1935: "By the testimony of all competent observers in Russia, these [Walker] articles were wildly inaccurate and prejudiced."

No sooner had the Walker series been completed (the Hearst papers characteristically printed nothing about Walker's arrest and exposure) than a new series by Fred Beals was begun. Again there was the familiar tale of horrible sufferings in Russia, and again the news did not square with the daily dispatches of such a competent

Moscow reporter as Walter Duranty of the New York *Times*. Beals, too, had a bad record.

He was a former labor leader who led the Gastonia textile strike of 1929. He was indicted for murder as a result of his activities in the strike, but jumped his bail and escaped, making his way by devious routes to Russia. He was given employment as a working-class fighter, but it appears that Beals did not like work. Beals had documents showing that he had actually been resident in Russia (which Walker had not been) and these Hearst published.

One of the documents was Beals' factory card from Russia and, written upon it in Russian was the legend: "Discharged for loafing," although as translated by the Hearst papers it read "Left on vacation."

The New York *Times*, apparently worried that it was missing real news from Russia, asked Walter Duranty, its Moscow correspondent, to inquire into the basis for these stories. Duranty wired back that conditions in Russia today, while not perfect, were the best ever seen in that land.

The "Old Guard" Socialist *Jewish Daily Forward* applauded Hearst's campaign of falsification about Russia and printed the Lang articles, apparently unconcerned by the fact that the campaign was merely the screen behind which Hearst attacked trade unions, academic freedom and the "New Deal," and fostered anti-Semitism.

When Hearst took up his anti-Communist campaign there were a number of victims within the Hearst organization itself. All the Hearst men who, on orders from Hearst, had become known as experts on Russia or Russian affairs, were abruptly discharged.

Emile Gauvreau, former editor of Hearst's *Mirror* and a well-known newspaper man, was fired in 1935 because of Hearst's new anti-Russian policy. Gauvreau had taken an extensive trip through Russia in 1932, when starvation was supposed to have been rife. He wrote a series of laudatory descriptive articles about the Soviet Union which was printed in the *Mirror* and other Hearst papers in 1932 and syndicated to fifty non-Hearst papers throughout the United States.

Early in 1935 the articles were published in book form under the

IMPERIAL HEARST 365

title, *What So Proudly We Hailed*. In the latter portion of the book were quotations from American newspapers about bad conditions in the United States.

On June 7, 1935, Hearst received this telegram: "PLEASE CONSIDER HOW YOUR ORGANIZATION KEEPS EMILE GAUVREAU ON MIRROR STAFF WHEN ABSOLUTELY CONTRADICTORY YOUR ANTI-COMMUNISM. GAUVREAU JUST PUBLISHED FILTHIEST ANTI-AMERICAN PRO-SOVIET PROPAGANDA BOOK EVER ISSUED IN AMERICA 'WHAT SO PROUDLY WE HAIL.' YOUR ANTI-COMMUNISM SHOULD NOT ALLOW THIS CONTRADICTION TO BECOME CAUSE CELEBRE. OUR PATRIOTIC DUTY COMPELS OPPOSITION TO BOOK AND AUTHOR TO LIMIT. WE ARE CONSTANTLY WORKING TO OBTAIN SUPPORT FOR HEARST PRESS FROM WOMEN'S AND OTHER ORGANIZATIONS. GAUVREAU'S EMPLOYMENT BY YOU BESMIRCHES AND NULLIFIES OUR EFFORTS. SURELY YOUR PATRIOTISM DICTATES YOU GET RID OF GAUVREAU AT ONCE BEFORE BECOMING A NATIONAL SCANDAL.

"AMERICAN DEFENDERS
"BY MAJ. FRANK PEASE."

Hearst replied: "THANK YOU FOR YOUR KIND TELEGRAM OF JUNE SEVENTH."

The next day Gauvreau was fired.

Major Pease, on whose solicitation Hearst discharged a trusted, highly paid employee, had a somewhat interesting history. In 1930 he campaigned against a film company when it brought Sergei Eisenstein, the Russian director, to this country. He has also carried on anti-Semitic propaganda. Although styling himself "major," the War Department records do not show that he is an army officer, active or retired.

Late in 1933 Hearst's *Mirror* carried a story from London about "Major" Pease and his wife. It was to the effect that they had palmed themselves off on the widow of Joseph Conrad, the novelist, as old friends of Conrad's. The *Mirror* said they took up residence with Conrad's widow, but were ejected by police when a physician came to believe they were attempting to drug Mrs. Conrad.

"Perhaps Scotland Yard would tell more about 'Major' Pease," said the *Mirror*, "but Scotland Yard is very quiet about the entire affair. Yes, 'Major' and Mrs. Pease were asked to leave the country and not to return, but the great detective refused to say why the request was made."

Pease, obviously, had a personal motive for moving against Gauvreau.

There were other reasons why Gauvreau had become *persona non grata* to Hearst. In 1933, a year before Hearst made the deal for $400,000 annually from the Hitler government, Gauvreau, as editor of the *Mirror*, had his reporters ferret out German Nazi intrigues in the United States. In November, 1933, Gauvreau was summoned to give evidence against Nazi agents before the House Immigration Committee in Washington, and his testimony was instrumental in forcing them into hiding. Gauvreau's life was threatened daily while this investigation was going on.

The Hearst stories coming out of Russia are all 100 per cent fakes. Even Lindsay Parrott, Moscow correspondent of Hearst's INS, when interviewed by the Moscow correspondent of the New York *Daily Worker* during the height of the campaign of falsification, declared that conditions were excellent in the Soviet Union. The blatant falsity of the whole Hearst anti-Communist campaign can be shown from evidence much nearer home, evidence which even the most incredulous could not presume to doubt.

On Monday, November 4, 1935, the New York *Journal* and other Hearst papers announced:

SECOND YOUTH KILLED BY RED'S BOMB

The morning papers had carried a story that a young Milwaukee racketeer was killed when a bomb he was manufacturing had exploded. The afternoon story, as reported from Milwaukee by Hearst's International News Service, was as follows:

"Four unidentified associates of Hugh (Idzy) Rutkowski, maniacal Red who was blown to bits yesterday by his own infernal machine in a terrific explosion which took at least two other lives, were being held today. It was reported they are about to confess aiding the vandal in the series of bombings which have terrorized Milwaukee in the last week.

"Detectives refused to name the men. They were taken into custody along with a number of others, also unidentified, but all known to be friends or relatives of Rutkowski.

"A third victim was disclosed today when bits of clothing found in the debris in the South Side garage explosion were identified by the parents as belonging to Paul Chavanek, 16.

"He was a chum of Rutkowski, who fell the victim of his own fiendish designs as he prepared a 'super-bomb' for a new outrage.

"An innocent victim of the Red terrorism was nine-year-old Patricia Mylnarek. Playing in her home, next door to the two-car garage where the explosion occurred, she was horribly mangled and died in an ambulance en route to the hospital. . . ."

Charges of a "Red" plot followed. There were also stories of "Communist" plots in Chicago and Boston. From Boston, where the Hearst machine is tied in with the political apparatus all the way up to Governor Curley, came the following Hearst story:

"Communist leaders were being trailed today by police detectives and plain clothes officers were assigned to guard important buildings as a result of the Milwaukee bombings, authorities fearing the midwestern outbreak a forerunner of a nationwide plot.

"From an unknown source, authorities were 'tipped' an outbreak was to occur in this city 'during the week.' . . ."

In the same issue of the Hearst papers was a special story from Milwaukee by Elliot K. Hayes of the International News Service, as follows:

"The truth about Hugh (Idzy) Rutkowski, Milwaukee's dynamic terrorist, lay in a youthful mind warped with the seeds of Red Russia's Communistic menace.

"He talked Russia—looked to Russia as the world's special paradise—saw in it great opportunity.

"In the opinions of Chester L. Mayer, juvenile court probation officer, and John L. Kenny, chief probation officer, Rutkowski was typical of other boys with good educations who are lending their talents to a misguided struggle for revolution.

"'I would say,' said Mr. Kenny, 'that most of the Communistically-inclined boys and girls with whom we deal are well educated. I may safely add, that they are excellent students. They apply themselves thoroughly to a study of economics and the social sciences. Rutkowski was of this type.[5]

"'He liked to talk about Russia,' said Mayer. 'He frequently told me that things in this country were all wrong. He said that here there was no job for him, but in Russia he would have opportunity to prosper—that there everybody could have a job . . . He associated with youngsters from families inclined toward Communism. He took long bicycle rides in the country. He read revolutionary literature and thought about it. All these youngsters who talk about Communism are thoroughly schooled in their specious economic creed. And because their plans are unsound they are almost unanswerable.'"

Indeed, the story was so sensational, as printed in the Hearst press that, obviously, all newspapers would want it. Unfortunately for Hearst, his men were the only ones who could find traces of Reds.

The Associated Press, however, sent this story from Milwaukee on the morning of November 4th:

"Hugh Frank ('Idzy') Rutkowski, twenty years old, believed by the police to have been the terrorist bomber responsible for five bombings here in the last week, was blown to bits today as he experimented with thirty-eight sticks of stolen dynamite.

"A nine-year-old neighbor girl, Patricia Mylnarek, also was killed when the terrific blast wrecked the home of her parents next door. Eleven persons, including the mother and brother of the Mylnarek girl, were injured.

"The two-car garage in which Rutkowski was divising a 'super-bomb' was completely demolished, as was an automobile in the building. Numerous homes in the vicinity were damaged and windows were shattered in other buildings about the area. Total damage was estimated by officials at $75,000.

"A hundred sticks of dynamite, stolen from the Estabrook Park C.C.C. Camp here October 3, were blown out of the garage and picked up by the police in neighboring yards.

[5] Other Hearst dispatches of the same day indicated that Rutkowski could scarcely write simple English—F. L.

"Police had not determined at a late hour whether other persons were in the garage with Rutkowski at the time of the terrific blast, but were searching for the dead youth's eighteen-year-old companion, who was believed on his way to the garage when the explosion occurred."

There were other details supplied by the AP, *but not a word about communist plotting.*

On the afternoon of November 4th the Associated Press stories still contained no reference to communism. They said the youth was a racketeer engaged in bombing stores. Even though the AP and other non-Hearst news services on subsequent days said nothing about communism, the INS on November 5th carried more lurid falsifications.

Accompanying a huge photographic lay-out showing the wreckage, the INS on November 5th said:

"Two young cronies of Hugh Frank Rutkowski, 21-year-old radical blown to bits by his own infernal machine, were being grilled by police here today.

"The pair have admitted, the police said, accompanying Rutkowski on minor crime expeditions.

"The youths, George Sujiwicz, 20, and Elmer Gritz, 16, are suspected of being accomplices of the young Communism-inspired dynamiter. They have been held incommunicado since their arrest Sunday night . . . Police sought to learn whether he made any attempt to organize a gang of Red terrorists to aid him in his campaign. . . ."

Still the Associated Press and other news agencies could find nothing of all this, for the simple reason that it was fabricated in the brains of Hearst editors who then procured persons willing to stand by their statements in return for the good-will of the Hearst office. This is the traditional Hearst technique.

On November 6th the INS sent out the following:

"Police today investigated the possibility that a third Communist perished in Sunday's terrific explosion . . . [The police] were determined to break up the Red terrorist organization. . . ."

At no time did the Associated Press or the non-Hearst Milwaukee papers find any traces of communism, radicalism or liberalism; at no time did any responsible public official make such charges.

The Hearst papers on November 5th carried the following editorial:

"Dynamite is Communism's weapon now in its open warfare against America and American institutions, as shown by the series of bombing outrages in Milwaukee, Wisconsin, which culminated Sunday in the killing of two persons and the wounding of thirteen.

"One of the dead, Americans will be pleased to hear, was the dynamiter himself.

"The other, they learn with horror, was an innocent nine-year-old girl—one who merely happened to be within the zone of the explosion.

"But a few innocent victims, more or less, cannot be considered of importance to the maniacal type of Red.

"Milwaukee, peaceful and well-governed city hitherto, knows more about Communism now than it did before.

"The United States, it is to be hoped, knows more as a result of Milwaukee's experience.

"The *Wisconsin News,* Hearst newspaper in Milwaukee, takes pardonable pride in the fact that by its offer of $5,000 reward for the capture of the dynamiters it has been singled out for special Communistic invective.[6]

"The truth of the exposure by that and other Hearst newspapers of Communist propaganda and plotting has never been more signally confirmed than by these threats from the Reds.

"The violence that Communism has preached *in* this country and promised *to* this country is now being practised *on* this country, as the Milwaukee bombings witness.

"The American people now have evidence by which to judge Communism *as it is in fact in the United States today.*"

A news story of this character, circulated among millions of people, was meant to inspire violence against somebody. If Communists are practicing terrorism, are bombing property, they must be re-

---

[6] This was a typically false Hearst innuendo, for the Communists did not denounce the reward, but did denounce Hearst's linking of Communists to the outrage.

pelled by violence. Hearst, however, has scrupulously withheld from his readers the fact that the Communist Party is the only revolutionary party in history which forbids terrorism. Any act of violence by a Communist brings instant expulsion from the party, for history has shown the Communists that the preponderant facilities for committing violence are in the hands of their foes. There is a difference between individual force irresponsibly used and political force responsibly applied, and this difference the Hearst reader is not equipped to discern, nor does Hearst point it out. All government consists of force responsibly applied in the interests of the governing class; all governments, not excepting the United States government, retain power by "violence." It is not the kind of violence involved in individualistic acts, however.

Hearst's own editors did not believe the stories sent out from Milwaukee. E. P. Mahoney, editor of Hearst's *Wisconsin News*, on November 4th sent to INS subscribers the following confidential telegram:

"Please be very careful not to say that the bombings in Milwaukee are the result of a Communistic plot. There is no evidence to support any such assertion. The men involved so far are too youthful to have enjoyed the confidences of any organization. It is perfectly true that Rutkowski did have strong communistic leanings as is evidenced by assertions of the probation officer who had him in charge.[7] But the evidence so far unearthed will not justify saying anything stronger than that this gang may have been inspired by communistic teachings. This information should be given to all editors."

Despite this warning, which made it possible for the Hearst organization to plead vigilance in the handling of news if any non-Hearst subscriber were sued for libel by the family of the dead, the Hearst papers played the story as a communistic plot. The family of the dead man denied to the other news services that the youth had any radical leanings. But the Hearst papers ignored the family, preferring the "impartial" testimony of an ambitious probation officer.

[7] The probation officer was talking about a dead man.

This series was a preliminary step in Hearst's deliberate campaign to create an atmosphere of violence in this country, not against Communists alone, but against militant labor leaders, progressive educators, writers and artists, unemployed demonstrators and rebellious farmers.

Hearst has been creating the same kind of passionate rancors he created before the war with Spain.

It will be an incident, either fabricated or real, such as the explosion of the *Maine* or the firing of the German Reichstag, which will suffice to release all the rage Hearst has been creating among the ignorant. It is not difficult to imagine what such an incident will be. In 1933 President Roosevelt was shot at by a demented foreigner who killed Mayor Anton Cermak of Chicago. Were such an occurrence to take place now it would be handled by the Hearst press as the Milwaukee bombing was handled. If the President or some other prominent political personage were slain by a fanatic, the assassin would automatically become an "agent of the Comintern" in the Hearst press. It would be shown, by "documents," that he had been sent forth by the Communist Party, with the endorsement of various labor leaders. A serious accident in the American Navy would similarly be laid to Communists.

On the basis of the Hearst charges and "evidence," there would be an investigation launched by ambitious public officials. Whether the charges were sustained or not would not be important; the charges against the Reichstag defendants were not sustained. Such an incident, coming at this late date on top of a whole series of Hearst incitements to violence, would provide the excuse for smashing labor unions, for quelling the demands of progressives in general. In an atmosphere of national tragedy it would be difficult for anyone to speak for the legitimate needs of the American people.

Even though investigation of a tragic incident would ultimately clear radicals, liberals and Communists, the occasion would make possible wanton terrorization by subservient officialdom, itself too inept to probe to the real causes. And when all the accused were exonerated, as were the Reichstag defendants, it would mean nothing. Hearst and his backers would have firm control of the whole situation.

It is well, in this connection, to recall that although history has exonerated Spain of the blame for the sinking of the MAINE, Spain nevertheless permanently lost Cuba, Puerto Rico and the Philippines. Although Hearst was proven 100 per cent culpable in the case of the Mexican forgeries, he nevertheless secured the cancellation of those portions of the 1926 Mexican land laws which withheld sub-soil rights from foreigners.

Another falsification in the Hearst pro-fascist campaign, in which Hearst was caught red-handed, concerned David Dubinsky, president of the International Ladies' Garment Workers Union.

On November 12, 1935, after the American Federation of Labor convention in Atlantic City had passed strong denunciations of Hearst despite the opposition of Messrs. Green and Woll, the New York *Journal* and the other Hearst papers quoted Mr. Dubinsky as saying:

"It is obvious that the purpose of these resolutions was to get even with the Hearst newspapers for their anti-communistic policies. American labor has no grievances against the Hearst newspapers."

Dubinsky, leader of one of the largest industrial unions in the country, issued the following statement on November 13, 1935, from headquarters of the I. L. G. W. U. at 3 West 16th Street, New York City:

"The statement attributed to me in the Hearst newspapers today is not correct. I have never made any such statement."

Mr. Dubinsky went on to point to internal evidence in the Hearst "quotation" indicating its falsity.

After the Milwaukee bombing story the Hearst press has done much quoting from Marxian literature, which is available to anyone. The quotations have been carefully selected, ripped from their context, and statements that Communists are calling for violence and vandalism have been interpolated.

In the Hearst press of Sunday, December 22, 1935, there was a big "exposé" of Communistic "documents" which have been on sale for years at five cents each. Linked with the Communists this time, and shown in photographs with acknowledged Communists, were Corliss Lamont, liberal writer and son of Thomas W. Lamont, the

Morgan partner; Dr. George S. Counts of Teachers College, Columbia University; and Professor Robert Morss Lovett of the University of Chicago.

Hearst singled these men out, hoping they would be terrorized. Counts is an editor of *Social Frontier* magazine, whose issue of February, 1935, unmercifully analyzed Hearst for the benefit of American educators. Lamont is the president of the American Friends of the Soviet Union, an organization devoted to spreading information about Soviet Russia that the newspapers refuse to carry, similar in all respects to organizations performing similar services for other countries. Lovett is an editor of *The New Republic*, which has written harshly of Hearst, and a leader in the American League Against War and Fascism. None of these men is a Communist. However, linking liberal democratic elements with Communism revealed whom Hearst and his backers aim to entangle when the moment is ripe.

Side by side with its assiduous falsification about the "Red Menace," the Hearst papers in certain localities, unknown to persons outside those localities, have, since early in 1935, carried on a campaign against Italian and German anti-fascists who are not in any sense radical. The Hearst papers have succeeded in having many of these thoroughly democratic and humanitarian persons held by the United States government for deportation to countries where prison or a firing squad awaits them. European fascist governments are anxious to lay hands on those of its nationals who agitate among naturalized Americans against the political régimes of the native country. In this work the Hearst press serves as an American arm of a foreign political police and cannot, by the remotest stretch of the imagination, pretend to be serving American interests.

Hearst's pro-fascist campaign has drawn up a huge phalanx of influential supporters, among them Matthew Woll, vice-president of the A. F. of L.; former Senator James A. Reed of Missouri; Governor James Curley of Massachusetts; Father Charles E. Coughlin; and Governor Eugene Talmadge of Georgia. These men have publicly endorsed the campaign; others have endorsed it by implication, by their silence, and among these are Alfred E. Smith, the Wall Street bankers, and those numerous American newspapers which have not joined issue with Hearst.

Father Charles E. Coughlin's connection with Hearst was never clearer than when the New York *American* of August 31, 1935, printed the following statement from Father Coughlin:

"The statement of William Randolph Hearst advocating a Constitutional Democratic Party is timely. I believe Mr. Hearst's influence will be felt for the good of the party at the next Democratic National Convention.

"It is an admirable characteristic of Mr. Hearst to put aside personal animosity, as he has done, in suggesting Alfred E. Smith for the Presidency.

"The President's [Roosevelt's] policies are un-American. Norman Thomas is a piker compared to Roosevelt. After all, Thomas stands for a fairly good brand of American Socialism, but Roosevelt stands for a poor brand of Russian Communism."

Of this Coughlin statement the New York *Post* of September 3, 1935, said:

"Consider this statement in the light of Father Coughlin's record. He preached doctrines far to the left of the restrained liberalism of President Roosevelt. Time and again he criticized the President's 'conservatism.'

"Now we find him supporting not only a conservative, Al Smith, but also speaking unctuous words of praise for William Randolph Hearst, who, as every literate American knows, is now trying to scare this country into Fascism.

"Now consider Father Coughlin in the light of another great orator, Adolf Hitler.

"Hitler preached an unscientific socialism far more 'radical' than that of the Marxists whom he attacked. And he denounced everything he opposed as Communism, especially as the 'Moscow brand of Communism.'

"And when the pay-off came, Herr Hitler, of course, turned out to be a dummy for Thyssen and the other great industrial interests in Germany.

"Now Coughlin, the 'friend of the common man,' turns out to be working with millionaire William Randolph Hearst.

"Forewarned is forearmed. America knows now in which direction the Fascist danger lies."

Under the guise of suppressing isolated Communists the forces of fascism will, after the few Communists are driven underground, proceed against the trade unions, teachers, writers, artists, actors, doctors, lawyers and the white collar workers. This is precisely what was done in Germany and Italy, by individuals and organizations which functioned precisely as Hearst and his cohorts have been functioning. It is necessary for the handful of millionaires at the back of the fascist movement to suppress liberals, trade unions and radicals so that all opposition to a wholesale reduction in the general standard of living and the elevation of corporate profits will be removed.

Hearst has been much more active in fascist directions than the evidence cited indicates.

The Nation of May 29, 1935, showed that Hearst inspired the formation of armed fascist groups in Los Angeles for use against discontented California citizens. Three units, the Light Horse Cavalry, the California Esquadrille and the Hollywood Hussars, had been launched and others were in process of formation. They were led by Gary Cooper, Victor McLaglen and George Brent, he-men film actors. After *The Nation's* exposure, Cooper announced his resignation, pleading that he had not known these armed groups were anything but parade units.

A feature of the mass recruiting meetings of these units was the appearance of speakers alarmed by the "menace of communism."

McLaglen was quoted in the Los Angeles papers as saying his unit "has offered its services to city, state, and federal authorities at any time it might be needed."

Cooper's Hussars had as their express purpose "to uphold and protect the principles and ideals of true Americanism" and its members "pledged themselves to make their regiment the model to inspire other communities to organize similar bodies of trained Americans throughout the nation."

"The organization reaches deep into local politics," said *The Nation*. "Judge Marshal F. McComb, of the Superior Court of Los Angeles County, is listed as a major (he was formerly of counsel for the Los Angeles *Examiner*[8] and was backed for judicial appointment by William Randolph Hearst). . . .

"Why, it may be asked, should Hollywood suddenly become so militaristic? It seems that Mr. Hearst was deeply impressed with Victor McLaglen's success in organizing the Light Horse unit. Mr. Hearst then induced Gary Cooper to try his hand at the game, promising liberal backing and support. . . .

"But the Hussars and their allies have other uses. They are designed to advertise the charms of fascist organizations to the American public. Through the publicity medium of the industry, the most powerful propaganda machine in America, these gaudy units sponsored by popular and well-known stars can be advertised to millions of Americans as the latest and snappiest fascist models. It is even rumored that a motion picture will be made, presenting the Hollywood Hussars in the act of suppressing a radical uprising in California. Also these groups have all volunteered their services to the authorities 'in case of trouble.' "

During Upton Sinclair's "Epic" campaign for the California governorship in 1934, the Hearst press joined with the motion picture industry and The Crusaders, a fascistic organization, in spreading the boldest sort of lies about Sinclair's intentions. Sinclair, the Democratic candidate, had received the endorsement at first of Senator McAdoo, but this was withdrawn as the Hearst press opened fire. Bogus newsreels were manufactured in Hollywood, notably by Metro-Goldwyn-Mayer, showing unemployed vagrants rushing to California in box cars to obtain the benefits promised by Sinclair's "Epic Plan." The Hearst press published excerpts from these films.

In the remote Philippines the Hearst fascist visage is also plain. *The Nation* of May 29, 1935, carried an article about Philippine affairs and about Manuel Quezon's *Philippine Herald*. The writer of this article said:

"Quezon's *Herald* has all the earmarks of a member of the Hearst

[8] A Hearst paper.

chain of newspapers. The campaign against radicalism, communism, the Soviet Union and militant labor organizations characteristic of the Hearst press forms an integral part of its policy. At the same time the *Herald* consistently indorses fascism and lauds Hitler and Mussolini. The issue of the *Herald* for March 30, 1935, illustrates Quezon's methods. First, there is an article . . . Nazi Germany at First Hand, which frankly exalts Hitler and Hitlerism. A second article extols the New Life movement of Chiang Kai-shek in China; a third reproduces a commencement address given at the University of Manila under the heading, 'The Youth Must Be Ready to Undergo Military Training.'

"The same issue ran two anti-red editorials, a cartoon, and a newsstory. The cartoon shows 'Sovietism' driving a huge wheel marked 'All-Absorbing State Capitalism' over the body of 'Labor.' The various spokes of the wheel are labeled 'political tyranny,' 'rigid discipline,' 'violence,' 'class hatred,' 'despotic laws,' 'control of private life,' and 'espionage.' A half-page editorial elaborates this theme. In a second editorial captioned Fighting the Agitators, the *Herald* boasts that 'the press is doing its part.' The news item warns that Quezon's lieutenants, Hayden, Sison, and the chief of the constabulary, are conferring 'on ways and means of curbing radical activity.' To round out the Hearstian character of the *Herald*, Arthur Brisbane contributes his weekly syndicated editorial, which on this occasion breathed jingoism and militarism.

"Quezon's kinship to Hearst is even closer than appears from their common stand on fascism and communism. Quezon is a disciple of Hearst. When Quezon was recently en route to Washington the *Herald* proudly proclaimed that the president of the senate would stop over to visit his 'personal friend' William Randolph Hearst. 'It is said,' the *Herald* continued, 'that whenever President Quezon passes by the Pacific Coast he always takes the opportunity to call at Hearst's San Simeon ranch.'

"The *Herald* also revealed that Quezon's visit [to Hearst] was not purely a social affair when it stated that 'Mr. Hearst, whose opinion on the Far East is known to be for a deferred Philippine independence on account of Japan's ambitions, may have interesting slants on the problem that President Quezon would want to hear at this decisive moment in Philippine history."

In neighboring Mexico, too, the Hearst fascist hand is plainly discernible. The leader of the fascist "Golden Shirts" of Mexico is General Nicholas Rodriguez, former gambler, who was associated with Hearst and Brisbane in a number of Los Angeles real estate speculations. The policies of the "Golden Shirts" are essentially the policies of the Hearst newspapers, the American Liberty League, Father Charles E. Coughlin, Governor Eugene Talmadge of Georgia and the Quezon Party in the Philippines. It behooves Hearst, as Mexico's biggest landowner, to be identified with Mexican as well as American political reaction.

Militarism is not fascism, but it is closely akin. The Hearst newspapers are the most militaristic in the United States. Not only have they called, day in and day out, for heavier Federal military expenditures, but Hearst has placed his organization actively to work in military directions. The Junior Birdmen of America is a Hearst organization publicized each day under a special column and "devoted to the interest of American youth in aviation.". It is also, manifestly, devoted to the interests of the United Aircraft and Transport Corporation, whose sponsor is the National City Bank. There is also a Hearst medal bestowed for military excellence each year on ranking classmen in all the numerous military "prep" schools of the United States.

Apart from this, a very large proportion, if not a majority, of the high Hearst executives, beginning with General Roy D. Keehn, president of the National Guard Association of the United States, hold reserve commissions in the R. O. T. C. or are members of the naval reserve of the various state national guards. These men carry the political gospel of Hearst and the Hearst newspapers into their military organizations and at the same time keep the lord of San Simeon posted on the state of affairs in the armed forces of the nation. These military-minded Hearst men, who actually number several hundred, are also potent forces in organizations like the American Legion and the Veterans of Foreign Wars.

While the Hearst newspapers were publicly advocating payment of the veterans' bonus at the expense of the funds appropriated for the unemployed, these executives were carrying on the same propaganda within the veterans' organizations.

The fascist intrigue of Hearst is not his alone. He is working in close collaboration with other groups and is obviously blessed by the Wall Street bankers (the writer knows of one very prominent banker who alluded to the "splendid" work being done by Hearst in the pro-fascist campaign). It is an alarming condition. Hearst has been called a "political failure" by shortsighted observers who have merely had in mind his vain attempts to achieve high public office. Hearst is one of the most powerful political figures in the nation.

His power today is infinitely greater than ever because he is receiving financial and industrial approval which has undoubtedly induced most of the non-Hearst newspapers to permit him to proceed without that sort of criticism published by the pro-Roosevelt New York *Post*. Many non-Hearst newspapers, obviously inspired from behind the scenes, have begun to quote him on every sort of matter. This, in the profession, is known as creating a "build-up."

To what purpose?

There should be a Congressional inquiry into the Hearst enterprises from top to bottom lest they smash American democracy. There should also be a national law making newspaper publishers liable for falsifying and circulating falsified facts. The American press can never be made free until it is made responsible to the people.

William Randolph Hearst's career has required the continuous deception of the American people, though his newspapers, magazines, movies and radio stations use the idiom of the people.

Down through the years he has played a great and ghastly part in shaping the American mind. He could, more truthfully than any other man, say, "The American mentality is my mentality." This is not because Hearst has become "the voice of the people," speaking their unformulated thoughts and desires. It has been because adequate, widespread and *popularized* criticism of his innumerable deceptions has been lacking. Time and again, as in the cases of the war with Spain, the sales tax, the income tax and military preparation, he has been able to make America accept his deceptions and his debaucheries of its political institutions.

At least half of Hearst's unquestioned power over the American mentality arises from the fact that the very elements in our society which should have been busy tirelessly exposing him, year in and year out, have been silent because, in either close or distant ramification, they profited by being silent. Organized labor has probably functioned better in this respect than any other agency except perhaps educational authorities, but it has been traduced by its leaders, many of whom have been Hearst tools and allies.

There is now only one way of combating the Hearst influence emanating from his newspapers, radio stations, magazines and films. It is by vigorous and unending effort. A large section of Hearst's audience, paralyzed by long exposure to the Hearst method, cannot be budged. But the winning of a large minority of this audience would bring Hearst to his knees.

Hearst, at seventy-three, is the weakest strong man and the strongest weak man in the world today. Without the support of bankers and industrialists for his last irresponsible and anti-social rampage, he would be merely a senile clown. Hearst, while powerful, is exceedingly vulnerable, a giant with feet of clay. Most of the Hearst readers, if confronted with proof of his misdeeds, could no longer be fooled. Basically, Hearst's power stems from the ignorance of his audience, and this ignorance in turn is fostered by fundamental economic forces in American society. The truth can make us free, and the truth about Hearst can expose, deflate and destroy a man who would doom this country to the death that inheres in political reaction, whether manifested as outright fascism, or concealed in the guise of Americanism, rugged individualism, or other demagogic appeals.

BIBLIOGRAPHY

OFFICIAL DOCUMENTS

George Hearst Memorial, Post mortem speeches in eulogy of Senator George Hearst in the United States Senate by Senators Stanford of California, Vest of Missouri, Bates of Tennessee, Dolph of Oregon, Morgan of Alabama and Felton of California; Fifty-second Congress, Second Session, Government Printing Office, 1894.

Compilation of Reports of (Senate) Committee on Foreign Relations, 1789-1901, volume 7, pp. 655-672, Government Printing Office, 1896.

Report of the Naval Court of Inquiry upon the Battleship Maine.

Hearings of the inquiry into the election of Senator William Lorimer of Illinois, Senate Document 484, Sixty-second Congress, Second Session, 1911. Government Printing Office, 1912.

Hearings of the Senate Privileges and Elections Committee pursuant to Senate Resolutions 79 and 386 on campaign contributions (1912-13), parts 1 to 45, Sixty-second Congress, Second Session. Government Printing Office, 1913.

U. S. Industrial Relations Commission (The Walsh Commission), Final Report, 1916; Sixty-fourth Congress, First Session, Senate Document 415, Volume IV. Government Printing Office, 1916.

U. S. Brewing and Liquor Interests and German and Bolshevik Propaganda: Report and Hearings on foreign propaganda, espionage and intrigue in the United States during the World War; Senate, Sixty-sixth Congress, First Session, 1918-19. Government Printing Office.

U. S. Senate Public Lands Committee. Leases upon Public Lands (The Teapot Dome Inquiry). Hearings, Sixty-seventh Congress, Second Session, Government Printing Office, 1923-24.

Report of the Select Senate Committee on Investigation of the Internal Revenue Bureau (The Couzens Committee), Senate Report 27, Sixty-ninth Congress, First Session, Government Printing Office, 1926.

Hearings Before a Special Committee to Investigate Propaganda or Money Alleged to Have Been Used by Foreign Governments to Influence United States Senators. Senate, Seventy-ninth Congress, First Session, in response to Senate Resolution 7, Government Printing Office, 1928.

Hearings Before a Sub-Committee of the Senate Naval Affairs Committee to Investigate Alleged Activities of William B. Shearer in

IMPERIAL HEARST

Behalf of Certain Shipbuilding Companies, Government Printing Office, 1929.

Stock Market Practices. Senate Banking and Currency Committee, Investigation of Wall Street, Seventy-second Congress, First and Second Sessions, Government Printing Office, 1933.

Investigation of Lobbying Activities: Special Senate Committee, Seventy-fourth Congress, First Session.

Hearings Before the Special Senate Committee (Nye Committee) on the Investigation of the Munitions Industry (incomplete), Government Printing Office, 1935, 1936.

Congressional Record, 1886-1936.

Court Records, Etc.

Property in the News, New York, 1919; transcript of the litigation of the Associated Press versus the International News Service, Universal Service, William Randolph Hearst, et al, from the Federal District Court of New York through the United States Supreme Court, being a prayer to permanently enjoin the defendants from stealing news.

Law of the Associated Press, New York, 1914-19.

Charter and By-Laws of the Associated Press.

Technical

Ayer, N. W., and Sons, Directory of Newspapers and Periodicals
Directory of Directors (New York)
Economist, The; London (weekly periodical)
Financial and Commercial Chronicle (weekly periodical)
Moody's Directory of Directors (national)
Moody's Industrial Manual (1915-1935)
Poor's Industrial Manual (1916-1935)
Poor's Public Utilities Manual (1924-1935)
Standard Statistics Index
Scientific American Supplement, May 13, 1905; Recent Exploration in Peru, by Enos Brown; An account of the Dr. Max Uhle-University of California (Phoebe Apperson Hearst) Expedition to Peru.

Reference Works

Appleton Cyclopedia of American Biography
Dictionary of American Biography
Encyclopedia Americana
Encyclopedia Britannica
Encyclopedia of Biography
National Cyclopedia of American Biography
Who's Who

Books and Pamphlets

Anonymous: *The Life of William Randolph Hearst,* pamphlet, N. Y. (?) 1909 (?)

Anonymous: *The Political Campaign of 1909,* pamphlet of newspaper excerpts, N. Y., 1910.

Anonymous: *The Shameful Life and Career of William Randolph Hearst,* N. Y., 1924, reported in the daily press to have emanated from Tammany Hall circles.

Allen, Robert S.: (with Drew Pearson) *Washington Merry-Go-Round,* H. Liveright, Inc., N. Y., 1931.

Atherton, Gertrude: *California, An Intimate History,* Boni & Liveright, N. Y., 1927.

Baker, Ray Stannard: *Woodrow Wilson: Life and Letters,* Doubleday, Doran & Co., N. Y., 1931.

Bancroft, Hubert H.: *History of California: 1542-1890,* History Company, San Francisco, 1890.

—— *History of Nevada, Colorado and Wyoming,* A. L. Bancroft, & Co., San Francisco, 1890.

Barrett, S. M.: *Geronimo's Story of His Life,* Duffield & Company, N. Y., 1906.

Barron, Clarence Walker: *They Told Barron;* Notes of Clarence Walker Barron, edited by Arthur Pound and Samuel Taylor Moore, Harper & Bros., N. Y. & London, 1930.

—— *More They Told Barron,* ibid., 1931.

Beals, Carleton: *Fire on the Andes,* J. B. Lippincott Co., Phila., 1934.

Beck, James M.: *The Enemy Within Our Gates,* an address delivered November 2, 1917, at Carnegie Hall, N. Y., American Defense Society, N. Y., 1917(?).

Bent, Silas: *Ballyhoo: The Voice of the Press,* H. Liveright, N. Y., 1927.

—— *Strange Bedfellows: A Review of Politics, Personalities and the Press,* H. Liveright, N. Y., 1928.

Bierce, Ambrose: "In Motley," *Works,* vol. 12, Neale Publishing Company, N. Y. & Washington, 1909-12.

—— *Letters;* edited by Bertha Clark Pope, Book Club of California, San Francisco, 1922.

Bishop, J. B.: *Theodore Roosevelt and His Time,* C. Scribner's Sons, N. Y., 1926.

Bleyer, Willard Grosvenor: *Main Currents in American Journalism,* Houghton Mifflin Company, Boston & N. Y., 1927.

Boettiger, John: *Jake Lingle,* E. P. Dutton, N. Y., 1931.

Bolton, Herbert E.: *California's Story,* Allyn and Bacon, Boston & N. Y., 1922.

Bonnet, Theodore: *The Regenerators; a study of the graft prosecution of San Francisco*, Pacific Printing Co., San Francisco, 1911.
Bright, John: *Hizzoner Big Bill Thompson*, J. Cape & H. Smith, N. Y., 1930.
Busbey, L. White: *Uncle Joe Cannon*, H. Holt & Co., N. Y., 1927.
Byington, L. F.: *The History of San Francisco*, by L. F. Byington, Oscar Lewis and others, S. J. Clarke Publishing Co., Chicago & San Francisco, 1931.
Carnegie, Andrew: *Autobiography*, Houghton Mifflin Co., Boston, 1920.
Chadwick, F. E.: *The Relations of the United States and Spain*, C. Scribner's Sons, N. Y., 1911.
Chambers, Walter: *Samuel Seabury—A Challenge*, The Century Company, N. Y. & London, 1932.
Cisneros, Evangelina: *The Story of Evangelina Cisneros by Herself*, The Continental Publishing Company, N. Y., 1895.
Clark, George T.: *Leland Stanford*, Stanford University Press, 1931.
Cleland, Robert G.: *A History of California*, The Macmillan Co., N. Y., 1922.
Cochran, Negley D.: *E. W. Scripps*, Harcourt, Brace & Co., N. Y., 1933.
Cole, Cornelius: *Memoirs*, McLaughlin Bros., N. Y., 1908.
Corey, Lewis: *The House of Morgan*, G. H. Watt, N. Y., 1930.
Cortissoz, Royal: *The Life of Whitelaw Reid*, C. Scribner's Sons, N. Y., 1921.
Counts, George S.: *School and Society in Chicago*, Harcourt, Brace & Co., N. Y., 1928.
Creel, H. G.: *Newspaper Frauds*, pamphlet, National Rip-Saw Publishing Co., St. Louis, 1911.
——— *Tricks of the Press*, pamphlet, ibid.
Creelman, James: *On the Great Highway*, Lothrop Publishing Co., Boston, 1901.
Croly, Herbert: *Marcus Alonzo Hanna*, The Macmillan Co., N. Y., 1919.
Daggett, Stuart: *History of the Southern Pacific*, The Ronald Press, N. Y., 1922.
Daniels, Josephus: *The Life of Woodrow Wilson*, Phila.(?), c. 1924.
Davis, Richard Harding: *Adventures and Letters*, edited by Charles Belmont Davis, C. Scribner's Sons, N. Y., 1917.
Dewey, Squire P.: *The Bonanza Mines and the Bonanza Kings*, San Francisco(?) 1879(?)
Fisher, H. A. L.: *James Bryce*, Macmillan Co., Ltd., London, 1927.
Flynn, John T.: *God's Gold, A biography of John D. Rockefeller*, Harcourt, Brace & Co., N. Y., 1932.

Forbes, W. Cameron: *The Philippine Islands,* Houghton Mifflin Co., Boston & N. Y., 1928.
Fowler, Gene: *The Great Mouthpiece,* Covici, Friede & Co., N. Y., 1931.
——— *Timberline,* Covici, Friede & Co., N. Y., 1933.
Gardner, Gilson: *Lusty Scripps,* The Vanguard Press, N. Y., 1932.
Gilbert, Clinton: *The Mirrors of Washington,* G. P. Putnam's Sons, N. Y., 1921.
Glasscock, Carl Burgess: *A Golden Highway,* The Bobbs-Merrill Co., Indianapolis, 1934.
——— *The Big Bonanza,* The Bobbs-Merrill Co., Indianapolis and N. Y., 1931.
——— *The War of the Copper Kings,* The Bobbs-Merrill Co., Indianapolis and N. Y., 1935.
Guinn, James Miller: *A History of California,* Historic Record Co., Los Angeles, 1915.
Hapgood, Norman: *Professional Patriots,* A. & C. Boni, N. Y., 1927.
——— *The Changing Years,* Farrar & Rinehart, Inc., N. Y., 1930.
With Henry Moskowitz: *Up from the City Streets: Alfred E. Smith,* Harcourt, Brace & Co., N. Y., 1927.
Harper's Pictorial History of the War with Spain, Harper & Bros., N. Y., & London, 1899.
Hearst, William Randolph: *Let Us Promote the World's Peace,* pamphlet, McConnell Printing Company, N. Y., 1915.
——— *On the Foreign War Debts,* pamphlet, reprinted from editorials by William Randolph Hearst, N. Y.(?) 1931.
——— *The Obligations and Opportunities of the United States in Mexico and the Philippines,* pamphlet reprint of editorials by William Randolph Hearst.
——— *The Truth About the Trusts,* pamphlet, privately printed by William Randolph Hearst, Rahway, N. J., 1916.
Hendrick, Burton J.: *The Life and Letters of Walter Hines Page,* Doubleday, Page & Co., N. Y., 1922.
Hibben, Paxton: *The Peerless Leader,* Farrar & Rinehart, Inc., N. Y., 1929.
Hichborn, Franklin: *"The System," as uncovered by the San Francisco graft prosecution,* J. H. Barry Co., San Francisco, 1915.
Howe, Winifred C.: *Putting the Poison in Columbia's Cup,* pamphlet, Allied Printing Trades Council, Milwaukee, 1920.
Hunkins, Ralph V.: *South Dakota; Its Past, Present and Future* (with John Clarke Lindsey), The Macmillan Company, N. Y., 1932.
Hunt, Rockwell D.: *California and Californians,* The Lewis Publishing Co., Chicago and N. Y., 1926.

Josephson, Matthew: *The Robber Barons*, Harcourt, Brace & Co., N. Y., 1934.
Kennan, George: *E. H. Harriman*, Houghton Mifflin Co., Boston & New York, 1922.
Kingsbury, George W.: *History of Dakota Territory*, S. J. Clarke Publishing Company, Chicago, 1915.
Leach, Fránk A.: *Recollections of A Newspaper Man*, S. Levinson, San Francisco, 1917.
Lee, James Melvin: *History of American Journalism*, Houghton Mifflin Co., Boston and N. Y., 1923.
Lewis, Alfred Henry: *Confessions of a Detective*, A. S. Barnes & Co., N. Y., 1906.
────── *The Boss and How He Came to Rule New York*, A. L. Burt & Co., 1903.
Lewis, Lloyd (with Henry Justin Smith): *Chicago: The History of Its Reputation*, Harcourt, Brace & Co., N. Y., 1929.
Lewis, Oscar (with L. F. Byington and others): *The History of San Francisco*, S. J. Clarke Publishing Co., Chicago and San Francisco, 1931.
Lindsey, John Clarke (with Ralph V. Hunkins): *South Dakota; Its Past, Present and Future*, The Macmillan Company, N. Y., 1932.
Lodge, Henry Cabot: *Letters of Theodore Roosevelt to Henry Cabot Lodge*, C. Scribner's Sons, N. Y., 1926.
Lord, Eliot: *Comstock Mining and Miners*, U. S. Geological Survey, Monographs, vol. 4, Government Printing Office, 1883.
MacGowan, Kenneth: *Coiled in the Flag, Hears-s-s-s-st*, pamphlet reprint from the New York *Tribune*, N. Y., 1918.
Mackenzie, F. A.: *Lord Beaverbrook: An authentic biography of the Right Honorable Lord Beaverbrook*, Jarrolds, Ltd., London, 1931.
Markham, Edwin: *California the Wonderful*, Hearst's International Library Company, N. Y., 1914.
McElroy, Robert M.: *Grover Cleveland*, Harper & Bros., N. Y., 1923.
Millis, Walter: *The Martial Spirit: A Study of the War with Spain*, Houghton Mifflin Co., Boston and N. Y., 1931.
Moskowitz, Henry (with Norman Hapgood): *Up from the City Streets: Alfred E. Smith*, Harcourt, Brace & Co., N. Y., 1927.
Myers, Gustavus: *History of the Great American Fortunes*, C. H. Kerr & Co., Chicago, 1911.
────── *History of Tammany Hall*, Boni & Liveright, Inc., N. Y., 1928.
Neville, Amelia Ransome: *The Fantastic City; memoirs of the social and romantic life of old San Francisco*, edited by Virginia Brastow, Houghton Mifflin Co., Boston & New York, 1932.

Newspapers Relating to the Assassination of President McKinley; bound in three volumes, N. Y. Public Library.

New York State Public Service Commission. *Brief on rate complaints brought by certain large users, William Randolph Hearst, the United Cigar Stores Company et al.,* N. Y., 1931.

O'Conner, Harvey: *Mellon's Millions,* The John Day Co., N. Y., 1933.

Ogden, Rollo: *Life and Letters of E. L. Godkin,* The Macmillan Co., N. Y., 1907.

Ogg, F. A.: *National Progress: 1907-1917,* Harper & Bros., N. Y., 1918.

Olcott, Charles S.: *Life of William McKinley,* Houghton Mifflin Co., N. Y., 1916.

O'Laughlin, Edward T.: *Hearst and His Enemies,* pamphlet, The O'Laughlin Co., Brooklyn, 1919.

O'Shaughnessy, Edith L.: *A Diplomat's Wife in Mexico,* Harper & Bros., N. Y., 1916.

Older, Fremont: *My Own Story,* the Call Publishing Co., San Francisco, 1919.

Older, Fremont Mrs.: *William Randolph Hearst: American,* D. Appleton-Century Co., N. Y., and London, 1936. With a foreword by Fremont Older.

Parkhurst, Rev. Charles H.: *My Forty Years in New York,* The Macmillan Co., N. Y., 1923.

Paxson, Frederick L.: *Recent History of the United States,* Houghton Mifflin Co., Boston, 1921.

—— *The New Nation,* Houghton Mifflin Co., Boston, 1915.

Pearson, Drew, *Washington Merry-Go-Round* (with Robert S. Allen), H. Liveright, Inc., N. Y., 1931.

Platt, Thomas Collier: *Autobiography,* McClure's Magazine, N. Y., 1910.

Quille, Dan de: *A History of the Comstock Mine,* American Pub. Co., Hartford, 1876.

Ramsaye, Terry: *A Million and One Nights: A History of the Motion Picture,* Simon and Schuster, N. Y., 1926.

Rea, George B.: *Facts and Fakes About Cuba,* G. Munro's Sons, N. Y., 1897.

Rhodes, James Ford: *The McKinley and Roosevelt Administrations,* The Macmillan Co., N. Y., 1922.

Roosevelt, Theodore: *Autobiography,* C. Scribner's Sons, N. Y., 1926.

Rosewater, Victor: *History of Cooperative Newsgathering in the United States,* D. Appleton & Co., N. Y., and London, 1930.

Salisbury, William: *The Career of a Journalist,* B. W. Dodge & Co., N. Y., 1908.

Seitz, Don C.: *Joseph Pulitzer,* Simon and Schuster, N. Y., 1924.
Seldes, George: *Freedom of the Press,* The Bobbs-Merrill Co., Indianapolis and N. Y., 1935.
Sherover, Max: *Fakes in American Journalism,* pamphlet, Free Press League, Brooklyn, 1916.
Shinn, Charles Haven: *The Story of the Mine,* D. Appleton & Co., N. Y., 1903.
Sinclair, Upton: *The Brass Check,* Published by the Author, Pasadena, 1919.
Slosson, Preston William: *The Great Crusade and After,* The Macmillan Co., N. Y., 1931.
Smith, Henry Justin (with Lloyd Lewis): *Chicago: The History of Its Reputation,* Harcourt, Brace & Co., N. Y., 1929.
Spring Rice, Sir Cecil: *The Letters and Friendships of Sir Cecil Spring Rice;* edited by Stephen Gwynn, Constable & Co., Ltd., London, 1929.
Steffens, Lincoln: *Autobiography,* Harcourt, Brace & Co., N. Y., 1931.
Stoddard, Lothrop: *Master of Manhattan: The Life of Richard Croker,* Longmans, Green & Co., N. Y., 1931.
Stone, Melville E.: *Fifty Years A Journalist,* Doubleday, Page & Co., Garden City, 1921.
Sullivan, Edward Dean: *Rattling the Cup on Chicago Crime,* The Vanguard Press, N. Y., 1929.
Sullivan, Mark: *Our Times,* C. Scribner's Sons, N. Y., 1927-35.
Thomason, Arthur: *The Conspiracy Against Mexico,* International Press, Oakland, Cal., 1919.
Tinkham, George H.: *California Men and Events,* Record Publishing Co., Stockton, Cal., 1915.
University of California: *Phoebe Apperson Hearst Memorial Volume on Archaeology and Ethnology,* University of California Press, 1923.
——— *Prospectus of Phoebe A. Hearst Architectural Plan of the University of California,* L. Roesch Co., San Francisco, 1897.
Villard, Oswald Garrison: *Prophets True and False,* A. A. Knopf, N. Y., 1928.
——— *Some Newspapers and Newspaper Men,* A. A. Knopf, N. Y., 1928.
——— *The Press Today,* reprinted from The Nation, The Nation Press, N. Y., 1930.
Werner, M. R.: *Bryan,* Harcourt, Brace & Co., N. Y., 1929.
——— *Privileged Characters,* R. M. McBride & Co., N. Y., 1935.
——— *Tammany Hall,* Doubleday, Doran & Co., Garden City, 1931.
White, Andrew D.: *Autobiography,* The Century Co., N. Y., 1905.

Wilson, James Harrison: *Life of Charles Dana,* Harper & Brothers, N. Y., 1907.
Wilson, Rufus R.: *Out of the West,* The Press of the Pioneers, N. Y., 1933.
Winkler, John K.: *William Randolph Hearst, An American Phenomenon,* Simon and Schuster, N. Y., 1928.
Young, John P.: *Journalism in California,* Chronicle Publishing Co., San Francisco, 1915.
────── *San Francisco: A History of the Pacific Coast Metropolis,* S. J. Clarke Publishing Co., San Francisco, 1912.

A mass of newspapers and periodicals, too extensive to mention individually, has also been consulted for the period from 1863 to 1936. Newspaper and periodical research has especially emphasized the localities of San Francisco, New York and Chicago. Previous books about Hearst by John K. Winkler and Mrs. Fremont Older have been used critically and sparingly. Abundant acknowledgment of indebtedness to newspapers and periodicals has been made throughout the text.

INDEX

INDEX

Abuse, use of against opponents, 40, 62, 82, 86-87, 93, 95, 111, 116-117, 213-214
Actors' Equity, 199
Addams, Jane, 175
Adam, James Noble, 110
Advance-Rumely Corp., 276
Advertising, in San Francisco *Examiner*, 24; valuable, achieved by Hearst, 31; spurious, 34-35; contract with Southern Pacific exposed, 37-42; why N. Y. *Journal* did not get it, 66; sensational, in N. Y. *Journal*, 84; losses sustained in support of Bryan, 85; "help wanted," 85; fake stock and patent medicine, 85, 107-108; not affected by Pure Food and Drug Act, 106; indecent, in New York *Herald*, 115; Rockefeller, secured, 124; Chicago Gas Company, secured, 144; received from German brewers, 218; cancelled in war-time boycott, 233; Doheny-Sinclair, 258; public utilities, 263; "scientific," in *Good Housekeeping*, 281-282
Agricultural Adjustment Administration, 276
Albert, Dr. Heinrich, 239-240, 243, 276
Alger, Russell A., 82
Alien Property Custodian, 234, 236
Altman, Vincent, 153, 156
American Federation of Catholic Societies, 186
American Federation of Labor, 46, 101, 112, 165, 166, 168, 170-171, 200, 360
American Friends of the Soviet Union, 374
American Historical Association, 264
American League Against War and Fascism, 374
American Legion, 361-362, 379
American Liberty League, 358, 361
American Magazine, 112
American Medical Association, 282
American Metal Co., 308-309, 341
American Newspaper Guild, 166, 196-199
American Newspaper Publishers' Assn., 167-169, 195, 279

American Newspapers, Inc., 311, 313, 315, 328
American Pressman, 169-171
American Trust Co. of San Francisco, 262
American Weekly, 166
Amherst College, 350
Anaconda Copper Co., 19, 50, 182
Anarchists, 32
Anderson, Louis B., 136
Anglo-American Treaty on Venezuelan Boundary Dispute, 64
Anglo-California National Bank, 320
Anglophobia, 90, 91, 217-218, 230, 233, 242
Annenberg, Max, 151, 155, 158-159, 162, 164, 291, 292
Annenberg, Moses, 151, 161, 164-165, 293
Annenberg, Walter, 165
Archbold, John D., 122-123, 125-128, 130
Armour, Charles, 105
Armour, Ogden, 105
Associated Gas and Electric Co., 261-263
Associated Press, 53, 74, 154, 201-209, 352, 368-369
Astor, Vincent, 333, 355
Atherton, Gertrude, 29
Atlanta, 87
Atlanta *Georgian*, 219, 358
Avila, Miguel R., 285-286

Babicora Ranch, 19, 220-221
Baer, Arthur ("Bugs"), 280
Bailey, Joseph W., 106, 123, 132
Baker, George F., 109
Baker, Ray Stannard, 211, 215-216
Baldwin, Stanley, 230
Ballard, H. W., 258-259
Baltimore Brevities, 164
Baltimore *Sun*, 198, 240
Bank of America, 320
Bankers Trust Co., 91, 175, 179, 309, 339
Bank of Italy, 320
Bannon, Joseph D., 164, 291, 295
Barbary Coast, 19, 32, 45
Barbusse, Henri, 231

393

INDEX

Barney & Co., Charles D., 176
Barr, H. W., 150, 151
Barrett, Charles, 159-160
Barrett, Edward, 153, 159, 160, 170
Barron, Clarence W., 50, 247, 248, 257-258
Beall, Jack, 296-298
Beals, Carleton, 177, 285
Beals, Fred, 363-364
Beck, James M., 232
Beaverbrook, Lord, 230
Becker, Alfred L., 234, 241, 242
Belgrano, Frank N., Jr., 362
Belmont, August, 100, 109, 216
Bendix, Vincent, 277
Bennett, James Gordon, 26, 49, 51, 85, 115, 117, 248
Bent, Silas, 247, 285, 293
Berger, Victor, 220, 234
Bergner and Engel, 234
Bernstorff, Johann H. von, 217-218, 238, 241
Berry, George L., 169
Biddle, Francis, 198
Bielaski, Bruce, 234, 238-240
Bierce, Ambrose, 23, 29, 31, 37, 90
Big Business, 35, 173, 212, 357
Birchall, Frederick T., 352
Black, Winifred ("Annie Laurie"), 29, 32, 51
Blackmail, 31, 37, 61, 124
Blair, Emily Newell, 275, 279, 280-281
Blair, Harry, 275
Blanc, George Le, 278
Block, Paul, 180, 235, 243, 250, 277, 330-331
Bloor, Ella Reeve, 105
Blue Ridge Corporation, 263
Boer War, 91
Bonzano, Archbishop, 186
Bookman, The, 109
Borah, William E., 287, 290, 359
Boston *Advertiser,* 180
Boston *American,* 352
Boston *Globe,* 20
Boulder Dam, 354
Boycotts, 37, 44, 82, 93-94, 205, 233, 246, 307, 350, 361
Breines, Louis, 296, 298
Bremen, S. S., 353
Bribery, indications of, 64, 82, 104, 109, 120-121, 202, 247
Brisbane, Arthur, 54-55, 57, 88-89, 95, 103, 107-109, 121, 149, 165, 233-238, 243-244, 249, 260, 280, 287, 333-335, 353, 378

British Foreign Office, 91
British Government, 91, 229, 230, 242, 246-247
British Intelligence Service, 246-247
Brodsky, Louis B., 353
Broun, Heywood, 196
Brown, Morris, 112
Bryan, William Jennings, 83-88, 93, 116, 215-216, 222, 226, 229
Bryce, Viscount James, 230
Buckley, Chris, 28
Buckley, George, 275
Buffalo, 110-111
Buffalo *Evening News,* 66
Bureau of Internal Revenue, 265, 270
Burgess, Louis, 197
Burleson, Albert S., 233
Burnett, Frances Hodgeson, 70
Burnham, James, 349
Burns, William J., 45, 46
Busch, Bishop Joseph F., 185-186, 188-190
Business Week, 279
Busse, Fred, 153

California, 19-48, 193
Calles, Elias Plutarco, 286, 289
Camara, Rear Admiral Manuel de la, 80-81
Canada, 137, 138
Canada Power and Paper Corp., 263, 336
Canadian Parliament, 138
Canadian Reciprocal Tariff agreement, 137-138
Cannon, Joseph, 99
Capone, Al, 173
Cardenas, Cuba, 71
Carlton, C. C., 37
Carnegie Hall, 111, 232, 254
Carranza, Venustiano, 222-223
Carvalho, Solomon S., 54, 65, 109, 114, 261
Caverley, John R., 159
Cecil, Lord Robert, 230
Censorship, 154, 164, 172-173, 180, 182, 232, 257-258, 301
Central Labor Union of Boston, 195
Cermak, Anton, 173, 372
Cerro de Pasco, 91-92, 166, 174-180, 219, 256; Corporation, 270, 308, 326, 336-337, 339-341
Cervera, Pascual de, 79, 82
Chamberlain, Sam S., 26-28, 36, 37, 51, 54, 58, 59, 65, 66, 72, 83, 92, 96
Chambers, Walter, 124

INDEX 395

Chandler, Harry, 259
Chase National Bank, 276, 309, 355-357
Chernow, Joseph, 298-299
Chicago, 139-173
Chicago *American*, 57, 139; description of office, 139-142; theft of news, 142-143; denounced by clergy, 146; circulation war, 151-162; locks out pressmen, 168; editor linked with Capone mob, 173
Chicago *Chronicle*, 139, 149
Chicago *Daily News*, 139, 152, 173, 359
Chicago *Daily Socialist*, 153, 154, 155, 158
Chicago *Daily World*, 158, 159
Chicago *Day Book*, 170
Chicago *Examiner*, 134; persecutes Standard Oil witness, 136; financial loss, 139; circulation wars, 154-162; locks out pressmen, 168
Chicago Federation of Labor, 170
Chicago *Herald*, 139, 235
Chicago *Herald-Examiner*, 162, 240, 293, 351
Chicago *Inter-Ocean*, 139, 149, 154
Chicago *Journal*, 139, 149
Chicago *Post*, 139
Chicago Publishers Assn., 166-168
Chicago *Record*, 139
Chicago *Record-Herald*, 149, 162
Chicago *Tribune*, 66, 139, 150; circulation war, 152-162; 172, 285, 291
Child Labor, 195-196, 275
Childs, Richard Washburn, 354
Chinese, employment of, 32, 193-194
Cigarmakers' Union, Local 144; 112
Circulation, 27, 35, 52-53, 66, 83, 85, 139, 141, 151; wars in Chicago, 153-162, 233, 280-281, 291-300, 306, 314
Cisneros, Evangelina Cosio y, 69, 70, 71
Cities Service Corporation, 262-263
Clapp, Moses E., 130, 131
Clark, Bennett C., 279
Clark, Champ, 212, 214-215, 233, 279
Clark, Edward Hardy, 49, 51, 55, 92, 114, 116, 176, 179, 181, 226, 253, 288-290, 309, 339
Cleveland, Grover, 31, 64, 90
Cleveland *News*, 202-208
Cobb, Frank I., 216
Coblentz, Edward D., 288
Cochran, W. Bourke, 121
Colby, Bainbridge, 331
College Editors Association, 347
Collier's Magazine, 96, 98, 107-108, 123, 125-129, 131-132, 214

Columbia University, 50, 348-350
Committee for the Nation, 243, 276-278, 339, 361
Committee on Pacific Railroads, House of Representatives, 37
Commons, John R., 188
Comstock, Anthony, 103
Comstock Silver Lode, 19
Confectioner's Journal, 279
Connors, W. J., ("Finkey"), 122
Consolidated Gas Company, 62, 262
Consumers' Advisory Board, 275, 279
Consumers' Research, 279, 281-282
Continental Illinois Bank & Trust Co., 320
Coolidge, Calvin, 257, 260, 264, 273, 288-289; administration, 137, 180, 264
Cooper, Gary, 376-377
Cooper, Kent, 208
Copeland, Royal S., 255, 263-264, 278-279
Corporate Structure of H. Enterprises, 308-342
Corruption, 45, 110, 120, 121, 125, 128, 150, 152, 157, 170, 173, 182, 202, 295-298
Cosmopolitan Film Corporation, 210
Cosmopolitan Magazine, 99, 100, 145, 261
Cotton, Joseph, 341
Coughlin, Rev. Charles E., 243, 277, 338, 358, 374-375, 379
Counts, George S., 349-350, 374
Couzens, James G., 265-269
Crane, Stephen, 54, 56, 59, 65
Crawford, F. Marion, 57
Creel, George, 182-188
Creelman, James, 54, 68, 69, 79, 81, 93, 112
Crimmins, Phil, 28
Crocker, Charles F., 38-41
Croker, Richard, 95-96
Crusaders, 361, 377
Cuba, and the "Cuban Question," 66-68, 77-78, 82; revolutionary party in, 67; junta, 67, 74; insurrectos, 73, 74
Cudahy, Edward, 105
Culberson, Charles A., 215
Cummings, Homer S., 275, 359
Czolgosz, Leon, 93-94

Daily Racing Form, 164
Daily Running Horse, 164
Daily Worker, 366
Dale, Alan, 54, 56
Daly, "Chicago Jack," 153

396 INDEX

Daly, Marcus, 50
Damage suits, 97, 113-114, 135
Darrow, Clarence, 47, 101
Dartmouth College, 350
Daugherty, Harry M., 260
Davenport, Homer, 51, 86
Davies, Marion, 199, 302, 326
Davis, Mrs. Jefferson, 69
Davis, John W., 255
Davis, Richard Harding, 52, 54, 64-65, 71, 74-75
Davis, Robert H. ("Bob"), 54
Davison, Henry P., 311
Deaths in N. Y. American election explosion, 96-97; at Cerro de Pasco, 178; at Homestake, 182, 188-189
Debs, Eugene V., 260
Decker, Karl, 70
Delmonico's, 58, 71, 121
Democratic campaign financed by Senator G. Hearst, 1886, 19; party, 98, 100, 105, 110, 122, 125; machine, in San Francisco, 28; '88 convention kept in East, 31; convention of 1896, 83; convention of 1904, 101; N. Y. convention of 1906, 110; convention of 1912, 215; convention of 1922, 254; convention of 1924, 255; convention of 1932, 173, 273-274
Dennison, Frank A., 135
Denunciations of W. R. H., 29, 31, 40, 42, 77, 93, 95, 102, 109, 132, 146, 170, 220, 230, 232-233, 251, 254
Dern, George H., 359, 360
Detroit *Times*, 277
Deutsches Journal, 225, 233, 240, 276
Dever, William, 153
Dewey, George, 78, 80
Diaz, Porfirio, 220
Dickerman, Don, 334
Doheny-Sinclair faction, 257, 286
Doherty, Henry L., 262-263, 335
Dorgan, T. A. ("Tad"), 29, 109
Drug Trade News, 280
Dubinsky, David, 373
Duke, Lloyd L., 150, 151
Dumaine, Frederick C., 257
Dunne, Edward F., 105, 152
Dunne, Finley Peter, 112
Dunne, Frank H., 28
Duranty, Walter, 364

Early, Stephen, 198
Eastman, John M., 149
Eat, Drink and Be Wary, 281
Eddy, John L., 123, 130, 131, 132, 136

Editor and Publisher, 283, 329, 347
Educators, 264, 347-352, 374
Egan, Martin, 311
Ehret, George, 234
El Caney, 79
Eldridge, Fred, 132, 136
Electric Bond and Share Co., 262
Elizabeth (N. J.) *Times*, 165
Elsey, Fred T., 262, 336
Empire Voting Machine Co., 150
Employees, status of, 25, 52, 58-59, 140, 142, 147, 149, 166-167, 174, 175-179, 183-199
England, 81, 93, 97, 138, 219, 230-234, 245
Enright, Maurice ("Mossy"), 153, 155-156, 158
Equitable Trust Co., 278
Evening Graphic, 294
Evening Journal, 57
Evening World, 57
Export-Import Bank, 355
Exposés, San Francisco *Examiner*, 28, 32, 36; by N. Y. *Journal*, 105; by *Hearst's Magazine*, 125; by Chicago *American*, 152
Exposés of W. R. H., 33, 37-42, 107-108, 113-114, 116, 214, 283-284
Extortion, 31, 33, 42, 150-151

Fair, James, 26
Fairfax, Beatrice, 109
Fall, Albert B., 258
Falsification, used in "exposing" Southern Pacific, 36; in N. Y. *Journal*, 63, 69, 72, 74, 76, 79, 103, 112; in N. Y. *World*, 66; on Chicago *American*, 140-141, 145-147, 171; on Wisconsin *News*, 199; in N. Y. *American*, 221-222, 224-225; during the World War, 228-229; in anti-Soviet campaign, 351-352, 363-366
Farley, James A., 274, 359
Farley, James S. ("Strikebreaker"), 116
Farm and Home Magazine, 99
Farmers National Bank, 180
Farnsworth, William, 303
Farrelly, Edward, 56
Fascism, 343-381
Federal Commission on Industrial Relations (Walsh Commission), 186, 188
Federal Housing Administration, 275
Federal Trade Commission, 282, 317
Federation Bank & Trust Co., 165-166, 294
Feigenspan, Christian W., 234-238

INDEX 397

Feldman, Harry, 291, 295, 298-300
Fickert, Charles M., 45, 47
Film industry, 199, 301-302
Financial & Commercial Chronicle, 175
Fireworks explosion, 96-97
First National Bank of San Francisco, 40
Fish, Stuyvesant, 118
Fisher, Bud, 29
Fisher, Harrison, 29
Flatiron Building, 96
Fleishacker, Herbert, 256, 316, 320
Flinn, William, 180
Flynn, John T., 123
Foley, Boss Thomas, 255
Foraker, Joseph B., 123, 124, 132
Forbes, B. C., 317-318
Ford, Henry, 50, 324
Foreign policies, 90-92, 217-246, 256
Forgeries, 112, 116, 124-125, 126-129, 282, 284-290
Fortune Magazine, 191-193, 310-315, 319-320, 323-328, 330, 332-337
Fox, Edward Lyell, 239
Franco-Prussian War, 26
Fredericks, John D., 46
Free Silver, 83, 88, 139
"French Restaurants," 45
Frick, Henry C., 176, 180
Fuehr, Dr. Carl A., 239
Funds, raised by San Francisco *Examiner*, 32; by N. Y. *Journal*, 73, 86

Gallagher, James J., 119
Gallagher, James L., 43-44
Galveston Flood, 101
Gangsterism, 43, 61, 103-104, 110-111, 133-136, 142, 153-164, 169-171, 291-301, 346
Garner, John Nance, 273-274, 359
Gassaway, Frank, 41
Gauvreau, Emile, 364-365
Gaynor, William, 102, 118-120, 212
General News Bureau, 164, 165, 173, 294, 305
Genesee Society, 121
Geneva, 282-283
Gentleman, "Dutch," 153, 156, 158
Gentleman, Gus, 153
Gentleman, Pete, 153
Geraghty, James F., 296
Gerard, James W., 121, 231
German Foreign Office, 228, 238, 353
Germanophilism, 90, 217-218, 226-227, 230, 238-239, 240, 244-246, 272-273, 344

Geronimo, 19
Gest, Morris, 302
Giannini, Amadeo P., 256, 309; Banks, 275, 276, 320
Gifford, Walter S., 325
Gilhooley, Martin, 155
Goddard, Morrill, 53-55, 84, 326
Godkin, Edwin Lawrence, 62, 77
God's Gold, 123
Goering, Herman W., 351
Goldman Sachs Trading Co., 262-263
Gompers, Samuel, 47, 101, 166, 200, 245
Good Housekeeping, 100, 219, 275, 280, 282
Grady, Thomas F., 110, 121
Graft, San Francisco *Examiner*, 23, 28; Ruef-Schmitz, 42; in Anaconda management, 50; N. Y. *American*, 99; in Chicago, 150-152, 173; news-stands, 296-297
Grant, Mrs. Julia Dent, 70
Graves, John Temple, 124, 211-212
Greco-Turkish War, 65-66
Green, William E., 165, 200, 331, 361
Grey, Sir Edward, 229, 245
Grosvenor, Chas. H., 125-127
Gruening, Ernest H., 287
Guldensuppe Case, The, 60, 61

Haas, Morris, 44
Haggin and Tevis, 50
Haggin, J. B., 176
Haggin, L. T., 176
Hale, William Bayard, 238
Halsey, Stuart & Co., 144, 172, 316, 323
Hamm, William, 234
Hanfstaengl, Dr. E. F. S., 344
Hanna, Marcus A., 76, 86, 88, 92, 125, 127, 152
Hanna, Mrs. Marcus A., 70
Hapgood, Norman, 107-108, 125, 214, 252, 258, 260-261
Harding, J. Horace, 176
Harding, Warren G., 257; administration, 268
Harper's Bazaar, 100, 219
Harper's Weekly, 101, 108, 182-183, 222, 225, 228-229
Harriman, E. H., 36, 109, 118
Harrison, Carter H., 105, 135
Harriss & Vose, 278
Harriss, Robert M., 278
Harte, Bret, 29
Harvard University, 20, 24-25

INDEX

Hauptmann, Bruno Richard, 306, 331, 352
Havana, 67-68, 72-75, 81
Hawaii, 78
Hawthorne, Julian, 54, 106
Hay-Pauncefote Treaty, 91-94
Hearst Consolidated Publications, 312, 315-316, 318-322, 327-329
Hearst Corporation, 311-316, 320-323, 327, 328
Hearst Estate, 62, 86-87, 270
Hearst, George, 19, 21, 24, 27-28, 36, 49; Estate, 176
Hearst, George, Jr., 103, 325
Hearst, Haggin, Tevis and Company, 19, 91
Hearst Hotels Corporation, 270
Hearst's Magazine, 123, 125, 127-129
Hearst Magazine Properties, 329, 331-332
Hearst Magazines, Inc., 323
"Hearst Method," 23, 34
Hearst Mercantile Co., 183, 187, 190, 193, 312
Hearst-Metrotone News, 302, 312, 316
Hearst mining properties, 336-342
Hearst, Mrs. William Randolph, 97, 100, 103, 186, 266, 303
Hearst newspaper group, 328-330; mergers, 331
Hearst, Phoebe Apperson, 19-20, 49, 51, 66, 91, 182, 185-186, 190, 222
Hearst power and paper properties, 336
Hearst Publications, Inc., 317-318, 321-322, 329
Hearst Real Estate Holdings, 332-335
Hearst, William Randolph, background, 19; parents, 19; birth, 19; schooling, 20; expelled from St. Paul's, 20; expelled from Harvard, 20; joins staff of New York *World*, 21; acquires San Francisco *Examiner*, 21; buys talent, 29; tries to bring Democratic convention of '88 to San Francisco, 31; charged with employing Chinese labor, 32, 33; absents himself in Egypt during Southern Pacific scandal, 37; excoriated by San Francisco *Call*, 41-42; political influence in San Francisco after 1901, 42-48; supports Ruef-Schmitz regime, 42-46; political alliances, 45-46; turns against union labor, 46; prosecution of McNamara brothers, 46; leads attack on union labor over the country, 47; purchases New York *Journal*, 49; takes staff from Pulitzer, 52-57; adopts "yellow journalism," 57; sell-outs to public utilities, 62-63; rôle in Spanish-American War, 66; greets Evangelina Cisneros, "the girl martyr," 69, 70, 71; arrives in Cuba, 78; plans to sink a vessel in Mediterranean, 81; espouses cause of Bryan, 83; tries to secure Vice-Presidency, 87; foreign policy, 90; tie-ups with German brewers, 90; anti-British bias, 91; opposition to Hay-Pauncefote Treaty, 92; political prospects (1901), 93; assailed after McKinley assassination, 93-94; charged with being "un-American," 95; elected to Congress, 96; marriage, 97; change wrought by election explosion, 98; activities in Congress, 98-99; called Socialistic, 99; aspires to Presidency, 100; favorable publicity in rival press, 101; loses bid for Presidential nomination, 101; asks Charles F. Murphy for Mayoralty, 102; campaigns on streetcorners, 103; cheated of Mayoralty by Tammany, 103-104; Murphy and the Gubernatorial nomination, 104; fights Pure Food and Drug Act, 104-106; attacked by *Collier's*, 107-108; makes pretence of suing, 109; nominated for Governor, 109-111; gets favorable notices again, 112; fakes union labor endorsements, 112; motives for wanting Governorship, 113; charged with tax evasion by Hughes, 114; denounced by Elihu Root, 117; loses Governorship to Hughes, 118; defeated for Mayoralty, 1909, 118; attack on Mayor Gaynor, 118; theft of Gaynor-Murphy letters, 121; theft of Standard Oil letters, 123; called before U. S. Senate, 130; defeats Canadian tariff agreement, 138; in Chicago, 139; challenges Chicago *Tribune's* lucrative lease-hold, 152; power over Chicago mayors, 152; tie-ups with Annenbergs, 165; loans from A. F. of L. bank, 166; responsibility for conditions at Cerro de Pasco, 179; responsibility for conditions at Homestake, 181; exploitation of labor in California, 193; transfers stock ownership from M-G-M to Warner, 199; enjoined from stealing AP news, 201; orders editorial attack on Wilson, 212; opposes war policies of Wilson, 217; his downfall predicted, 219; supports Socialists in New

INDEX 399

York and Milwaukee, 220; prints pacifist editorials, 230; discussed in Senate investigation into German-American activities, 235; German intrigue in U. S., 238; friend of Bolsheviks, 243; opposes U. S. entry in League of Nations, 245; adopts anti-Soviet policy, 245; begins real estate operations under Hylan, 249; abortive attempt at Gubernatorial nomination (1918), 251; feud with Al Smith, 252; rebuffed in second try for governorship, 254; record in Teapot Dome scandal, 257; defends Harry M. Daugherty, 260; supports Hopson and Associated Gas, 261; buys control of Kansas public utility corporation, 263; another try for Presidency, 263; tax rebates under Mellon regime, 265; attacks Hoover on pro-English bias, 271; deported from France, 273; supports Garner for President (1932), 273; contacts in Roosevelt Administration, 274; connections with Committee for the Nation and Father Coughlin, 277; opposes Tugwell Bill, 278; accepts forged Mexican documents for publication, 285; early interest in motion pictures, 301; participant in race track racket, 304; responsible for Lindbergh leaving U. S., 306; corporate structure of his enterprises, 308; endorses Hitler regime, 344; raises "red scare" in San Francisco general strike, 345; attacks "intellectuals," 348; sells news services to Nazis, 352; begins campaign against U. S. S. R., 355; ties up with opposition to Franklin D. Roosevelt, 358; uses Socialist "Old Guard" against Soviet Union, 363; inspires military units in Hollywood, 376
Hearst, William Randolph, Jr., 326
Heflin, Thomas J., 287
Henderson, A. B., 26, 39
Henderson, W. J., 54
Hendrick, Burton J., 216
Heney, Francis J., 43-44
Herrin, W. T., 39
Higgins, Frank W., 113
Hillquit, Morris, 220, 260-261
Hisgen, Thomas, 124
Hitler, Adolph, 245, 344, 375, 378; government, 243, 352
Hoffman House, 26, 57
Homestake, 19, 49, 166, 174, 176, 181-193, 219

Homestake Mining Co., 270, 274, 308, 326, 336-339
Home States Telephone Co., 42
Hook, Sidney, 348
Hoover, Herbert C., 264, 271-272; administration, 180
Hope, Jimmy, 28
Hopson, Howard, 261-263
Horner, Henry, 173
Houghton, A. J. Company, 234
House, E. M., 215
Howe, Julia Ward, 69
Hoyne, Maclay, 154
Hugenberg, Alfred, 343
Hughes, Charles Evans, 109-110, 113-114, 117
Hull, Cordell, 359
Huntington, Collis P., 36-37
Hupfel, G. C. W., 234
Hylan, John S., 233, 248-252, 260-261, 263-264

Ickes, Harold L., 251, 357, 359
Illinois Manufacturers' Assn., 105
Illinois National Guard, 171, 172
Imperialism, 87-88, 217-220, 222, 228
Impostures, 59-60, 133-134, 136-137, 159, 161, 224, 229, 349
Independence League, 111, 124, 150
Ingalls, John H., 63
Insull, Samuel, 144, 172, 242, 263
Insull Utilities, 262-263
International Harvester Co., 152, 244
International Intrigue, 238-243, 245-247, 355-357
International Magazine, 258, 260-261
International Magazine Co., 266, 270
International News Service, 201-209, 229, 272, 294, 304-305, 328, 351, 353, 366-371
International Newsreel Corporation, 247
International Publications, 166
International Typographical Union, 169
International Stereotypers Union, 169
Irving Trust Company, 91, 175, 179, 309, 339

Jacobs, Mike, 303
James, Henry, 56
James, William, 20-21
Japan, 93, 179, 223-225, 227, **239**
Jeffries-Johnson prize fight, 119
Jennings, Dean, 197
Jerome, William Travers, 97, 110-111, 113

INDEX

Jewish Daily Forward, 364
Johnson, Grove L., 253-254
Johnson, Hiram, 45, 233, 245, 256-257, 274, 287, 355
Johnson, Hugh S., 345
Journalism, Continental, 26-27; Anglo-Saxon, 27; American, 34, 290

Kaiser Wilhelm, 90, 217, 231
Kallet, Arthur, 281, 301
Keehn, Roy D., 171, 172, 234, 241, 379
Keeley, James, 150, 155, 157, 158
Kellogg, F. W., 247
Kelly, Edward F., 173
Kelly, Marshall, 240
Kelly, Martin, 28
Kennedy, John A., 274
Kerensky Government, 355
Kidnapping, 133, 134, 135, 158, 307
Kilpatrick, William H., 349-350
King Features Syndicate, 312, 316
Knowles, Freeman, 182
Knox, Frank, 139, 359
Kravif, Hy, 311
Kuhn, Loeb & Co., 116

Labor Policies, 166-169, 174-200
Laborite, The, 298-299
Laffan, William M., 117
La Follette, Robert M., 257, 260, 287
La Guardia, Fiorello H., 298, 335
Lamar, Joseph R., 223
Lambert Pharmacal Company, 280
Lamont, Corliss, 373-374
Lamont, Thomas W., 311, 357, 373
Lampoon, the Harvard, 20, 26
Landon, Alfred, 330, 358-359
Lane, Franklin K., 28
Lang, Harry, 363
Langdon, William H., 43-44
Lardner, Ring, 52
Lawrence, Andrew M., 28, 124, 134, 149-151, 153, 162, 167, 171, 219
Lawrence, Frederick, 28, 67-68
Lawson, Victor, 152, 162
Lead, S. D., 181-193
League of Nations, 245, 256-257
Leases, Chicago School land, held by Chicago *Tribune,* 152; Illinois Publishing & Printing Co., 267-268
Léguia, Augusto, 181, 309
Lehmann, Frederick W., 223
Lenin, V. I., 48, 244
Lester, George B., 234, 240
Lewis, Alfred Henry, 54, 88, 212-214, 222

Lewis, James Hamilton, 173, 233, 263-264
Libel, defended by Brisbane, 121
Libel suits, 34, 109, 113, 116, 287, 299
Liberty Loan, 227, 231, 242
Liberty Magazine, 164, 331
Liebman, Julius, 234
Lindbergh, Charles A., 306
Lingle, Jake, 172-173
Loans, 165, 166, 181, 219, 235-238, 245, 268, 356-357
Lobbying, 282-283
Lodge, Henry Cabot, 95
Logan, Mrs. John A., 71
Lôme, Dupuy de, 70-72
London Budget Company, 130
London Daily Telegraph, 225-226
London, Jack, 29
Long, Huey P., 358
Long, John Davis, 72
Lorimer, William, 157
Los Angeles, open-shop, 47
Los Angeles *Examiner,* 199
Los Angeles *Times,* 289-290
Los Angeles *Times,* Bombing of, 46
Louis Napoleon, 26
Lovett, Robert Morss, 374
Lowden, Frank O., 242, 257
Lowell, A. Lawrence, 230
Lund, Robert L., 280
Lusitania, 226, 228, 239

Macfadden, Bernarr, 164, 294, 331
Macfadden Publications, Inc., 331
MacGinnis, John, 50
Macgowan, Kenneth, 232
Mackay, John W., 26, 36
Madison Square Garden, 71, 96
Mahoney, E. P., 371
Maine, The, 71, 72-75, 81-82
Maison Riche, 25
"Man with the Hoe," parody, 29-30
Manila, 80
Mansfield, John C., 294, 298
Manton, Martin T., 201
Markham, Edwin, 29
Marriott, Edward E., 150
Mason, Redfern, 197-198
Mayer, Dora, 175, 177, 178
Mayer, Levy, 105, 212, 233, 235
Mellon, Andrew W., 180, 257, 264
Metro-Goldwyn-Mayer, 199, 302, 377
Metropolitan Life Insurance Co., 244
Metropolitan Street Railway, 62, 116

INDEX

401

Mexican-American Peace Conference, 222
Mexican "documents," 282, 284-290
Mexico, 220-224, 286-290, 379
Miami *Daily Tribune*, 165
Milk Fund, benefits, 303-304
Miller, Fred, Brewing Co., 234
Miller, Nathan L., 254
Mills, Darius Ogden, 36, 176
Mills, Ogden L., 180, 255-256, 265, 339
Mills, William H., 38, 41
Milwaukee *Leader*, 189, 234, 238
Milwaukee *Sentinel*, 165
Milwaukee *Wisconsin*, 240
Misrepresentation, 28, 61, 70, 74, 76, 78, 80-81, 102-103, 107, 112, 124-125, 158, 224-225, 229, 253, 281-282, 289-290, 363-371
Mitchel, John Purroy, 120
Mitchell, Charles E., 273
Mitchell, Roscoe Conklin, 222-223
Mooney, Tom, 46-48, 256
Moore, Alexander P., 179-181
Morgan, J. P., 109, 116, 176, 253
Morgan, J. P., & Co., 91, 176, 227, 242, 262, 286, 309, 337, 339, 356
Morgen Journal, Das, 90, 107, (*Deutches Journal*), 217
Morgenthau, Henry, Jr., 359
Morning *Advertiser*, 53
Morris, Edward, 105
Morris, Edward S., 133, 135, 137
Morris, R. N., 105
Morro Castle, 72
Morrow, Dwight W., 286, 306
Municipal Ownership League, 102, 104, 111
Munitions investigations, 282-284
Munsey, Frank A., 234, 292
Murders in Chicago circulation war, 156, 157, 158, 159, 161, 162, 170, 173
Murphy, Charles F., 95-96, 102, 104, 110, 114, 118, 120, 212, 215-216, 254-255
Murphy-Gaynor Letters, 120-122
Mussolini, Benito, 347, 354

McAdoo, William Gibbs, 233, 241-242, 255, 273-274, 335, 377
McAndrew, William, 264
McCabe, Patrick A., 122
McClellan, George B., 102, 113
McComb, Marshal F., 377
McCooey, John H., 254
McCormick, Medill, 152, 153, 293
McCormick, R. R., 291
McCormicks, of International Harvester Co., 152, 162

McEwen, Arthur, 26, 51
McIntyre, O. O., 280
McKinley, William, 71, 76, 83, 86, 88-89, 92-94, 117, 120; administration, 67, 69, 90, 92
McKinley, Mrs. Nancy, 70
McLaglen, Victor, 376-377
McLaurin, J. W., 123
McLean, John R., 49
McNab, Gavin, 28
McNamara brothers, 46
McWeeney, John, 154

Nash's Magazine, 247
Nation, Carry, 141
Nation, The, 62, 77, 198, 287, 351-352, 376-379
National Association of Democratic Clubs, 87, 102
National Association of Manufacturers, 280
National City Bank, 50, 181-182, 273, 275-276, 309-310, 320, 324, 356-357
National Labor Relations Board, 198
National Recovery Act, 360
National Security League, 166, 361
National Surety Co., 179
Naval investigation into Maine sinking, 73
Negroes, 124, 132, 136, 141, 162-163
Nelson, Knute, 237
"New Journalism," 59
Newark *Star-Eagle*, 235, 243
Newlon, Jesse H., 350
New Republic, The, 172, 308, 363, 374
Newsboys, 154, 155, 156, 161, 195-196
Newsdealers, 291-300
Newsdealers Protective and Benevolent Assn., 297
News fabrication, 33, 67, 68-69, 72-75, 140-141, 220-222, 223-225, 228, 351-352, 363-366, 373, 377
Newspaper & Mail Deliverers' Union, 291, 298-300
Newspapers, English, 92; American, 92; Chicago, 164; Pittsburgh, 180; South Dakota, 182
Newspapers, State of, in California, 21; Parisian, 27
New York *American*, election celebration and disaster (1902), 96; censors hearings on Pure Food and Drug Act, 105; makes light of passage of act, 106; rejects G. O. P. letter under peculiar circumstances, 118; berates Gay-

nor for permitting fight pictures, itself possessing exclusive rights with *Journal*, 119; accepts proffered Standard Oil letters, 123; recipient of loans from Federation Bank and Trust Co., 166; W. R. H., Jr., tries to break Guild chapter, 197; violates A. P. contract, 203; fakes anti-Mexican stories and photos, 221; carries false reports of Niagara Falls Peace Conference, 223; raises false issues to weaken U. S. support of Allies, 227; editorials on sinking of Lusitania, 228; anti-British editorials, 230-231; charged with weakening U. S. position, 232; upholds Bolshevik revolution, 243; pushes men's wear to increase advertising lineage, 280; competition with *Daily News*, 292; used to puff theatrical interests of H., 302; gets photo that causes Lindberghs to flee, 307; used to puff H. securities, 317; brands Student Union as "radical," 348; attacks college professors, 348; prints Coughlin's endorsement of W. R. H., 375

New York Association for the Blind, 298
New York *Daily Mirror*, 180, 294, 303, 306, 364-366
New York *Daily News*, 164, 196, 291-294
New York *Evening Mail*, 243, 276
New York *Evening Post*, 76
New York *Herald*, 86, 115-116
New York *Herald-Tribune*, 296
New York *Journal*, purchase of by Hearst, 49; reputation of, 49; copies the N. Y. World, 51; circulation stunts, 52; initial losses, 53; gains in circulation, how bought, 53; "lifts" news, 54; known as "yellow Journal," 57; early practices, 59-60, 61-62; inaugurates fake campaign against utilities, 62; bribes "beat" on Venezuelan treaty, 64; fakes, Cuban news, 67; sends F. Lawrence to Cuba, expelled, 67; creates "girl martyr," Evangelina Cisneros, 69-71; demands American warship for Cuba, 71; attacks McKinley for peace policy, 71; raises Maine Memorial fund, 73; sends staff to Cuba, 77-78; banned from Cuba, 82; scoop on Spanish peace treaty by under-handed methods, 82; sponsors William J. Bryan, 83; leader in "help wanted" advt., 85; editorials inciting to assassination, 88; copy of, reported found on assassin of McKinley, 94; names changed to *American* and *Journal*, 95; *Evening Journal* used to campaign for Hearst for Mayor, 103; editorial found in pocket of Gaynor's assailant, 119; prints purloined Murphy-Gaynor letters, 120; average salary for reporters, 196; starts editorial attack on Al Smith, 253; Lee Olwell of National City made publisher, 275; "advice to investors" column proves embarrassing, 317; features alleged "red" bombing in Milwaukee, 366; fakes statement of David Dubinsky, Pres. International Ladies Garment Workers Union, 373
New York *Morning Telegraph*, 97, 165-166, 294
New York Newspaper Guild, 326
New York *Post*, 196-197, 294, 307, 350, 375
New York *Sunday American*, serializes falsified translation of Japanese book on war with U. S., 224-225; serializes Ambassador Gerard's *My Four Years in Germany*, 231; cancels serialization of Barbusse's *Under Fire*, 231
New York *Sunday World*, 55
New York Telephone Co., 62
New York *Times*, 98, 114, 150, 256, 270, 279, 298, 344, 352, 364
New York *Tribune*, 71, 195, 221, 232-233
New York University, 348-350
New York *World*, 20, 21, 24, 51, 52, 53, 54, 55, 56, 57, 61, 66, 74, 75, 77, 82, 104, 118, 122, 181, 239, 315
New York *World-Telegram*, 197, 294, 315
New Yorker Herold, 225
Neylan, John Francis, 181, 309, 326, 342, 345, 347
Niagara-Hudson Combine, 262
Nicaragua, 284
Nicaraguan Canal, 88
Noble, F. H. L. ("Cosey"), 51, 58
Nolan, Jack, 153
Norris, George W., 287, 290
Northwestern University, 350
Noyes, Frank B., 329
N.R.A. Code Authority, 195-196, 198
Nye, Gerald P., 283

O'Bannion, Dion, 162-163
O'Brien, John P., 334
Ochs, Adolph, 117, 292

INDEX

O'Connor, Joseph W. 296
O'Connor, J. F. T., 274
Official investigations into activities of W. R. H., 68, 90, 130-137, 154, 234, 248, 264, 287
Older, Fremont, 43, 48
Older, Mrs. Fremont, 43, 48, 81, 145, 236
Oliver, Geo. T., 131, 180
Olson, 135
Olwell, Lee, 275, 324
100,000 Guinea Pigs, 281
Oquendo, Spanish warship, 80
O'Rell, Max, 29
Osborne, Thomas Mott, 110
Otis, Harrison Grey, 46, 47
Outcault, Richard F., 54
Overland Monthly, 112
Overman, Lee S., 236-237

Pabst, Gustave, 234
Pacha, Bolo, 241
Pacific Gas and Electric Co., 262, 336
Pacific Tel. and Tel., 42
Page, John, 285
Palermo Ranch, 194
Palmer, Charles M., 38-39, 49
Palmer, Frank, 301
Palmer, Frederick, 60, 98
Panama Canal, 91-93, 216, 225
Papen, Franz von, 218, 239, 344
Parker, Alton B., 101, 111
Parkhurst, Rev. Charles F., 103
Parrott, Lindsay, 366
Patent Medicines, 35, 84, 106-108, 275, 278-282
Patria, 241
Patterson, J. M., 291, 293
Patterson, R. W., 152
Pearson's Magazine, 112
Pease, Frank, 365-366
Penrose, Boise, 123, 126-127, 129
People's Press, The, 301
Perkins, Frances, 359
Persecution of individuals, Huntington, alleged, 37; Spreckels, 40; Heney, 44; Pulitzer, 52, 62; Admiral Sampson, 82; Hanna, 86-87; McKinley, 86-87, 93; Murphy, 95; Hughes, 110; Osborne, 111; Gaynor, 118-120; Stewart, 133-136; Morris, 137; Knowles, 182; Wilson, 213-214; Al Smith, 253; Tugwell, 281; Chernow, 299; Lindbergh, 307
Pershing, John J., 220
Peru, 91, 174-181, 218, 264, 273, 340

Phelan, James D., 43
Philippine Herald, 377-379
Philippine Islands, 67, 78, 81, 87, 223
Phillips, Jennings J., 43
Phillips, M. C., 281
Pierce, Franklin, 118
Pinar del Rio, 67
Pittsburgh, 180
Pittsburgh *Post-Gazette*, 180-181
Pleasanton Ranch, 194
Polachek, Victor H., 134, 135, 136
Political ambitions of H., Vice-presidency (1900), 87; Congressman, elected (1902-1906), 96; Presidency (1904), cost of campaign, 100-101; nominated for mayoralty by Samuel Seabury (1905), 102; cost of campaign, 102; gubernatorial nomination (1906), 104; convention fight, 110-112; defeated, 118; defeated for mayor again (1909), 118; seeks Lieut. Governorship as "Independent" (1910), 118; aspiration to governorship, abortive (1918), 251; second abortive attempt at Governorship (1922), 254; attempts at Presidential boom (1924), 264
Pomerene, Atlee, 131
Pope Leo XIII, 69, 103
Pope Pius X, 103
Poth, F. A. & Sons, 234
Potter, Bishop Henry C., 97
Powers, T. E., 55-56
Preparedness Day Parade, bombing of, 47
Pressmen, Chicago, 157, 160, 166-169
Princeton University, 214, 350
Printer's Ink, 107, 279
Printing Worker, The, 299
Product of Labor Bill, 99
Prominent names, use and abuse of, 63-65, 69-70, 103
Propaganda, anti-Spanish, 66-70, 81; pro-German, 218, 230-234, 238-241, 246-247; pro-Soviet, 243-244; anti-Soviet, 245, 363-366, 378; anti-Allied, 218, 225-233, 239-240; anti-Mexican, 220-224; anti-Japanese, 224-225, 227, 239, 241; Italian, 354; Nazi, 344, 351
Property in the News, 201
Proprietary Association, 107
Proprietary Press Bureau, 107
Publicity "stunts," 32, 52, 63, 66, 70, 73, 83, 96-97, 101, 103, 105, 141, 280, 303
Public Utilities, 28, 61-63, 104, 142-144, 261-262

INDEX

Pulitzer, Joseph D., 20, 24, 26-27, 34, 49, 51, 53, 55-57, 59, 66, 116-118, 139, 141
Pure Food and Drug Act, 104-106, 281

Quay, M. S., 126
Quezon, Manuel, 377

Racing Record, 164
Rackets, commemoratory, 33; signed statement begun, 63; continued, 69-70, 141, 145-146, 305; circulation, 295-300; prizefight, 303-304
Radio Guide, 164
Raines-Murphy Recount Bill, 113
Rainey, Sam, 28
Ralph, Julian, 51, 65
Real Estate, 29, 46, 78, 249-251
"Red Menace," 166, 277, 345-352, 361-370, 373-374, 378
Reed, David A., 285
Reed, James A., 218, 233, 242, 245, 263, 374
Reid, Whitelaw, 292
Remington, Frederick, 68-69
Reporters' Union, Chicago, 142; Boston, 166
Republicans, 86, 88, 109-110, 114, 118, 254-257; Republican machine in San Francisco, 28; in California, 256; convention of 1920, 259; convention of 1928, 264
Reuter & Company, 234
Revolution, Hawaii, 78; Peru, 179; Russia, 243
Rice, Sir Cecil Spring, 229, 230
Richberg, Donald, 198
Rickard, Tex, 303-304
Ridder Brothers, 225
Ritz Towers, 270
Robinson, Joseph T., 280
Rockefeller, J. D., 50, 104, 123, 195, 275, 355-356; Rockefellers, 109, 124, 152
Rogers, H. H., 181
Rolph, James, 256
Roosevelt, Franklin D., 198-199, 255, 274, 276, 281, 283, 358, 360; administration, 197, 250, 270, 276, 278, 280, 355, 362
Roosevelt, Mrs. Franklin D., 281
Roosevelt, Theodore, 66, 76, 95, 109, 117, 137, 232-233
Root, Elihu, 109, 117
Roper, Daniel C., 273, 274, 359
Rosenberg, Alfred, 344, 351

Rosenwald, Lessing, 277
Rothermere, Lord, 230, 343, 347
Rothschilds of London, 50
Ruef, Abraham, 42; Ruef-Schmitz machine, 42-44
Rukeyser, Merryle S., 271
Rumely, Edward A., 243, 276
Rumsey, Mary Harriman, 275
Runyon, Damon, 281
Ruppert, Jacob, 234
Russell, Charles Edward, 101, 145
Russia, effect of on Mooney case, 47-48
Russian Revolution, 243-244
Rutkowski, Hugh (Idzy), 366-371
Ryan, Thomas Fortune, 109, 215-216

St. Donat's, 335-336
St. Joan Estate, 100
Sales Tax, 258, 343
Salisbury, William, 139-148
Saltus, Edgar, 54
Sampson, William T., 80, 82
Sander, Albert O., 240
Sandino, Augusto, 284
San Francisco, 19-48, 100, 141, 256, 345-347
San Francisco *Argonaut,* 289
San Francisco *Bulletin,* 43, 44, 46, 48
San Francisco *Call,* 37-40, 44
San Francisco *Call-Bulletin,* 43, 198
San Francisco *Chronicle,* 45
San Francisco *Examiner,* 20-21; taken over by W. R. Hearst, 23; staff parties, 25; bids for circulation, 27; assails crime and corruption, 28; styled "Monarch of the Dailies," 33; advertisements, 34; "exposes" Southern Pacific, 36; is itself exposed, 37-42; threatened by outraged citizens, 37; assails prosecution Ruef and Schmitz, 44; in league with underworld, 45; tapped to aid N. Y. *Journal,* 53; espouses Philippine annexation, 78; attacks McKinley, 90; locks out pressmen, 171; center of anti-Guild terror, 197; tax evasions, 266-267
San Francisco General Strike, 345-347
San Francisco Industrial Association, 345
San Francisco *News Letter,* parody, 29
San Quentin, 47
San Simeon Ranch, 271, 277, 285, 357
Santiago, 77-78, 82
Saturday Review of Literature, 311
Sausalito, 25
Sbar, Jake, 296
Schley, Winfield S., 82

INDEX 405

Schlink, F. J., 281
Schmidt, C. & Sons, 234
Schmitz, Eugene E., 42
Schuman, Frederick, 350-351
Schwab, Charles M., 325
Scotland Yard, 365
Scripps, E. W., 34
Scripps-Howard, 197, 294, 314
Seabury, Samuel, 102, 124
Seitz, Don, 118
Seldes, George, 131
Senate Foreign Relations Committee, 68
Senate Indian Affairs' Committee, 19
Senate Privileges and Elections Committee, 122-123, 130, 135
Sex, exploitation of, 27, 32, 34-35, 60, 69, 84, 302, 306
Shafter, William Rufus, 81-82
Shearer, William B., 282-284
Shearn, Clarence J., 99, 113, 114, 248, 252
Sheffield, James R., 285, 286, 289
Shenandoah Corporation, 263
Sherman, James S., 118
Sherman, John, 69
Sherover, Max, 221
Sigsbee, Charles Dwight, 73
Sinclair, Upton, 105, 164, 183, 377
Singer Sewing Machine Co., 244
Skin Deep, 281
Smith, Alfred E., 102, 220, 251-256, 271, 274, 358, 374
Sloane, W. D., 176
Social Frontier, 350, 374
Socialist *Call*, 219
Socialists, 145, 184, 220, 260-261, 363, 364
Socony Vacuum Oil Co., 356
Southern California, labor, 47
Southern Pacific, 36-43, 98
Southwick, Alfred L., 352
Soviet Union, 244-246, 285, 353, 354, 355-357, 362-367
Spain, 66-67, 71-72, 74, 77, 79-80, 87
Spanish-American War, 66, 77-82, 85
Sporting Times, 164
Standard Oil Co., 99, 106, 122-123, 129
Standard Oil Letters, 122-128, 130-135, 137
Star Corporation, 214, 318
Star Holding Co., 315, 318, 321
Star Publishing Co., 265-266
Spreckels, John, 37, 40, 43
Spring Valley Water Company, 42
Stanfield, Robert N., 259
Stanford, Leland, 36

Steffens, Lincoln, 112, 124
Stern, J. David, 196, 294
Stevens, Walter, 154
Stewart, Gilchrist, 132, 133, 134, 135, 136, 137
Stock transactions, 50, 199, 263, 265-267, 315-325, 337-341
Stockyards, 105, 164
Strauss, S. W. & Co., 316-317, 320
Strikebreaking, 166-171, 189, 199
Stump, Charles, 122, 123, 135
Stump, I. C., 40
Suez Canal, 81, 217
Sullivan, Edward Dean, 163
Sullivan, D. G., 28
Sullivan, F. H., 168
Sullivan, John, 165
Sullivan, John A., 98
Sullivan, Johnson, Barry and Roache, 256
Sullivan, Matt J., 256
Sullivan, Roger, 212, 216, 233
Sulzer, William, 251, 253
Sûreté Générale, 273
Survey, The, 175, 176, 178
Swanson, Claude A., 359
Swenson, Eric P., 273
Swift, Edward C., 105
Swift, Louis, 105
Syracuse *Journal*, 348
Syracuse University, 347

Taft, Wm. Howard, 137, 138
Taggart, Tom, 233
Talmadge Eugene, 358-359, 374, 379
Tammany, 95-96, 99, 102-103, 110, 120-121, 248, 254-255
Tampa, 77
Tampico, 220
Tarbell, Ida, 112
Tax evasion, 114, 116, 187, 193, 265
Taylor, Myron C., 325
Taylor, Phineas, 29
Teapot Dome, 257-259, 282
Tebbs, Charles, 51
Teresa, Spanish man-of-war, 80
Theft, of news, N. J. *Journal*, 54, 57; Chicago *American*, 142-143; International News Service, 201-209; of letters, N. Y. *Journal*, 71; Murphy-Gaynor, 120; Standard Oil, 123; French Foreign Office papers, 272
Thomason, L. C., 150
Thompson, William Boyce, 246
Thompson, William Hale, 163, 233, 263-264

INDEX

Time Magazine, 311
Tolley, H. R., 276
Towne, A. N., 38, 41
Towne, Charles A., 112
Townsend, Edward W., 29
Triangle Factory Fire, 31
Trude, A. S., 152
Tugwell Bill, 106, 275, 278-281
Tugwell, Rexford G., 278, 357, 359
Twain, Mark, 29, 65
Tweed Ring, 34
Twombly, H. McK., 176

Union labor, 46, 142, 157-158, 160, 163, 166-168, 170-171, 182-184, 189, 194-200; faked endorsements of, 112, 373
Union-Labor Party, 42
Union Public Service Co. of Kansas, 263
United Corporation, 262
United Railroads, 42
United States Congress, 78, 104, 138, 261
United States Navy, 73, 77
United States Secret Service, 234, 238-340
Universal Service, 353
University of California, 21, 42, 45, 91
University of Chicago, 195, 350
University of Illinois, 350
University of Wisconsin, 350
Untermyer, Samuel, 252

Vance, Louis Joseph, 210
Vanderbilt, Consuelo, marriage to Duke of Marlborough, 51
Vanderbilt, F. W., 176
Vanderlip, Frank A., 276, 277, 338
Varges, Ariel, 246-247
Venezuelan Boundary Dispute, 64, 91
Vera Cruz, 220
Verne, Jules, 33, 141
Veterans of Foreign Wars, 361, 379
Vidal, Eugene L., 274
Viereck, George Sylvester, 239
Villa, Pancho, 220-221
Villard, Oswald Garrison, 117, 209, 287

Waldorf-Astoria Hotel, 97, 121
Walker, James J., 250, 330
Walker, Thomas (alias), 363
Wall Street, 64, 86, 90-91, 116, 218, 227, 236, 258, 278

Wall Street Journal, 50, 247, 258
Walsh, Charles A., 150-151
Ward, Paul, 198
Warner Brothers Pictures, 199, 302
Warren, George E., 278, 338
Warwick Hotel, 270, 277
Washburne, John N., 348
Washington, D. C., 67, 70, 81, 88, 91, 99, 106, 180, 198
Washington Naval Conference, 282-283
Washington Times, 235-236, 238
Watson, Victor, 248, 285, 288, 351
Wayman, Charles, 154
Webster, Sidney, 118
Weimar Republic, 244
Wells Fargo Bank, 38, 219
West, George P., 25
Western Federation of Miners, 182, 189
What So Proudly We Hailed, 365
Whelan, George, 248
Whitman, Charles S., 251, 253
Wiley, Harvey, 281
Williams College, 350
Williams, James T., 274
Williams, John Sharp, 98
Williams, T. T., 39
Willson, George, 97
Wilson, Woodrow, 47, 93, 102, 211-217, 220, 222, 226, 231-232, 241, 245; administration, 268
Winchell, Walter, 303
Winfield, Willie W., 122-123, 132-137
Winkler, John K., 28
Wisconsin News, 199, 234, 330, 350, 370-371
Wise, James Waterman, 301
Wolcott, Josiah O., 236-237
Wolff Bureau, 352
Woll, Matthew S., 166, 200, 331, 361, 374
Wood, Leonard, 257
World War, 217-218, 225-243, 246-247
"Wrecking Crew," N. Y. Journal, 58, 77-78
Wyntoon, 327

Yale University, 350
Yellow Journalism, 54, 57, 121, 289

Ziegfeld, Florenz, 303
Ziegfeld Theatre, 270
Zittel, C. F. ("Zit"), 109

ST. MARY'S COLLEGE OF MARYLAND LIBRARY
ST. MARY'S CITY, MAR

33164

DUE	
DEC 11 '70	
4-22	
DEC 16 '74	
MY 7 '84	
MR 4 '85	
MR 17 '86	
	PRINTED IN U.S.A.